CASE STUDIES IN
CULTURAL ANTHROPOLOGY

GENERAL EDITORS
George and Louise Spindler
STANFORD UNIVERSITY

APACHE ODYSSEY

A Journey between Two Worlds

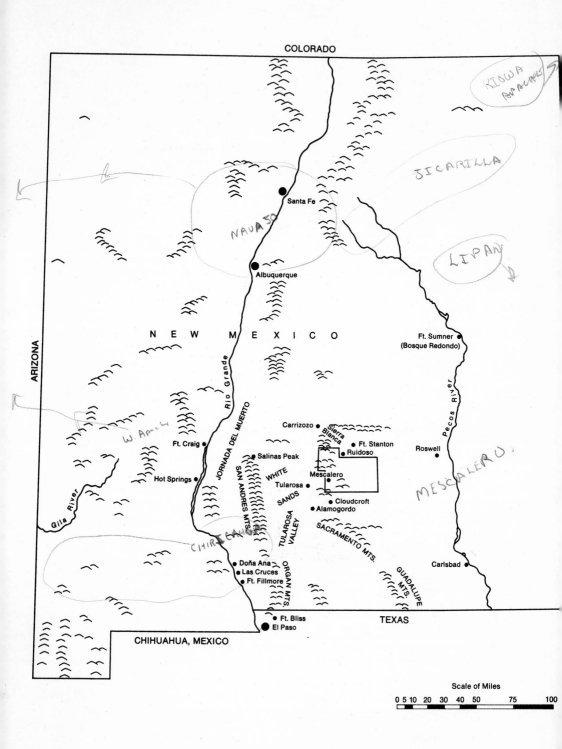

COLORADO

KIOWA APACHES

JICARILLA

NAVAJO

• Santa Fe

• Albuquerque

LIPAN

ARIZONA

N E W   M E X I C O

Ft. Sumner
(Bosque Redondo)

Rio Grande

Pecos River

W. Apache

Gila River

Carrizozo •

Sierra Blanca

• Ft. Craig

• Ft. Stanton

Roswell •

JORNADA DEL MUERTO

• Salinas Peak

• Ruidoso

• Mescalero

MESCALERO

SAN ANDRES MTS.

WHITE SANDS

• Hot Springs

• Tularosa

• Cloudcroft

• Alamogordo

TULAROSA VALLEY

SACRAMENTO MTS.

CHIRICAHUA

Carlsbad •

GUADALUPE MTS.

• Doña Ana
• Las Cruces
• Ft. Fillmore

ORGAN MTS.

• Ft. Bliss

TEXAS

El Paso

CHIHUAHUA, MEXICO

Scale of Miles

0 5 10 20 30 40 50   75   100

APACHE ODYSSEY

A Journey between Two Worlds

By

MORRIS E. OPLER

Cornell University

HOLT, RINEHART AND WINSTON

NEW YORK   CHICAGO   SAN FRANCISCO   ATLANTA

DALLAS   MONTREAL   TORONTO   LONDON   SYDNEY

Library of Congress Catalog Card Number: 79–81690
SBN: 03–078905–2
Printed in the United States of America
1   2   3   4   5   6   7   8   9

To Harry Hoijer,
genial and helpful companion
of field-work days among the Apache,
in affectionate nostalgia

Foreword

About the Series

These case studies in cultural anthropology are designed to bring to students, in beginning and intermediate courses in the social sciences, insights into the richness and complexity of human life as it is lived in different ways and in different places. They are written by men and women who have lived in the societies they write about and who are professionally trained as observers and interpreters of human behavior. The authors are also teachers, and in writing their books they have kept the students who will read them foremost in their minds. It is our belief that when an understanding of ways of life very different from one's own is gained, abstractions and generalizations about social structure, cultural values, subsistence techniques, and the other universal categories of human social behavior become meaningful.

About the Author

Morris Edward Opler received his M.A. degree in anthropology from the State University of New York at Buffalo in 1930 and his Ph.D. in the same subject in 1933 from the University of Chicago. In 1929 he first visited the Apache and has been devoted to their study ever since. He is the author of over fifty books, monographs, and articles about the Apache; the best known, perhaps, being his Chiricahua Apache ethnography, *An Apache Life-Way*. He has also published widely on the topics of village India and anthropological history and theory. Dr. Opler began his professional career as an official of the U.S. Bureau of Indian Affairs and subsequently taught at Reed College, Claremont Colleges, and Harvard University before coming to Cornell University, where he has been Professor of Anthropology since 1948. He has been a Fellow of the Social Science Research Council, a Fellow of the John Simon Guggenheim Memorial Foundation, a Fellow of the Center for Advanced Study in the Behavioral Sciences, and holds a Senior Fellowship of the National Endowment for the Humanities for 1968–1969. He has been an officer of the American Folklore Society and Associate Editor of the *Journal of American Folklore,* and has served on the Executive Board of the American Anthropological Association whose president he was in 1962–1963.

About the Book

This volume departs from the established format and character of the series as it has developed to the present. Each of the studies has brought into focus a single culture "case" in a relatively brief book written especially with students in mind. These cases have taken essentially the form of short ethnographies, although most have focused upon certain aspects or processes rather than summarizing the whole cultural round. The title of the series Case Studies in Cultural Anthropology, however, implies that the ethnography is not the only form of presentation and interpretation of culturally relevant material allowable within the range of its format and purposes. When we started the series in 1960 it was our intention that "case studies" should cover a wide range of possibilities.

Apache Odyssey is a departure in a direction appropriate to the series in its broader conception. It is the biographical narrative of a single individual, a Mescalero Apache, who grew to maturity when his people, like most American Indian tribes through the turn of the last century, were experiencing defeat, confinement, and profound cultural readjustment. His is "a journey between two worlds." He is, compared to his father, a marginal man, and yet he is clearly a Mescalero Apache. His imagery, his beliefs, and his world view contrast dramatically with Western norms and are identifiably Mescalero, in the comparative context of other Apache tribal cultures.

Apache Odyssey is a study of the relation of the individual to his culture, a study of the effect of cultural change and social dislocation upon the individual, and also a study of Mescalero Apache culture during a critical period of change. It is a study of an incipient shaman, and of shamanism among the Mescalero when religion was all that the people had left for protection. It is, as the author points out, also a "window" into the history of the West, and into Indian-white relations.

The notes provided by the author are as fully a part of this volume as the narrative. It is essential that the reader study them carefully as he reads the text, since in them Dr. Opler provides the necessary explicit connections to Mescalero culture and to history. With them, and through the words of the single informant, we have a unique opportunity to see a way of life as it is always seen by the native—from his point of view, uniquely. Anthropologists complain that there is a lack of this kind of material available to students—that culture in the abstract is not the equivalent to culture in particular. This case study is designed to help provide the needed material.

Since this study includes both a detailed biographical narrative and its running interpretation, it has not been possible to confine it to the limitations of length of the established case study format.

GEORGE AND LOUISE SPINDLER
General Editors

San Diego
Estepona, Spain, 1969

ACKNOWLEDGMENTS

In launching this attempt to enlarge and deepen the anthropological sub-fields of ethnology and of culture and personality by combining their materials in one book, I am conscious of many debts. It was Edward Sapir, one of my teachers in anthropology, who persuaded me that life history material could contribute not only to our knowledge of the content of culture but to our understanding of the dynamics of culture change. It was due to his urgings that I sought to collect autobiographical accounts, of which Chris's story is one, of Apache of different age groups and interests. Later, Clyde Kluckhohn continually prodded me to treat some of these life histories separately and to demonstrate what they can indicate concerning the interplay between individual proclivities and cultural demands. In at length acting upon the advice given through the years, I have been encouraged by the faith of Louise and George Spindler in the experiment. My wife, Lucille Opler, has given continual help at every stage of the venture. The manuscript was completed while I held a Senior Fellowship of the National Endowment for the Humanities of the National Foundation on the Arts and the Humanities. My most profound obligation is, of course, to Chris and his people, who took me into their confidence and who taught me that part of anthropology which no curriculum can convey.

MORRIS E. OPLER

Contents

3. Unsettled Years

APACHE ODYSSEY

A Journey between Two Worlds

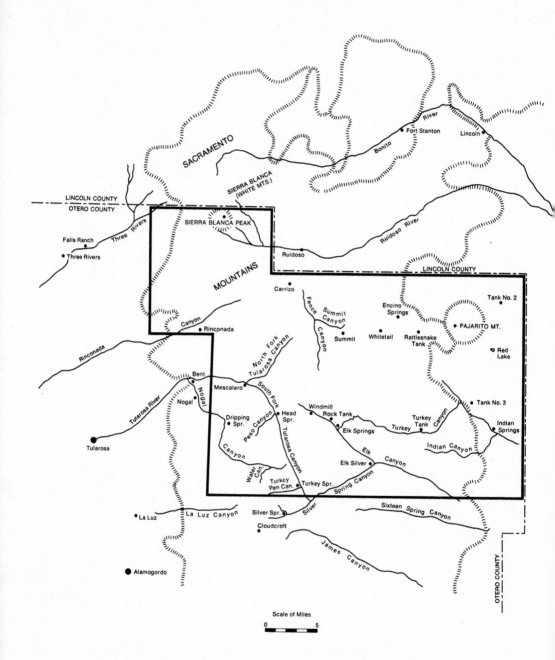

Map of the present Mescalero Apache Indian Reservation and environs showing the most important places referred to in the text.

Introduction

I BEGAN MY ETHNOLOGICAL FIELD STUDIES among the Apache Indians of the Mescalero Indian reservation in southeastern New Mexico in the summer of 1931 and continued this initial work until the early fall of that year, when I had to return to the University of Chicago to complete the final phase of my graduate program. During this early period in the field, I heard references to a Mescalero Apache to whom I have given the pseudonym "Chris," especially when hunting techniques and plant and animal identifications were being discussed, but I did not succeed in meeting this knowledgeable Apache that summer, for he was hunting and trapping far from the agency center and was constantly on the move.

In September 1932, after my academic work was completed, I returned to Mescalero for a longer stay. On Monday, January 16, 1933, I was at the lodge, the recreation hall and meeting place attached to the Protestant church, interviewing a prominent Mescalero whose name is given as Big Hat, when Chris appeared. He had a double errand in mind. His wife was in the hospital, and he had come to get some magazines for her "with lots of pictures." He also wanted Big Hat's advice and help and mine, too, in framing a claim against the government. The government had removed the Chiricahua Apache from their lands in the West following Geronimo's surrender in 1886 and had held them as prisoners of war until 1913. The Chiricahua were now petitioning for compensation for false arrest and detention, since most of those punished had not been involved in Geronimo's hostile action and many had actually acted as Indian scouts for the government forces. Because his father was a Chiricahua (he was one of the Indian scouts serving the United States armed forces), Chris and his family had been caught in the removal net. Therefore he had joined with the Chiricahua in a claim for $25,000 in compensation for every individual involved. However, as he put it, "In case that doesn't work, I have another claim. I have a claim against the government different from any of the others. My mother was a full-blooded Mescalero, and therefore, counting myself a Mescalero, I consider that the government did a double wrong to take me prisoner." Chris asked me to take down the account of the imprisonment of his

1

The author taking down Chris's life story.

family, which I readily agreed to do. After he had finished his recital, he indicated that he could use several typed copies of these remarks. He mused over possible strategies, saying, "I guess I'd better wait and see what happens to the Chiricahua bill. No, I'll send it in. This is the first time I made out the history of it. I'll send it to Senator Thomas because I can't separate this from the Chiricahua bill. [The Chiricahua expected Senator Elmer Thomas of Oklahoma to sponsor a bill for the redress of the wrongs they had suffered.] He can show it to Senator Bratton. They all know me. And I'd like one for Chavez, too."

This opportunity to meet Chris in a context that permitted discussion of his family connections and affairs was extremely timely for me. One of the devices I was using to build up a picture of Apache culture through the years was the gathering of life histories of Indian friends of different age groups and interests. I found that Chris was willing to cooperate with me in such an undertaking. The serious sickness of his wife (she died in May, 1933) kept his family close to the agency and the reservation's medical facilities, and, because of added family responsibilities following his wife's death, Chris wandered about the reservation less and was much more accessible for interviews than would otherwise have been the case. The essential part of the personal narrative was told in 1933 and early 1934; a few episodes and embellishments were added when I returned to Mescalero for a third time in the summer of 1935 and for a fourth time in the summer of 1936.

Chris's love of the outdoors and his restlessness imposed certain conditions of work upon our undertakings. Unless the weather made it impossible, he insisted on staying outdoors, preferably in some isolated, wooded area. A tree trunk or log was the usual desk for the taking down of Chris's story, and the personal account was often interrupted to call attention to some bird or animal that came into view and to give some information about its place in Mescalero usage or belief. Chris kept his pact and gave his autobiographical account. Yet he sometimes found the routine monotonous, and it became necessary every now and then to turn to different tasks, such as the gathering of specimens of plants used by the Mescalero for food, medicine, and ceremony.

Though his father was a Chiricahua Apache, Chris had little or no exposure to organized Chiricahua life. Even before his birth the Chiricahua had been removed from their tribal lands and concentrated under close military supervision on the Western Apache reservation. His father, who was his Chiricahua link, was away most of the time, performing his duties as an Indian scout for the United States army. By the time Chris was six years old, he and his family were uprooted and transferred, first to Florida and then to Alabama, with the Chiricahua prisoners of war. During the initial period of this relocation Chiricahua life was greatly disrupted. Men and women were separated, supervision was close, older children were isolated from adults and sent away to schools. Less than three years later, in 1889, Chris and his family were returned to the West, to the Mescalero Apache reservation. His father soon began to wander about again, as the narrative indicates. His other paternal relatives were still being held as prisoners of war in the East. Chris's Mescalero relatives took responsibility for him, and he grew up in a Mescalero Apache cultural environment. It was not until 1913, when he was approximately thirty-three years old, that the Chiricahua were released from their prisoner-of-war status and those who so wished were allowed to return to the West and settle with the Mescalero Apache on the Mescalero Indian reservation. Consequently, regardless of his dual tribal parentage, Chris was culturally a Mescalero Apache when I became acquainted with him.

Anyone familiar with comparative Apache ethnography would recognize that in terms of culture Chris could not be anything other than a Mescalero Apache. His kinship usages and his attitude toward peyote, for instance, would establish this. Yet Chris differs from every other member of his tribe. One of the impressions I hope this document will convey is some sense of this interplay between culture and the individual. Chris is not presented as *the* Mescalero of his day but as *a* Mescalero whose adventures throw light both on cultural requirements and expectations and on the individual effort to thread a path through them.

Though Chris pauses to explain some matters which he thinks may be obscure, he obviously takes much of Mescalero culture for granted, partly because he is talking with an anthropologist who has been among his people for some time. Consequently, in order that the reader may understand what aspects of Mescalero usage Chris accepts or defies or manipulates, I have supplied extensive notes to fill out the cultural dimension. It is my hope that, as a result, this volume can be as much a guide to a culture, to the Mescalero way of life, as it is a personal record. Many of the events to which reference is made occurred on the Western frontier during a strenuous period of American history. For the benefit of those who are interested in the development of the American West, I have included rather full historical notes to mesh with the text. I call attention to the fact that, besides being a guide to a culture, a document useful in culture and personality study, and a window on the history of the West and Indian-white relations, this book should have considerable interest for those engaged in research in comparative religion. Chris grew up in a period when Apache arms and prospects had collapsed before American military power. The one recourse left to a troubled people was the protective and predictive forces of religion. Consequently shamanism flourished for a time, and shamans vied with each other to stem the white man's inroads and diseases and to expose the witches within the tribe who had weakened the Apache will to resist. Chris's father, mother, and mother's sister were all renowned shamans, and Chris was serving his apprenticeship in the practice of ritual when the white man decreed that he go for five consecutive years to schools they had established in Albuquerque and Santa Fe. There, where Indians of various tribes argued their separate beliefs and the white supervisors scoffed at all their claims, his confidence in his ability to summon and control supernatural power in the Apache context became undermined. Though he approached the threshold several times during his life, as we shall see, he never dared take the final step and proclaim himself a full-fledged shaman. His struggle with himself over this matter took the form, rather, of an obsessive curiosity about shamans and their ceremonies. Thus, while he remained on the fringe as a ritualist and performer, he was the most fascinated and tenacious of beholders. If his faith remained imperfect, his fund of information about the Mescalero ritual pattern and the practices of numerous individual shamans grew impressively. Out of his self-doubts and search for religious affirmation has come one of the most complete and penetrating pictures of the psychology and mechanics of shamanism of which I know.

In many ways Chris is an excellent representative of Mescalero Apache traditional culture. His stamina and physical strength, though less crucial after the inauguration of the reservation period, were greatly admired by his fellow Apache. His hunting skills and talents as a woodsman were highly esteemed. He honored the avoidance and polite form usages to kin and affinal relatives without question. He was a competent horseman. He could recount the traditional stories to the young effectively, with all due gestures and voice modulations. He had a large fund of dance songs with which to enliven social occasions and a good strong voice with which to project them. He had a healthy enough attitude toward sex, but this did not dominate his life. He was a faithful husband and a devoted father. He drank, but usually not to excess. He was generous to kinsmen and to sick and indigent tribesmen.

Yet, as each of us is to some degree, Chris was unique. He was the product of a Mescalero-Chiricahua marriage at a time when such marriages were much rarer than they were later to become. Each tribe saw his idiosyncracies as the result of his inheritance from the other group. These allowances and the lack of solid identification may well have encouraged deviation and experimentation on Chris's part in respect to some matters.

At the age of seventeen, after fairly complete exposure to Mescalero practices and ideals, Chris was sent away to the white man's school for a term of years. The period when his meaningful contact with his people was broken is the time when a Mescalero youth ordinarily marries, acquires some supernatural power, and accepts the responsibilities and attitudes of the adult. Instead, for Chris it became a time of contrast and questioning, resulting in less than full participation in aspects of Mescalero culture. In ceremonialism and curing, Chris retained sufficient belief to become an avid observer and even a shaman's helper, but his own efforts ended at the point where herbalism begins to take on the trappings of ceremonialism. He makes sure that shamans are willing to teach him their ceremonies. Yet something inhibits him from taking the final step of determining whether supernatural power will ratify and implement their choice. As a sop to his empirical American education, he sloughs off minor Mescalero items of belief. He is willing to eat during a thunderstorm and dine on the meat of a deer killed by an eagle. Yet he does not challenge the major premises of Mescalero religion. He does not question the existence of supernatural power and witchcraft or the reality of the struggle between the two. His deviations from the Mescalero belief pattern, though they make him feel worldly and critical, go only deep enough to irritate his fellow Apache and move them to gossip.

In some respects it is Chris's conservatism, rather than his daring, that has made difficulties for him. He was determined to make a living by hunting at a time when some monetary income was needed for the clothes and utensils which had become a family requirement. Consequently he had to hunt and trap animals which white traders, dealers, and officials wanted for the fur trade or as bounties. Many of these, such as the fox, snake, coyote, and wolf, are strongly feared as vehicles of sickness, witchcraft, and disaster by the Mescalero. This willingness to handle the unclean and dangerous, on the one hand, and the disclaimer of supernatural power which would make such behavior understandable, on the other, have done more than anything else to make Chris stand out in the minds of fellow tribesmen as a suspicious and perplexing person. The distrust that exists might have taken more pointed and menacing form long ago if Chris were not so formidable physically and so well connected to powerful families by blood and marriage. The fact that he is no glum, chronic dissenter, that he is good-natured and outgoing and makes friends easily among Indians and white men alike, has also helped keep criticism to a reduced pitch. The white man's law, which deals so severely with acts of vengeance or retaliation based on charges of witchcraft, has probably also helped to keep antagonism toward Chris at the muttering level.

It is interesting that those with some scientific training who have come to Mescalero—the agency doctor, the museum man, the anthropologist—have usually managed to locate Chris and find in him a helpful and kindred spirit. I have often wondered whether his powers of observation, his flare for evidence and detail, and his willingness to experiment do not mark a man who would have become a first-class scientist in the white man's world. As it was, time and events led him on a journey along a shifting border between two cultural worlds. Neither one of these worlds fully claimed him. From the one he knew best he felt a certain isolation. The curtain of the other he penetrated only occasionally. It was his nature to be happy and active. It is surprising how well he accomplished this in spite of codes that raised warning signals at so many turns in the trail.

A word about the arrangement of the parts of this book may be in order. Chris is a representative of a particular culture, and much of his behavior would seem bizarre indeed if the broad affirmations to which he was responding were not kept in mind. Therefore, as background for the action, a sketch of Mescalero culture and its historical vicissitudes is provided immediately following this intro-duction. The autobiography is divided into four chapters, representing major periods in Chris's life. Every attempt has been made to present the story as it was told. The narrator was allowed to emphasize, embellish, and ignore as he chose, for it was felt that the degree to which he developed a subject was an index of his emotional investment in it. Annotations through which the particulars of Chris's account are given historical depth and wider ethnographic meaning are woven into the narrative in a manner that makes them an integral part of the whole and yet distinguishes them by type and format. In this way the text and notes are kept in close proximity and can be conveniently used together for fullest perspective and clarification; yet the explanations need not intrude upon Chris's life story if one finds it useful to give the autobiography a first reading without regard to supplementary material. My intention has been to present within the covers of a book a number of facets of the human condition: the shifting historical matrix in which a culture is found, the culture to which a man is born and with which he must make his peace, the individual who is always less than his culture and always more, too. What is uni-versal in all this—what transcends time and place, the particular culture, and the given individual—I leave to the empathy of the reader.

PART ONE

THE CULTURAL
AND
HISTORICAL BACKGROUND

Traditional Mescalero Practices

THE MESCALERO APACHE TRIBE is one of seven linguistically and culturally related peoples whose aboriginal territories stretched over large sections of present-day southwestern United States and northeastern Mexico. That portion of *Apacheria*, as it came to be known, in which the Mescalero made their homes was bounded on the west by the Rio Grande and extended eastward beyond the Pecos River. On the south the Mescalero range included a portion of northwestern Texas and parts of the Mexican states of Chihuahua and Coahuila. Mescalero living sites were to be found as far north as the thirty-fourth parallel, and hunting and raiding parties penetrated even farther north.

The western neighbors of the Mescalero were the Chiricahua Apache, the group closest to the Mescalero in language and culture. These two tribes were normally at peace, had a reasonable amount of contact, and not infrequently offered a haven for each other's members during the troubled times immediately before the modern reservation period. The father of the narrator of the life story with which we are concerned was a Chiricahua who several times wandered into Mescalero territory and twice married there. To the east and southeast of the Mescalero lived the Lipan Apache. The linguistic and cultural differences between these two groups were of considerable magnitude, and they had little contact until military pressure in the late historic period restricted their movements and forced them to make common cause. To the north and northeast of the Mescalero was the territory of the Jicarilla Apache; but again rather pronounced linguistic and cultural differences had developed, and there was little interaction between the two until the policy of concentrating Apachean-speaking peoples on the same reservation was begun by the United States government. With the other three Apachean-speaking tribes—the Kiowa Apache well to the east and the Navaho and Western Apache (White Mountain, San Carlos, Cibecue, Northern Tonto, and Southern Tonto) beyond the Chiricahua to the west—there was still more spatial and cultural separation. Never-

9

theless, in spite of the tribal similarities and differences that have been noted, it should be understood that there is a common underlying Apachean pattern of institution, behavior, and precept, which is quite apparent to anyone who carries on comparative work among these tribes.

The heartland of Mescalero territory, the west side of the great plains of New Mexico, Texas, and Mexico, was a region consisting of majestic mountain ranges separated by flats and valleys. Through the valleys ran the Rio Grande and the Pecos River. Between these major waterways were enclosed areas of higher ground, such as the Tularosa Basin, the site of the modern Mescalero Apache Indian reservation. The aboriginal Mescalero country provided the greatest variation of geographic and climatic features. A mountain peak of the Sierra Blanca (White Mountains) was over 12,000 feet high, and Salinas Peak of the San Andres range reached an elevation of nearly 9,000 feet. The descent to alkali flats and white gypsum sands was broken by hills, buttes, and ridges. Precipitation and temperature fluctuated with elevation. The lowland plains received an average annual rainfall of approximately ten inches. The winters there were mild and sunny, and the summers blistering. Sagebrush, cacti, yuccas, mesquite, and Mormon tea were characteristic vegetation of these lowlands; rabbits, antelope, and prairie dogs were the common fauna. Until approximately 1875, when the southern herd was exterminated, there were bison on the plains to the east. The high mountains at the edges of the basins received more precipitation than the flats and were covered with forests. The banks of the streams that rose in the heights and flowed through the basins provided favorite home sites and bases for the Mescalero. In the low hills just above the plains, mescal and sotol were plentiful. The foothills of the mountains were covered by such vegetation as the one-seeded juniper, piñon, and the three-leaved sumac. Aspen, western yellow pine, and spruce dominated at the higher elevations. Deer, elk, and bighorn were available to the Mescalero hunters in the mountains. Because of its contrasts and ruggedness, Mescalero Apache territory was not easy for the uninitiated to traverse. In fact, much of it was very imperfectly known by the Spaniards, Mexicans, and Americans until well after the middle of the nineteenth century. The lowlands were hot, dry, and thorny; water sources in them were few. The sudden rains of the surrounding mountains cut deep washes and arroyos that made passage difficult. The tangled brush of the foothills was an impediment, and the many high ranges were a formidable barrier to any not familiar with the passes. The river valleys were vulnerable to raiders from the mountains. The valley of the Rio Grande became known as the *Jornada del Muerto*, and for a long time forts were established along it and punitive expeditions were repeatedly launched in a vain effort to keep the route open to commerce and travelers.

The Mescalero were characterized by an economic, political, and social order that harmonized well with their challenging environment. They were familiar with the agricultural practices of the Pueblo Indians and of the Mexican and American settlers. In late historic times they even did a little desultory farming along some watercourses, but the severe weather and short season of the mountains and the precarious water supply of the lowlands did not encourage cultivation of the soil. Instead, they depended on hunting and the gathering of the wild harvests. Such an economy required great mobility; there had to be readiness to follow the food harvests when and where they matured and to move from one hunting area to another when the supply of game dwindled. A concentration of population was, of course, inappropriate to such techniques of food procurement; as a result, the population was thinly dispersed over the immense range. Since most economic errands were carried out in small groups, there was little incentive for highly centralized leadership. It is probable that never in its history did the tribe have a single leader who was recognized and followed by all. Rather, the Mescalero leader, or "chief" (literally, "he who speaks"), was, as his title suggests, a respected adviser drawn from the heads of the families who tended to camp and move together.

A leader usually benefited by having a large and cohesive family which was related by blood and marriage to other prominent families of the vicinity. Age (within limits), experience, and a reputation for sagacity were prime attributes of a leader. To a large extent the leader was a spokesman for the group and the one who sensed and summarized sentiment. Since he had no coercive power and no way to enforce an unpalatable decision, he had to understand what his followers were willing to do. No other family head was obliged to follow him blindly or to remain with the group; therefore serious misjudgments or unpopular counsel might cost him his position or a portion of his followers. One of his acknowledged functions was to prevent or mitigate friction in his group. To succeed in this was obviously to his advantage, for if a feud persisted it was only a matter of time before some of those involved would move away. Despite his lack of absolute authority, the Mescalero leader was a useful and important figure in the social and political setting. Once he had gauged sentiment and acted as a catalyst and spokesman, the tendency in the group was to close ranks and work together toward the stated objective.

Theoretically the office of leader was not hereditary; in practice there was a tendency for the sons of leaders to succeed their fathers. The Mescalero explain this by saying that a leader was likely to train his son more carefully than did others and that the leader's son often accompanied and assisted his father and therefore quietly took over the functions of the older man. If the son showed marked leadership qualities, the group members interposed no objections to his gradual rise in importance and transferred their respect and allegiance to him at the death or superannuation of his father. On the other hand, if a leader's son demonstrated none of his father's qualities, he received little deference at times of council and crisis, and some more vigorous family head moved to the fore and assumed leadership. The process was informal but decisive.

Typical situations which involved a leader included the questions whether to move to another site because of poor luck in hunting, repeated deaths, epidemic disease, or the proximity of enemies, whether to sanction a raid or war party, whether to sponsor an important social or ritual event to which outsiders might be invited, and what to do about charges of witchcraft or gross misbehavior which were disrupting or dividing the group. The ability to lead successful raid and war parties, as well as to sanction them, was, of course, a great asset for a leader; such expeditions meant booty, and this, in turn, made it possible to distribute favors widely. In a society where generosity was one of the cardinal virtues, such activity built and sustained the good will so important to a leader.

The body of people with which the leader was associated could be termed a local group, since it was ordinarily identified with some specific place or locality that served as a center or base from which the people moved out, usually in small parties, to forage or hunt. Such a site was most often in the mountains and was chosen with an eye to defensibility, water supply, fodder for mounts, and accessibility to hunting and gathering areas.

The local group was comprised of from ten to twenty families, and normally this was enough to supply the necessary hands for most economic and military tasks. When an ambitious revenge or raiding party was planned against a strong antagonist, or if a buffalo hunt was contemplated, the members of other local groups might be invited to participate. In multigroup enterprises one local group leader might defer to another who was especially rich in experience and standing, and something like a united command might arise on a temporary basis; but more often a leader continued to direct his own men, and when the leaders conferred among themselves, the members of each local group received the advice or the substance of the decisions from its own leader. If a successful joint venture resulted in a celebration, the affair might be held at the headquarters of one local group, which then played host to its allies. Just as frequently, though, the members of a large expedition scattered to their own territories before celebrating.

Though the local group was often referred to by the name of its base or head-quarters or by the name of some geographical feature near this spot (alternatively it was referred to by the name of its current leader), its territories ordinarily included an area large and varied enough to provide most of the staples of Mescalero diet. Local group boundaries did not overlap seriously, nor were they jealously defended against other Mescalero local groups. In general, they were so spaced that each had sufficient room for living and carrying on its economic pursuits. Thus, though a Mescalero was extremely mobile, he usually moved on his economic and social errands within local group boundaries. The main exception to this pattern was the buffalo hunt; since buffalo were to be found only to the east, the local groups of the western part of the tribal territory had to leave their customary hunting grounds to obtain this important food. Thus for many local groups an annual eastward journey was added to the many expeditions within the more familiar territory. Consequently Mescalero social and economic life was marked by great fluidity; a Mescalero had to be psychologically prepared to move or to join some enterprise at very short notice.

Although local group membership was not hereditary and might be terminated at will, the local group was a reasonably stable unit. Successful exploitation of difficult terrain by hunting and gathering techniques requires an intimate knowledge of the area. No Mescalero hunter wished to sacrifice his long acquaintance with the favorite haunts of the various animals in familiar territory for the hazards of hunting in a district relatively unknown to him. Moreover, in the local group in which he had grown up and had been trained, a Mescalero was likely to have special hunting companions with whom he was used to cooperating. A Mescalero woman who was well acquainted with the natural timetable of wild food harvests in one area did not relish the idea of familiarizing herself with the resources of another local group area. The economic pressures were too constant and the margin of survival too slight to encourage such risks. Social as well as economic bonds often inhibited changing affiliation. A married man whose parents-in-law were alive could not easily move his immediate family from the territory of one local group to that of another. As we shall see, he was bound to his wife's relatives by the strongest ties of economic and social obligation and could not change residence unless his wife's father also wished to move and, indeed, initiated the move. By the same token, a Mescalero woman was trained to share household and economic tasks with her mother and sisters, and she would not be likely to leave local group territory unless the entire extended family, of which she was an important economic cog, had determined to change location. Consequently, in spite of the lack of hereditary membership in the local group and the absence of local group endogamy, because of the demanding natural setting and the need for mastery over the particular environment, certain Mescalero families have been identified with definite territories for long spans of time. Genealogical and historical inquiry verifies this, and the pattern of identification with leaders and localities has continued among the Mescalero even into the modern reservation period.

Whether there were social and territorial units within the tribe larger than the local group—that is to say, whether there were bands or moieties—is more difficult to determine with certainty. The local groups to the east spent more time on the plains and relied more than did the others on the meat, hide, and sinew of the buffalo. This resulted in more dependence on the horse and the horse travois, a greater use of the portable, conical skin tent or tipi, and a greater concentration of people for the hunt and for defense. Mescalero elders have occasionally taken note of this more eastern position of a part of the tribe and its greater orientation toward the prairies by making a distinction between the "plains people" and the "edge-of-the-mountain people." Though there has been some vague talk of separate leadership for the "Plains" Mescalero and the "Mountain" Mescalero, there is no strong proof that the men named were more than local group leaders who occasionally acted as spokesmen when a larger than usual concentration of people was involved. All agree that there were no significant differences in speech, dress, or custom between the "Plains" and "Mountain" Mescalero. Whether the distinction was ever more than a reference to geographical position and to the slightly different response to plains life that it stimulated in one section of the tribe is difficult to determine at this late date. The likelihood is that it was not and that the Mescalero did not have a band organization or a dual division. If this is true, they contrast in regard to this social feature with their Apachean-speaking neighbors—the Chiricahua, the Jicarilla, and the Lipan—all three of whom had well-defined band or moiety arrangements. However, it must be remembered that the ruthless and determined invasion of Mescalero country by United States forces in 1862, the evacuation of all members of the tribe who could be found to Bosque Redondo (Fort Sumner) on the Pecos and their detention there for the three years that followed, and the severe repression of the tribe until 1881 greatly disturbed social and spatial conditions and make it most difficult to reconstruct the relations of the aboriginal groups in every detail.

Regardless of questions about the reality and function of other social units, there is little doubt concerning the characteristics and importance of the Mescalero extended domestic family. Ideally this social unit consisted of an older married couple, their unmarried children, their married daughters and sons-in-law, and their daughters' children. In other words, marriage was matrilocal: the daughter continued to live in the encampment of her parents after marriage, while the son left at marriage for the encampment of his parents-in-law.

The consequences of this arrangement for the Mescalero are quite evident. It gave a good deal of security to the women. A girl was a member of a work group which consisted of her mother and sisters (and often her mother's sisters and their daughters, too), not only until marriage, but throughout her life. No matter whom she married, she was likely to remain in her local group territory, for it would be the husband who would have to make the move in case of a marriage between members of different local groups. After her marriage the girl's knowledge of the food resources of the area would continue to be useful; there would be little interruption of her work habits and no major adjustment in her contribution to the economy. Though, as a married woman, she would set up a separate dwelling near those of her mother and sisters, food would continue to be cooked at one place by the women of the cluster and would be carried from the place of preparation by the wives to their husbands and children. Moreover, the Mescalero woman had considerable psychological security. It was the man and his family who initiated marriage overtures. Before the marriage, presents passed from the prospective groom and his family to the family of the girl as an earnest of the support and aid that could be henceforth expected from the suitor. These gifts were ordinarily distributed among the close relatives of the girl in gratitude for the assistance they had rendered in supporting, training, and safeguarding her until she reached marriageable age. Once a spokesman for the young man had received an affirmative answer from the girl's parents (usually after a conference with her close relatives) and the presents had been proffered, the couple were free to live together. No formal ceremony marked the establishment of the new family unit. The bride and her close female relatives simply erected a wickiup or tipi near those of her parents and married sisters. As soon as all was in readiness, the groom joined his wife in this extended family encampment.

Obviously, therefore, it was the groom who had to make the major adjustments at marriage. He had to join his wife's encampment. Formerly he had hunted and worked with his father, unmarried brothers, and brothers-in-law. Now he was under the discipline and at the beck and call of his wife's parents and her other close relatives. If he married within his own local group (and this was quite possible because there was no rule of local group exogamy), he would be familiar with the terrain and the hunting grounds. If not, he would have to gain an acquaintance with the nature and resources of the region as quickly as possible. He was expected to be a willing replacement for the sons whom his parents-in-law lost through marriage, to defend the camp, to show the greatest deference to his affinal relatives, to cooperate in economic and military ventures with the men of the extended family, and to heed the requests of his parents-in-law, regardless of the burdens they imposed. The married man was constantly reminded of his obligations to his wife's relatives by elaborate conventions of behavior and speech. He had to avoid coming face to face with his mother-in-law and his wife's maternal and paternal grandmothers. Still other female relatives of his wife might, as a compliment to his wife and him, also request "avoidance." To other relatives of his wife, including her father, he was required to use "polite" speech, a special form of address that implies deference and respect. Polite speech, too, might be requested by some with whom it was not obligatory. In such cases the option lay with the wife's relatives, and a request for an observance that was not strictly required was considered a sign of approval of the marriage and of affection for the newly married couple. Avoidances and polite forms were not empty gestures; they were taken most seriously. They were supposed to continue for the lifetime of those between whom they had been established. Even the death of his wife did not allow a man to terminate the avoidances and polite forms that had been established at the outset of his marriage. For good reason, as we shall see, insistence on compliance with these forms was even more pronounced after her death. Avoidance and the polite form of speech implied respect, loyalty, and fullest economic cooperation. One could not listen with equanimity to any unfriendly comments about an affinal relative from whom one hid or to whom one used the polite form of speech. In any factional dispute, one's place was with those relatives-in-law with whom these forms of respect had been established. No reasonable request for goods or economic services could be denied such affinals. Consequently, a man was forced to be most circumspect in his new residence after marriage, for he was surrounded by his wife's kin, who expected a good deal of courtesy and service from him. The Mescalero youth was truly on trial after his marriage; his behavior and work habits came under close scrutiny. Not infrequently the relatives of the wife decided they had made a misjudgment in admitting a young man to their circle and drove him away on some pretext. This constituted a divorce.

The subordination of her husband to her relatives, the requirement that he be respectful and obedient to them, and the fact that she was constantly in the company of her mother and other female relatives during the discharge of economic tasks fairly well guaranteed a woman against physical abuse by her husband. Any great unhappiness she felt was soon noticed; any complaints she was impelled to make found the ear of those who could make their displeasure quickly and effectively known.

From what has already been said, it is plain that the woman held an important and secure place in Mescalero society. Since sons departed for other households soon after maturity and there was dependence on sons-in-law for defense and hunting, girls were as welcome as boys at birth. The women's contribution to the economy was acknowledged to be large; great pains were taken to train the girl in household tasks and in food-gathering techniques. Since women were more familiar with plants and their properties than were men, herbalism and the treatment of minor ailments were largely in female hands. There was little in the cultural domain from which women were barred. They attended celebrations and ceremonies with men, and they sought and obtained supernatural power on a par with men. Many of the great shamans mentioned in Mescalero "power stories" are women. A culture heroine, the mother of the culture hero, rivals her son in importance in Mescalero religion. It is not an accident that the most intricate, public, and sustained Mescalero ceremony is the girl's puberty rite and that it is so structured as to afford entertainment and bring benefits to the whole group. It is true that the men represented the extended families in council and that the leaders of local groups were always men; but women participated freely in family councils, and no one denied their influence on the stands that the male family spokesmen took. There were a few concepts and observances which tended to emphasize male attributes and prerogatives. The hoop and pole game (played by sliding a long pole after a rolling hoop) was reserved for males, and women were barred from the level grounds prepared for the sport. Males, including male horses, had to be protected from menstrual discharges. The sexual division of labor was dramatized by requiring that baskets such as women used in gathering wild vegetable foods be absent during any hunting expedition. Yet women had their equivalent discriminations. It was considered unmanly for any grown male to linger around the place where women were playing the stave game, their favorite form of gambling. And the women, under the pretext that their efforts would be "spoiled," kept males at a distance when they carried on certain kinds of work.

In cultural practice and concept, however, it is the joint contributions of the sexes to the food supply and group welfare that stand out most vividly. Women accompanied the men on the buffalo hunt to prepare the meat and hides. Men attended the women when they went to gather the hearts of the century plant and bake them in an underground oven. On these occasions the men afforded the women protection, helped transport the heavy and cumbersome plants to the baking pit, assisted in preparing the oven, and hunted in the vicinity while the "mescal" was slowly baking.

It must not be thought that the Mescalero man was an abject and browbeaten creature. If he married into a strong family, he had ample help in his economic tasks and bright prospects for a comfortable future. The avoidances and polite speech usages did not disturb him; he had grown up in the midst of such practices, responded easily to them, and considered them appropriate. He had been reminded again and again by his own relatives that at marriage he should obey and cooperate with his relatives-in-law. In fact, he was told that he would bring shame to his blood relatives and call his training into question if he proved to be troublesome in his wife's encampment. Nor was the young man completely isolated. If he had married within the local group, as was often the case, his blood relatives lived nearby, and he could visit them frequently. The marriage had been initiated by him and his relatives, and ordinarily he would not have sought an alliance with persons with whom he had reason to think he might not be able to live in harmony.

Though the affinal relatives of a young husband exercised a good deal of control over him, they were careful not to be too demanding or arbitrary. Their safety and their food supply depended on the presence, the good will, and the efforts of young men such as these who had been drawn into the family circle. A stalwart worker was a great asset to them, and it would not do to discourage or alienate him. Divorce for reasons of infidelity or incompatibility was allowed either marriage partner. Consequently, if the man was a valued member of the group, his wife's relatives took pains to indicate their good opinion of him and to extend moral support to him. They did not hesitate to scold or discipline his wife if she was jeopardizing the union by her failings.

It has been mentioned that a man's obligation to support and honor his relatives-in-law continued even after the death of his wife. Moreover, a man was not free to go his way immediately and contract another marriage following his wife's demise. Death was an anxiety-provoking crisis at best for the Mescalero. The social rules were calculated to prevent a double loss to a family whenever possible in such situations. A widower was said to "belong to" or "be at the disposal of" his deceased wife's family. After a period of mourning the kin of the dead woman pondered their relative-in-law's future. If he had been a good husband and provider and they had a marriageable girl for him within their ranks, they invoked the sororate and requested that he marry a sister or cousin (a terminological sister) of his dead wife. He could scarcely refuse, and if he did he would have had a most difficult time finding another mate, for it was believed that a marriage to one still "bound" in this manner to another family could only end in tragedy for the principals and any issue of the unsanctioned union. Mescalero culture provided the smoothest possible transition to a sororate arrangement. Sisters were accustomed to working together and were familiar with each other's households. As they grew up, they were often reminded of their common loyalties and lot. An unmarried but nubile girl would probably have already been assisting her married sister in household chores and in caring for the children and could easily, in the Mescalero view, slip into her sister's place. Of course, if a family had no girl of marriageable years to offer him, after a decent interval of mourning, it would have to allow a widower to remarry elsewhere. In such a case, presents and sentiments of regard were exchanged before the man took his leave. Children usually remained with their maternal relatives. Unless there was great need, a man was not expected to continue to provide for the relatives of his deceased wife. The avoidances and polite forms of speech which marked the marriage were perpetuated, however.

The incidence of sororal polygyny among the Mescalero was another indication of the strength of the bond between sisters and the influence of matrilocal residence. Polygyny was permitted among the Mescalero, but it was rare; it was difficult enough for a Mescalero hunter to provide adequately for one household and the progeny from one wife, without compounding his obligations. In most cases it was only prominent men, usually local group leaders, who sought a second wife. If the first wife were barren, a man might suggest that a second wife be taken; if the first wife were too fecund and therefore overworked, the initiative might come from her. Almost inevitably the rule of matrilocal residence, the difficulties of providing for affinal kin in two encampments, and the sensibilities of the man's relatives-in-law by his first marriage dictated that his second wife be a sister or cousin of the first.

The responsibilities of a woman to her husband's kin at the time of marriage were not particularly arduous. If she and her husband were of the same local group, she might know them well. If they lived at a distance, they might be and might continue to be virtual strangers to her. The marriage was considered a means of cementing bonds of friendship between the two families. In times of danger or crisis such ties might be the basis for an appeal for assistance. A common interest in the children born of the union brought these families still closer together. Not infrequently members of one family attended the social events or rituals of the other. The married woman owed her husband's kin no economic support. She did not practice avoidance with any of them. A few of the collateral relatives of her husband had the right to request the polite form of speech of her, but they rarely exercised the privilege.

It was at the death of her husband that certain rights of the husband's kin over the widow came into play. Again, the practice seems designed to safeguard and perpetuate the family and to provide the children with an appropriate father substitute at the earliest possible moment. The manner in which this was achieved in Mescalero society was to have the principle of "belonging to" or "bound to" cut both ways. When a married man died, his wife automatically became "bound to" the deceased husband's kin. If they had no suitable mate to offer her or if she had been a faithless or indifferent wife, they would probably tell her she was free to make her own future arrangements. If she had been a good wife, however, and they respected her family and valued the tie that the marriage had created, they invoked the levirate and asked her to accept a brother or cousin of her dead spouse in marriage. She had no recourse but to accede, and the scars of death were healed according to the precepts that the Mescalero thought best. For the Mescalero taught their children that brothers, too, should work together whenever possible, should share pleasure and danger, and should substitute for one another in case of need.

It is important to understand how the social system that has been outlined influenced the contacts and affiliations of the growing child. In theory, the Mescalero had a bilateral kinship system: there were no unilateral kinship units, and there was no doctrine or conscious feeling that the mother's line was more significant for the individual than that of the father. Yet, in practice, because of matrilocal residence, the mother's relatives exercised a dominant role in shaping a child's life. The mother's mother, maternal great-aunts, mother's sisters and female cousins constituted a group from whom willing hands could be drawn to help the mother care for an infant. The mother's sister's children were available to watch or play with toddlers. The young married men of the group were individuals who were attached by marriage bonds to the mother's sisters and female cousins, and they were accountable in behavior to the mother's line. Thus the early training of the child was mediated by the members of a group of kinsmen of the mother. Even if divorce or death struck a family, the child's position in this unit was not threatened; the group closed ranks to shield him, as we have seen. As children matured, the girl spent a greater amount of time in apprenticeship with the women of this group and gradually became aware that these were lifelong associations for her. The boy received his first instruction in the tasks of the male from the men of this group. In time he came to understand that his prime duty after marriage would be to his parents-in-law and other affinal relatives, but he was urged to make the transition manfully and to prove his worth in a manner that would reflect credit on the encampment in which he had been reared and schooled. In practice, then, the Mescalero women were the stable core of the society, and the maternal line was the base on which the small family, the extended family, and the local group were solidly built.

Although the Mescalero woman was in a strong and protected position socially, her share in the division of labor pointed to an arduous life. Besides gathering the wild plant harvests and preserving and storing any surplus meat and vegetables, she had numerous other responsibilities. She fleshed and tanned skins for clothing, blankets, and tipi covers (men might help to stake out and work very heavy skins), cut and sewed the skins for tipi covers and clothes, and made and painted the parfleches, or flat, rawhide containers in which family possessions were stored. It was the woman who was expected to build the wickiup or erect the tipi, gather the firewood, keep the camp supplied with water, and prepare the meals. She cared for the children (though old men or young boys might watch the toddlers in her absence or when she was busy with other chores) and fashioned the baskets and woven, pitch-covered water containers which were always in evidence in a Mescalero household. Many other utensils and such objects as the baby carrier, by which a mother cradled a baby on her back, were also her handiwork. Not the least of her tasks was to brew *tiswin*, the corn beer that was the staple for any important social gathering. (The maize used in making this was obtained by trade or raid from Pueblo Indians and Mexicans.) A woman might earn an enviable reputation as an expert in this art.

The man, too, had many duties to occupy him. His concentration on the hunt has already been mentioned, and the procurement of meat for the encampment took a good share of his time. In addition, he was responsible for the defense of the camp and the safeguarding of the precious herd of horses from thieves and raiders.

Two traditional Mescalero tray baskets and one basket of modern form (Courtesy, the American Museum of Natural History).

In times of danger this meant long periods of vigil and scouting. In order to augment the supply of horses or to compensate for losses, a man was expected to catch and break wild horses or to obtain them by raiding enemies. He was expected to participate in raids on foes for booty and, when the Mescalero had suffered greater losses in warfare than those inflicted on the enemy, to join war parties for revenge. The Mescalero man fashioned and embellished his weapons, tools, gear for horses, and ceremonial paraphernalia. If all other chores were attended to, he would probably be found braiding strands of rawhide into rope or winding buffalo hair or horsehair into rope with a distaff-type twisting tool.

In the food quest a wide variety of the animals and plants of the area were sought and utilized. The men hunted deer, elk, and the bighorn, or wild sheep, in the mountains. In the plains the buffalo, antelope, and cottontail rabbit were the principal game. Opossums and woodrats were eaten when they could be obtained. In post-contact times horses, mules, and wild steers were utilized. There was a difference of opinion about the acceptability of the squirrel, prairie dog, ringtail, and peccary as food; some Mescalero hunted and ate them, and some would not. The same division of sentiment existed in regard to the turkey, quail, and dove. In general, birds were not an esteemed article of diet, and while fish was eaten by some, it was rejected by others. The flesh of some animals, such as the bear and mountain lion, was occasionally eaten, but as a rule only in connection with ceremonies.

Head masks were sometimes employed in stalking antelope and deer, and once in a while deer were snared in head nooses strung along the trails. Relays of men mounted on swift horses occasionally ran antelope to exhaustion. Rabbit surrounds occurred in which young and old, men and women, took part. However, game was usually hunted by men, singly, in pairs, or in small groups, who depended mainly on a knowledge of the habits of the animals and a familiarity with their haunts and watering places.

The rules of the hunt, as did so much else in Mescalero Apache culture, emphasized generosity toward one's tribesmen. If a Mescalero came upon a hunter who had made a kill, it was the custom for the latter to step aside and offer a share to the new arrival. This person might take as much as half of the meat and the hide, too, if his need was great. A sense of proportion ruled, however, for every man knew he was subject to the same treatment and that overreaching on his part would only result in excessive demands upon him at a later date. Even if a hunter killed and butchered his kill undetected, he was expected to be open-handed with widows, the elderly, and the infirm who might approach him on his way into the camps with his load. Those who were unable to hunt or who had no one to hunt for them might even appear at the encampment of a person reported to have been very lucky, and they were seldom turned away empty-handed.

The Mescalero were quite particular about the birds and animals they would consume; they took into consideration the food habits of the species, and those, such as the turkey, which ate insects and "nasty things" were likely to be rejected. They also reacted against the utilization of certain other birds and animals because of unsettling ritual associations. The exploitation of the wild plant food harvests of the region, on the other hand, was considerably more thorough and less subject to taboos. The full inventory of plant foods utilized would make an unduly long list; only a representative selection will be offered here.

The agave, or mescal—the plant after which the Mescalero tribe is named—was, of course, a most important food staple. Its crowns were baked in an underground oven, and its flowering stalk was roasted and eaten, too. Sotol, a plant that looks like a smaller edition of mescal, was utilized in the same way. Other stalks that were used for food were those of bear grass and of the amole (*Yucca glauca*). The flowers of another yucca, the soapweed, were consumed as a vegetable, as were the flowers of datil (*Yucca baccata*). The fruits of datil and of the palma were the so-called Indian bananas common in Mescalero diet. After the thorns of the prickly pear tunas were removed, the fruit was eaten with relish. Many other cactus fruits were enjoyed, too. Mesquite pods, the screw bean or tornillo, the pods and flowers of the locust, the pods of vetch and the wild pea, and the podlike fruits of the white evening primrose were all utilized. Wild potatoes, the Indian potato or *camote de raton,* rootstocks of the cattail, and the tubers of the sedge were welcome additions to the larder. Juniper berries, the fruits of the three-leaved sumac, and algerita berries were gathered in quantity, too. Acorns, walnuts, and the nuts of the piñon pine, western yellow pine, and western white pine were eagerly sought. Red root or tumbleweed, purslane, lamb's quarters, pigweed, osha, wood sorrel, and shepherd's purse yielded greens. Seeds for a baked, unleavened bread came from tumbleweed, pigweed, and grasses such as dropseed. Sunflower seeds were harvested also. Some of the berries and fruits that entered the diet were strawberries, raspberries, mulberries, hawthorne fruits, gooseberries, currants, grapes, chokecherries, elderberries, and hackberries. Mint, horsemint, pennyroyal, hops, wild onion, sage, and wild celery served as flavorings. The inner bark of the pine and aspen and the inner bark and sap of the box elder maple were the sweeteners. The women knew when and where each of these foodstuffs was at its best and regulated their movements in a way calculated to gain most from the natural harvests. They exercised a great deal of ingenuity in processing some of the foods they gathered in order to make them palatable or to preserve them. The women and the men, too, utilized plants and trees for artifacts and medicines, purposes that required a good deal of knowledge of their locations, their properties, and their growth cycles.

The practical needs of the Mescalero did not absorb all of their time, energy, and thoughts. Religion played an important part in their lives and, in fact, permeated most other aspects of their culture. For instance, there were ceremonial overtones at the time of the baking of mescal: the largest crown was marked with sacred tule pollen, prayers were uttered, and restrictions on behavior were observed while the baking was in progress. In another context, men wore amulets and called upon supernatural helpers to aid them in the hunt.

The Mescalero did not worship a large pantheon of gods and goddesses. The main supernaturals whose characteristics were known to all were the culture heroine, White Painted Woman, and her divine son, Water's Child, the culture hero. These models for Mescalero womanhood and manhood are frequently mentioned in prayers and ritual songs, and the Mescalero girl impersonates White Painted

Children after the spring haircutting ceremony.

Woman during her puberty ceremony. Yet these holy figures belong essentially to the mythological period, to the early days of mankind's existence, when the culture heroine miraculously gave birth to a son who would vanquish the evil beings that were threatening the extinction of mankind. These powerful supernaturals preserved the Mescalero, taught them ceremonies and wholesome knowledge, and left. After that they intervened very little in earthly affairs.

As one might expect in a nonagricultural, mobile society, there were no calendrical rites, or ceremonies that had to occur at a specific time each year. Rather, the established or required rituals were associated with the individual life cycle and constituted a series of observances designed to guide a child through life's hazards from birth to maturity. The first of these was the cradle ceremony, in which the the infant was placed in the carrier prepared for him with prayers and appropriate ritual gestures. When the child began to walk, he was dressed in new moccasins and was led through a trail of pollen to the east, symbolic of the long and fortunate life it was hoped would be his. A little later his hair was cut for the first time; a few patches were left to encourage new and luxuriant growth. This ceremony, suitably enough, was held in the spring, when new growth was apparent everywhere, and the symbology throughout indicates that it was a prayer for the vitality and long life of the child. Though there is a generalized pattern to each of the life cycle rites referred to so far, they are considered to be an individual acquisition of those ritualists who perform them. This is decidedly not the case in regard to the girl's puberty rite, the one ceremony which is considered to be a public and tribal event, rather than an individual and personal matter.

It was believed that a girl who did not celebrate the puberty rite could not live long or bear healthy offspring; consequently no man would seek a marriage alliance with her. In sponsoring the rite, the girl's close relatives were expressing their gratitude that she had lived to maturity, and they played host to as many distant kinsmen, neighbors, and friends as they could afford to entertain. The guests came to congratulate their hosts and to wish the girl well. These occasions were among the largest and most satisfying social events of the Mescalero, and their continuance was a matter of great public interest. The ceremonialists who knew the songs, prayers, and procedures of the rite acquired their competence by being understudies of a previous generation of priests. Young men were urged to "sit with" the "big tipi" singers so that they might perpetuate the event that "gave a good time to the people." The fact that those who presided over the girl's puberty rite gained their credentials by study and application, rather than through inspiration, is to be noted, for, as we shall see, shamanism, or the acquisition of a ceremony by personal contact with supernatural forces, was the more usual method of becoming active in Mescalero religion. In fact, the girl's puberty rite is the one clear example of priestcraft among the Mescalero, the sole instance in which a rite was handed down through instruction, rather than having its origin in a mystical personal experience.

The girl's puberty rite not only differed psychologically from other ceremonies, but it was also the most complex ritual event in the Mescalero repertory. The girl's dress, modeled after that anciently worn by the culture heroine, had to be made in a prescribed manner. A female ceremonialist was engaged to dress, advise, and care for the girl throughout these proceedings. A male ceremonialist was hired to sing the songs of the rite while the girl carried out her role according to directions. The sponsoring family had to construct the "big tipi," a large structure in which a good many of the ritual episodes took place, and had to extend hospitality to the many guests. The song cycle of the rite pictured a long and successful career for the girl and blessed in advance every substance and experience she might encounter on her life journey. Masked dancers, impersonators of the Mountain Spirits who, from their stations in sacred mountains, protected the Mescalero, carried on animated dances around a great fire for each of the four nights. Their performance was considered part of the entertainment, but their presence safeguarded the camps from sickness and evil, too. Each night social dancing between men and women followed the appearance of the masked dancers.

The essence of Mescalero religion, however, was the individual power quest. The universe was believed to be suffused with supernatural power, eager to be associated with human affairs; but power could not approach man in undifferentiated form—it had to reach man through some channel, some natural phenomenon, animal, or plant, with which man was familiar. Moreover, it could appear only to believers, to those receptive and responsive to it.

The acquisition of supernatural power at some point in life was considered a normal Mescalero experience; the Mescalero was taught that he was infinitely better prepared to cope with danger if he had a supernatural helper. As he grew up and had to fend for himself and especially after he married and had responsibilities for others, he thought more and more of the added assurance that warnings and responses from the supernatural world would bring. Then, at a time of stress and anxiety, he might very well have a dream which he would interpret as a vision experience and power grant. The usual pattern was for the individual to be accosted or signaled in a dream (interpreted as a vision experience) by the source of power, which then changed into a person dressed in the Mescalero manner and led him into a "holy home," often a cave in the mountains. There the uses of the ceremony were divulged, and the songs, prayers, and particulars of the rite were rehearsed and learned. Assurances were given that supernatural power would appear and lend help when it was summoned and when it heard its songs and prayers.

The relation of an individual to supernatural power in Mescalero religion was a very intimate one. No social conventions intervened. This was the one context in which the Mescalero could unburden his soul. Support and satisfaction were considered to be mutual: supernatural power was gratified to find a human collaborator through whom its potential energies could find realization, and the human being was equally pleased to find a divine advocate who would respond to his needs and pleas. The actual relationship established between a Mescalero and his supernatural helper differed from person to person and fluctuated over time. One person might expect no more of supernatural power than to be warned of impending danger. Another would desire a healing ceremony to conduct over family members in time of illness. Still another hoped for a ceremony by means of which he could cure the sickness of fellow tribesmen who appealed to him. Some Mescalero, too literal-minded to believe that they had been approached by the supernatural, never claimed to have obtained ritual aid of any kind. In some cases supernatural help was initially granted for limited purposes only, but as a Mescalero's enthusiasm for his power grew, he might begin to feel that he was being given sanction for increased scope for his ceremony. On the other hand, in specific cases, a series of ritual failures would lead to a sense of rejection and dejection, and a shaman would abandon his ritual work. In other words, the Mescalero ritual world was an area of great fluctuations. The attachments of supernatural powers and their human agents ebbed and flowed; shamans rose in reputation and were eclipsed; ceremonies were born and died.

As a whole, Mescalero ceremonialism reflected an anxiety that so often haunts a hunting and gathering people whose margin of survival is narrow—the concern over debility. Consequently most Mescalero ceremonies were curing rites. In the explanation for sickness certain dangerous and polluting agents loomed large: lightning, which could sicken by striking close; the bear, whose odor could cause a serious ailment; the snake, whose sloughed skin could be lethal; the owl, the embodiment of the malignant ghost; the coyote, who visited disfigurement on those who touched his carcass or crossed his trail.

Another source of uneasiness ran through Mescalero ceremonialism, one that contributed tension and drama. This was the consciousness of the existence of evil, the realization that though supernatural power is attainable by all men, it will sometimes fall into the hands of malicious men. Thus a good deal of sickness was attributed to the manipulation of power by witches, and a considerable share of ceremonialism was devoted to exposing and confounding the witch. During the dark days of confinement and physical suffering following military defeat, a black mood prevailed among the Mescalero, and charges of witchcraft multiplied. Peyote meetings in particular (the peyote cult became established among the Mescalero about 1870 or a little before) became vehicles for the witch hunt on the part of persons whose inhibitions had been reduced and whose suggestibility had been stimulated by the drug.

Before leaving the subject of Mescalero ceremonialism, special mention should be made of two matters. The first is that there were no formal Mescalero rites of marriage and death, events so often marked in other societies by elaborate observances. Marriage among the Mescalero was less the founding of a new social unit than it was the absorption of the couple into an on-going extended family. It was therefore the social forms which bind the husband to his affinal group that were emphasized; the emergence of the new social unit was lightly touched upon and was not dramatized by ritual. As far as the absence of Mescalero funeral rites is concerned, it must be understood that in the Mescalero conception death was the ultimate foe and its triumph was not to be celebrated. Burial was hasty, the home and possessions of the dead person were destroyed, the grave was avoided after the burial, the name of the dead person could not be uttered, and references to him were deemed affronts to his relatives. There is a sharp and deep cleavage between the symbols of vitality and life and those of debility and death in Mescalero thought. The former are constantly mentioned and invoked; the latter are stubbornly repressed.

The second matter which deserves attention has to do with the place of women in Mescalero ceremonialism. As in other aspects of the culture, Mescalero women have a secure place, one comparable to that of men, in religion. Women did not act as the peyote chief, or the leader and moderator of a peyote meeting, though they attended such rituals. They did not impersonate the mountain-dwelling super-natural guardians of Mescalero country against enemies and epidemic disease. Yet they acquired ceremonies from the Mountain Spirits and directed the activities of the young men who did impersonate them. Women were never the singers of the girl's puberty rite who presided in the large ceremonial tipi each of the four nights while the girl danced. Yet they had another important ritual office in connection with this ceremony. The one thing with ritual overtones from which the women were excluded was the sweat lodge. This may be due to a certain association of ideas. The sweat lodge was much used by men as a remedy for rheumatism, an ail-ment often associated with inadvertent contact with menstruating women or menstrual blood. In all other aspects of Mescalero ceremonialism the women were active and prominent and were often approached by men who sought relief through their ceremonial knowledge.

The key to the understanding of Mescalero ceremonialism is the relationship between the activities and manipulations of the Mescalero shaman, or religious prac-titioner, and the accomplishments of his supernatural mentor. The Mescalero shaman has a reciprocal understanding with his source of supernatural power. He has been directed to request that the patient offer four ritual gifts (downy eagle feathers, a piece of turquoise, a bit of abalone, a small bag of pollen, and so on). Though these are presented to the shaman, they are considered to be payment to the power—evidence that the shaman is as concerned about recognition of power's role and compensation for power as he is about his own reward. These ritual pay-ments to power and the songs and prayers of the ceremony signal power that its ceremony is being employed and that its presence is required. It hastens to fulfill its part of the pact. Of those present, only the shaman is fully aware of what is taking place, but behind the scenes the exertions of the power parallel and match the activities of the shaman. When, as he is directed to do by his supernatural helper, the shaman brushes pain away with a bundle of feathers, this is the outward, visible symbol of the healing manipulations of the unseen power which is in attendance. When the shaman sucks some noxious object from his suffering client, this is the gross objectification, for the benefit of earthlings, of the elimination of disease from the body which supernatural power has achieved. To speak of Mesca-lero gullibility in the face of legerdemain is to confess ignorance of the ceremonial role of supernatural power, of which the performance of the shaman is the shadow and the accompaniment, not the substance. The psychology and, in fact, the theology of shamanism is still very imperfectly understood.

In the light of this very compressed overview of some of the main features of their life-way, what can be said of the cultural position of the Mescalero? Some orientation, especially in material traits, to the culture of the Indians of the great plains is evident. Yet how deep does it go? There was some dependence on the buffalo, but there was no organization or discipline on the buffalo hunt comparable to that of the typical plains tribes, and no great accumulation of lore and ritual concerning the buffalo. Dress and hairdress showed plains influence. A plains-like tipi was used on the flats, but it was usually replaced in the foothills and the moun-tains by a brush-covered wickiup. The horse travois was employed for dragging tipi poles and carrying the tipi cover when on the prairies, but the Mescalero travois was crudely made and seldom used to carry people or baggage. Parfleches, or flat rawhide containers, were made, and geometric designs were painted on some of them. The peyote cult, which had and still has great popularity among the tribes of the plains, existed among the Mescalero; but it was adapted to their ritual, some common plains features of the sect never took root, and it was virtually abandoned by them before 1910. It has continued to have much more vitality on the plains. The Mescalero war complex offers some elements that show plains influence, such as the use of the feather headdress and the round, covered shield. On his return from battle the Mescalero warrior publicly described his war deeds and called upon others to bear witness to the truth of his assertions. The victory dance of the Mescalero resembled Plains Indian counterparts. Some scalping of enemies took place, but it was directed toward Mexicans rather than toward Indians, and it was stimulated mainly by the bounties the Mexicans had offered for Apache scalps. Actually, because of Mescalero fears relating to death and the dead, these trophies were not retained, as they were by the Plains Indians, and did not figure importantly in victory celebrations. Thus, even the elements reminiscent of plains culture were weakly developed in the Mescalero context. On the other hand, the camp circle, the sun dance, men's and women's societies, and graded war deeds—all characteristic features of Plains Indian life—were completely absent. It has been suggested that the Mescalero system of restraints toward affinal relatives is due to plains influence; but the system of "polite forms" and avoidances practiced by the Chiricahua Apache, who lived farther west and had little or no plains contact, is even more elaborate. Certainly in social attitudes and social organization the Mescalero are far from plains-like. For one thing, the status of the woman among the Mescalero differs conspicuously from her standing on the plains.

Since the features of Mescalero culture which suggest plains contact and influence are mainly in the material sphere and are more readily discernible, they have over-shadowed equally important elements that are probably inspired by the Pueblos. Many of these, such as the presence of masked dancers who impersonate the super-naturals, the liberal use of color-directional symbolism, and the employment of pollen, turquoise, and abalone in ritual contexts, have become an integral part of the religion. It may be that even the witchcraft cult can be traced to Pueblo sources. Such material traits, too, as the mano and metate and the false boomerang very likely have a Pueblo origin.

However, the great preponderance of Mescalero possessions and concepts can be traced neither to Plains Indian nor to Pueblo origins; they belong, rather, to a general Apachean pattern, from which they have diverged in interesting and subtle ways in the course of time.

Though there is always a risk of oversimplification in such a procedure, it may be worth while to attempt to characterize the essence of the traditional or aboriginal Mescalero life-way in a convenient summary. Mescalero life was marked by a very simple material culture consisting mainly of artifacts that were light in weight, unbreakable, transported without difficulty, and simple to replace. Such a material adjustment fitted in admirably with an enthusiasm for mobility, a readiness to leave on errands of hunting and gathering at short notice, and a willingness to break camp in response to seasonal needs or to profit by a buffalo hunt. This ability to "travel light," to exploit a large territory, and to react to pressures or opportunities had its psychological repercussions. The attitude of the Mescalero toward his world was marked by a love of freedom and of movement and by a strong dislike of restraint and settled routine. There was a training correlate to this: the constant circulation of people for economic or social purposes, often singly, in pairs, or in small groups, required hardihood and confidence. Therefore the young were taught to be self-reliant, and the training of boys for strenuous and dangerous physical tasks, since the boys went farther afield, was an especially exacting process.

The accent on mobility and on making the best use of present opportunities and the de-emphasis on the accumulation of material possessions was adhered to thoroughly and consistently. Goods and booty were sought primarily for immediate use or to give away. Generosity was acclaimed as one of the cardinal virtues; property was used as a means of cementing friendship or insuring future assistance, rather than to impress others. Possessions, which were mainly personal, were destroyed at death. The dwelling in which a death occurred was abandoned, but it could easily be replaced. Household articles that were associated with the deceased were destroyed, too, but there was no great problem in procuring new baskets, water jars, and the like. Supernatural sanctions reinforced the ban against the inheritance of property. It was believed that the ghost of the departed would return to claim possessions that the living had selfishly retained and that "those who thought more of possessions than of their relatives" would become afflicted with ghost or owl sickness (the ghosts of the aggrieved as well as those of the evil and the unrequited returned as owls to trouble the living). A thinly spread, mobile population with a zest for untrammeled freedom of movement offered little incentive for a strong, centralized government. Political organization was extremely loose. The local group, from which a family might separate itself at will, may have been the largest recognized social and political unit within the tribe. Certainly bands or moieties, if they existed, were very nebulous bodies. The chief, or leader, of a local group was much more a spokesman for the family heads or an adviser than a person in whose hands unlimited authority was vested. His post was not hereditary; it was not even guaranteed for his own lifetime; it had constantly to be validated by accomplishment.

The absence of wide political bonds stood in sharp contrast to the strong family ties. Women of a family were linked together by common residence and joint work obligations and habits as well as by the blood tie. The mature men, who entered a family at marriage, were bound to it by very formal and exacting respect relations and by such institutions as the sororate, sororal polygyny, and the "belonging to" relationship that became effective at the demise of a mate. The extended domestic family with matrilocal residence which was brought together by these arrangements was the basic work group, the social and economic unit in which productive efforts and consumption were centered. The family was also the unit which protected the individual when he was accused or threatened and which avenged him when he was mistreated or slain. The average extended family, consisting as it did of a number of small or elementary families, was normally large enough to discharge its economic, social, and protective functions. If it lacked the numbers to cope with a situation, there was always the possibility of a temporary alliance with other extended family groups. As a result of the pivotal position of the extended family among the Mescalero, it had primary responsibility for the training of the children of its members and exercised a disciplinary function over those affiliated with it. The enthusiasm for freedom and self-reliance which was fostered by their natural and social environment frequently collided with the requirement that a Mescalero subordinate his own personal inclinations to the best interests of the extended family. There were strong sentiments against showing resentment when family needs overrode personal desires, but there is also evidence that the irritation or anger, though repressed, sometimes found a vent. Tales, fantasies, and the structuring of fears indicate that there was a good deal of alarm on the part of an individual over the possibility that the supernatural power of a relative, bent on prolonging his own life, might be used against him or that, if one was not "sacrificed" in this way, he might be persecuted by the ghost of a deceased kinsman. Thus we see that, though in many ways the extended family was effective and helpful, like so many other human arrangements, it harbored unresolved conflicts and ambivalences.

Any discussion of the Mescalero extended family and its importance brings to mind the anchor role played by the women, not only in this social unit, but also in other cultural contexts. Matrilocal residence held a group of women together. They had ample opportunity to cooperate in exploiting the resources of the area, and their contribution to the economy was significant. They took an active part in ceremonialism. In fact, there were few aspects of the culture in which they did not participate fully.

It was ill health, rather than human enemies, that caused the Mescalero most alarm. Very likely the narrow margin of subsistence and the incessant need for vigor and mobility fed this concern, for nothing was as threatening to the Mescalero as the inability to hunt and gather in order to provide for the family. Rites to locate and control the enemy, ceremonies to find lost objects, ceremonies to help on the hunt, ceremonies to attract and influence persons of the opposite sex, and religious exercises for still other purposes were practiced. Nevertheless, in response to the overshadowing health anxiety, the great majority of Mescalero ceremonies were curing rites. Life was conceived of as an arena in which the forces of health and life struggled with the forces of sickness and death. Old age was honored, and its symbols were much invoked in ceremonies because it was considered a triumph over death. Life cycle ceremonies were important because they preserved a person in health and good fortune to the next stage of life. Ceremonies to confound witches were pictured as warfare against the forces of illness and death; the very vocabulary that was used ("arrows of the witch") drew from the terminology of warfare. Disease was the hated enemy, comparable only to the darkest forces of the natural and supernatural world.

The crux of Mescalero religion might be characterized as evangelical or devotional shamanism. It conceived of a universe permeated with supernatural power which must realize itself through man or not at all. If he were to be long-lived and successful, man had equal need of power. As a result of this dual necessity, power and man met in a mystic experience in which man learned the details of a ceremony and in which power acquired a human representative and advocate. The relation between supernatural power and the shaman was a warm and intimate one. The shaman sang the praises of his power and ceremony and demanded faith and compliance with his directions of anyone who sought his help. Any cure or success was credited ultimately to supernatural power, but the shaman was buoyed up by the conviction that it was only through his mediation that the beneficial effects of supernatural power could be released. Obviously a ceremony was effective only so long as power and the shaman cooperated. If they quarreled, if either lost faith in the other, if one made suggestions or demands that outraged his coworker, the ceremony would be withdrawn, would be abandoned, or would lose its effectiveness. And since the best of friends sometimes quarrel or doubt each other, ceremonies often became dormant or passed out of existence. Shamans gained and lost in renown; like so much else in Mescalero culture, it was effectiveness, not theory, that counted. A Mescalero shaman had to succeed and continue to succeed in order not only to command the faith of·others but to still his own doubts.

Mescalero Culture under Siege

What has been pictured is traditional or aboriginal Mescalero culture, and, as every condensed account tends to do, it emphasizes modality and goals, and not the actualities of every situation. There were many families that did not have daughters to attract stalwart sons-in-law or that did not have sons through whom to cement alliances with other families. There were individuals who never were inspired by a vision experience or who soon became disillusioned with the supernatural power they did acquire. There were those who were indiscreet in their threats at a moment of anger and who were dogged thereafter by rumors that they dabbled in witchcraft.

Not only did individual fate, even in aboriginal times, often depart from cultural prescription, but forces were gathering three centuries ago that were to threaten and modify the on-going culture itself. Before the end of the seventeenth century the Mescalero were horsemen, and we can only speculate on the degree to which their culture was modified by the acquisition of an animal which has since figured so prominently in their economy, warfare, social life, folklore, and religion. By the beginning of the eighteenth century the advancing American frontier pressed tribes westward and southward, and the conflict with the Comanche for the buffalo, horses, and territory loomed. In the eighteenth century, too, the Spanish frontier moved northward. The Spanish crown recognized no Indian claim to land, and the Mescalero found themselves increasingly engaged in hostilities with the soldiers sent to protect or avenge the colonists. The struggle with Spanish forces came to a peak by 1789, after which there were three decades of comparative calm. Thereafter Spain was preoccupied by the Mexican independence movement, which succeeded in 1821. In 1824 New Mexico was made a territory of the young republic and, with an eye to the rapid expansion of the United States, an attempt was made by Mexico to encourage and hasten its settlement. This meant further intrusion into territory which the Mescalero considered their own and a sharp increase in the number and ferocity of the clashes between Indians and settlers. The creation of the Republic of Texas in 1835 presented the Mescalero with a new claimant to some of their tribal lands. The annexation of Texas by the United States in 1845 and the quarrel over the western boundary of Texas precipitated war between the United States and Mexico. Much of the territory in dispute, land in Texas between the Nueces and the Rio Grande, incidentally, was viewed by the Mescalero as belonging to them. By the Treaty of Guadalupe-Hidalgo, which ended the war between Mexico and the United States in 1848, and by the Gadsden Purchase of 1853, the United States acquired most of the lands which the Mescalero considered to be their tribal territory. A struggle between American settlers and the Mescalero was inevitable. By 1849 an Indian agent was appointed by the United States. In 1850 a proclamation of President Fillmore created the United States Territory of New Mexico, and the governor was named to the additional post of Superintendent of Indian Affairs. At this moment thousands of prospectors were crossing the territory on their way to the California gold fields. In the eyes of the Americans it was imperative that the Indians be controlled and contained. Various means were used. Between 1852 and 1855 treaties of peace were negotiated with the Mescalero—treaties which were either not approved or not implemented by Washington. Military posts such as Fort Fillmore, Fort Bliss, Fort Craig, and Fort Stanton were built to protect travel routes and settlements. By 1853 United States military forces were making forays into Mescalero mountain strongholds "to divert" and overawe the Indians. Already the idea of isolating and confining the Indians had taken root. A treaty of 1855 designated a reservation near Fort Stanton for the Mescalero. The treaty was not approved, but an agency was maintained at Fort Stanton for a long time thereafter. By 1856 the territorial legislature was requesting reservations on which the Indians within its boundaries could be housed. As a result, the federal appropriation acts of 1856–1857 made provision for the establishment of Indian "reserves" in New Mexico.

Just before the outbreak of the Civil War the stream of settlers became a flood. The discovery of gold in Colorado brought 100,000 miners to the new fields, and many of them drifted south. The expanding cattle industry, the prospecting, and increasing activity along the trade routes introduced a good many unruly and violent elements to the area. In obedience to the directions of their agents, some of the Mescalero tried to farm in the fertile valleys of their domain. Frequently their stock was stolen by white cattle thieves, and, on a number of occasions, they were attacked without provocation by white vigilante groups.

At the beginning of the Civil War, Confederate sympathizers among the American military cynically announced a punitive thrust through Mescalero territory; their real objective was to join rebel forces at El Paso. After some initial successes the Confederate forces were driven south and did not seriously threaten the territory during the last stages of the war. While the white soldiers were engaged in their fratricidal struggle, the Mescalero had a respite and an opportunity to strike back at the prospectors and settlers, but in 1862 General James H. Carleton of the United States Army turned his attention to them. He planned and executed a massive three-pronged attack into their mountain strongholds and ordered that all Mescalero men who did not immediately appear at Fort Sumner on the Pecos River for surrender should be killed. A good many were slain in a vain attempt to reach the fort; others escaped to the plains or to the west or made their way into northern Mexico. Eventually four hundred and seventy-two Mescalero were concentrated at Fort Sumner, or Bosque Redondo, as it was alternatively called. Here the Indians were set to agricultural work under strict military supervision.

Having subdued the Mescalero, General Carleton began a campaign against the more numerous Navaho. Though he had promised the Mescalero that Bosque Redondo would be reserved for them alone, he decided to send the defeated Navaho there also. Before the influx was halted, he had sent nearly ten thousand Navaho to Fort Sumner. Land and resources for so many people were lacking at this site, natural disasters compounded the difficulties, the Mescalero and Navaho fought pitched battles, and want and desperation ruled. General Carleton's policies came under sharp attack, and he was relieved in September 1866. Even before this the Mescalero stole away one night in a body, leaving behind only nine tribesmen who were too old or infirm to travel with them. For the next several years there was little contact between government representatives and the Mescalero. An agency was maintained for them, but they sedulously avoided it.

It was not until 1870 that any Mescalero were willing to trust themselves to white "protection" again. In 1872 a first attempt was made to define the boundaries of a reservation for them; a year later a reservation comprising the eastern slopes of the White and Sacramento Mountains was set aside by executive order. The Indians complained bitterly that the area was too small and that it forced them to remain in high mountains in severe weather. Yet the boundary lines were enforced; a pass system was instituted, and any Indian found outside the reserve without written permission was deemed a "hostile." In spite of their restricted lands the Indians were still the targets of white plunderers and of settler hostility. The horses of the Indians were considered fair game; at the same time a band of horse thieves at a town some distance from the reservation made it a convenient practice to raise the cry of "Apache" to cover their own trail. Greater concentration of population and confinement left the Mescalero ready victims of disease, too. In 1877 there was a serious outbreak of smallpox, a scourge that was to return to decimate the tribe a number of times. In 1878 the notorious Lincoln County war, a contest between two factions of cattlemen, reached its height. Agency personnel were engaged in the struggle. The agent was identified with one of the factions and lost his position; the agency clerk was killed by Billy the Kid. A new agent started for his post but turned back at Santa Fe when the prevailing conditions were described to him. Two hundred persons are reputed to have lost their lives in this "war" that raged in and around the reservation and kept the Indians bewildered and apprehensive.

An even heavier blow was soon to fall. The Desert Land Act of 1877 had opened still other Western lands to settlement, and a move for even greater concentration of the Indians on fewer reservations was being pressed. In spite of the promise of a reservation in their own country that had been made to them, the Eastern, or Warm Springs, Chiricahua were ordered to make ready to move to San Carlos, Arizona, to live with the Western Apache. This they refused to do, and a contingent of them, under the leadership of Victorio, fled to the Mescalero reservation. When Victorio departed southward, some Mescalero who were similarly disillusioned and disenchanted went with him. To prevent further aid to Victorio from the Mescalero, the military decided to disarm and virtually imprison them. They were assembled at Fort Stanton under false pretenses and surrounded by a thousand troops. Their arms were taken from them, their horses were driven away, and they were crowded into a corral in which the manure lay several inches deep. Fourteen Mescalero who resisted were killed. Most of the Mescalero property fell into the hands of the Indian scouts who accompanied the troops. The Mescalero were confined in the corral until spreading sickness forced their release. Even after that they were not allowed to stray far from the fort. Their pleas to be allowed to hunt and gather to supplement their slender rations were disregarded, and the restrictions remained in force until Victorio died in battle and all danger of Mescalero belligerency was considered to be past.

It was just about at this moment of Mescalero defeat, humiliation, and serious property loss that Chris, the narrator of the life story presented here, was born, probably in 1880. The next year the Albuquerque Indian School, to which Chris was eventually to go, was founded for the education of Mescalero and Pueblo children especially. In 1882, not without difficulty, the tribe was persuaded to send three children to the young institution. In this same year gold was discovered in a northern district of the reservation, and there was a surge to the area by miners and prospectors, who considered the presence of the Indians a nuisance and a threat to the riches they hoped to find. Demands for the removal of the Mescalero arose once more and were stilled only by the revision of the reservation boundaries to accommodate the mining interests. The boundaries of the reservation were to be altered on several more occasions, each time to the consternation of the Indians. Mescalero fears of removal were temporarily relieved when the Jicarilla Apache were sent to live with them in 1883, but the Mescalero were to be unnerved by constant invasions of their land and range by settlers and cattlemen, and they repeatedly asked for a clear title to their reservation. It was not until 1922 that Congress confirmed the Indian title to the reservation.

In 1883, also, the first serious attempt to missionize the Mescalero was made when one hundred and seventy-three of them were baptized into the Catholic faith, the religion to which most of them nominally adhere to this day. At this time the white man's medicine began to be applied; in 1886 all the school children were vaccinated. But crowded dormitories and restrictions on movement were encouraging diseases for which Western medicine as yet had no cure; the incidence of tuberculosis, which was to grow to alarming proportions, was on the increase. From the reports of the agents it is evident that the boarding schools and the off-reservation schools were being used as a device to reduce the influence of the traditional culture. The policy was to separate the school children from their elders as soon as possible for as long as possible and to hold them in school the year round so there would be no backsliding. Meanwhile the attempt to house the Jicarilla Apache with the Mescalero was failing. The Jicarilla exodus began in 1886, and by 1887 all of the Jicarilla had drifted northward to their former territory.

Another effort to oust an Apache tribe from its ancestral lands was causing even more difficulty. The Chiricahua Apache had been concentrated with the Western Apache at San Carlos, an arrangement resisted by both tribes. There were a series of unsanctioned departures of Chiricahua groups, each followed by a military campaign to intercept and return the fugitives. The last of these military confrontations involved Geronimo and his small band of followers. Chiricahua scouts and Mescalero, too, were employed in helping the United States military forces to trail and subdue the so-called hostiles. In 1886 the Mescalero agent reported: "The commander of the military district has made repeated requisition upon us during the year for scouts to assist in the campaign against Geronimo. To all of these the Mescaleros have responded cheerfully, until now more than half their men are in the field. . . ." At the end of the conflict all who could be identified as Chiricahua Apache, whether they had acted as Indian scouts for the American forces or were insurgents, were taken into custody and removed from the West. It is easy to see how Chris's father, a Chiricahua married to a Mescalero woman, a man urged to join the scouts by both tribes, fell into the removal net. The number of Mescalero males available for scouting, incidentally, should not be exaggerated. In 1887 there were 438 Mescalero on the agency rolls, of whom 185 were males and 253 were females. Many of the males were very young or very old; the number of males in the middle-age range had been much reduced by the pitiless campaigns to contain and reduce the Mescalero that lasted until the death of Victorio.

The defeat of Geronimo and the removal of the Chiricahua to eastern prisons and barracks ended open Apache resistance to reservation life and white domination. The reports of the Indian agents for the Mescalero indicated that their efforts were increasingly directed toward enrolling children in school, sending older children to off-reservation boarding schools, and encouraging farming practices. There is a good deal of evidence in these reports of much unhappiness and of aggression turned inward. Homicidal outbreaks among the Indians resulting in several deaths at a time are frequently reported. References to charges of witchcraft and executions for witchcraft become more common. A people used to a sprawling existence was adjusting painfully to living at close quarters under stress. The local group was a prime target of white officials. A determined attempt was made to induce family heads to fan out as individual homesteaders. The influence of the women of a family was an irritant to the white personnel. They were mystified by its presence in a virile people and looked upon it as a device to keep the girls out of school. Some aboriginal institutions were probably reinforced by historical events. There was a good deal of headshaking in official circles over the large number of polygynous marriages; the campaigns of extermination of the men and the resulting skewed sex ratio no doubt contributed to this. Reverses, disease, and uncertainties made for a greater dependence on religion, too.

The Indian policy of the United States fluctuated wildly. At one period Indian agents were nominated by religious groups, at another school superintendents were expected to act as agents as well, and at still other times it was considered advisable to fill the post of agent with army officers. The last-named course brought a series of smug martinets to Mescalero, the most famous (or infamous) of whom was Lt. V. E. Stottler. This worthy refused to give any gainful employment or to issue any goods or equipment to Mescalero men who would not cut their braids and adopt the white man's style of apparel. He achieved 100 percent school attendance by employing starvation and the guardhouse against recalcitrant parents. He decided he could better maintain discipline by "summary action" of his own and abolished the court of Indian offenses on which Mescalero judges sat. Thereafter Indians lost their positions or tasted the guardhouse for such offenses as "working against the policy of the agent." When his methods were questioned, as he candidly reports, he "dispensed with the services of the [school] superintendent and assumed personal charge of his duties." Indian dances, *tiswin* parties, and ceremonies were banned. Shamans were allowed to attend the sick only in "cases where death would inevitably take place," and they were forbidden to accept payment for their services. Stottler was enraged and contemptuous over the "hen-pecked" condition of the Mescalero, and he did not hesitate to decree the guardhouse and hard labor for the "mother-in-law who interferes." Like other agents, he acted to keep the children in school over the summer so they wouldn't "return to camp ways."

Yet, as far as his warped vision permitted, Stottler was eager to protect the assets of the Indians and make them self-supporting. He sought to reduce squatting and running cattle on Indian lands without paying for the privilege. He established a sawmill so use could be made of the timber resources. He advised that the claims of white men to four hundred acres of improved reservation land "be extinguished by purchase or otherwise." He was determined to move Mescalero families from the tipis in which they were living to log cabins he ordered them to erect. In casting around for enterprises that would help make the Mescalero self-sufficient, he settled upon a combination of blanket-weaving by the women and sheep-raising to furnish the materials. Five thousand sheep were purchased and issued, a house was built where the girls could be taught to weave, and a number of expert Navaho weavers were imported to demonstrate the art. When Stottler retired in June 1898, he was confident that he had done much to "civilize" the Mescalero, and he basked in official praise. The alleged "advance" of the Mescalero was taken seriously enough so that in 1899 all rations and annuities were cut off except for the aged, blind, and infirm.

Yet many of Stottler's "reforms" expired at about the time he left the reservation. No example of Mescalero blanket-weaving exists. Not long after his departure the flocks had decreased so seriously that the remaining sheep were put in the hands of the few Indians who had shown some interest in the industry. By this time the first field matron had been assigned to the reservation. She started a class in lace-making for the young women and made an abortive attempt to revive an interest in weaving. Neither effort lingered long or added much to Mescalero economic salvation.

The stringent controls over the Mescalero were relaxed very slowly. It was 1898 before the pass system was abolished and the Indians could come and go without penalty. Rules of behavior continued to be promulgated by the agent. In 1901 Agent Luttrel set aside certain holidays and feasts for the Mescalero. Curiously enough, most of them coincided with such standard American festive occasions as the Fourth of July, Thanksgiving, and Christmas. In reporting his action to his superiors, the agent asserted with evident self-satisfaction: "So now they have six civilized gatherings each year, where they enjoy themselves in innocent amusement and recreation. This takes the place of those things we have taken away from them." The Stottlers and Luttrels at Mescalero were neither in advance of nor behind their times. In 1901 W. A. Jones, Commissioner of Indian Affairs, instructed all agents to see to it that their male charges cut their hair and that both sexes adopt "citizens' clothing," abandon face-painting, and cease dancing and feasts. The commissioner attributed "the majority of the cases of blindness among the Indians of the United States" to face-painting! In the same year the commissioner proclaimed that "it shall be the duty of each Indian agent to keep a permanent register of every marriage which takes place among the Indians under his charge. . . ."

In 1902 it was reported that there were still Mescalero in northern Mexico, remnants of those who fled during the troubles of 1880. The group turned out to be Lipan, but nevertheless arrangements were made to bring thirty-seven of them to Mescalero in 1903. Again members of more than one Apache tribe were housed together on the Mescalero reservation. In 1902 the first grazing permit was issued to an outsider, and at last some compensation was received for what had been arrogantly used without compunction or payment before. In 1903 grazing permits yielded $7,600. By this time Chris had returned from school, and his narrative describes in some detail the events that impinged on Mescalero culture until he ended his recital in 1935 at the age of fifty-five. In 1912, the year New Mexico was admitted to the Union as a state, negotiations were in progress which would return most of the Chiricahua to the West as residents on the Mescalero reservation. The willingness of the Mescalero to admit still others to the reservation was due in part to renewed nervousness over the possible loss of the fraction of their former territories that had been set aside for them. There was a persistent rumor that A. B. Fall, whose ranch adjoined the reservation in the Three Rivers area, had designs on the Indians' land. From 1912 to 1922 Senator Fall sponsored legislation that would have made a public park of the Mescalero reservation. A large contingent of Chiricahua arrived in 1913, forming the third Apache tribal component in residence. The tribal differences and the greater worldliness of the traveled and better-educated Chiricahua created tensions, some of which Chris was to feel acutely. Now greater sources of income were needed to support the larger population, and a cattle herd for the Indians was begun. As it grew, the leases to white cattlemen were cancelled. At the outbreak of World War I a fairly large number of the young Apache of the reservation enlisted. For the Mescalero youth this was a rare break with reservation life, and at the end of the conflict all Indians who had served in the armed forces were admitted to citizenship. The influenza epidemic of 1918 did not spare the Mescalero, as Chris's account pathetically reveals.

The depression of the early 1930s cut off sources of credit and outside income for the Mescalero. New Mexico was part of the dust bowl, and the privations of both the whites and the Indians of the region were severe. A phase of the New Deal was a massive program to help the Indians. It brought the Indian Emergency Conservation Work (ECW) to employ the Indians in the building of roads and facilities throughout the reservation. It included the Indian Reorganization Act, which freed funds for economic, medical, and educational purposes. It was while these new attempts to treat with the Mescalero, quite different in tone and spirit from what had gone before, were being implemented, that the writer first met Chris and began to record his odyssey. As the comments of no outsider could, it conveys the indignities, the buffetings, the bewilderments, the hardships, the misunderstandings, the strivings, the satisfactions, and the burgeoning hopes that made up life as the Mescalero experienced it between 1890 and 1935.

PART TWO

CHRIS'S LIFE STORY

1

Child of the Vanquished

War and Raid in the West

"IN THE MIDDLE" is my real name. I don't know who gave it to me. They just started calling me that, I guess. My father was a Chiricahua Apache. "Hide the Moccasin" was his Indian name. My first name in English is after his. Then a cowboy gave me his name for my last name. He was a great friend of my father's. My mother was a Mescalero Apache. She was called Compra. I call myself Mescalero in spite of my father.[1] My mother was one of the kinfolk of Peso, the Mescalero chief, who died here on the Mescalero reservation.[2] My mother carried Peso around in the cradle when he was a baby.[3]

[1] The Mescalero Apache trace relationship through both mother's and father's line. But residence is matrilocal: women are the stable nucleus of the family group; children grow up surrounded by maternal kin, ordinarily remain with the mother and her relatives in case of separation or divorce, and usually continue to live with maternal kin at the death of the mother. Accordingly, in spite of a theory of bilateral kinship, in practice there is a greater reliance on maternal relatives and more contact with them. Consequently, in intertribal marriages, when the mother is Mescalero, there is a strong tendency, as in this case, for the children to be considered Mescalero. On another occasion, in the course of genealogical work, the narrator claimed, though he could not justify his assertion by convincing evidence, that his father was "part Mescalero." This may merely have been an attempt to identify himself still more completely with the Mescalero tribe. Yet, if it is true, it may help to explain the tendency of the narrator's father to visit and seek refuge in Mescalero country and his marriages to Mescalero women.

The name is often virtually a nickname bestowed on an infant or a young child, arising from something distinctive in appearance or behavior. If a name proves inappropriate as time goes on, it is replaced by one that seems more fitting or that refers to some major event in which the person has been involved. Names associated with their exploits are sometimes conferred on children by warriors. The name is not used in direct address except in pleading for help, in emergencies, or in anger. Etiquette decrees that even in discussing a person his name be employed sparingly. The use of teknonymy, kin terms, and various circumlocutions makes it possible to avoid frequent use of the name.

[2] The Mescalero did not make elaborate status distinctions, but it was a matter of pride to be connected with the families of political or military leaders.

[3] The kindred living in one place formed what might be called a "work pool," exchanged services, and cooperated in various chores and enterprises, as this passage suggests.

Do you remember the time we were on the White Sands with my cousin, Tom? You recall that he pointed to a certain place in the San Andres Mountains. He was saying, "That is the place where your father was left when he was a novice on his first raid."[4]

[4] During his first four raiding and martial expeditions the Chiricahua youth was considered a novice and was subject to various rules of behavior and speech. For details see Opler and Hoijer 1940. The San Andres are in south-central New Mexico. The White Sands, a part of which is now used as a United States testing ground for rockets, is a large area of gypsum sand dunes in Doña Ana County in southern New Mexico. It lies southeast of the San Andres Mountains.

When my father was about thirteen, some Chiricahua Apache were making a raid to steal Mescalero horses. They were both Apache tribes, but they were doing this anyway.[5] They left my father at that place that Tom pointed out and they never came back for him.[6] He waited and waited. He got pretty cold and hungry. At last the Mescalero found him and brought him in. That is how he came to the Mescalero people the first time.

[5] It was unusual for the Chiricahua and Mescalero to raid against each other. But these were troubled times. Owing to the incursion of white settlers, tribal ranges were shrinking, Indian tribes had been dislocated and set against one another, and horses were in great demand.

[6] The novice was trained on the journey but was not to be endangered by being involved in direct action or fighting if this could be avoided. Very likely this is why the boy was left at some distance from the scene of action in this instance.

Afterward he went back to his country. Choneska was a little boy then. He was playing outside the camps and he was the first one to see my father. He called out, "That boy that they say is dead is back again!" His family told him, "Don't say a thing like that! That one must have died!"[7] But he went and told my father's family too, and they came running out and saw my father there.

7 Choneska was one of the oldest living Chiricahua Indians at the time this narrative was recorded. Note the indirect manner of referring to one thought to be dead and the reluctance to discuss death at all. Such taboos and cautions are related to acute fear of ghosts.

My father said that the women had their hair cut for him with just a patch in front and back left.[8] He didn't like to see it. He said, "I'm not dead. They just threw me away. They got a lot of good horses, and they didn't want to give me any, and that's why they left me."[9]

8 Haircutting, especially by women, was one of the symbols of mourning. About this practice the narrator added: "If a person is lost and they think he is dead, they wait four days and then cut their hair. Like the time my father was left— they waited four days and then cut their hair. Then he showed up. The Mescalero women just cut their hair a little in back and front for mourning, but this is the way my father said he saw it over among the Chiricahua Apache. For mourning, the Mescalero men used to cut off one braid and leave the other. I often saw this."

9 It is improbable that the boy was callously abandoned. It is more likely that the raiders were discovered, cut off from him, and forced to flee without him.

My Father's Supernatural Power

My father's father was a leader in those days, and he was pretty angry when he heard how my father had been left behind. He was going to kill those two men who took my father out on the raiding trip and left him.[10]

10 In threatening revenge against those who had endangered his son, this man was reacting as a family head and not as a leader of a larger social unit. Ideally leaders were expected to try to keep the peace. There is other evidence that the narrator's father had Chiricahua relatives who were prominent members of the tribe. The grandson of the Chiricahua leader, Cochise, said: "I gave a gun to Chris once. He is a relative of my father. I feel he is kin to me if he is a relative of my father."

Later my father was given power by the bear, the wolf, and others when he was on a journey. He went to Mexico and then to the Victorio band and then to Hot Springs where his tribe was living. Loco was not yet head of the eastern band of Chiricahua Apache.[11] My father went across the plains twice, and the second time he slept at a place near the White Sands.[12] It was close to the springs. He was a little up the hills and on a rock. He built a fire and went to sleep. He had made a mattress of grass.

11 This identifies the narrator's father as a member of the Eastern Band ("red paint people") of the Chiricahua Apache tribe. Both Victorio and Loco were

Eastern Chiricahua Band leaders. Warm (or Hot) Springs Apache, Ojo Caliente Apache, Coppermine Apache, Mimbreños Apache, and Mogollones Apache are other names by which reference to this band or parts of it has been made in the literature.

[12] "The plains" mentioned here are the flat lands of the Tularosa Valley and Jornada del Muerto in New Mexico, west of the present Mescalero reservation.

While he was sleeping at this place, something came to him. This happened toward morning, and he was sound asleep. Something touched him and told him to awake for it had good things to tell him. He pushed the cover off his head, and there beside him sat a silver-tip bear. It spoke in a human way to him and told him it was time for him to get up, that it was here he would get something to know and to travel by.[13]

[13] Both Chiricahua and Mescalero Apache conceive of the universe as being suffused with supernatural power, potentially useful to man for curing illnesses, confounding the enemy, finding lost objects, and so on. Power reaches man through animals, plants, and natural phenomena which take human form to instruct an Apache man or woman in the appropriate ceremonies. This account, with its vision experience, guided journey to a "holy home," and acquisition of power and ceremony, follows the typical pattern for the obtaining of supernatural help and ritual among Chiricahua and Mescalero Apache.

He got up. He knew that a door was open to him. He just walked right in, into the rocks. He was led into a room, and the grizzly bear changed itself into the form of a man and told him to follow wherever it went.

He showed my father through a gate where striking rocks were hitting against each other all the time. Then they came to a place where four points of rock went back and forth. They also walked through that. They came to another rock that was rolling and was in the form of a round ball, just like a hill. It hit the bank on the other side all the time. But they walked over it and didn't even notice it strike the bank. Then they came to a swinging rock door and passed through it safely.

They now saw two big bears, one black and one white, at a gate. The leader said to continue, and they went between them. Further on they came to two big snakes, a black one and a white one, but they went between these also without trouble. This time something that was never seen before [in accounts of the acquisition of supernatural power known to the narrator] was present in the cave. It was the wolf, the big timber wolf. There was a black one and a white one. In all the holy caves the shamans describe, they never speak of seeing the wolf at all. They tell of coyotes, skunks, and other animals, but not wolves. The wolf spoke to my father, but still he went on. Now they came to the geese. There were a black one and a white one there. When they saw my father they tried to fly but came to the ground all the time, because they felt so good. They said, "We know you. We have known you all the time."[14]

[14] In the vision experiences that lead to the acquisition of supernatural power, tests of the courage and determination of the seeker for ritual aid are common. To make his choice seem more discriminating and important, supernatural power other than that which the shaman (the individual recipient of supernatural power and ceremony) finally obtains is often offered but is rejected or ignored.

Next they crossed a place where two moving logs were used for a bridge. Beyond this bridge they reached another more beautiful place. My father asked the guide what this place was and was told this was Summer's home. They left it, crossing a spider thread that acted as a bridge. They came to an even more beautiful country with many flowers growing. All these spoke to them. My father asked what this place was, and the bear told him this was the home of the flowers and the herbs used for curing men all over the world. "This is Medicine's home."[15]

[15] Herbalism is extremely important in Apache ceremonialism. Plants can act as a source of supernatural power, and, in any case, almost any power advises the shaman about the proper use of medicinal plants in his curative rites.

They went on. Then they came to the humans. The humans were working out in the fields. They ran towards my father and tried to show him many supernatural things.[16] He paid no attention to them.

[16] These "humans" can be thought of as the essence of shamanism, symbolizing human beings who can manipulate supernatural power in extraordinary ways. What "work" these human beings were carrying on in the fields is not specified. The Eastern Chiricahua were among the first Chiricahua Apache to attempt to farm, and the narrator's father tried his hand at farming in the early reservation period between military episodes. Therefore he may have agricultural work in mind.

Then he came to a place where there was nothing but beautiful young women dressed like White Painted Woman, like the girls who have just gone through the adolescence ceremony.[17] The puberty rite was shown him there. That was the "home" of that ceremony. But he paid no attention to this either.[18] On he went. He came into another land, and you could hear the drums beating steadily. It was even more beautiful. There he saw Black One and the Mountain Spirits with different markings. This also belonged to the adolescence rite.

[17] White Painted Woman is the culture heroine, the mother of the culture heroes. Every young Apache girl is dressed to resemble White Painted Woman, enacts the role of White Painted Woman, and is referred to as White Painted Woman during her adolescence ceremony.

[18] This suggests that he could have become a priest of the girl's puberty rite if he had halted here and accepted instruction. In this context the word "home" has the force of a ritual center at which religious knowledge and understanding of the rite can be obtained.

His guide said to him, "If you want to be a leader of the Mountain Spirits you can take those four Mountain Spirits there. They are used in every way. They are the leading ones, stronger than any you saw in any other caves." There were twelve altogether. He was told, "You can use only four in one night. If sickness is in the country, you can use them." But my father said no and went on.[19]

[19] The Mountain Spirits are mountain-dwelling supernaturals, protectors of the Apache and their territories against enemies and epidemic disease, who are impersonated in ceremonies by Apache masked dancers. Black One is a special kind of Mountain Spirit. Ordinarily the impersonators of the Mountain Spirits dance in groups or sets of four. The masked dancers always appear at a girl's puberty rite.

Then he was led farther and before him was a big man. There were four tables.[20] The man showed him all the kinds of power there, but my father said, "No, I want to go to one stronger than you."

[20] Note the modern touch; the assorted powers are displayed on tables!

The man said, "But they usually go no farther. This is the best."
But my father refused and wouldn't take any of it.
He went into another room, and there in the middle sat another man with a chair that turned either way. From him shone light, and all around him was green fruit.[21] The man studied my father. He said, "There is no human being who has come this far, passing the first man. What do you come for? You see fruits here, and there are things here that are valuable above all. What you ask for your own good, for rearing your children, I will give to you."

[21] The narrator's father had apparently seen a swivel chair as well as tables. He acted on a number of occasions as a scout for United States military forces and was familiar with the furnishings at military headquarters and posts. The Chiricahua-Mescalero color-directional ceremonial circuit begins with the east, the most important ritual direction, and moves clockwise, or sunwise, around the cardinal directions. The usual combinations are: east—black; south—blue (green); west—yellow; north—white (or variegated). Though it was not mentioned, it can be assumed that the first room to which the narrator was led stretched to the east and that its contents were black. In sequences of ritual songs, prayers, or gestures, the east is always mentioned first or given priority.

My father said, "I come for the power that is strongest. Are you the strongest?"[22]

[22] The use of supernatural power may be confined to the protection and needs of the recipient and his immediate family, or it may be employed more widely in rites to cure or benefit unrelated tribesmen. The implication here is that this man was seeking power strong enough to use in all contexts.

"No, there are two above me."

Then my father went on. He came to another man who was shining with a yellow light before him. The light made it seem as though the wind was blowing pollen from the trees around him. But it was not. This man knew that my father was not going to stop there. So he brought before him two yellow horses with white tails. And a sort of wagon was there.

My father got in the wagon with the guide, and they came to a gate, a big, white gate. Everything was white, even the trees and fruit; and the faces of the people there shone, and before him he saw many things. He bowed down four times, and the fourth time he was before a man in a big white chair who had a white staff in his right hand.[23] This man was the last one.[24] He asked my father how he got there, and my father told him.

[23] Four is the most important Apache ritual number. Note that the white man's wagon has become a part of this Apache ritual account.

[24] These "men" who offer ceremonial knowledge represent supernatural power in personified form. In reality they are symbolically offering themselves and their capacities to the narrator's father.

"We must hurry," the man said, "for it is almost daylight." He listened to my father and said yes to everything my father asked him. Everything my father wanted he got.

My father told him, "I hate to see poor people sick. I hate it when people are walking along the road, poor and without horses. I want to know what is best to do for them. You can give me what you think is best."[25]

[25] In his vision the seeker after power is here asking for a curative rite and for ceremonial aid in the acquisition of horses, the main symbol of wealth.

This man sang and performed the ceremony that was given my father. And it raised my father as though he had wings. There was nothing but clouds around him. Before him everything shook, and there was lightning and thunder. Much was shown my father, terrible things, and how to stop them.[26]

[26] The "terrible things" are undoubtedly witches and witchcraft. Note the reluctance, for fear of "drawing" the attention of witches to one, to refer to witchcraft directly. The recipient of power is being taught a ceremony that, among other things, will be effective against sickness and disaster caused by the machinations of witches. Not all ceremonies are "strong" enough to counteract witchcraft, and not all shamans care to or dare to challenge witches.

The man handed my father a staff. "You'll always have this. It will speak itself. It must never be lost." So this man had told him what was best to be done. This power he received, they say, was the power of Bear. And this same man also told him, "All these are yours," and named Goose, Wolf, Lightning, Horse, and many other powers.[27]

[27] A shaman usually wears or carries something which acts as a link between himself and his source of power. It might be the feather of the bird from which power has been obtained, a piece of lightning-riven wood if the ceremony is from lightning, and so forth. At a time of crisis or in answer to a request, power often speaks through this object or gives some sign through it. Not infrequently a Mescalero obtains power from more than one source, though his main dependence may remain on one ceremony or power source. Bear was the guide and mentor of the narrator's father in this quest for supernatural power. In ceremonial matters the narrator's father was mainly noted for his rite from Bear, though he claimed to have supernatural help from other sources as well.

On another occasion, in order to illustrate his father's possession of power from Horse, the narrator described this "horse ceremony." "It is a real true story I am about to tell you. It happened after we came back to Mescalero from Alabama. A few Indians went down to Wilson's store where they sold lots of booze. Old Flint was in one bunch. A burro threw him and he hit a rock with his head.

"My father was there. He said, 'Turn away and don't look at that man.' Tom was a little drunk and put his hand right on the head. My father said, 'Pull him away.'

"My father made his ceremony. This man who was dead was made alive. My father kicked him under the feet and told him to get up, and he got up.

"Tom says there was blood and hair all over his head. Tom was pretty sure that man was dead. 'I felt it. His head was just like jelly. I couldn't be fooled,' Tom says. Tom tells that story yet. Everybody heard the crack when Old Flint went down."

After this my father knew all the people and their ways and their thoughts, and what was going to be done, and what was going to happen to them. He cured the sick among his own people and even among the whites and Mexicans, and he was known in Comanche country and by the Navaho people.

My Father Marries and Has an Accident

My father came to Mescalero again. It was during the period of much raiding. He wanted to see other relatives here. While he was in this region, some Navaho came, and he joined them and went to Navaho country.

My father's first wife was a Mescalero woman also. He had some children by her, one boy and one girl. The boy went to school in Albuquerque. He came back sick and died. My father, Kanasgo, and Swinging-Lance buried him. My mother and I didn't go. I never found out where they buried him. This boy had never married.[28] The girl married a Mescalero and had three girls of her own. Two are living today, one married to a Chiricahua and the other to a Lipan Apache.

[28] The dead were buried by adult male relatives in rocky crevices in the mountains. Children were considered particularly susceptible to the contamination associated with death. The place of burial was not disclosed, discussed, or revisited, for malignant ghosts, witches, and "ghost" sickness are associated with graves, and persons who take an interest in grave sites are suspected of witchcraft. Witches are believed to use bones, hair, or possessions of the dead in their evil practices.

My father not only had power from many sources but knew his herbs from the ceremony showed him in the cave. Power showed him how to use the herbs for each ailment and how to use them in a ceremonial way too when a man is sick from an animal and the healer doesn't want to use his other powers. There were many things my father did and told, not only at our camp but among other people. He was never alone. He was always a leader till the accident.

My father's brother got drunk and was going to shoot another man. My father saw that he was drunk and tried to stop him.[29] My father's brother was on horseback, and my father was on foot. In the struggle for the gun, it turned towards my father's brother and went off. It shot him right through the chest. They went after my father and were going to kill him. He did not run away but stood there. He said, "Do what you want with me."[30]

[29] Since there was collective family responsibility and family feuds were common, persons who did not want to be involved in difficulties would attempt to control their hot-tempered relatives.

[30] The relatives and friends of a slain person usually try to retaliate against the murderer. In this instance the situation was complicated by the fact that the narrator's father and his slain brother were married to sisters. The common set of relatives-in-law had both formal obligations of revenge and obligations of protection in respect to the narrator's father and could not act decisively. This probably saved the life of the narrator's father or at least made it unnecessary for him to flee at once for safety.

Muchacho Negro was there. He was in the height of his manhood, twenty-five years old or so, and not a scratch on him. He said, "If you shoot that man, you will have to kill my whole family, for that man didn't kill his brother on purpose."[31] So they let my father alone.

[31] Family solidarity is so strong that Muchacho Negro was able to pledge the support of his whole family when he came to the aid of the narrator's father. Muchacho Negro was later to become the father-in-law of the narrator.

But he was so mad over what had happened that he said, "I might as well leave for good." So he left home and went to Hot Springs, leaving his first wife here. Then he went to San Carlos.

My father scouted against the Mescalero. He scouted against the Navaho too. Another time, hearing of trouble on the Comanche reservation, he went there. A few of the Comanche were still outlaws, and he joined the government forces and scouted after them. Then he was brought back to the Navaho country as a scout, and they went after the Navaho and brought them in. When the Navaho were brought to a reservation around Fort Sumner, he helped bring them there. Later he helped transfer them to their own country again.[32] Then he came down to Mescalero country with a few Navaho scouts. A few Mescalero had gone from the reservation, and he was one of the men who brought them back.

[32] The Navaho were concentrated at Fort Sumner or Bosque Redondo on the Pecos River in New Mexico in 1863. The Mescalero had already been sent there. In 1865, after economic difficulties and constant friction with the Navaho, the Mescalero deserted the place and moved south. The Navaho were kept at Bosque Redondo until 1868.

At this time, after he had done all this work for the government, he married my mother. His first wife was not to be found; that is why he married again. She had been captured by the Victorio band.[33] Later she came back, but she never lived with my father again. She married the Mescalero leader, Natsili.

[33] The abduction of the first Mescalero wife of the narrator's father presumably occurred in 1879. Victorio, a leader of the Eastern Chiricahua Band, had refused to submit when the Apache from the Hot Springs Reserve were removed to San Carlos in May 1877, and he and his followers found refuge on the Mescalero reservation in 1878 and 1879. Indictments were found against Victorio for stealing and murder; and upon learning this, he and his band fled from the Mescalero reservation.

My father took my mother back with him to San Carlos. I was born there at San Carlos.[34]

[34] The narrator is not too sure of his place of birth, for on another occasion he said, "I was born at Fort Stanton." Possibly he was born on the Mescalero reservation and taken to San Carlos as an infant. Genealogical work brought out that the narrator's father, in the course of his wanderings, was married to two other women, one a Chiricahua and one a Plains Indian, for brief periods. The narrator explained that though he doesn't know their names or whereabouts, he has been told that he has two half sisters as a result of these unions.

In spite of previous failures the attempts to concentrate Apachean-speaking tribes on the same reserves continued. The Chiricahua were ordered to a reservation in Arizona set aside originally for the Western Apache. Their presence was deeply resented by the Western Apache, and continual friction resulted. Mistrust of American intentions, fear of the more numerous Western Apache, and nostalgia for their old range led to a series of unsanctioned departures by small groups of Chiricahua. Apache scouts were recruited to help locate the escapees. The narrator's father took his family to Western Apache country in response to the concentration order, served as a scout for the government, and tried to make an adjustment to the situation. The last and most serious outbreak of the Chiricahua from the Western Apache reservation was in 1885 when Geronimo and his followers left and were pursued. Geronimo's final surrender came in September 1886.

At San Carlos my father joined the scouts who were going out after hostiles. He joined for the term of a year as a member of Crawford's group.[35] During this time the government helped us in every way. The government gave us a few farming tools and also some fences. We started in. My father bought some horses, and horses were pretty high at that time too. We lived peaceably all during my father's first term of scouting there. We had almost everything we needed. Then he started in on his second term. He worked for the government until Geronimo surrendered.

[35] The reference is to Captain Emmett Crawford. In the fall of 1885 he led an expedition of soldiers and Indian scouts in pursuit of Geronimo and his followers. The trail led south of the Mexican border. Crawford's party twice overtook the hostiles, but each time the main body escaped. Then a Mexican column which was also in search of Geronimo came unexpectedly upon Crawford's command and, mistaking the Indian scouts for the enemy, opened fire. Crawford, who exposed himself in an attempt to halt the attack, was shot and severely wounded. He died before the discouraged party reached San Carlos.

Geronimo had wanted him to go out with him too, but he wouldn't go. The scouts saw that the outlaws didn't have any show, so they tried to save as many of them as possible. The rest of the people hated those scouts who went after them and said they'd get even some day, but that day never came. The scouts made friends with the whites and knew what life was like. They knew it was best to surrender. If I had been a grown man then I would have gone wild. The ones who went out, like Geronimo, were more scared than the ones who stayed in.

Exile

At the time of Geronimo's surrender we were thrown in as prisoners with the hostiles. At that time we had nice crops waiting to be harvested. We had been issued cattle and had a nice bunch of them and a good team of horses to work with. We had a good start.

I did not know why I was taken to Florida, being so young. I cannot say how old I was then, but I was just old enough to know everything that was going on. At the time we were taken away my father had pay for a month and a half coming to him that was never received. It was money that was already earned.[36]

36 In spite of the fact that most of the Chiricahua had refused to follow Geronimo and that many of them had served as scouts in tracking him down and inducing him to surrender, all of them, hostile and peaceful members of the tribe alike, were removed from the West and held as prisoners of war for twenty-seven years.

We were taken after that with the Chiricahua Apache to St. Augustine, Florida. Later we were taken to Mount Vernon Barracks near Mobile, Alabama. While we were there we corresponded a whole lot with the leading men of the Mescalero. Also we did a lot of talking with the chief men who were with us there. We were trying to get out of that place. We wanted to know why we were prisoners, for we belonged to the Mescalero tribe.

Our agent in Alabama found out that we were Mescalero. I guess it was found out through the interpreter, George Wratten.[37] My father went with some Chiricahua to Washington and saw Grover Cleveland. Shortly afterward we were brought back here—my mother, my father, and I, and another brother now dead.[38]

37 George M. Wratten was closely associated with the Chiricahua for many years. He was fluent in the Chiricahua dialect and served as interpreter when Geronimo agreed to surrender in 1886. He accompanied the Chiricahua into exile and played an important role during the period when they were stationed at Mt. Vernon Barracks, Alabama, and at Ft. Sill, Oklahoma. He married a Chiricahua woman who bore him two daughters. Both of these girls married Chiricahua men. The Chiricahua accepted Wratten as one of them and agreed that he be accorded the same share of tribal property as any adult Indian. As a result, Wratten received an allotment of land in Oklahoma at the time when the Chiricahua were given their choice of accepting allotments in severalty in Oklahoma or of removing to the Mescalero Indian reservation.

38 Because of intertribal marriage or other circumstances a number of Mescalero were removed with the Chiricahua in 1886. In the spring of 1889 five families, the narrator's among them, were allowed to return to the West, to the Mescalero reservation. The narrator had still another brother who died before the family was released. See the Annual Report of the Commissioner of Indian Affairs for 1900: 289–290.

First Impressions of Mescalero

When we got back to Mescalero, the people were living in round houses thatched with grass or covered with skins and in tipis covered with buffalo hides. By that time some people were using canvas too.

They were still making baskets and many other things in the old way then. Very few women made pots, but my mother's sister and a very old woman who is in the hospital now used to do it. I couldn't get near very often. She said that a boy or a man couldn't be around or the pots would break, and she ran me off. But I would

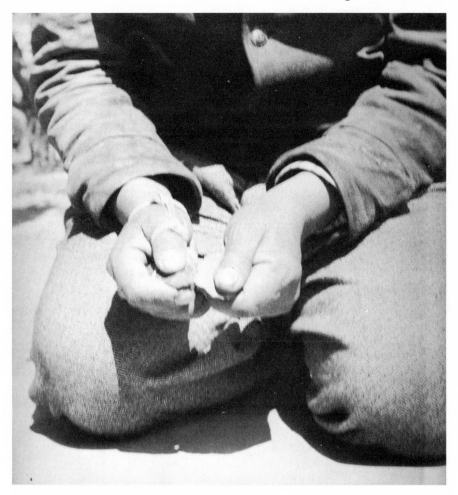

Chris demonstrating the chipping of arrowheads.

sneak up and look; then she would take a stick to me sometimes and chase me out. She made little round pots with Mescalero designs. The old lady who is now being taken care of in the hospital made the same designs but colored them differently.[39]

[39] There is no evidence that the Mescalero made clay pots anciently. It is possible that the few women who made pottery during the period described by the narrator were stimulated to do so by the example of the Jicarilla Apache, who did make fair pottery and who were stationed upon the Mescalero reservation from 1883 to 1887 as a result of the concentration policy.

The old woman who is now in the hospital was here when there were no white towns around. She knew about Carlsbad Caverns before any whites were around here; lots of the Mescalero people did. She was in a good many fights and she's lucky she never got shot.

The women worked at making baskets all the time in those days. A basket is made of the black stem of the unicorn plant[40] for the girl's adolescence rite. Once my grandmother was making a basket out of these. It's slow work. I grabbed one from her, I got so tired watching. She took a stick and went after me. I said, "Why work so hard?"

[40] "Martynia althaeafolia."

I used to watch my father making spears from mountain mahogany or another wood we call "hard wood." He made them to sell to the traders after he got back here. In the old days these were used as much as arrows; they were even used for killing cattle and buffalo. On rainy days the spear is better than the bow and arrow, for when the bowstring gets wet, you can't use it; if it gets too wet, it breaks apart.

I also saw my father make arrows. He used to chip the arrowheads, sometimes using a hard bone for chipping. I learned how to do it. He showed me how, and Shorty showed me how to do it too. But I am not in practice. It takes a delicate touch and lots of practice to make good arrow points like the ones my father and the other old men made.[41] We boys liked to have arrows to play with, and I remember that the men used to give us a few arrows so we would watch out for a wild potato patch for them.[42]

[41] In spite of his disclaimer, the narrator fashioned a rather good arrowhead in a relatively short time in the presence of the author. The narrator's father evidently was a better than average craftsman. The American Museum of Natural History has in its collections a war bonnet made by the narrator's father and acquired by P. E. Goddard at Mescalero in 1909. In aboriginal times, incidentally, the Chiricahua did not make or use such bonnets.

[42] "Solanum fendleri" and "Solanum jamesii" are the wild potatoes to which reference is made.

They used to get brass bracelets from the traders. These were used as money among us for a while. They paid five bracelets for a horse at one time. We kids used to steal them. We would watch to see who had them and take them when they were gone, then we'd trade them for cartridges.[43]

[43] The narrator presented one of these bracelets, which had somehow been preserved, to the author. It is a thin band of brass, not completely closed, decorated with incised, slanting lines.

The Mescalero used to go buffalo hunting in the fall; the meat is best then. I have eaten buffalo meat I am told, but I was so young I don't remember it. They used to eat the unborn of the buffalo. Some of the old people still eat foetal calves, but the young people don't. I tried my best to eat one, but it tasted funny to me.[44] I didn't like it at all.

[44] The narrator's venturesome spirit and willingness to attempt the unusual are in evidence here.

The Mescalero people were still eating a great deal of mescal which was baked in a pit.[45] I have helped with mescal, for the men and boys used to go with the women when they gathered it and help dig the pit and get the rocks. Then the men usually went off to hunt while the mescal was baking. When the mescal is in and the pit is ready to close up for the baking, they take the youngest child present, have him stand to the east of the pit and throw four stones into the pit. Then it is covered over. A rock is placed on top of the mound and a cross is drawn with charcoal on the rock. Then they let the mescal bake for two days. While the mescal is baking, the women are supposed to stay away from their husbands. If the mescal is not cooked through they say that the women disobeyed. They say that the men should have known better too.

[45] Mescal is a century plant, "Agave parryi." It was the crown which was used for food. The tribal name "Mescalero" reflects the extensive use of this plant by this Apache group. For fuller details of the preparation and utilization of this food staple see Castetter and Opler 1936: 35–38.

In my early days the hair of the Mescalero boys and girls was gathered at both sides and tied there. I used to have it like this. It was worn this way until it grew pretty long, until the boys were novices training for the raid. I knew many of these old men still living when they had long hair. When they combed their hair they put the combings away somewhere. They were afraid to let anyone touch that hair they had combed out.[46] They used to pull out their whiskers. Long ago men and women pulled the eyebrows too. I tried to do it once. It sure hurts and makes you wink too.

[46] It is believed that witches use the hair of the persons they wish to sicken or destroy in their evil rites. See chap. 1, note 28 (henceforth referred to as 1 [28]).

The flute was used in many ways. I've heard it played. It was used in love ceremonies sometimes.[47] It was also used in a ceremony to suck sickness out of a wound. I've seen it used like that a lot. The old men did it to the wounded. I couldn't see much of it. Just the wounded man and his family were allowed in there. They chased children away.

[47] Ceremonies to attract and influence individuals of the opposite sex were not uncommon. See pp. 74–76, 154–156, 179–181, 204–206.

A basket was put over the head to cure homesickness in those days. This happened to me one summer. I was at Nogal, staying with my sister and two brothers. My father and mother had gone away, had gone to Three Rivers.[48] I got very homesick. They put a basket over my head four times and sent me out to play, and I forgot all about it. But I ran to meet my parents when they got back just the same. This was the last time it was done to me.

Once when I was little I saw Black One perform. They use Black One only in time of sickness or trouble. He is dressed partly like the clown but has a headdress.[49] He wears a gee string around his middle and has white clay on the upper part of his body. He has on a whole face mask like the masked dancers but wears a headdress with the longest wing feathers of the eagle as the upright pieces. He carries the middle tail feathers of the eagle in his hand or the longest feathers of the wing. He has charcoal markings.

[49] Usually a shaman with the right to "make" (paint, costume, and ceremonially prepare) the impersonators of the Mountain Spirits readies a set of four dancers. If he cannot persuade as many young men as this to lend their services, he may "make" only three dancers or even two. The set of four dancers are usually costumed alike and do the same dance steps in unison. Another impersonator, the clown, is sometimes present. His costume and his behavior are quite different from those of the others. He grotesquely imitates the other dancers, makes believe he is picking up objects they have dropped, and engages in various bits of buffoonery. The clown probably ideologically represents the freedom from ordinary conventions, restraints, and limitations that marks the supernaturals.

Some outlaws, the Oliver Lee bunch, were coming and were going to clean out certain camps of Indians. We heard of it through the whites. Cherokee Bill was with us and was going to fight with the Indians against them.[50] One old lady, who died of old age later, prepared one Black One and two masked dancers.[51] They built a fire with the fire drill. The masked dancers and Black One circled the camps four times. Sometimes Black One led and sometimes he was behind. He was watching out. The people were not to say anything bad during the whole time. They can't mention who Black One is while he is working. Everyone has to let him alone.[52]

[50] Cherokee Bill, a white man, was butcher and stockman on the reservation for many years. White outlaws found refuge in the area over a long period. Indian stock suffered from their depredations, and, to add insult to injury, the Indians were often charged with the crimes these outlaws committed. The famous and bloody "Lincoln County war," between two rival groups of white cattlemen, was fought in the vicinity of the Mescalero reservation.

[51] The impersonators of the Mountain Spirits do not dance for their own satisfaction or at their own pleasure. The only person who can select, costume, and instruct impersonators of the Mountain Spirits is a shaman who has received a power grant from Mountain Spirits in a vision experience. This shaman sings and prays while the impersonators are being prepared and when they are dancing in a curative rite or at a girl's adolescence ceremony.

[52] Even after easier ways of igniting a fire were common, fires to be used in

ritual contexts were kindled by the fire drill. There are tales of the supernatural punishment of anyone who reveals the identity of a supernatural
impersonator.

After the ceremony, the old lady said the outlaws would stay just one day
around there. And that's all they did stay. Those outlaws didn't fight us that time.
They went on.

Among my people, some use polite forms of speech to a cousin of the opposite
sex; some who are related in this way hide from each other. You can't sit on a girl
cousin's bed or use her blankets. You can eat out of the same food bowl, but you
can't use any of her things. If she is in a card game, you can't play. You can't play
in a stave game with her.

I had a girl cousin. Her mother called my mother "sister." When I was very
little I played all the time with her. But when she was about nine and I was a little
younger, they spoke to her about it. She came to me and said, "We can't play
together as we have been doing. I'm growing up now and we'd better turn to the
polite way."

So from then on we talked in the polite way. She didn't want to hide from me.
She hid from some of my brothers.[53] My brother said, "It's best that I hide from
her. I don't want to talk to her." So he hid from her. I talked to her only when it
was really necessary. Most of the time I stayed away from her. I had to deliver
messages to her for my brothers who hid from her; that was about all I saw of her.

[53] The individual Mescalero may choose to avoid a cousin of the opposite sex
entirely or may decide to continue to see this relative but to treat the kinsman
of this category with restraint. In the latter case, polite form, a special third
person form of address which lends obliqueness and reserve to the conversation, is used. Cf. 4 [5].

The Power of a Bird

Old Lady Yube died quite a while back. One day I was at her camp at Rinconada.
I used to stay with these people. I was a little boy, but old enough to know things.
I was lying in the shade. A cedar waxwing was coming towards me. I was just about
to shoot it when she looked up (she was weaving a basket) and said, "Don't
shoot!" I put down my arrows.[54]

[54] The small Mescalero boy was encouraged to acquire skill in using the bow
and arrow by shooting birds and small mammals.

The bird stayed there and sang. She said, "I hope it means nothing but good."
It looked like she was talking to that bird. She said, "Don't say anything against
that bird. It's coming to help me, to help me make baskets and to sell my baskets,[55]
and to tell me about the herbs and about the bites of animals and how to cure them."

[55] These baskets were sold to the trader, who in turn sold them to visitors to the reservation.

"Can I shoot these birds?"

"No, do not shoot them. Shoot any other birds but these."

"All right, as long as you tell me not to, I won't shoot them."

She said to me, "That bird is good in many ways. Good birds like these we should not bother. To shoot birds that we have no use for is no good. They sing around camp. If you are sad and don't feel well, when they sing you feel better." She put her basket away and spoke to me, and I listened. "Life-Giver sends us these birds.[56] They tell us many things. They are too small to use. So it's best to leave them alone. It's just like you, now. Suppose that you were small and the bird was large and it came for you and wanted to eat you. How would like it?"

[56] Life-Giver is a shadowy creator deity. Though the Mescalero refer to him in contexts such as this one, he is seldom a source of personal supernatural power and does not figure prominently in the ordinary ceremonial round.

"Oh, I wouldn't let any bird eat me. I'd kill it."

"No, I'm telling you this for a lesson, to show you that you should leave birds alone."

Chris demonstrating the Mescalero arrow release

The only toothache I had was right there. It happened to me right where she spoke to me that time. I couldn't stop crying. She said, "Now watch and that bird will come."

I was wishing and wishing that it would come. It didn't come all day. Then it came. It looked at me and was afraid to light. I said, "Bird, I'm sick; I can't hurt you." The bird sat there and sang.

Then the old woman came out. She heard it singing. She talked to it and it sang on the palm of her hand. She spoke to it, and it took something out of its mouth and put it in her hand.[57] She took it and rubbed it all over my jaw where it was sore. It was sticky and felt good. It felt as if the pain was all being pulled out. That night I slept soundly, and the next day the swelling was down. She did this four times, and then my toothache disappeared. I didn't go to the doctor at all.[58] When she did it, she sang songs and the bird sang also.

[57] There is often a difference between what objectively takes place in a ceremony as an outsider might see it and a description of the activities of the source of power given by shaman, patient, or believer. It must be remembered that the supernatural power source is considered to be represented by and present in the ritual music and prayers and that allusion to events in song and prayer grants them a kind of "religious reality." Therefore we need not be astonished at the unusual behavior attributed to birds, animals, and even inanimate objects in accounts of ceremonies.

[58] The agency doctor is presumably meant.

I often think of this. The other day I was telling these stories to my boy. He said, "Did you ever tell the one about the cedar waxwing to Mr. Opler?"

I said, "Naw, what would he do with it?"

"You ought to tell him. When that book comes out, you'll be glad to see it in there. It's pretty good to have had just one toothache."

"The next time I see him I'll tell him about it." So here I am telling you the story.

Whenever I see this bird I thank him. I say, "Thank you for curing that toothache so many years ago." Ever since then I like to watch the birds all the time.

I was told to throw my teeth to the east when I lost them. I did this when I was a boy. I was also told to throw them toward the sun, wherever it was. Once I ran against someone and knocked out a tooth. I threw the tooth up to the sun and said, "Give me a good tooth in its place." I got a good one.

Chief Natsili

Natsili lived during his young days on the other side of Silver Springs Canyon, in Sixteen country.[59] It was wild then. When he remembered these things, you could see tears running down his cheeks, for he wanted those ways back. His father was a war chief, a leader in war and raiding.

[59] This is the southeastern part of the present Mescalero Apache Indian reservation.

Natsili had an older brother who had the right to be a war leader, but during a hunt he happened to meet a bear which killed him. His mule, which he had tied, got loose and came back to camp early in the morning, and then they sent out a searching party. This party trailed him. They found nothing but bones at the end of the tracks. The bones were still red, and the head was gone. The clothes were scattered on the bones in little bits, and his moccasins were there.

Then they found the bear waiting for them in a hole, for it was time for him to hole up. The searchers sent back word of this. While the band was all getting together, the bear poked out his head and looked at them. They circled around the bear, and a man came close to him, but the bear chased him.

Natsili told the others to stand back. "He killed my brother; let him kill me too!" His father warned him not to go too close, but through the power he had learned by means of peyote he knew very well what to do with this bear.[60]

[60] The Mescalero used peyote ("Lophophora williamsii"), a small cactus with narcotic qualities, ritually. In fact, the Mescalero were one of the first Indian groups north of Mexico to use peyote and probably had a good deal to do with its transmission to the central plains, where an important religious cult arose involving its consumption. Natsili, as a person who claimed power or special knowledge from peyote, arranged and conducted meetings at which peyote "buttons" were chewed and at which attempts to cure the sick or gain favorable visions of the future took place. Peyote also acted as a guardian spirit or supernatural monitor for Natsili, as in this instance. For additional details of the Mescalero use of peyote see Opler 1936a.

But the others chased the bear and did not give Natsili a chance to do the killing. They killed the bear. Natsili jumped off his horse, took a knife from his belt, and started cutting up the bear in small pieces. Another bear appeared and was surrounded and held. Natsili said a few words; the bear fell, and, dragging its hind legs, tried to crawl up to a bush. But Natsili overtook it and killed it with his spear. They cut up the bear in small pieces. A man who knew the power of the bear fed this meat to the people. They cut both bear scalps off to have a war dance over that night.[61]

[61] Bear was not only considered to be a dangerous animal in the ordinary sense but was thought to be a potential source of pollution and sickness. The eating of bear meat or even the sight or smell of bear would make the ordinary Apache ill. But a small piece of bear meat fed to a person ritually by one who has obtained supernatural power and a ceremony from Bear is considered to be a prophylactic against contamination from Bear and other dangers. A victory dance could be held only when the score was evened by a triumph over an enemy who had inflicted a loss on the Mescalero or when the Mescalero were clearly "ahead." Here the bear is being treated as a tribal enemy.

Back at camp they held a big council. And then they decided that young Natsili should be second chief. The war bonnet was placed on his head, and the bear scalp was fixed up nicely for a headdress with eagle feathers and two buffalo horns on the sides. They put on two stars, one on each side in beadwork to show he was second chief.

Natsili was a great leader after that. He was a chief when I came back from being a prisoner of war. He was one of those who was forced by the agent to have his hair cut, but he didn't say anything, and he was issued clothes and blankets.[62]

[62] See 1 [91].

His band had been the last of all the Mescalero bands to surrender. There were many Mescalero still outside raiding. They were said to be from his band, and he tried to bring them all in. He was taken prisoner because he was supposed to be leader over these raiders, and he was kept at the agency. He was told to bring them all in or he would be made a prisoner again. So he moved his band back to the mountains and gathered all the rest of them together and led them all back to the agency.[63]

[63] A favorite means of the United States military in dealing with hostiles was to threaten or punish their alleged leaders. Actually the Mescalero leader was essentially a respected adviser or arbiter rather than a chief with absolute control over his followers. Often a Mescalero "chief" would be obeyed without question only by his close relatives. Others would dissociate themselves from his group if they questioned his actions and advice. Much friction between American officials and the Indians resulted from a misunderstanding of the limitations of authority of Mescalero leaders. Actually the Apache word that is usually translated "chief" literally means "one who speaks."

He never had any children. Through his power he was a peyote chief and held meetings and used peyote in many different ways. We made many visits to his place and saw that he practiced his peyote power. He used it toward the white man to make friends instead of trouble and used it for rain and to bring good summer weather, for he loved to see many fruits growing.[64] I have never known him to use his power for healing. He said he knew his power through Life-Giver, Water's Child,[65] and White Painted Woman, and for this reason he was present at most girls' puberty ceremonies even though it might take him a long time to get there. He would be in the tipi where White Painted Woman was dancing and would stay through the four days and nights.[66] He was the one who went after peyote or told others where it grew. He encouraged youngsters to learn about peyote, for he said peyote was more powerful than any other ceremony. He sang many songs for me when I was at his place visiting him.

[64] During periods of fluctuating policy and tension between Americans and Indians much ritual was directed toward fathoming the intentions of the unpredictable white man and attempting to influence his decisions in a direction acceptable to the Mescalero.

[65] Water's Child is the culture hero of the Mescalero, conceived miraculously by

the divine culture heroine, White Painted Woman, when she stood under a waterfall and water dripped upon her head. Water's Child is sometimes accompanied by a weaker, less heroic brother, Killer-of-Enemies. In Mescalero thought Killer-of-Enemies has come to be regarded as the sponsor and friend of the white man and so is seldom mentioned. Interestingly enough, some other Apache groups such as the Jicarilla and Western Apache make Killer-of-Enemies the principal culture hero and allot the subordinate role to Water's Child.

[66] During the adolescence rite the pubescent girl is addressed and referred to as White Painted Woman, as has been previously mentioned. Natsili apparently felt that his peyote visions brought him in touch with supernaturals such as Life-Giver, White Painted Woman, and Water's Child.

Natsili claimed that he knew the ceremony of summer in the peyote way and in the way of power. He also knew the crow.[67] He liked to hear the crow when he was out hunting. That's why he always sang of the crow.

[67] That is, he gained ceremonial knowledge about the control of weather and rainfall (ceremony of summer) and ceremonial knowledge useful in the hunt (there is a ritual association between the crow and hunting in Mescalero belief and mythology) through visions induced by the use of peyote.

One year at Silver Springs it was getting dry. Some places were burned to bare ground. The grasses were burning. So one night he held his ceremony with his own family. He called on the places where he was living. In his prayer he named Elk Springs, Silver Springs, Turkey Springs, and James Canyon. That was his range where he lived all his days till he was old, except for a few days when he was off for the buffalo chasing. It was along about the month of July. They did not have the Fourth of July celebration those days,[68] but it was before the deer's horn starts to get hard; they were not quite grown yet.

[68] Formerly the adolescence rite was performed over the individual girl whenever she came of age. More recently white agency officials have insisted that the adolescence rite be held once a year, beginning on the first of July and ending on July fourth, and that all girls who have become mature during the year and wish to have the ceremony carried out for them go through a collective rite at this time.

He felt sorry for the people, who were suffering. He spoke about these things and started beating his drum. He usually did beat a drum in his ceremony. While he was beating his drum he began to sing in a low tone, for he had a way of singing in a low tone to bring the rain. In his song he said he hoped his song might spread out and be a cloud and bring rain.

It was close to noon. His wife was cooking. He said, "I want it to rain more than I want to eat. I want the rain to come so that the grass will be green and the horses and cattle and deer fat, so that we'll have plenty to eat this winter." His wife told him that everything was about done.

He paid no attention to her and went right on. There was one little cloud in the sky. It started to spread. He heard a crow caw from the cloud, and then he saw a lot of crows rising in the air from the fields as if it was going to rain. And he also saw the buzzards gathering and swinging to the tree tops as if it was getting dark and they were getting ready to roost. He knew Buzzard and Crow. His wife put everything away because everything was well cooked and he was making a ceremony for rain. She put the food near the door to cool, brought the cooking utensils inside, and sat by her husband.

Then she thought it best to go after water before it rained, so she went with the jug to the arroyo, filled it, and when she was on the way back it began to sprinkle.[69] It was just a little way to the arroyo too. She heard the drum again and she heard him singing. She saw that the birds were gathering. She looked to the east and there she could see heavy rain. She looked in all directions, and everywhere there was heavy rain. She was afraid to be caught in it and she hurried. At the doorway she stopped a moment and looked at the pine trees close by. She saw the lightning come down at the pine trees. And then it began to hail. She got in safely.

[69] The Mescalero water "jug" is a woven receptacle made waterproof by giving it a coating of the pitch of the piñon pine tree inside and out.

Natsili was still singing. He took off his shirt, took off his chaps and moccasins, and walked out in the rain with only his gee string on, singing, because he was so happy. He said he had done this because his land was drying up and to cool off the country. That is not the only time he did it. He did it several times. They were our neighbors, and I was right there.

Not long ago it was getting pretty dry around here. I was asked what shaman would be good for it. I remembered Natsili and said, "A man who knows something of Summer[70] and who knows the fruits and things like that would be good for it."

[70] It will be noted that the summer season is personified and considered animate. Everything in the Mescalero universe is thought of as potentially animate and a possible source of supernatural power.

First Teachers

Natsili was really a good leader in all things. He showed us how to hunt, to ride horses, to make saddles, bows and arrows, ropes, quirts, head bonnets, shields, and many other things; and in the making of these things he showed us what to use, the stoutest buckskin and sinew that would last a long time. He also told stories, such as the Coyote stories, the moccasin game stories, the tales of the killing of the monsters, the rearing of Water's Child, and of the Foolish People, and also some stories about one of the Chiricahua Apache bands.[71] And we sat there days and nights listening. Sometimes we'd get sleepy. A head would begin to go forward; a boy would be asleep. Rap! he'd get it on the head, and that head would come up again. He tapped me on the head many times. I stayed longer than any of them. All the other youngsters would go, but I would stay. My father, Swinging-Lance, and others also used to tell us boys stories.

71 The Coyote stories are a cycle of tales about the misadventures of a foolish animal, Coyote, whose gluttony, pride, disobedience, and lubricity constantly get him into difficulties. The moccasin game story tells how the harmless birds and animals and the dangerous ones played a hidden ball game against each other in the earliest period of the earth's existence to determine whether there should be perpetual night or whether there should be sunshine and daytime as well. The story of the killing of the monsters is an important myth dealing with the exploits of the culture hero, Water's Child, and detailing how he made the earth habitable for man by slaying the monsters who were preying on humankind. For an explanation of the stories about the Foolish People, see 1 [83].

I didn't care so much for the war stories, but I just couldn't listen enough to the animal stories.72 I often stayed up all night to hear them. Some of the stories used to scare us. When they told a story about Owl and Coyote, Owl's part would be spoken in a loud voice, and we would be quiet. When we'd hear an owl out in the woods after that, we'd sure scatter and go for camp.73

72 The narrator is a skilled hunter, trapper, and woodsman, as will appear. His bent in this direction apparently developed early.

73 The owl is associated with death and is believed to be the form assumed by the spirits of dead witches. Consequently its hoot, which is often interpreted as a threatening message in the Mescalero Apache language, is feared and disliked. In telling the stories, the personality of the protagonist is often portrayed by the tone of voice employed.

They always made some boy who wasn't paying attention chase after something they called "that which one smokes with."74 They had me chasing it once. Natsili told me, "You go and get it." I kept asking for it at one camp after another. They kept me going! At every place they told me they had just given it to someone else. It was what you call a wild goose chase. I was pretty well tired out. Finally I came to my own camp, and I asked for it, and the whole family laughed and said old Natsili had it. When I got back to him he said he'd already used it. They always say they want it quick.

74 This is comparable to the "left-handed monkey wrench" for which American children are sometimes sent to tease them.

Natsili said the power of peyote is good in all forms; he told us that for use in hunting it is really at its best. He said, "My children and my relatives, there are many things I'd like to say to you. But we never come together as in the old days, so I like to tell all I have learned and can still remember to the few who come to me. I'm always glad to let you know. Remember that to kill your own people is not right, or to steal from them. Especially you, the youngest one here," and he meant me. "Now roll this up in your ear and don't forget it." "Yes," I said. He said, "Some day my time will come when I join those who went before me."

But he lived till I went away to school at Albuquerque. I never saw him after that. I heard he died while I was away at school.

Old Man Luntso and his wife, who knew power from Goose, were good story-tellers too. They said that Goose was the best of all powers and led the others.[75] We used to get these old people to tell us about Goose. I'd go to their camp and say, "Uncle and Aunt, tell us stories." They were no relatives to me, but I'd call them this just so they wouldn't refuse.[76]

[75] It is characteristic of a Mescalero shaman to make extravagant claims on behalf of his source of power. It is expected that there will be a strong bond of loyalty between the shaman and the power source which is "working through him" or helping him.

[76] Mescalero relatives were expected to share goods and fortune. To put a person symbolically in the position of a relative is to make it hard for him to refuse a request. Those in need of his services often call an unrelated shaman by a kinship term to make sure that he will consent to perform his ceremony on their behalf.

If they were willing, a whole bunch of us would come to their camp. Then they'd begin the story and take turns telling it. They would often stop right in the middle of a story to explain the meaning and give a lesson. In the story of Goose, where the smallest goose does not obey, they would say, "Don't laugh at us. We have lived long. We know what happens to young people who don't say good words. Look what happened to this little goose! Never say that you are going to do a thing at a certain time in the future or that a thing will surely happen at a certain time. Say 'bye-and-bye.' "[77]

[77] This refers to a story of a journey to the end of the world by a flock of geese. On the way they meet Crane who tells them they are going to a dangerous place and advises them to use words such as "bye-and-bye" in a protective magical formula. One gosling fails to do so and falls victim to an eagle.

They would tell stories till dawn. During the night when anyone got sleepy or wanted to go, they'd say, "We've got some yucca fruit we'll give you pretty soon." They promised us chokecherries, dried fruit, and everything else that children like. But it never came. At dawn they'd say, "That's all. Now you can go. We're not going to feed you. All you do is sleep." Some would hang around, but I was always the first one to go. When I got home, my folks would ask me where I had been, and I'd say, "Over to see Old Man Luntso." Then we'd go to bed and sleep all day.

Before Luntso died he told the people that before he was dead four days—it might be the first or the second or the third or the fourth day—Goose would come to his grave, circle it four times, and then carry his spirit away. After he died every-body watched. He was buried on the side of White Mountain. Sure enough, on the fourth day we heard geese. They went straight for that spot. They circled it four times and flew off. As they went, we said to each other, "There goes Luntso." I saw this myself.[78]

[78] There is a vague belief among the Mescalero that the soul of a powerful shaman may go, at death, to the holy home of his power, usually the cave or place where the power and ceremony were first acquired in the original vision experience.

I was sitting in my little camp here the other night and I heard the old lady, my mother-in-law, tell Luntso's goose story to my children and some others.[79] She told them about his death too.

[79] The narrator was in a separate brush shelter but close enough to hear his mother-in-law's voice. A Mescalero mother-in-law and son-in-law cannot, of course, come into each other's presence. For a listing of other avoidance and restraint relations, see 4 [5].

Luntso knew Goose for curing. He sang and prayed in his ceremony and gave the call of the goose. He used pollen and made pollen markings.[80] He cured all kinds of disease, but he didn't show much about his power. He was like Old Nogal, he kept it to himself. It was the Canada goose that Luntso knew. My father knew it too. My father ate goose. I never noticed Luntso eating it.

[80] As will be abundantly evident, pollen is the most important ritual substance of the Mescalero and appears in every ceremony and religious context. The pollen generally used was from the cattail tule ("Typha latifolia"), but a shaman may be directed by his power to use pollen from other plants also and from various trees.

Early Training

Novices training for raiding wore one feather in the hair. It was easy to recognize them by this, one eagle tail feather, that's all. A novice does not scratch himself with his fingers; he has to use a stick. The rules that the novice follows hold around camp as well as in raid or war. He is required to do the jobs, to build fires in camp when they are out on a raid. He takes the water bag made from intestines and fills it. Whether or not it is rainy or dark or dangerous he has to do it. They tell him that the way he acts as a novice is the way he is going to be through life. If he minds and is prompt, that's the way he will be. In the old days a boy had to be a novice whether he wanted to or not.

They tell the novices, "Never be mean to old people, never make fun of them, never throw stones at them." They talk to them; they give them lessons.[81]

[81] The novitiate of the Mescalero boy can be thought of as a boy's puberty rite, for it is the counterpart, in many ways, of the girl's adolescence ceremony.

Many of the associated practices and concepts are the same. For instance, both the pubescent girl and the boy who is a novice use a scratching stick and may not scratch themselves with their fingernails. Both are told that the characteristics they display during this period will mark them through life. Both must use a hollow tube in drinking water. And both, of course, are watched to see how they respond to advice and discipline.

Before I went to the white man's school, I stayed up all one night listening to these things. Three or four old men were talking. They got all the boys who were novices together and talked to them. I was just a little kid. They told them, "Hold your arrows tight. Don't waste them. Make them count. Shoot first at the white man who is aiming at the Indian. Don't get excited. Save your friend's life."

After listening to such advice, we used to do lots of crazy things to toughen ourselves. We used to go naked where there were wasps. Another thing was to get hold of some bullets, throw them in a fire, and keep running past the fire. Another thing: if a place on the body pains, they take the pulp from the inside of a dried sunflower stalk, put it on the spot, set fire to it, and let it burn down and go out by itself. It leaves a scar. I've seen people do it many times. I've never used it myself to stop pain, but when I was a boy we used to try it just to see whether we could stand it. My cousin Tom has plenty of scars all down his arm. He did it to show how tough he was. The pith from borage and elderberry are used in the same way.

The boys used to get lots of instruction to keep away from women and live right. When I was a kid I was told that women have teeth in there that would bite my penis off if I didn't keep away from them. Sometimes an old woman used to get the boys together and talk to them. An old man might say to the old woman, "You're spoiling those boys." She'd say, "No, it's a lesson."

The old women told us, "You mustn't go with old women like us. We've had our day. If you have anything to do with old women, you get a big penis and testicles; you have to straddle to cover it up as you go along the road. If you do it to old women, worms will kill you."

They believed they got "worms" (that is the word for tuberculosis) from old women and from nothing else in the old days, especially from white and Mexican women. They thought you caught worms from the vagina of a woman and that was the only way. You might be sitting where a woman had sat, but you wouldn't get it from that. They are worms and crawl to your lungs. The boys sure listened! We asked, "Do the worms really kill you?" Often women would talk to the girls about such things, and men to the boys. Sometimes an old woman would talk to the boys. I've heard it lots of times.[82]

[82] Some of the standard Mescalero notions about sex are reflected in these passages. The Mescalero believe that initiation into sexual activity at too early an age is debilitating and that a young man invites sickness by sexual intercourse with an old woman. Tuberculosis was considered a venereal disease, and shame and secrecy about it made effective treatment difficult for a long time. Most Apache groups formerly saw some connection between venereal

disease, tuberculosis, and "worms." It was also believed that the Mescalero Apache male was especially vulnerable to sickness if he had sexual intercourse with Mexican or American women. Consequently these beliefs supported tribal endogamy. For generally similar Jicarilla Apache beliefs see Opler 1947.

When they told the story of the Foolish People, they told the children, "Animals are animals. They are used in a different way, to eat. You should have nothing to do with them otherwise. Marry in a decent way. If you do bad things your children will follow you and do the same. If you want to raise good children, be decent yourself." They never tell these stories just for fun; they tell them for a purpose, to teach the young people how to live. They wouldn't tell these things to boys and girls together though.[83]

[83] The stories of the Foolish People are a set of tales about a simple-minded group who were constantly doing the senseless or inept thing. In some of the stories they are also represented as committing shameful and bestial acts. These stories of sexual misconduct are not told to mixed groups of boys and girls because there are likely to be siblings or cousins of opposite sex present, persons between whom a restraint and embarrassment relationship exists.

They used to get the girls together too. There would be a bunch of girls. The mother of one would be there giving lessons. Lots of the girls hated to come; they hated to hear it. Some would cry.

The woman would tell them, "Look at the spruce tree. It's pretty, isn't it? But it's more than that. You have to know how to use it. You use it for bedding. Now what would you use on the prairies?"

One girl does not think and says, "Mesquite."[84] "No, how could you use thorns to sleep on?"

[84] "Thelypodium longifolium."

Then another girl says, "Grass." "That's a smart girl! Who told you that?"

Then the woman would tell them, "You must learn how to cook. The man takes care of you. He goes out and gets deer. You must know how to prepare it when he brings it back.

"Look at the wild seeds. This is the way you pick them. This is the way you grind the seeds. This is the way you cook the bread, in ashes or on hot rocks. Then, when you take it out of the ashes, scrape it off and wipe it and you've got the best bread you ever had. Just cover it with ashes when you put it in. It's easy to clean. Just wipe the hard crust off, and it's just as clean of dirt as anything.

"Look at this plant. It is medicine. That woman over there is a good doctor. I'm going to call her. Remember what she tells you. Some plants make you crazy. Be sure you make no mistake. If you are not sure you have the right one, ask. Remember the names she tells you. Then use these herbs. Help others to gain strength. Feed the sick. Don't make fun of old people."[85]

Parfleches (Courtesy, the American Museum of Natural History).

85 The respect and attention due the elders is a constant refrain in informal
Mescalero education of the young.

That's the way they talked. Then they would take the girls to another woman, an
artist in painting parfleches, and to another who was good at making needles.[86]

86 The parfleche or "Indian suitcase" is a flat container made of rawhide.

Sometimes a boy or a girl would fall asleep. They would hit him a lick on the
head and he would wake up and cry. They would say, "We aren't trying to be mean.
This stick is your lesson. Keep awake. You are listening to something you'll need
and it's something you may not hear any more."

Now it's different because the white man is educating them. But they go away and learn trades and when they come back the trade jobs aren't given to them. The white man's got in the lead of them, and when they want jobs as mechanics or with the cattle they can't get them.

Now the old people tell them that the old teaching is past, that their bows and arrows are past. "The white man tells you to have farms and support children and learn trades. There is nothing else now," the old ones say. "Stick to the trades. Do your best at school when you are learning a trade or the language of the white man." They tell them not to try to marry too young either.

The young ones say, "The whites don't give us trade jobs." But the older people tell them, "Keep to the trades. It's bread and butter. Some day we'll have the right man as commissioner or agent and you'll get your chance."

They teach them to keep clean and try to do away with sickness. But that's one thing around here we can't stop.

Now they tell them, "Be kind to all. Even the whites are your people, even the Negroes. Feed them if they need it. Look at these old men here. All of you are just one family. If they've got no pants, give them pants. If they are hungry, give them something to eat. Be with good company. Don't make your family watch you, but watch what you are doing."[87]

[87] The canons of generosity and openness with material goods and of collective responsibility—both very important in Mescalero thought—are emphasized here.

I was trained in the old way before I was thirteen. I wanted to be tough. The trader's son wanted to be tough too, and we sure toughened him up! We'd fall off trees and do all sorts of things. My son hasn't had this training. Big Hat, Julio, and I used to whip each other. Just about the time I was toughened up, I went to school at Albuquerque. It's an easy way to kill yourself, trying to be tough, but when you're young you try everything. There were buckskin whips to use on the runners. Some runners would cry out on hearing the whip, without being hit.

I was trained with Hummingbird to be a good runner. When I went away to school it all went away. Some of the young boys were trained with Goose, some with Weasel, some with Deer. All were trained with something to make them fast runners. Their relatives saw to it. They hired a man who knew about it. The girls were trained too with different things. Some used White-collared Swift. It was a great thing to see us practicing running. You saw all kinds of ceremonial objects; horse tails and all sorts of things were tied to our legs.[88] Some didn't want to be seen. They went off alone and practiced.

[88] Nothing important in Mescalero culture was attempted without recourse to supernatural help. The prevalence of imitative magic in Mescalero ceremonialism can be gathered from this description.

My older brother used to get me out, cut a hole in the ice in winter, and push me in the cold water. He ordered me around too. I had a younger brother. He had a tough time too. He was taller than I was, but he died. I used to try to help him. Another younger one had an easy time. They were not doing this any more when he was growing up.

I'd be sent to carry water jugs a long way to learn how to pack them. When I had jugs and met women, I'd be ashamed, so I used to go at night for water.[89] I used to wish I'd meet a mountain lion and he'd kill me and end all this.

[89] One of the tasks the adult man never performs, unless he is out camping with other men, is to get the water. The young boy is here being prepared for situations in which no women will be available for the errand. It is a test of the obedience and humility of the boy, as well, for it is a disagreeable task to be forced to perform near the regular campsites.

One winter, just after New Year's, some other boys and I took an icy plunge. Our folks made us do it. It was right at the agency. We were naked. I was the first to go in. They had cut a hole in the ice. How it did hurt! I ran two hundred yards and came back. They hit me with willow switches, lots of the big fellows did it. Not one of us cried. They say you're no good if you cry. We toughed it out. I thought I was going to cry on the last lick, but I didn't say anything. We didn't want to do it, but my folks said I should. The ones who hit you don't care. They say, "Some day you'll be tough." They use the palm of their hands, too, to hit you. There was a big crowd there. The women watched from the top of the hill. They asked who stood it best. The men said that all were pretty good and didn't cry. Julio gave just one yell, "a-i-i-i!" when he went in.[90]

[90] Julio later became a transvestite. Either he showed less manly characteristics than others from an early age or they are being attributed to him retrospectively.

When Stottler came as agent everything like this stopped.[91]

[91] Lieutenant V. E. Stottler is the man to whom reference is made here. In the early 1890s a policy was inaugurated of appointing army officers to the posts of Indian agent as these fell vacant. Lieutenant Stottler, who assumed his duties at the end of 1895, was the second officer to serve on the Mescalero reservation as a result of this. He was an uncompromising disciplinarian who was determined to "civilize" the Mescalero by forcing him to cut his hair, wear white man's clothes, farm, and give up his traditional customs. He even brought Navaho to the reservation to teach the Mescalero to weave blankets. Stottler remained as Mescalero agent for approximately two and one-half years.

A Victory Dance

I saw a victory dance once. Old Man Sito and Running Water were there. They had a cowhide out there, and several men beat on it and sang. Then the two men

Mescalero water jars (Courtesy, the American Museum of Natural History).

came out. They faced each other. They had shields on their arms. Running Water wore a war bonnet, Sito wore a fox cap. This was just to show that a dance was going to be held that night. They faced each other and sang. They motioned as though they were shooting arrows at each other. Then that night at dark they built a big fire. They drummed and danced. There was a big crowd there. The warriors were painted. Soldiers from Fort Stanton and Mexicans looked on.

This is the way they start these dances. The men will be out there. They will be dressed in their best clothes. They show up with spears, guns—all their weapons. They are all ready to dance. They put things out there, matches, maybe a pocket knife, different things.[92] If the people all make a rush for them, if they want it all themselves, that ends it, the dance is off. If they take it slow, just pick up things one at a time, the men go in and dance. Everybody wants to see the dance and so they go slow. If they get fooled, they go slow next time. This time there were twenty-five men and they put on a real dance.

[92] These represent the booty taken from the enemy. The Mescalero victory dance was greatly influenced by the practices of the tribes of the Western Plains area.

One fellow got out. He made a big talk. He said, "We have killed all your enemies. We did it with these," and he held up his arrows. He told what brave deeds he did. Then he called on another man. This one was a witness for him. He told that he saw it and added what he did. Their faces were painted. We saw a great show. I just saw it once. After that they never had this dance any more, but many stories are told of it.

Some man who has done something big is the first one out, then the witnesses. This first man doesn't dance right away. He just walks right out and talks first. There are three or four who talk. Then they yell out and shoot and the big dance commences. Sometimes it lasts till morning.

The victory dance is very vigorous. They use the knife, then the spear. Some go out there jumping back and forth, sideways, with a blanket, to show what they did in battle. Some use the shield as they did in the fight, and some the spear and other weapons. They call one man and then another to come out and do this dance. Pretty soon they are all strung out there dancing. Some will be resting and some dancing after this. They take turns for the whole night. They just do this dance after the war's over. The way they talk, the Jicarilla Apache did just like this too.

I thought it was great fun. I thought maybe my time to show off would come, but it never did.

When they came back from a good hunt, a buffalo hunt or any kind, they danced too. When they danced, they told how they got the animals, and they put things out there for people the same way. I never saw one of these, but I heard about it from Muchacho Negro and others. Some people still tell of it.

When they were going out to fight, they took a cowhide[93] and sang war dance songs till midnight. Then any fighting to be done was done the next morning or the next day. They didn't let children see the fighting. They ran you off if you were a child.

[93] The cowhide was beaten with a stick to provide a crude but effective "drum."

Witchcraft and Death

It was about this time that Eye-Covered, a shaman with strong supernatural power, came to cure a half brother of mine.[94] He came to my people. He said the boy had a witch's weapon in him. "It is not supposed to be taken out, but I'm going to do it no matter what happens to me. I love this boy."[95] He said this right across from that store down the road, on the hill, before a big bunch. My mother hired him to perform his ceremony.

[94] Eye-Covered was killed in 1908 by Indian police after he murdered an American youth who presumably discovered him butchering a stolen steer. An account of his death is given in McNeil 1944.

[95] Battle terminology and psychology rule in ceremonies to cope with sickness due to witchcraft. A witch is said to "shoot" his "weapon" or "arrow" into the body of his victim. A successful shaman removes the missile and "shoots" it back into the witch, who may then sicken and die. A shaman who fails to vanquish a witch is always in danger, for the triumphant witch, knowing he is stronger than his challenger, may decide to take his revenge on the interfering ceremonialist.

The boy was eighteen or nineteen years old, just starting his manhood. He was good looking. Finally one day he got sick, and he lay in bed for quite a long while.

They tried every kind of Indian doctor, but they couldn't do anything for him at all. When they found out about this fellow healing several sick people, they hired him. My mother begged to have him come up and heal her boy. He said he was coming to see what he could do.

He came up, and there was a crowd in the tent this time because we had lots of relatives. He pointed out the way that they were to ask him to perform the ceremony, and they did as he commanded.[96] Then he said a prayer, and it was a long one. When he finished his prayer he said that the boy was witched and a strong witch weapon was in him, and whoever took it out was going to die afterward. He said, "Someone has witched him because of his good looks. I'm going to take it out; it won't kill me, but I'll lose an eye." He had two eyes then.[97]

[96] A shaman must be asked in a polite and ceremonious way for his services, and four ritual gifts must be made to him. These may include feathers, pollen, red ochre, yellow ochre, turquoise, white clay, flint, abalone, etc. These gifts are conceived of as a payment to the source of power, without which the supernatural will refuse to cooperate. When a shaman acquires a ceremony, he is told by the power what preliminary ritual gifts of this kind he should demand before beginning the rite. Thus these gifts are a recognition of the rights and claims of the power source. The shaman is given additional payment or gifts for himself at the conclusion of the rite. The friends and patients of a shaman usually inform others about the manner in which he must be approached and the ritual objects to give him. Otherwise the shaman has to explain his requirements when his services are requested.

[97] This is probably a case of "post hoc, ergo propter hoc." A picture which I have reason to believe was taken in 1883 shows this man with a patch over his eye. Yet this ceremony could not have taken place before 1889, the year in which the narrator and his family were sent to the Mescalero reservation.

So he sang, and at the end of the fourth song he told them the same thing that he had told them in the first place. "It's a hard one to take out," he said, "but I'll take it out and show it to all of you, and then you'll have to believe." He showed them his clothes, his hands, even his mouth. There was nothing on him.

"The thing I'll take out will be something that you can see, and I'll show how witches kill." Witches not only kill in a way that can be seen but put things in where it will kill you sooner. He said he was going to sing four songs and was going to try it the fourth time. He told them to keep a good fire up, to put a white cloth near it, and to watch what kind of looking thing it was going to be that they call a witch's weapon.

So he sang till the fourth song. At the end of the fourth song he went up to the boy and put his mouth to his head. And here he pulled out of his head something which was a very peculiar-looking thing. It was a bone, shaped into an arrow, with the arrowhead painted red. The arrow was blue and it had hair wrapped around it. And he claimed that the bone was a human bone and the four strands of hair were human hair.[98]

[98] "Sucking shamans" are common in Mescalero ceremonialism; much sickness is attributed to the presence of foreign objects in the body. Note the web of unpleasant associations in regard to witchcraft: the witch's missile is a miniature arrow; it is of human bone; it has four strands of human hair on it; it is covered with red material (blood). These are familiar motifs of recitals involving witchcraft.

While the shaman was working, he was talking with his power. His power said, "Don't take it out. That witch is stronger than we are."[99]

[99] The audience hears only one half of the conversation between a shaman and his power. From this the nature of the exchange can often be inferred. At intervals the shaman usually reports the content of his messages from his source of power.

He answered, "Why do you talk this way? We can't let this boy die of witchcraft. Here you've been telling me how strong you are and now you are backing out on a little piece of work like this!"[100]

[100] The shaman often shows his interest in and good will toward his patient by special appeals to his power on his patient's behalf and even by attempts to shame his power into exerting its strongest efforts for the benefit of his client. This, of course, evokes feelings of gratitude and confidence in the sick person and his relatives.

But the power said, "We can't do it. This witch is too strong for us. If you take it out, four days from now your eye will burst."

But the shaman said, "I'll do it anyway, no matter what happens to me." And he went right ahead with his work.

After he took that one out he said he would wait two days and then take out the other weapon of the witch. But when he came back to try the other one, it was too much for him. But anyhow it shows that there is really witchcraft, for there it lay on the handkerchief before all of them, that bone with the four human hairs around it; and the arrowhead was red, and the notch was red, and it was blue in the middle. It was about three inches long, and nice work on it, a deadly-looking weapon. When he took it out, instead of keeping it, he burned it, and it made a noise like a gunshot.[101] This was during the day, in the morning. He took it out and burned it right away.

[101] Witchcraft is considered so "strong" and tenacious that nothing but fire will entirely destroy it. Consequently objects of witchcraft are consigned to flames. A "pop" or explosion signals the destruction of the evil influence. Witches are executed by burning; and they, too, are said to "pop" as the witchcraft principle in them is destroyed by the flames.

Eye-Covered claimed that the one who did this witchcraft was a man who went south long before to join the Lipan Apache.[102] And there the man who did the witching was killed by another Indian who claimed he found out this man was a witch.

[102] When a shaman diagnoses sickness as being due to witchcraft, he not infrequently identifies the witch as someone of another tribe, someone who has left the area, or someone who has since died. In this way an open conflict between the friends and relatives of the accused and the accuser is avoided, and the issue becomes essentially a test of strength between good and evil power.

The boy never got well. He died of the one witch weapon that was left in him. And the shaman lost one eye. His eye burst after he tried to take out the second weapon. So they told him not to try any more, and he left it in the boy, and the boy died.

In this way some shamans lose everything. They have disagreements with their power. They say that if you fight with your power, it is so much less strong and it gets weaker and weaker each time till there's nothing left. It is as if you cut off a stick shorter and shorter. If you tell a lie against your power, it's bad, they say—for instance, if you say you got your power over at some other mountain instead of mentioning the right one. Then the power hates you. It says, "Why don't you tell the truth about me instead of working against me and telling lies? We should be pulling together, and instead you balk and pull the other way."[103]

[103] The relation of a shaman to the source of his supernatural power and ceremony is a very personal and delicate one. Power can become increasingly fond of the shaman, may grant him more ritual knowledge as time goes on, and give him more aid. Or it may grow angry with the shaman to the point where the songs he sings and the prayers he utters are no longer effective, for the power has withdrawn its presence and support. Consequently an unsuccessful shaman wonders whether his power has deserted him. The relationship may be likened to that between two friends which may become warmer and closer with time or which may cool and terminate in mutual recrimination.

A Successful "Charming" Ceremony

One family used the warbler for charming, and they used red ochre and white clay on the face of the one they wanted to charm. The white paint stood for the white markings on the breast of the bird. So if you wanted to influence anybody, you put the white clay up to her breast and throat. Yellow ochre stood for the yellow markings of the bird.

I was there and saw that they were trying to charm for one of the boys to be married. It was during his young days. This is how it started. My mother knew that this woman knew charming. Once when they were drinking corn beer at a little party, she said to her, "There's your son. Why don't you marry him off? You know how to charm." The boy heard it and asked his mother to help him.

They say when a person knows charming he has nothing but his gee string; he is sure to be poor.[104]

[104] Mescalero "charming" ceremonies or love magic have much in common in psychology and detail with hunting ritual, especially with the deer ceremony. In both instances the intention is to draw the "victim" to one and to make the pursued amenable to one's wishes. If a person chooses to use this type of ceremony to attract the opposite sex, he pays an economic penalty. The underlying idea is not so far removed from that expressed in our own saying: "Lucky in love, unlucky at cards."

This young man liked someone who didn't care for him much. She was a young girl, a little crippled, still in school. I had heard talk about this ceremony from other people, and I was a little afraid of what they were doing. I thought they might make me crazy.[105] I had always heard it was dangerous for a child to be around a charmer. But they told me it wouldn't hurt me, that it was not for me, so I made up my mind I'd be there every night, and I stayed there with them.

[105] The danger in the use of a love ceremony is that if a person toward whom it is directed resists it, he is likely to become mentally unbalanced.

The first night nothing happened. This boy's mother had the tail and breast of the bird in her hand, and she marked them with pollen. In the middle of the ceremony she asked her son, "Do you want that girl to come to you or do you want to go to her?" "I'll go to her myself." "All right, I'll tell you how it will be done."

Next night I was there again. My mother was there too. After half of the ceremony the charmer told her boy, "The girl is willing to come to you."

"I didn't want it that way. I wanted to go to her!"

The second day that boy was out in the fields. His mother sent me after him. I brought him back, and she told him, "Go to the agency right now. It's the warbler's word, and you must go. In a week you'll see what's going to happen. Never mind the other two nights of the ceremony. We'll take care of that later. You know what that means."

I went with him. I rode a white horse and he rode a bay horse. Before we started she marked his face with white, red, and yellow ochre. She wanted to mark me too. I said, "I'm not going after a girl. I don't want that!"

She said, "It doesn't matter. When you're with someone you must be marked like him. A pair has to be marked when it's like this."

We stopped at my cousin Tom's on the way. I stayed and told this fellow I'd wait there for him while he was gone. He left for the agency. I don't know what happened there. I was watching a hoop and pole game and forgot all about him.[106]

[106] The hoop and pole game is a favorite gambling game of men. It is played by two men on a level field. A hoop with markings around the rim is rolled

along the ground. Poles which are marked at the butt end are slid after it. The object is to make the hoop fall on the butt end of the pole in such a way that the markings on the hoop and the pole overlap. A count is made according to the relative position of the markings. Women may not approach the hoop and pole grounds or watch the game, and the game has ceremonial overtones.

It was Saturday noon. I saw a couple coming down the canyon. It was this boy riding with his girl on the saddle. I thought to myself, "It's a great thing! I'll do that myself some day."

That evening he said, "We must go back. Mother is working hard for me there." He left the girl at the agency. We went back.

That night his mother went on with the ceremony. "You don't have to tell me what you've been doing, son," she said, "I see it all. It's all coming out well."

The next night was the fourth night of the ceremony. It must be done at night. She said, "It's this one that's doing it for you," and she showed him the warbler feathers.

Nine days after she began her ceremony they were married. It was the first Catholic wedding on the reservation. This woman is still living and has children. The man has been dead two or three years, but she has not remarried yet.

I think his mother used the warbler for healing too. She worked on a man's eyes once, using the warbler ceremony, but it didn't do him any good at all.[107]

[107] It is somewhat ironic to discover that Mescalero love magic paved the way for a formal Christian marriage. It is obvious from a number of accounts that the performance of a love ceremony makes a timid swain bold enough to approach and impress his beloved. Thus, though its aid was nothing more than psychological, it was nevertheless effective in some instances. Note that the warbler was used ceremonially for more than one purpose. Note also that some failures as well as the successes of ceremonialism are acknowledged.

Early Lessons in the Importance of Power

These little birds are often very powerful. One time one of the schoolboys chased a California towhee and killed it. He tried to cook it on the stove, but the boys scared him, and he stopped. But they claim he ate it. A few days later he got sick. I looked at him. He had clap. I was only thirteen or fourteen years old then, and he was just twelve. I don't know how the world he got it! They say it was from this bird. They took him to the doctor. He died of it. I saw this happen. Since then I have been afraid of this bird.

About this time my brother got sick and was treated by a shaman. This man usually worked on the head of his patient. He used the golden-crowned kinglet power for healing. He used pollen with it. He made a queer noise when he worked. He marked the tail feathers with pollen and put the tail of the bird on the head of the sick one and left it there. He also put pollen in the mouth of the sick person.[108]

> [108] When the source of power is an animal or bird, a shaman usually uses some part of the body of his power source in the ceremony or imitates its calls, movements, or habits.

My brother had the measles, as I found out afterward. This old man said it nearly turned out to be nine-day sickness (pneumonia), but he said he took out everything, and the boy was safe. All he asked of us was a buckskin, a gun, and a horse. This man was a great healer before he entered the peyote meeting. There it was taken away from him.[109]

> [109] It was considered dangerous for a shaman who had power from some other source than peyote to go to peyote meetings, for under the influence of peyote he was likely to reveal too much about the nature of his power, become involved in a contest of supernatural strength with another ceremonialist, and as a result lose it. For an account of the episode in which this shaman lost his power see Opler 1936a: 154–155.

Earning the Right to Smoke

In the old times smoking was mostly for a ceremonial purpose, though there was some smoking for pleasure. But some of the old people do not smoke for pleasure even now. Then they wouldn't let you smoke till you caught a coyote. I did it. I was about fifteen or sixteen years old then.

It happened at Three Rivers. There was a whole bunch of us. We had nothing but moccasins on. They got a coyote started, and we tried to head him off. Two other boys and I were there when he came toward us. Some boys were chasing behind that coyote. He was six feet in the lead of one fellow. He came straight for me. We missed him the first lick and started chasing and heading him off the second time. I got him by the tail and swung him, and they all yelled. I went down in an arroyo with him and held him till the others came up.

They came up and said, "You can smoke." I wanted to try it right away. I hunted tobacco in the crowd and felt pretty satisfied as I puffed away. Now I could smoke anywhere like a man.

Some of the other boys wanted a try at that coyote, so we let him go, and they started chasing again. This time he got away, though. The next day they had another run, and another boy got his coyote. The day after that they treed a fox. One boy got him and could smoke then. We were called men after that.

I smoked four or five times before I got home that night. I was sick that evening. They had said, "Put that smoke through your nostrils; let's see it." It made me sneeze at first, but I got used to it.

After catching that coyote, I had to wash myself and throw my clothes away, it smelled so bad.[110]

[110] The Mescalero have an ambivalent attitude toward Coyote. Coyote appears in the myths as a buffoon and trickster. Useful supernatural power for war, hunting, and running can be obtained from it. Yet it is also classified with evil animals of the night; and to touch, smell, or to be frightened by it can bring sickness to anyone who does not have power from it. Because of this the narrator was concerned over the consequences of touching and smelling a coyote, and he washed thoroughly afterwards. Actually it was not the intent of the elders to induce the young boys to handle a coyote. It was assumed that no boy could keep pace with the animal and that this would be a brake upon smoking at an early age. In this case the boys upset such calculations by organizing a surround. Note that the fox is treated as the equivalent of the coyote for this purpose.

First Hunting Experiences

The Mescalero boy, when he makes his first kill, whatever it is, is instructed to take out the heart and eat it raw. Then he can always kill. This is still done. I saw some schoolboys do this. Four boys killed a pigeon. One looked at it. He took the heart out. He said, "It's too big for me to eat. I tell you what we'll do. I'll cut it in four parts, and we'll put a cross on it and eat it." They did it. The boy just put a cross on with a motion of the hand; it was not a real cross.[111] Then they swallowed it raw. The boy said, "Now we'll always be able to kill something any time we want to and we'll have all the pigeons we want."

[111] Most objects used or consumed in ceremonies are marked with pollen in the form of a cross. Here the gesture stands for the cross of pollen. In Mescalero ideology the cross symbolizes the four corners of the earth or the entire world.

When one of my friends was a kid he was just going to swallow his first heart. He had it in his mouth. Just then I hit him on the back as hard as I could. That heart came up. You could see it hit the roof of his mouth, and he nearly choked on it. The old men told him he had to do it over again and keep it down. You're not supposed to have any trouble when you swallow it.[112]

[112] The narrator has apparently long shown, and continues to display, a mixture of reverence and irreverence toward ceremonial matters. Ritual matters should go smoothly to be most effective, and it was bad manners for him to play a prank in this context.

There are all sorts of rules and stories about hunting and the animals. I can't remember all of them. We say that when the moccasin string becomes untied on either foot while you are out hunting, it means that you won't make a kill, that you won't find anything or will miss a shot. Then you might as well go back. If your moccasin comes off entirely it is good luck. You won't have to go far. I caught my moccasin in a bush once and it came off. I said, "That's good. I won't have to go far." I put it on, went just a little way, and found a big deer. If you meet a mountain lion, a coyote, a wolf, a wildcat, or a fox when you are hunting, it means good luck.[113] It means that you won't have any accident.

[113] Presumably this is related to the hunting prowess of these animals.

They taught us to put the head of the deer toward the sunrise before butchering. Alfred did it when I killed those two deer the other day. I laughed at him.[114]

[114] The narrator again makes light of a ritual injunction.

I've heard lots of times that if you shoot an elk, at the very time you hit him, you must fall down and roll around as though you were shot. If you don't do this, that elk will just keep running. If you roll, it will not get very far but will fall dead soon. I thought I would do this if I ever shot an elk, but I have never shot one. My father used to eat elk. The last one they killed, they found up at Peso's place. Maybe I ate some of it. If a witch eats elk he will have to throw up. They tell a witch by this.[115]

[115] The witchcraft anxiety is great and pervades many contexts. All kinds of behavior are watched for any telltale signs of witchcraft.

Running Water chased an elk doe at Turkey Tank. I chased it too but it got away. Kakas saw it last. He saw it going to a little cave at Pajarito where they say there are elk horns lying. The elk walked in that cave and never came out. I have seen that cave.

They say that after almost all the elks had disappeared from around here, the Jicarilla Apache found one at a cave at White Mountain. They killed it, butchered it, and hauled the meat up with ropes. After that all the Jicarilla people who had eaten the meat died off. It showed that the cave was a holy home of the elks.[116]

[116] There is a general belief that animals are the gifts of the supernaturals and are released from holy caves or homes in the mountains for mankind's use. The animals must not be hunted until they are released; that is, the holy homes should not be invaded. A lack of game is taken to mean that for some reason, such as impiety of the people, the supernaturals are withholding the animals of the chase.

You can't just come through a lot of camps with deer that you've killed. If you do, when you get to your camp, you won't have a thing left but the head. When I went out hunting big game the first time, I didn't know this. I killed a big buck and was coming back through a lot of camps. Everyone stopped me, and the women came out and took what they wanted. This was over at Three Rivers. By the time I came back I had nothing but the head.

My mother said, "Don't say anything. They are poor people and they need it. This is the way of our people."

So when a hunter wants to bring his meat in, he passes far from all the camps and cuts in to his own camp the shortest way. Other hunters are easy on you. They know how hard it is to get the deer, and they know if they take your meat, you'll ask them for some too when they have been lucky. So they take just a little. They might take a rib and say, "This is all I want. I know you have worked hard." Then when you see them, you do the same thing to them. But the poor people, like women who have no one to hunt for them, take what they want. They say, "It's all right. I am poor and have no one to hunt for me."[117]

[117] The Mescalero tenet of generosity and sharing is indicated by this account.

At Three Rivers Tom had the same thing happen to him. His first time out he came through the camps, and they took everything but the hide.

Power from Squirrel

Turquoise was a man who was pretty strong in a ceremonial way, but for a long time no one knew what he had. Everybody tried to find out what it was. They tried to find out at peyote meetings, but they never could find out what he knew. He always had a bracelet on his wrist. This bracelet was a buckskin one with a little white bead, a red bead, turquoise, and other things on it.[118] I didn't know what they all were. He always brought a peyote button and something else to peyote meeting. He carried them in his hand there. This is the only man whose power source they couldn't find out and who told it himself.

[118] Often something a shaman wears suggests the source of his power. A person who begins to busy himself with ceremonial matters and at the same time starts to wear the feather of a certain bird will be suspected of having had a supernatural experience with that bird and of having obtained power and a ceremony from it. Sometimes the symbols give little clue to the identity of the power source, and the source of the ceremony does not become public knowledge unless a shaman reveals it himself.

At last he explained what he knew. He said, "Squirrel sits in the tree and never looks on the ground at all. He looks into the sky. He fixes his eyes like a field glass, and nothing can hide from him at any distance, whether it's behind the mountain or on the ground." He said this just one time, and that was during a peyote meeting in Nogal. They did not know what he had till he mentioned the squirrel. Then they did not think the squirrel amounted to anything, for there were other big things there, elk, bear, and others.[119]

[119] That is, there were shamans present who had obtained supernatural power from large animals such as the bear and elk.

While he was talking, he suddenly stopped short. Then the drum was handed to him. They looked at him but could not see anything. When you are at peyote meeting you are supposed to carry a red stone. It hides everything, and they can never find out what power you have.

He said, "That's the reason you can't find out what I have although you know I am pretty strong. I'll tell you how I got it. In my young days I was very, very poor. Many had power of all kinds, and one day I was thinking of power. I wanted to be out raiding and have good things and horses just like the rest.[120] One day I sat crying. While I was sitting crying, a little animal ran up to my shoulder and sat there. 'Don't cry, I've come to help you. I'll give you a little power that I know.' This squirrel talked to me. He gave me four things. 'Swallow these.' I did and they went in my body. You'll never find out what they are at all."

[120] As material already introduced has suggested, almost every adult Mescalero Apache, man or woman, was likely to have some supernatural help and ceremony, of greater or lesser scope and importance. The traditional view is that for success or even survival a person needs strength greater than that with which nature has endowed him and knowledge and guidance that his senses alone do not afford. A Mescalero feels that his own efforts must be supplemented by supernatural help, and he feels confident and safe only when he has a supernatural source to which to turn at a time of crisis. Individuals who have some supernatural power but desire more of it may seek increased power or knowledge of the supernatural from one source or may seek power from several sources. Such individuals with a proclivity for pursuing religion are said to be "loaded up" with power. They usually are willing to display their ceremonies publicly and are not loath to attempt to cure sick persons outside their own families. Others are satisfied with less power and less responsibility and use their ceremonial knowledge only for their own needs or those of their close relatives. Religious practitioners rise and fall in prominence and reputation. If a shaman is credited with a series of successful cures, the sick flock to him, and he is showered with payments of horses, buckskins, and food. If he has a series of failures, his clientele fades away, and he himself may come to feel that his power has lost interest in him. Through loss of patronage and self-confidence he is reduced to the ranks, so to speak. Thus, though the pattern of Mescalero ceremonialism remained reasonably constant, the personnel of shamanism and the relative positions of shamans changed rapidly.

I saw a ceremony that he performed over one of his own daughters when she had pneumonia. It was the first time I had seen pine pollen used. He did this quickly. He motioned four times with the pollen and then gave his daughter something that he took out of a leather case. He put it in water and gave it to her. He did it four times, and each time he did it the same ceremonial way. Then he began to sing.

The girl got well and was put back in school, but the same disease attacked her for the second time. He lived in Nogal and was not notified till she was in bad condition. That night she died. This death happened in my very young days. It was the first time I had seen a burial. I felt very, very sorry; but it could not be helped.

One time we were playing the moccasin game close to this man's camp. He talked about his power. He said, "I have been through Mexico and among all peoples who know different things in a holy way. I've done my best in every way and never gained much. What I gained was lost in turn. I outran even the bullets. I joined the Victorio bunch but was never even touched. I have been fired on at close range by infantry and never got a scratch. Victorio spoke to me many a time. When Victorio surrendered I was right by his side. 'You're a man,' Victorio told me that day, 'but the end will be at sunrise.' "[121]

[121] Victorio was killed in 1880 in an engagement between his followers and Mexican military forces.

Though there was heavy firing, the surrender of the women, children, and some men came because they had no more ammunition. They couldn't help it. But even though they were surrounded, Turquoise escaped with a few others. He got away from that place with his life.

"I do not know why I can't cure," he told us. "I can run. Even the horses can't stand up to me, for I go like the wind. And at the peyote meeting when they tried to see what I had they couldn't catch me. This shows I'm pretty strong. But this little thing, sickness, I cannot cure. I have tried it many times and have failed. But my power told me to hold on to him and I wouldn't die a painful death."[122]

[122] It is possible that failure to cure his daughter caused this shaman to lose faith in the efficacy of his ceremony for dealing with sickness. It is evident from what he says that he toyed with the idea of giving up his ceremony altogether.

And he died without knowing it. An automobile fell on top of him.[123] He's the only one who ever had power from the squirrel that I know, and that's what he said about it. His Squirrel power was good in war and running but not in curing.

[123] When automobiles became available, because of the limited financial resources of the Indians and their inability to cope with the white man's sales tactics, they acquired a good many used cars in dubious condition. The combination of mountain roads, illicit sales of bad liquor to Indians, and cars in poor repair resulted in a number of fatalities.

2

Following Two Trails

Civilization

W HEN I WAS YOUNG I was afraid of the whites. I used to just look at them from behind trees and run when they came near. I had to be caught to go to school. I didn't want to go. But when they got me there, they gave me bread, and I liked it pretty well. It was that big white bread. I wanted to stay then. I said, "That white man's bread is pretty good." They had an awful time getting some of the children to school. There were some big girls they were trying to catch to take there. The whites couldn't get them. So they even sent some of the big schoolboys to catch them. But they couldn't get near them. I saw one girl caught by the police on horseback. You'd think her heart was going to break, the way she cried.[1]

---

[1] The Mescalero boarding school was opened in 1884 with accommodations for fifteen pupils. Its staff consisted of one teacher, a matron, and a cook. The Annual Reports of the Commissioner of Indian Affairs for 1886, 1887, 1893, and 1896 contain vivid descriptions of the seizing of the Indian children for the boarding school, of the consternation of parents and unwilling pupils, and of the resistance of Indian police to the performance of this unpleasant duty. Fletcher J. Cowart, agent in 1886, writes: "I found the attendance at boarding school about half what it should be, and at once set about increasing it to the full capacity of the accommodation. This I found extremely difficult. . . . Everything in the way of persuasion and argument having failed, it became necessary to visit the camps unexpectedly with a detachment of police, and seize such children as were proper and take them away to school, willing or unwilling." (Annual Report of the Commissioner of Indian Affairs 1886: 199). In 1887, "considerable trouble was experienced" in filling the boarding school, "and it was necessary to withhold rations and use force before it could be done." (Annual Report of the Commissioner of Indian

Affairs 1887: 168). In 1893, after twenty-six pupils had been transferred to other schools, the agent notes: "So much intimidation had been used in procuring pupils for the transfer that the strong prejudice of the old Indian life against the home school was severely stirred up." (Annual Report of the Commission of Indian Affairs 1893: 217). In 1896, V. E. Stottler, First Lieutenant, Tenth Infantry, Acting Indian Agent, lists among the duties of the police "collecting and returning children to school." (Annual Report of the Commissioner of Indian Affairs 1896: 210). The boarding school was considered a device for separating the children from the camp Indians and "civilizing" them. Many agents would not let the children return to their families in summer lest they backslide. The worry of parents and relatives about the children and the homesickness of the children were most acute.

All during this time the white agents were trying to get the Mescalero to give up their own customs. About 1896 Boneska, the leader of the Lipan people, was chief of police here. The agent offered to cut his hair. This was my first year in school.[2] Later I went to Santa Fe for nine months and then went to Albuquerque to school. I stayed there until 1901.

[2] The campaign to compel the members of the police force to have their hair cut short is described from the agent's point of view in the Annual Report of the Commissioner of Indian Affairs for 1896: 209–212.

This police chief said to the agent, "I'm no white man. I won't cut my hair."
The agent said, "Why don't you want your hair cut?"
"It was meant to be long."
The agent said, "I'll give you a dollar," and the police chief told him, "I'll do it for five."
So the agent cut it, and the police chief got five dollars. All the police force had their hair cut.
Old Man Augustine ran off because he didn't want to have his hair cut. The agent said he would pay him well. Old Augustine lived around Alamogordo, La Luz, and Three Rivers. The agent got after him. He said, "You're not turning back to the Indian life. It's best for you to turn white." He was very strict.
He taught these people how to farm, how to put up houses. He ran all the white men off the reservation, their cattle and their mines. He issued blankets, clothing. Before his time they just issued food rations. Since his time the Indians have not worn Indian clothes.[3]

[3] The cattle from ranches adjoining the reservation had been seriously encroaching upon Indian land. Miners, too, were a constant source of difficulty. Lieutenant Stottler and his successor made a determined effort to oust intruders from the reservation.

Old Man Hoosh was wearing a blanket one time. This agent jumped on him. Hoosh won the fight, but he ran away. He never wore a blanket after that.

The agent distributed cattle at the time of the girl's adolescence rite. Everybody was invited. The agent came to watch the dance. The Indians all had rifles and bows and arrows at this time. I would hide from the white men often; I was scared of a few I didn't like.

Rivalry and Defiance

During this time when the whites were trying to rule these Indians, some funny things happened. Running Water knew power in a way towards the rifle or arrow. It works either when you're drunk or sober, and they claim that it brings luck in hunting. The men who knew it were great hunters and riflemen.

Once when they were showing off, two men were present who knew this power, Running Water and another Mescalero. There were white soldiers, a soldier and an officer, on the other side. They were going to see who was the best shot. And there was heavy betting.[4] On the Indian side there was little money. They all knew one of the white men was a good shot, one of the best in the country. And they had seen both of them shoot, and the white soldier and officer had seen the Indians shoot.

[4] Not infrequently soldiers and Indians found occasion to bet against each other. I secured a number of accounts in which soldiers and Indians competed in horse racing for high stakes.

They said, "Let's try it out now." Both Apache knew the ceremony of weapons pretty well. They could make the other fellow's gun shoot crooked, while they, themselves, would shoot true.

The white men tried to bet their lives on it, but the Indians wouldn't call it. The leading white officer wouldn't allow it either, for the law was pretty strong among us then.[5] They told those white men to make their own targets at any distance they wanted. Some of the white soldiers bet on the Indians and some on the whites, and the same for the Indians. This was to be one shot apiece, four shots altogether. They put up four stones, small targets, at a distance of about two hundred yards and were shooting off the hand, that is, standing with no rest.

[5] It is most unlikely that the white contestants offered to forfeit their lives if they lost. This sounds more like a projection of an Indian folkloristic concept. In the Mescalero tale of the playing of the first moccasin game, for instance, the losers were to die at the hands of the winners. See pp. 106–108 for details of the moccasin game.

An Indian was to shoot the first shot. So Running Water took the first shot. Army guns were being used. Running Water said it was a hard thing to do. "I've got to use my power," he said. So he rolled a cigarette and smoked. After he had done the proper things and smoked, he put his cigarette on the ground.[6] Then he stood and shot at the first target, and the rock went off and was gone.

⁶ This was ritual smoking in which Running Water engaged. One can be sure that the smoking was accompanied by prayer.

Then the white man was called. He was ready. He shot. That stone also fell off.

The other Indian, a little fellow, came up. He said, "That gun's too heavy. Give me a carbine." It's the same kind but has a shorter barrel. A cavalryman gave him a gun that they said would not shoot true. He said, "I'll make it shoot true." So they gave him a cartridge and told him to go in and shoot. He went in front carrying the rifle that was loaned him. He told them that his shot was going to be true.

Then a white man told him, "I'll give you a dollar if you hit it."

So the Indian said, "Give it to me. That rock is as good as gone."

The white man said, "No, you have to hit it first."

The Indian told him to give it to the white captain to hold. So he did. Then the Indian shot, and the target was gone.

The white man who had a shot left said, "You Indians have won your bet, because I can't shoot." He had got a little shaky when he got up before the crowd. They all noticed it. He aimed, then he put his gun down again. "It's going to be pretty hard," he said.

Then the rest of the soldiers made fun of him. He tried a second time. "I've lost the bet," that's what he told his partner. "I can't shoot." Then he tried for the third time. He couldn't stand it any longer. They saw that he was trying to pull the trigger. He pulled, and the shot went wild. He missed the rock. His soldier partner came near jumping on him. He said, "You missed on purpose!" The captain, without saying anything, handed the Indian the dollar. And so the Indians won.

Both these Indians knew Rock Crystal power. That's what did it. If you know that, you never lose out in a shooting match or a fighting match. If a man knows power from Rock Crystal, he sure knows the gun! That's all it's for. You don't use it in healing or in any other way, but just with the gun. Rock Crystal talks right up to them, and they sing to it.⁷

⁷ Rock crystal is colorless, transparent quartz. Note the personification of rock crystal and the attribution of power to it.

One time when Running Water was holding a ceremony over Rock Crystal, it told him he had only one more chance and his time was up. He would have to pay his own life then. There was no other way, Rock Crystal told him, for someone was stronger than he was. The fourth day after he talked to his power he was to get drunk and have a row with the whole police force. Swinging-Lance was a policeman at that time, and he was down husking corn.⁸ Also some of the other police were away. There were about fifteen there. Peso was the chief of police.

⁸ The agency police were often given practical tasks by the white officials. As a result some of the Indians sneeringly called them "janitors." The Indian police force at Mescalero was organized in 1881.

Leggings was a brother-in-law to this man who was going to start the trouble. Leggings was said to be one of the last of the Foolish People.⁹ He once tried to shoot a man and hit me when I stopped him. He thought it was a joke, a funny thing that happened. This time he and Running Water were both drunk with two women. The women were caught and placed in jail, but the two men were carrying rifles and were not very easy to place under arrest, for they started fighting.

9 It is sometimes said that a remnant of the Foolish People married into the Mescalero tribe and have had descendants. Leggings, who is considered eccentric and none too bright, is often pointed to as a descendant of one of these marriages.

This fighting began right in the middle of the agency. At the first shot everybody disappeared in the ditch, behind the woodpile, or back of the buildings. The one left in the open was Leggings. He was shot through the hams by the second shot, a deep flesh wound. Later he was chained, treated, and put in jail.

Running Water fired a few shots and went down the road singing. He started to run and told them they were shooting crooked; he asked them why they didn't shoot straight. He took a few shots at the white police captain and some Indians but was too drunk and couldn't shoot straight. The captain was shot through his shirt, which was sticking out from behind a tree. Running Water shot at the school disciplinarian and came two inches from the top of his head.

They caught up with Running Water at the cottonwoods near where the Catholic church is now. He shot his way through. He paid no attention to those shooting at him. There was a big tree there, and he shot from behind it. He got across the bridge. Our school cook had his hand shot right across. He was crawling through the oats when it happened. Running Water shot another Indian's hat off. George Kos was just missed. When the shooting was all over, Running Water went around the hill and hit for his camp. He disappeared from that place for a long time. Then finally he came in by himself.

Then in 1897, the next year, he was killed. Jake Bead killed him. He was knifed first and then shot. So what Rock Crystal told him came true.[10]

10 The fact that the prophecy of Rock Crystal was considerably delayed has not shaken the narrator's faith in it.

Yearnings

Even when we were in school we used to think about our own people and our own ways. Someone in the dormitory would start telling a Coyote story. While it was being told everyone would be quiet. Then, at the end of the story, all would break out laughing.

One time about twelve of us stole out of the dormitory and went up to camp.[11] We sat up and listened to stories told by the old men all night. Some couldn't stand it and went to sleep, but I listened all night.[12] We planned to get back before daylight and started back about six. But some missed their breakfast by not getting back on time.

[11] To leave the dormitory without permission was a daring thing to do and usually resulted in severe punishment.

[12] The narrator's avid interest in the myths and tales is evident here. As a result of his continuing fascination with this aspect of his culture, he has a large fund of stories of all kinds and is an excellent raconteur.

Another time I was out at Diego's camp. He didn't want us to go back to the school. He told us that there would be a big storm and we would get caught in it if we went. I had to get back to school, so I left. It was very clear when I started from his camp. But I got caught in one of the worst storms I was ever in before I got back to the agency. I was late for school and got in trouble, for I was not supposed to go away like that. They say Diego was a witch and that he admitted it when he was dying. Then he gave up feathers and lots of things he had worked with.

Sacrifice

One day a boy was watching some blackbirds just as school was out. One was sitting on the fence. It called four times. Then a grackle came in its place. This one was blacker than the other, with white eyes. Then a third, then a fourth came. The last one was the smallest one. It called four times. He did not know what it meant, but it meant something by the four times, he thought.

He asked one of the biggest boys, and this boy said, "The blackbird was trying to tell you something."

I was in school at that time. That night the blackbird came to him in the form of a man. Light shone on his bed. It looked as if someone held a light to his face, and he saw a beautiful man dressed in buckskin and with a feather in his hair like the novices of the raid wear. "I am the one who spoke to you four times today," he said. Then another came, and another, and another. There were four young men, good looking and dressed as Mescalero. They told him to sit up. He did. My cousin Tom and I were in the next bed to him, but we were sound asleep. Tom was about twenty years old; I was just a boy. Everything seems to be aged right now when I think back on this.

Blackbird told him not to show this to anyone till the right time came or he would be gone before his good times came.[13]

[13] At the time a Mescalero has a vision experience and acquires a ceremony, he is often told by his power to refrain from practicing the rite for a certain length of time or until he receives a sign that it is proper to use his gift. To disregard such directions leads to a conflict between the shaman and his source of power which may result in the loss of power or some supernatural punishment. Note that the boy was put in a receptive mood toward the possibility of a supernatural experience by seeing four birds, one of which he thought called four times.

His mother got very sick. He was worried and wanted to try his power. He went to the blackbird and asked to be allowed to practice. The blackbird told him not to worry, that his mother would be all right, and that he should not practice before he told him to. But that boy sneaked out of the dormitory and found his mother very sick. So he used his power anyway.

Before he started in with his ceremony, the grackle came to him. "Are you going to use your power?"

"Am I not old enough to use it?"

"No, you are just entering your manhood.[14] You should wait until you are told that it's all right. I've told you your mother will be all right."

[14] The acquisition and use of ceremonies were considered, in the main, the perquisites of adults, though there are references to pre-adolescents and pre-adults who were precocious in this respect. The need for supernatural power is most keenly felt when an individual has adult responsibilities and a family to protect and support.

"I want to see her well now."

"Are you going to practice? Do you think more of your mother than of me, even after I tell you your mother will be all right?"

"I will practice."

Blackbird told him four times not to do it. Then he got mad. "All right, I'm going to leave you. Do what you want. Go ahead!" And he left.

The boy used his power for his mother. While he was using his power, the blackbird told him, "You have given your own life for your mother."

"That's what I have done," he said.

Then his mother began to get well, but he got sick. Many different shamans were hired, but he died. He gave up his life for his mother.[15] He was supposed to go to the Fort Lewis Industrial Training School in Colorado in September, but he died before that.[16]

[15] The mortality rate of the Indians on the reservation was extremely high during this period. This was particularly true among the students at the boarding school, among whom tuberculosis was the great scourge. A psychological factor may have been involved in this boy's death. It is believed that power which is angered will withdraw protection and leave a shaman exposed to witchcraft or the evil forces he has challenged. Failure in ritual and fear of the consequences lead to despondency with the usual psychosomatic complications.

[16] The first Mescalero children to attend the Fort Lewis Industrial Training School were sent in June 1892. This episode probably occurred about this time.

Epidemic

This is something hard to believe, the way this power was shown. Not the form of the animal appeared, but its sign. The young fellow who learned this ceremony must have been seventeen or eighteen or younger when this was shown to him.

Four or five of us at the school were sick with typhoid fever. I was among them.

The worst one was Bob Eddy. I had been out herding cows. The boy I herded with said, "You look sick; your face is yellow. You should go back." I did and was put to bed and told I was getting typhoid fever. Then Bob got sick. The doctor came around three times a night. In the daytime our families were there and in the night too.

Everybody else got well and there were only Bob and I left there. My younger brother, Edgar, was four years old then. We kept on staying there and finally I was getting a little better too. But the boy, Bob, was just a skeleton. I told him, "Eat and get strength or you'll die."

He said, "If I die I'll meet you down at those cottonwoods at the bridge, and be sure to come and visit me."

I said, "All right, and if I die, I'll meet you there too." I felt weak and sick.[17]

[17] A frank discussion between Apache about death and afterlife is most unusual. The fact that the boys were in the hospital, a place which at this time was associated with death and ghost fears, may have been involved. Although there was no hospital on the reservation at this time, a room had been set apart for sick boys and one for sick girls at the school in 1897. See Annual Report of the Commissioner of Indian Affairs 1897: 194.

So we made these promises, and that night a man beat the old drum around there and we were scared to death.[18] The doctor had to come over to us and work on us, and we pulled through. The doctor said, "Don't be scared or you'll lose out." The doctor stayed up that night with us.

[18] Drumming is usually an accompaniment of ceremony, and most Apache ceremonies are curative rites. Consequently, the drumming reminds the boys of their sickness and danger.

My mother was there. Bob was very weak. My mother helped to put the poor boy on the bed pan. His mother never came around. We told him to eat. He said, "Oh, I'm all right. I got lots in me." He talked up like a man, but he was just skin and bones. It put life in me to hear him.

Then I said, "If you talk like that, I'll talk like that."

The doctor motioned us not to talk. I said, "Doctor, it's the best thing. If we talk, we'll forget our sickness, and we'll get well faster."

When we were just a little better, Bob said he was going to try to walk. He got hold of the bed. He couldn't make it. I tried it. I sank down. The doctor got after us for getting out of bed. Then Bob got up in the night time. I saw him walk just like a drunken man. "Someone is beating that drum again," he said and woke me. The doctor woke up and scolded us.

One time nobody was there. I was sound asleep. Bob heard something come in. It touched him on the head. "I've come to make you well. I want you," it told him. I didn't know what was going on. They put a big sleep on me so they could have their talk. I didn't know it at all.

In the morning Bob was a different person. He walked, but I was at the same place. He told me about it and said, "I'm going to ask him to come tonight again and come to you too and make you better. I'm better now."

Night came. It came to visit him the second time. I heard them talking. I thought Bob was talking in his sleep. Then all at once something touched me on the head. I wanted to touch it. I put my hand there, and it growled. I put my hand up and put it to its head and mouth, and it caught my hand. Then I had strength. My back felt different. I had a good feeling. It was Raccoon. He was giving his power to this boy.

Bob said, "Both of us will get well. I'm going to see much country. You, too, will see many things, but not what I will see." It came true all right.

For four nights we didn't have visitors. Of what my mother brought, I gave some to Bob. We got well and both got out at the same time. Instead of meeting a dead man at the cottonwoods, we met there alive and laughed over it.

Bob had said, "I long to see that big place they call Niagara Falls. I'll see it. I'll see Kansas City, Chicago, and all sorts of places."[19] He did; he traveled and worked in all those cities. His power gave him this. But he got tuberculosis. He came back here and was going to try to make it to the Jicarilla reservation, but he died here instead.[20] His ceremony could not help him with this part.

[19] For the circumstances that led to this man's travels see p. 189.

[20] This sick man had heard of a powerful ceremonialist on the Jicarilla reservation and planned to go there for ritual treatment. After the beginning of the reservation period it became quite common for those with lingering illnesses to travel widely to obtain ceremonial aid. The enforced peace, the concentration of different tribes on the same reserves for periods of time, the meeting of young people of various tribes at off-reservation boarding schools, and the new and more convenient modes of transportation were among the factors that stimulated these ceremonial interchanges. For a number of examples of this kind of activity see Opler 1942a.

Ceremonial Protection

I was still just a schoolboy when Look-Around-Water performed a ceremony for me. His power from Morning Star shows good visions too. This ceremony was held with his wife, his daughter, and myself present. I was invited to his camp. He was right at his top then.

He just volunteered to do this for me. I didn't hire him, because I was pretty young and didn't know anything then. We were still dressed in the old way and we had bows and arrows. We'd go out shooting birds during vacations. I think my father gave him something for doing this for me, but I don't know what it was. I don't know whether my father asked him to do it for me.[21] He just called me over, that's all. It was just for that one night. We were camping down there. We were living with San Juan's relatives. Old San Juan had died about 1886.

[21] It was common for a family to have a protective rite performed over a child who was going away to school. Since this shaman had power for coping with the enemy, it was particularly appropriate for him to attempt to safeguard a child going to the school of the white man. It is almost certain that he was hired by the narrator's family for this purpose.

I went to his camp, and he was getting ready to perform his ceremony from the morning star. He motioned to me to sit in a certain place where there was a goat hide, and I sat there. It was next to him, on his right side. The girl and the woman were on his left. He put out his pollen and things in front of the fire. A peculiar-shaped turquoise representing the morning star was there, and a downy feather was tied to it.

He said, "Because of this power I was never hit during the war time. I was hit two times by bullets before I learned it. This Morning Star pointed himself out to me in the form of a human. He came and talked to me. I did not know who he was or what he was, but he told me he was Morning Star himself. He was dressed in beautiful buckskin and wore only two feathers on his head. He was representing a Mescalero. He asked me whether I wanted the power of the morning star or the power of the sun. I said, 'You're here, and I will take you. I will believe in you and in what you are going to do for me and give me. I will take it all.' "

And so Morning Star gave this man his power. But he told him he was not to use it for four years, except in war; he was not to use it for sickness until the fourth year had come.

He traveled all over. He was in several fights with outlaws, Americans, and Mexicans. He was shot at from pretty close distances but never had a scratch until the fourth year had come. Then instead of using it in war only, he used it against sickness and against whites and Mexicans to keep them away from himself. Then the fourth year, bad luck seemed to strike him.[22]

[22] A disaster is frequently rationalized in terms of failure to heed some direction of supernatural power. When a shaman is about to perform his ceremony, in order to stimulate faith and an affirmative attitude on the part of patient and spectators, he often, as in this case, relates the story of his acquisition of power and episodes describing its efficacy or successful use in the past.

He was never hurt by Indians, but during a raid down in Mexico he was shot right through and through and left for dead. There was nothing in sight. While he was lying on the prairie as though dead, something told him to awake. He came back to his senses and was talking to himself. He found he was hit through and through. But he had his medicine of the Morning Star power and took the medicine. Then he hit the road back toward home.

The fourth day he came into camp. There was nothing but a big scar left on him where he had been shot through and through. He was well. They all wondered how in the world he got well. But he never said anything about it.

A second time he was on a raid for horses. At that place there was a big herd of horses. They took them. They were with them at a water hole two days later. They heard a shot fired. The bullet came whistling, and it sounded as if it hit a rock. But instead of hitting a rock, it pierced that same man through and through again. The man had his shirt off, and they saw it hit him in the chest in the flat place between the ribs and come out the back.

He sat there and tried to untie something that was around his shoulders. He was bleeding. He untied it, and it was like a looking-glass, a peculiar thing shaped like a star. He mashed it in his hand and put it in his mouth. In a little while he took another dose. Then they brought a horse up to him, because the Mexicans were coming. They put him on the horse; the others fought while they took him over the hill. He got off the horse and told them to go. They left the horse there tied for him in the bushes. He lay down. The other people went on. They said, "He won't live; it's no use to come back for him." One man said he was shot through the heart.

While he was lying there, Morning Star came to him and told him what had caused all the trouble. He had not used the power in the right way. It told him, "You can use me and use me right, and I will be with you all the time."

He said, "Didn't I use you right?"

"No, you know what you did."

"What have I done? I thought I was doing right with you all the time."

His power told him, "There's a song that you are using that doesn't belong to me."

He asked him which one. "You're using a deer song in place of the song you should use. I'm against everything in the world. I stand for myself, and I'll stand by you if you use me correctly. That's what those two bullets were for, because of the songs that you are trying to place with me. No Deer, no Coyote, no Bear, nothing from this country is greater than I am. I'm stronger than you, and if you use me properly you will be as strong as I am."[23]

[23] Some supernatural power sources are quite willing to be used in combination with others. A power source, however, may be extremely exclusive, as in this case, and may punish a shaman who does not give it his undivided allegiance and attention.

"All right," he said, "I'll use you the right way this time."

"This may be your last chance." Then Morning Star pointed out to him the song which was causing the trouble. Morning Star sang the songs as they should be. He sang one song, two, three, four. "Now," he said, "be on your way. There's nobody around. There is nothing wrong with you."

The man looked at himself. There was nothing wrong, but there was a bullet scar on his chest and another right by his spine. So he went to his horse, untied him, and got on. Then Morning Star pointed out the way that he should go to head off the others.

He was just five minutes behind where they passed. They were resting on the hill and looking on their back track, and they saw him coming. They waited till he came up. When he came he spoke to them. He said, "Let's go back and get those horses back." That's what Morning Star had told him to do. He led them back to the place where the horses were and they tried to get them for the second time. The Mexicans had driven off the horses they had left at the water hole. They caught up and drove these horses off again. This time there was no trouble all the way through, and they came back. And so the power was strong with him and stayed with him all the way through. This is what he told me before he held his ceremony.

It was evening. He pointed out to me that he was going to hold a ceremony toward all things in this world: against diseases, against witches, to influence white men, and also in connection with the gun. He said, "I know the gun. When you speak for the gun in the way of Morning Star you never miss a mark at all. It hits and never misses. No matter what the distance is, the gun that carries that far will always make the hit." He pointed out also that it works on the white man as well as the Mexican. If you know this power you talk to them and they do just what you say.

He also gave me some kind of a medicine or herb. He mashed it in his hand and gave me four doses of it before he started to pray and sing. He said, "This medicine I give you is only against witchcraft. I am going to start to sing just four songs before I pray." There was a pollen motion, standing up.[24] He marked all of us with the pollen and rolled four cigarettes. He gave me the cigarettes and told me to hand them back to him. Then he told me to cross one of the cigarettes with a match and give it to him. I gave it to him the way he asked for it.[25]

[24] That is, a motioning with pollen or the throwing of pollen to the cardinal directions in clockwise order, beginning with the east.

[25] To hand a shaman a cigarette in this manner or to put it on the moccasin of his right foot is to request ceremonial help from him.

Then he started to sing, and the song seemed to get me to want to help him sing. I had never heard the song before, but I felt like singing it. He told me not to be afraid of singing, but to sing right up. So I sang with him. I sang all through the four songs. Then we sat for a while again, and he started to say something in prayer. I tried to catch on to all the words he said, but he was going too fast, and I couldn't remember the words at all.

From what he mentioned, he fixed up everything for me. He sang till midnight, and about half way he marked my hand in the way of a four-pointed star. He said it was the morning star. He sang a short song while he was marking my hand, then another song, short, and so for four songs. Then he told me to look around.

I looked and looked and saw a lot of good things. He talked to me while I was seeing these things, but still I saw these things. Then he started to sing again and kept it up till midnight. I could see good things all this time. I saw a wife and children, fruits, lots of shoes, and friendship with the white man.[26] All these things came true. Yet I was only seventeen years old. I saw these things a long time ago, but I have never told any of it. This is the first time I have ever told about these things that I saw through Morning Star power, and they came true.

[26] The narrator is rather proud of his ability to get along well with the white man. Despite a few unpleasant incidents which he recounts, his relations with agency personnel have been prevailingly good. He claims to have worked with P. E. Goddard, the anthropologist, in 1909. Since the narrator was only twenty-seven or twenty-eight years old at that time, it is likely that he acted as an interpreter or guide rather than an informant. There is evidence that Goddard was in contact with the narrator's father during his stay at Mesca-lero. There is also evidence that the narrator had mixed feelings concerning Goddard and his mission. On one occasion he said, "Goddard worked with

Boneska when he was here. I didn't like it. I wouldn't go near him [while he was doing this]." Not long before the writer began his researches at Mescalero, the narrator found employment with an American naturalist who came to the reservation area to gather bird and animal specimens for an Eastern museum. It is significant that when the naturalist inquired about a helper, he was directed to the narrator, whose hunting and trapping abilities made him the logical candidate for the position. As a result of this contact, the narrator learned and remembered the scientific and common names of a large number of the birds and mammals of the region. Since aiding the writer, the narrator has assisted at least two other anthropologists.

A dream or vision of fruit is a symbol of good fortune and plenty. The shoes probably stand for success at the white man's school and in the undertakings education will make possible.

The ceremony went on. We felt pretty good over what we saw. Before the singing and the prayers were over, he spoke to us and told of the future. He did not mention me this time but told of his wife and daughter and himself. He first told of his daughter. He said she was not going to bear any children at all. And the way he saw all these things was true. The daughter was the first one that died, then he himself died, and the old lady died the last, of old age. He saw that too. I was the only one he saw that was going to live all the way through after they were gone. That was what was shown me, and it came out true.

The star he made was of blue paint. He used the turquoise too and always had a downy feather attached to it. The turquoise was shaped like a four-pointed star. I remember the place where he held that ceremony for me. It is in Nogal, and every time I go there I stop at that place and look at that old camp. That's quite a while back. Here I am, an old man, fifty-three now, and there he is turned to dirt, and the old lady and the girl too. The girl died while I was away at school. Grasshopper was the old lady's name. She died two or three years ago.

This man who sang for me began to go to peyote meetings. He claimed that peyote stole all of his power. All of them said this. They said this man didn't have any business going to peyote meetings.[27]

[27] During the early reservation period peyote was much used, and peyote meetings were frequent. This was a period of defeat, economic hardship, sickness, and internal dissension for the Mescalero. Aggressions were turned inward, and many antagonisms were fought out in terms of supernatural power. Charges of witchcraft were common. Because the eating of peyote relaxed normal inhibitions, much competition in regard to supernatural power and a good deal of alleged interference with the supernatural power of others occurred at peyote meetings. See Opler 1936a.

Witchcraft and Dream

They say that Nogal Canyon was witched. There was a girl walking backward; she fell and broke her leg. My father fell there and broke a leg. Swinging-Lance fell on a cornstalk, and it went up his nose and nearly killed him. Another man fell while walking on a hill, went into some yucca, and got his hip hurt. There were all sorts of serious accidents from little things like that. I was there and saw it. They got discussing why it was. Then they got a man who knew the power of different things, and he worked against it. Diego worked against it too.

These men found out that it was over a child who was lost there. It was a Lipan Apache, a dangerous man who did all this.[28] This man, when his child died, said that his child was not the only one who was going to die there. Only one tree at the south end would live, he said. And by George, it looks true! All those who lived there died off. Bronco moved because he was afraid when it was shown. All the Swinging-Lance family who lived there died off. Many people moved to Elk. Now only Mexicans live there. It doesn't look as if much was cured about the place. Now only that tree is sticking up there among those Indian fields. That prophecy was made long ago when I was a boy.

[28] In 1903 thirty-seven Lipan Apache were found in the mountains of Chihuahua, Mexico, and a year later were allowed to make their home on the Mescalero reservation. The Lipan were just different enough in habits and outlook to arouse Mescalero animosity and suspicion and became the target of repeated witchcraft charges.

I've had many a dream about it. I dreamed that all of Nogal was burnt up. To dream of fire is very bad; you can't do anything about it. I dreamed that I was the only one who was fighting that fire. But I could not stop it, and it was all popping.[29] I dreamed I went to the agency then. I looked back and there the fire was still going. I dreamed about it twice. I told the old men about it at that time. I said, "I dreamed that Nogal was on fire. Some day no one will live in that place." This was just before rations were being given out. Now it is true. The place is deserted.

[29] It is a general belief that to dream of fire is a very bad omen. It is significant that the narrator sees himself as the only person fighting the fire. As we shall see, he has some reason to consider himself a lonely and isolated figure. The "popping" of the fire suggests that it is associated with witchcraft.

Not all my dreams have been reliable. Some people get power from Water Controller. It is a man sitting at the water gate. He holds the water together. He stops all the water. They say he is dressed in buttons.[30] I used to hear about him when I was a little kid. I had lots of dreams about him. They say if you see him you get power. I went to the water many times just to see him. It was all foolishness.[31] I never saw him.

[30] Water Controller is more properly described as being covered with abalone shell, which is itself a symbol of water. Since commercial buttons of abalone shell were familiar to the narrator, he describes Water Controller as dressed in "buttons."

[31] The narrator here, again, shows some impatience with an item of belief.

Masked dancers ready to perform.

Temporary encampments for the girl's puberty rite.

Some people take dreams very seriously. They say that to dream of a bull chasing you is very bad. To dream of losing teeth is bad; it means the death of relatives or one of your own family. If you should dream this, take corn, chew it, and throw it to the west, or do this with a stone you pretend to chew instead of the corn.

At the Girl's Adolescence Rite

When I was growing up, boys never missed attending the girl's adolescence rite. There was a lot more to it then than there is now. The trees for the big tipi poles were gathered in a special way. The singer performed a ceremony for the building of the big shade. All this was done four days ahead of the main ceremony. This part is now left out. You do not see it any more, and I think it will never come back. The masked dancers' home was not supposed to be around the camp. The masked dancers would come from the hills in the evenings. They did not mind how far they had to come. It is all different now; they make them right near camp. And there was another thing during that time—the ceremonial tipi had to be away from the regular camping places.

The first and last days, when the girls ran, boys and girls and even old women and old men used to run with them. They say you get long-winded when you do it. Julio always used to run with them when he was young. I used to run with them lots of times. That's all left out now, but we are trying to get it back.[32]

Pubescent girls preparing for the ritual running.

[32] The running of the pubescent girl symbolized a long and successful path of life for her. Those who ran behind her shared in the benefits. The girl's adolescence ceremony is one of the very important Mescalero ritual events. It does not rest upon shamanism, that is, the acquisition of power by an individual, but is a traditional ceremony which may be considered the property of the entire tribe. The priests of the rite teach the songs, prayers, and details of the ceremony to interested younger men who are willing to "sit with" them, and they thus recruit personnel to perpetuate the ceremony. A large conical-shaped structure, the "big tipi," is raised for the event. Masked dancers, or impersonators of mountain-dwelling supernaturals, appear and dance each of the four nights of the rite. Actually, most of the practices to which the narrator refers, such as special ritual practices at the time of the selection of the main poles and the preparing of the impersonators of the mountain-dwelling supernaturals far from the camps of the people, were still being carried out at the time this account was recorded.

If a man is really a witch and goes into the big tipi of the girl's puberty rite, he can't go on with his witching. If he wants to learn the tipi songs and be a singer of the ceremony he has to give up his witching, for he cannot use the two things at the big tipi.[33]

[33] There is no question about the sanctity or positive character of the girl's adolescence ceremony, and therefore it is entirely incompatible with witchcraft or anything negative.

Once when Jicarilla, who was one of the leaders of this ceremony, was singing, he stopped and looked at a man sitting beside him. He said, "I see something evil

The big tipi of the fifth morning of the girl's puberty rite.

Ceremonial run while the big tipi is being dismantled on the fifth morning of the girl's puberty rite.

in you. You'd better throw it away. You can't do the two things at once." I saw this man he was speaking to at the girl's ceremony many times. He was trying to learn it and couldn't. "I see that something bad is coming. Your day is nearly here," Jicarilla told him.

During that summer some people were drinking corn beer when a heavy rain started.[34] This man was leaning against a tree. Lightning hit him and the tree at the same time. He was killed. There was the mark of the lightning on the side of his head, and all down his body they saw it.

[34] For the details of the manufacture of this corn beer see 3[81].

Jicarilla, who warned this man, had sat with Old Patricio and learned his songs of the girl's ceremony. Old Felix knew the songs at the same time, and he and Jicarilla sang together. Bronco sang with Jicarilla too. Then Julio learned the songs and ceremony from Jicarilla. Once I sat up a whole night with a singer of this ceremony. He told me many things about it. He sang a number of songs for me. I tried to catch them and did catch a few.[35]

[35] Here the narrator is hinting that he once began to learn the songs of the ceremony. Like many of his other ventures into religious activity, the experience was interrupted or never completed.

Julio knew more songs of this ceremony than anyone here now. He had a woman's sex organ too. Once at a party where they were drinking corn beer he showed everybody. The cowboys used him. One white cowboy who used him said he was just as good as a woman. Julio talked like a woman and acted like a woman. He always did the work of a woman; he tanned hides, made baskets, sewed moccasins, cooked, and made corn beer. He was out with the women most of the time. He was married twice but never had children.[36]

[36] Transvestites and hermaphrodites were permitted to live reasonably unhampered lives among these Apache. There was some ridicule of them behind their backs, but they were treated respectfully enough to their faces. Often they compensated for physical deficiencies by addressing themselves vigorously to ceremonialism. This was the case with Julio. A former agent at Mescalero told the writer that Julio did women's work and spoke like a woman. He added that this case was the only one of its kind that came to his attention during his period of service on the reservation.

Julio used to tell a story about the "chief bird," which is the Mescalero name for both the plain titmouse and the tufted titmouse. His family, he said, knew it in the way of healing, but he said he never learned its power. I see it yet, the way Julio was sitting and the way he was telling it. He said one of his relatives knew this bird in a way that helped him in the playing of the hoop and pole game and in card games too. His father learned most of this from his relatives long ago and used it down in the Guadalupe Mountains.[37]

[37] There is some expectation that ceremonies will be carried along in families, but, as this passage suggests, this often does not happen.

Treating Illness and Injury

My mother used the moth in curing, any kind of moth. Whenever she needed something, she called Moth, and it always came and told her what herb to use. She cured a woman who had typhoid fever. This woman came and stayed with us until she was well. My mother sang for her, and the moth came. It carried a plant named "rising star" which you call catchfly.[38] I saw this ceremony. Since then I have used this plant for bad cases of diarrhea.

[38] "Silene laciniata."

You can get power from plants, just as you do from insects and animals. My mother had different songs and ceremonies for them all and different ways of giving them. She taught me a lot about the power of plants. The plants talk to you. They have to be given in a ceremonial way. There are songs and prayers which go with the ceremony; you can't just give the herb. Sometimes the plant talks to you and tells you just what to do.

I believe the plants and the grasses are good. I have specialized in using them.

Quanah Parker, the Comanche chief, came here once with his boy. He had heard about my father from Beaver Hat, another Comanche. He hired my father. Tom was here this time. The doctor told Quanah Parker there was no hope. The boy had diarrhea and no lungs left. The diarrhea alone was enough to kill him.

My father looked at the boy. He took two eagle tail feathers and stuck them down the boy's throat. He wobbled them around. He took the feathers out, and big worms were there on the white calico. They were big and fighting, showing they were hungry. My father said, "They are hungry. That means no lungs are left. I can't do anything for you. If you had come earlier I could have cured him. But it is too late." He burned up the worms.

This happened at night. I didn't see it because I was at school. I was around during the day, but nothing was going on then.[39]

[39] If supernatural power so directs, ceremonies may be carried on during the day and for varying lengths of time, but the usual Mescalero pattern is to continue a ceremony for four nights. The ceremonial activities ordinarily start some time after dark and continue until midnight. In severe or difficult cases the ceremonial activities may continue until sunup.

My father gave him a little help, enough strength to last a little while. They took him back. Tom took him in a buggy. He died about at Roswell. The doctor asked my father what he did for that fellow. My father said, "I showed them the worms." But the doctor wouldn't believe it.[40]

[40] Roswell is in southeastern New Mexico, near the Pecos River. Note the implications of rivalry and mutual curiosity between the agency doctor and the Apache ritualist. Note also the conception of disease as something intrusive which must be extracted from the body by the healer. The association of tuberculosis with worms and shamanistic legerdemain are familiar elements in Mescalero curative practices.

There was a man at Nogal Canyon who knew a lot about plants too. One time he lent me his gun and gave me some ammunition. Then he told me this story. He said a long time ago he was in Mexico and got into a fight and was badly hurt. He was trying to make his way back to his people, but he became weak and exhausted from his wounds and had to give up. He fell to the ground and lay there a long time. Then he thought he heard a voice saying, "Why do you lie on me? Get up." Four times the voice spoke to him, and the last time he looked up. It was a plant talking to him. It directed him to cut a piece of its root off, cut this in four pieces, and put those on his wounds. He did this and got his strength back. Soon he was able to go on, and he got home in four days. The scabs fell off and all his sores were healed.

Finding the Happy Mean

There was one boy who was very, very quiet. They always wondered what kind of good time he could have, for he was always out alone. They worked over him.

So one fellow said, "Why not get a man who knows Vireo for him and put some life in him?"[41]

[41] The benefits of supernatural power often show a close correspondence to the characteristics of the power source. This is especially true of power obtained from a bird or beast. Thus the power of a fast-flying bird or a swift animal is particularly useful in making an individual a good runner; a person who "knows" Bear is certain to be physically strong; and, as in this case, an active and lively bird can, through ceremonial procedures, transmit its qualities to a timid and withdrawn human being.

Iyeho knew the power of this bird. He was a great joker, always making someone say something he ought not to say. He was a one-eyed fellow. He was a funny one. He talked about the white man's bread and teased us youngsters for liking it. He would say, "What do you want to eat this white man's bread for? It's got no strength." He would go in and make fun of the white cook this way. He'd say to the cook, "Those worthless baking powder biscuits!" The cook would get mad. "Men made of sand" he called the men who wouldn't talk and just look mad. "There's the man of sand coming. You fellows just leave him alone. He won't talk to you." He would say, "You fellows talk a lot about power. Just learn power from the vireo. That's enough. Then you'll talk a whole lot."

So they hired this man, and he made his ceremony over the feather of this bird. And once when this boy was sleeping, the man put the feather to his mouth and brushed his lips with it. The man told him, "Sing and talk and say things you ought not to say."

And in the morning that boy was different, I tell you! He was a hard one to get rid of then. "From now on," the shaman had told him, "you talk to women, you stay out, you sing; you can sleep during the day." And after that he sure did sing! You couldn't stop him. He'd yell.

But the mother didn't like that. The boy was causing too much trouble. So they turned around and tried to stop it. She went and got a man who knew Poor-Will, to get his quiet ways back for him. The poor-will stopped the vireo. They had a fight, these two birds, and they agreed to let him talk some but not to give him his old ways back. Then he was all right. He was not afraid to talk, but he was not too noisy.

Persecution

I always had hard luck getting blamed for things I never did. While I was at school here I was helping in the kitchen. There was a girl working there too. She was in another part of the kitchen by another window. An old woman was the chief cook. Her husband, a Civil War veteran who had had one toe shot off, was the disciplinarian. She came in and accused me of having improper relations with that girl. She said she found me on top of her.

The disciplinarian came over and said, "You'd better get your blanket and go right down to the agency jail. You can't get out of a thing like that!"

I said, "See here, old man, I wasn't near that girl. If you put me in jail, you put me in for nothing. And I can't see why that woman should say a thing like that about me."[42] But they put me in jail, and they put that girl in jail too.

[42] Positions on Indian reservations were often political favors bestowed on persons of dubious qualifications. Because of the isolation, loneliness, and danger, it was not easy to recruit personnel for Indian Service work during the early period. Disgruntled individuals and the failures of white society sometimes found a haven on reservations. Since the Indians were subordinated, without influence, and greatly restricted, an Indian reservation was an ideal theater of operations for an authoritarian or a petty tyrant. Consequently, some very strange representatives of white culture congregated on Indian reservations to mystify, perplex, and embitter the Indians.

Strong Tonic

When a man is sick and is losing his weight and strength, someone usually tells him that fresh deer's blood will make him a different man. If you drink it right along whenever a deer is killed, it will keep you healthy. It is drunk warm and uncooked. If you want the blood, you stick the deer in the neck. The blood spurts out. Then you catch it and drink it. Usually they catch it and bring it in, in the stomach. You can drink it raw only when it's warm, when it is still alive, when the animal is still warm, before the blood dies. Some can't drink much of it, but what little they get helps them, they say. I've tried it, but I don't know whether it made me a stronger man. The blood that is caught and kept in the stomach of the deer is boiled in the stomach. It thickens and is like liver when you eat it. Nowadays they fry it, or mix onions with it, or put brains with it. They also advise the boy to drink the hot blood of the deer if he doesn't like hunting or is afraid.

Jose Maria, an old man, drank deer blood for his health. He used to pay well for it when you brought it in. But he wanted it warm right after the kill if he could get it. Once I asked him for ammunition. He gave me five shells. He told me that if the deer was crippled not to kill it but to call him; he wanted to drink the blood warm. I tried my best. I had a chance to kill a deer close. But instead I tried to run it to the clearing near the road so Jose could get to it. That's where I lost out. The deer made off across the canyon and got away.

Drinking the blood helped that old man. He was down; they said he couldn't live. The doctor gave him up for dead. The doctor told him, "You can stay here at the agency but we can't do anything for you. We'll give you a good burial. That's all we can do for you."[43]

[43] American medical personnel are usually described by the Mescalero as being negative and pessimistic, for these Indians are unfavorably impressed by the

caution of the trained medical practitioner, which contrasts so markedly with the enthusiastic and hopeful diagnosis of a shaman who accepts a case.

He said, "They say I'm going to die. I'm not going to stay around here for the white men to look at me. If I'm going to die I want to die off in the hills and be buried like my people.[44] So he went back to Nogal.

[44] According to the Annual Report of the Commissioner of Indian Affairs for that year, the first Mescalero to be buried in a coffin was a little schoolgirl who died in June 1888.

I was out with him; four of us were going along. One killed a deer. It was still kicking. They saved it for him. He cut the throat and told us, "They say I'm going to die but I'm going to try this." And he drank all the blood warm. He lived for four years after that.

Later I went off to school. While I was there I sent word back to ask if he was still alive. He sent word to me that he was still living but didn't expect to see me any more.

In those days when you went off to school you stayed your whole term without seeing your folks. I was away for five years without seeing my people. I nearly died of homesickness the first year. When I came home I was a man, like my son is now.[45]

[45] The narrator was sent to boarding schools at Santa Fe and Albuquerque from 1897 to 1901.

Old Juan was another old Mescalero who drank deer's blood. But he wasn't sick when he did it.

Sport

Old Elk used Owl along with Road-runner in playing the moccasin game, and he was hard to beat. Once we were playing. I was on his side. It was my first experience at the moccasin game. We were just about beaten. I sat by this old man. He knew me well. He showed me all kinds of things about the game.[46] I don't know why, but he said, "I'm going to show you the moccasin game and why I'm never beaten."

[46] The moccasin game is a gambling game which supposedly derives from its prototype in the legends. See 1 [71]. In playing the game, the members of the two sides face each other, and each side buries in the ground four moccasins or containers which are left open at the top. A blanket is raised between the contestants, and one side hides the bone in one of its "moccasins." The blanket is then lowered, and a representative of the other side strikes the moccasin which he thinks contains the bone with a stick. If he is correct, the

side which unsuccessfully tried to conceal the bone must surrender it to its rivals. If a wrong guess is made, those who have hidden the bone successfully are given some of the tallies from a bundle. The number of tallies obtained depends on whether the bone was one moccasin, two, or three moccasins removed from the one struck. The side which hides the bone successfully continues to do so until the opponents guess its correct position. When the opposing players retrieve the bone, they, in turn, hide it and hold it until a correct guess forces its surrender to the opposition. The game ends when all the tallies have come into play and into the possession of one side.

He touched my eyes with owl feathers, then with road-runner feathers,[47] and then with a horsetail. They handed me the stick to knock the bone out with. When I looked at the four "moccasins," I could see the bone. Elk said the moccasin I saw fire come out of was the one that had the bone. And he put four dollars down that I was going to knock it out. And so the other side got four dollars and called it. And Carlos came forward and put down a dollar more that I was not going to make it. That made me mad, and I dug down in my jeans and pulled out two dollars more and bet that I was going to hit it. Then you heard the biggest howling ever. Everybody threw hats in the air and yelled. There was plenty of side betting going on.

[47] The owl and the road-runner were prominent participants in the legendary first game of this kind.

Then Carlos, who was hiding the bone for the other side, thought I knew where the bone was. He put the blanket up and wanted to change it. So they sang some more. I stepped back with the stick in my hand. They yelled in my face and made fun of me, for they thought sure I was going to miss and give them ten points.

John Elk bet a lot on me too. He bet a horse and saddle that I was going to hit the moccasin with the bone in, for he saw what his stepfather did to me. This horse had to be called before I started to hit. So Short-Leg called his bet. He said, "I've got a horse outside; it's up to you." And Boneska, who knew Old Elk too (he claimed he was "brother" to Old Elk) put up some money and a sack of corn.

Then when everything was called, they threw the blanket aside. I stepped up to hit, and then old Leggings grabbed me and came near taking the stick away. He wanted to hit instead of letting me do it. Old Elk caught him and threw him back.

They said, "Leave him alone. He will get it. He bet on it himself."

Then Jack Marsh came up. He said to me, "You've bet already?" "Yes." He gave me one more dollar, and it was called and raised. Tom had a six-shooter; he put it down also. I found something to bet against·it.[48]

[48] During the moccasin game side bets can be placed on any play. There is a set of songs which is sung during the game. These are songs which describe the legendary first moccasin game played to determine whether there should be daylight or perpetual night; individual songs are identified with the animals and birds which were the protagonists of the first game.

Now everything was called. I looked at the four "moccasins." I saw plenty of sparks coming out of the one next to the last on the right. The old man was singing. He started his song when I was going to hit it. He was shaking the blanket up and down. And so I whacked it, and the bone rolled out of the sack. I just picked it up and threw it to the old man, but he went right on singing.

Tom threw me the six-shooter. He said, "You've wanted it a long time. Now you've got it for keeps." And that was right; I kept it for a long, long time.

It took us a long time to count out the winnings. Then the game went on. They beat us twice. We beat them two games back and then by morning we beat them two more games. We got buckskins, rings, money, blankets, everything. All on our side were glad. We played on into the morning, and at sunup everybody put charcoal all over his face.[49] And there was dancing and singing and dust so thick you couldn't see. About noon the game ended, and we all went to bed.

[49] The original game ended with the triumph of the side that was striving for the existence of day. Therefore daybreak came when they won. Consequently, if a game is not over by sunup, all contestants have to blacken their faces so that, at least in a symbolic sense, darkness will prevail until the end of the game.

The people playing the game were all split up; some from Carrizo and Whitetail and Three Rivers were on our side. We had almost all the Lipan on our side. The power of the owl and the road-runner were shown in this moccasin game, and they were good ones.

Everyone enjoyed the moccasin game. Once when I was in school the bigger boys got out and played the moccasin game all night against the policemen in one of the canyons.

The white people have a game something like the moccasin game. We had one teacher who let us play it in school. She took four hats and hid something under one of them, and we had to guess which one it was under. We took a lot of interest in that game because it was so much like the moccasin game.[50]

[50] This is a good indication of how a little knowledge of Indian culture can aid in contemporary situations.

As soon as I grew up I played the hoop and pole game too. I've played it with many of the old men here. Carlos was a champion at it. Some of these men gambled every time they played. I was just playing it without gambling.

The Web of Sorcery

There was a man known as Neck. He knew Mountain Spirits through the power of the deer and the elk. He was a great shaman. What killed him was the one that was stolen; she was his daughter. He died of worry or a broken heart. He never lived to see her come back. But she did come back and married Jacinto.[51]

51 The material relating to the Mescalero agency in the Annual Report of the Commissioner of Indian Affairs for 1895 mentions this abduction incident. The abductor was a Chiricahua Apache known as Massai, who escaped in 1886 from the train in which his people were being taken as prisoners of war to the East after the surrender of Geronimo. The escape was made somewhere in Missouri. Massai found his way westward and was never captured. He is said to have forced the girl to accompany him when he found her gathering piñon nuts alone in the Rinconada area of the reservation. He took her farther west to former Eastern Chiricahua Band territory, where the couple and the four children born of the union lived in hiding until 1911. In that year, while hunting with his oldest son, Massai was surprised and fired upon. He was separated from his son, who fled to the parental camp. Massai was never seen again. It is presumed that he was killed or fatally wounded by the gunfire. After some time his wife and children made their way to the Mescalero reservation and identified themselves to their mother's kinsmen. See Betzinez and Nye 1959: 143–145.

The last time I saw him was when I went away to school. He shook hands with me and embraced me, and I could see the tears in his eyes. He said, "You'll never see me again." In those days I was young and took to school, thinking of the good I could do for this reservation. But all this changed. Then at school I got a letter saying he was dead. I never forgot him though, for he said, "If I live, when you come back I'll show you all these ceremonial things before a big crowd. You won't have to sit up nights to get it. I'll give it right to you, and it's a good thing to have." So I missed this right there. They say he never gave it to his relatives, never offered it to them. He asked just for me. They tried to get me, but it was too far. He was already unconscious.[52]

52 In theory supernatural power and a ceremony are given directly by a supernatural source to an individual. In practice many ceremonies are passed along from an older shaman to a younger person. The explanation and rationalization is that, if the power is not favorably disposed toward the younger person and does not want to "work through" him, he will not be able to learn the songs and prayers and will get no messages or aid from supernatural power. Consequently, the selection of the practitioner—or at least veto rights in regard to the selection—is felt to be the prerogative of the power source. All that the older or original shaman can teach is the mechanics. The influence and intentions of the power source are seen at all stages of the arrangement. It is felt that the supernatural source normally wishes to continue to be represented among mankind even though the shaman through whom it is working at the moment is growing old. Therefore, if a younger person shows an interest in the older shaman's ceremony, it is assumed that supernatural power is probably stimulating this concern. Both the older shaman and the young person may then have dreams or visions which tend to support this notion and to suggest that power would accept the younger person as a representative and ceremonialist. The older shaman is expected to be enthusiastic about his cere-

mony and his power source and desirous of seeing their benefits perpetuated beyond his life span for the good of his people. Consequently, there is a willingness to teach the ceremony and a willingness to receive instruction in it which operate within the conception that ceremonies of this kind are really always grants of power to individuals by a supernatural source. Once an individual learns a ceremony from another, his ritual knowledge may diverge from that of his teacher. Supernatural power may be more enthusiastic over the new recruit and may reveal more religious knowledge to him than was conferred upon the original recipient. On the other hand, matters may move in the opposite direction. At any rate, the relationship with power remains an extremely personal and changing phenomenon, whether the ceremony has been learned from another or obtained directly from the power source. Thus the individualistic or shamanistic flavor is preserved.

It will be noted that the narrator became interested in Neck's supernatural power just before he was sent to off-reservation boarding schools for a term of years. Had this interruption not occurred, his interests and his religious and intellectual history might have developed quite differently.

He gave many a performance of the power of the Mountain Spirits, of the elk and the deer. He usually used all these three and never one alone. They claim he was a strong man against witches. He would take out the witchcraft weapon with his mouth or else he used his Mountain Spirit power in the first place to make it easier and to be sure to get it out. He wasn't the only man who could do this. There were other Apache like him.

He used his power against sickness. Also he claimed that when a woman charmer is trying to get you it shows in many ways. Your head will feel funny. You'll get crazy if you do not go to her. Yet you're not exactly sick. He was strong against both men and women charmers.[53]

[53] The Mescalero Apache ambivalence in regard to "charming" or the use of the "love ceremony" is evident here. The practice is not considered witchcraft, but it is felt that there is something dangerous and distasteful about it. The ill effects, when they occur, are not the usual sicknesses but take the form, rather, of mental and emotional imbalance. Cf. 3 [132].

He healed many a sickness among these Indians. He used all three powers at the same time; he knew all of them very well; they worked very well together. He got along with it all the way through till his end came. Not one of his powers was jealous of the others. He healed not only Mescalero people, but also Lipan, Jicarilla, and even some of the Comanche.

He said lots of things about this Mescalero country—how they used to go anywhere and be absent for months, how they used to go to Oliver Lee's ranch, to Alamogordo, the Guadalupe Mountains, the San Andres, and the Organs; how they went out to kill antelope, deer, and things like that.[54] In those days there was plenty of game. Before he died he talked about all these times. He said, "All this is coming to an end." He said, "You will have to stay on your reservation, and it will all be fenced." He said this long before it happened. And he told them about the leasing of the reservation land to cattlemen, about selling the grass to outsiders.[55] He saw that, and it all came true. He said, "You'll have good houses and farms, but you will not go the way you used to go, and the hoe and the plow and the horses and the wagon, all these will be put in your hands. This is the white man's road. That's what is going to be done to your children, but I will not live to the time when it will come, my time is very short. In less than a year I'll be dead." And that all came true.

[54] From the time of the establishment of the reservation until 1898, the Indians had to obtain a pass in order to leave the reservation with impunity. Alamogordo is in southern New Mexico, near the present White Sands atomic proving grounds. The mountain ranges mentioned are in south and south-central New Mexico. Note the wistfulness over the "old times" and the tone of resentment over restrictions of movement.

[55] The grazing permit system of pasturage on the Mescalero reservation was begun in April 1902.

He knew where his daughter was and that she was well and would return sometime to the reservation with lots of children, and that she would not see her father, her mother, and her close relatives, for they would all be dead. All this came true. She brought several children back with her. Besides she got five more from Jacinto and had one before she was stolen. She did lots of good for her people.

There was one man who was very sick, and everybody else had worked for him. He tried every kind of shaman, even my father. But my father knew he couldn't do much for him because he was sick with the disease from a woman.[56]

[56] That is, venereal disease.

Then this man hired Neck, but his time was coming pretty short. When Neck used his power the first night, he looked him over and said, "You're sick, and you're hiding some kind of sickness. Why don't you tell it straight?"

"I'm not sick from women."

"Well, I can tell you the facts. I can tell you where you got it, who you got it from, the day you got it, and what time of the day you got it, and I can show you the place where you got it. I am one man you'll never tell anything to that is crooked about yourself. Nothing hides from me. Don't you know this thing kills if you hide it?[57] Now you tell me the truth about this, and I'll get someone to cure you. It's up to you. It's your life."

[57] It is believed that a ceremony or treatment for venereal disease will not be effective unless the patient reveals the identity of the person from whom he has contracted the ailment. In this case Neck did not intend to treat the venereal disease but was going to learn through his power who could treat it successfully.

"But I've hired everybody, and they never did any good."

"It's because you're hiding the facts about this disease from woman. If you had told them where you got it and from whom, you would have been cured. You've got a chance to get well yet." That's what he told him. "I'm not going to argue with you. If you don't want to tell, we'll quit right here. Now is your chance. What do you say? Shall I get that healer for you?"

His wife said, "You'd better do it. They say you monkeyed around some other woman, but I'm not jealous. Tell them. It's your life." He had a good woman.

He spoke up to his wife. He said, "That man is a witch, the worst one of the reservation! He wants to kill me! We'll go."

Neck was angry. The sick man went out of his head that night. He sent his wife over, and she begged Neck to do something for him. He said, "No, it's too late if he's out of his head now."

The doctor also came to see him and said he was too far gone. It was a colored doctor, a sure enough good doctor.[58] The man died next morning at ten o'clock.

[58] The Mescalero had considerable contact at one time or another with Negroes. Negro troops were used against them in military campaigns in 1880. Another Mescalero informant has mentioned this Negro doctor and has said his name was Peterson. For the use of Negro troops in operations against the Apache see Betzinez and Nye 1959: 25, 44–46, 149.

There was a woman who was very sick. She had trouble with her stomach and didn't know what was wrong. The colored doctor said it would take time. She wanted to be cured in a quick way, so she came to Neck in Rinconada.[59] She said she had little, but would give what she had. She came and told us about it. So Jack Marsh went to Neck, because the woman was a relative of his, and one of mine too (she calls us "brothers"), and said, "We'll give you whatever you ask if she can be cured." Jack and my father did their best for her. My father said, "I've got a horse." And Jack said, "I've got a gun." And each said, "I've got buckskin and the things that the man needs for his pay."

[59] Many Mescalero explained to me that, while both white and Indian methods of curing are ultimately effective, the Indian method through ceremony gives much faster relief. This, of course, was before the discovery and use of the "miracle drugs" of modern medicine.

The shaman said, "I did not ask you for pay. I'll look at her first, and then I'll tell you what is best to be done."[60]

[60] The Mescalero shaman usually asks no specific fee in advance. He simply suggests that the patient or his relative give him what they want at the conclusion of the rite. He knows that, if the patient feels relieved or if the diagnosis is favorable, his grateful clients will be as generous as possible. Substantial gifts are often given a shaman in the hope that he will continue to pray for the patient after the conclusion of the rite and protect him by means of his supernatural power until a full recovery is achieved.

He looked her over. He said, "Some time ago you had trouble with some woman, I don't know where, but you were living at Mescalero. You had a party and there were women there. I will describe the dress of this woman, but I will not call her by name. You will remember this woman and the place, and you will know who it is. There was a dark-complexioned woman, not very tall, with a blue skirt and a blouse, black with white dots. And her swinging sleeves were red.[61] She had a little red ochre on her face, and she had no grey hair. This woman asked you for a drink of corn beer. You did not look at her. You passed drinks to all the men who were present and to some of the women, but to her you didn't give a drink at all. You thought you did, but you missed her.

[61] Since the same outer garment was kept and worn by a woman for a number of years, this description positively identified the individual whom the shaman intended to accuse.

"Under her hand this woman had a spider's web, one of the strongest and most dangerous witchcraft weapons of all. This spider web represents the ropes of the sun. It is black, blue, white, and yellow.[62] That spider's web is wrapped around your arms and legs. It is not a very pleasant thing to show you, but it is a killing thing, because the sparkling of the web is the fire that is eating you, and she meant it to hold you till you were down in bed wasting away.

[62] The association between the strands of the spider web and the rays of the sun occurs in a number of ritual contexts. This is not the usual color sequence, perhaps because witchcraft is involved.

"And I ask you to wait four days until I can begin to work on you. That's the way it is when you are working against something as strong as this. And if I can't cure you, I've got someone even stronger. I will not tell you who this man is until I see that I can't do anything. I am strong in every way. Do not give me anything until I tell you when I want it. So come in four days."

And so they waited. The fourth day came. He said, "Bring her to me."

The queer part of this ceremony is that the shaman undressed himself, took off his moccasins, and left only his gee string on. He put red ochre on his face and all over his hair and on part of his body. He put white clay on the soles of his feet and then sat down and talked with his power.[63]

[63] Red ochre and white clay are sacred substances much used in Mescalero ritual. There is a basic pattern to Mescalero shamanistic ceremonies. On the other hand, in answer to his power's bidding the shaman often introduces an individual or unusual note. These departures from pattern lend interest to the ceremony and are considered a demonstration of the intimate relationship between power and the practitioner. In this instance the disrobing of the shaman is the unusual element.

That year there were very few elk. He told my father, Jack Marsh, and Edwin Bird, who was son-in-law to this woman, to get a horn of elk or any little piece of the horn. Close to noon my father came in with Jack. They had a small elk horn.

Neck put the elk horn right before himself. Then he got a deer horn and set it before him. Then he got a masked dancer headdress and set it in front too. He had two eagle feathers in his hand. He sat down and was talking to himself or praying. He was using the power of the elk. He raised the elk's horn upward four times and then towards the patient four times. Then he set it down. He did likewise with the deer horn. But the headdress raised itself and moved up close to him. It raised itself up four times and moved toward the woman four times. Everybody saw it.[64]

[64] It must be remembered that these shamanistic performances are carried on at night in the dim light of a campfire before anxious relatives and friends of a sick person. It is standard practice for a shaman to engage in legerdemain. In so doing, he does not feel that he is perpetrating any fraud. What he does is symbolic of the strength of his supernatural source and is done at the bidding of the supernatural source. His interest is in creating an affirmative state of mind and a feeling of belief and acceptance toward his supernatural source, for supernatural power will not lend its aid unless those present believe in the power, the shaman, and his rite, and are thinking "in the right way." Often the shaman describes the unseen miracles that the power source is performing or they are depicted in his songs and prayers. Afterwards, in recounting the story of the curing rite, these events are described as though they were actually witnessed by those present. Also, the dramatic and unusual manifestations of supernatural power tend to become enlarged with the repetition of an account. I have descriptions of ceremonies recounted by people who were present which are rather prosaic. When these same rites are described by persons to whom they were told, they tend to become embroidered with more extraordinary elements.

Then he passed the headdress around the fire and put it in the place of the elk horn, in the lead. He took the horns of the elk and deer outside and placed one in a tree to the east side and one on the south. He took the eagle feathers and went up to the woman and gave her something he had placed on the end of the feathers. He told her to take it in her hand and drink it in water. It was to kill the witchcraft, he said.

Everybody there knew the way of the ceremony because they'd seen it before. I was there and saw it too. He called to me and said, "Some day you will be just like I am right now, curing these poor people."

He handed me the feathers after marking them with pollen. I had them in my right hand. "Now," he said to me, "you sit still. Don't try to get up unless I tell you." When you have a feather like this, it tries to move you, to make you get up. And it tried to raise me up several times, but I did not move. Other people were watching me and saying, "Keep still." And I did.[65]

[65] A shaman will often have an assistant who drums while he sings, sings while he sucks out noxious objects, manipulates ceremonial paraphernalia according to his directions, or otherwise aids him. This assistant may be an understudy, one who is being groomed to carry on the ceremony in the future, or he may

be someone whom the shaman is trying to interest in his ceremony. In the case here described the feathers are a symbol of one of the sources of power being used in this ceremony. Such material symbols serve a number of possible functions. By fixing one's gaze upon them, one may see visions sent by the power source. They may speak to the person who is holding or watching them and thus be a medium for messages from supernatural power. They may move the one who holds them in a certain direction, thus calling attention to something hidden from others. Note the influence of the suggestions of the shaman and the attention of the audience upon the behavior of the narrator.

And then the light of the sun hit me. I'll tell you what I mean; you do not know. Remember it was in the night that this ceremony was going on. It was very dark and cloudy. I heard a whizzing sound, just like the purring of an engine. Neck said, "Now do not move around or try to look, but just keep to yourself what you see. I will ask you. Don't say it right out here. I will ask you outside."

I saw the sun rise out of the east, and it got up a pretty good ways. Then the sun moved pretty close to me, and then light fell on me. Through the power of the sun, I could see all over; there was nothing that could hide from me at all. I looked in this camp, looked at the one they called my sister,[66] and she was in pretty bad shape, but I saw that she still could stand quite a bit. I looked at her bed, at her feet, head, eyes, and under the bed. I saw a big spider lying right at her back, a dangerous one, such as I had never seen in this country. Everywhere I go now I watch the spiders. I have never seen anything like it yet. On its pincers was flesh and on its feet was flesh. From its mouth poured something like fire or blood. This spider was as big as my hand. But it did not scare me. And another thing: I looked at her arm, and I saw millions of little spiders wrapping her up in their web. It was nothing but red spider web.[67]

[66] This girl was actually a distant cousin. A Mescalero boy uses one term for sister and female cousin of any degree.

[67] The narrator, of course, is seeing what the shaman has described and predicted he would see.

Then I looked at the fire. The fire burned all the time as it always did. Then the eagle feathers started to lift me up. That man caught me by the arm and lifted me up. He said, "Keep still till I tell you. I'm looking at everything." Then he took the hat off my head and put water four times on my head. He told me, "Now cross the feathers and look closely at the spider and then bring them together and point them at him."

When he said that, he took downy feathers from the band which he wore around his chest and brushed me all over. He was singing. "Now go," he said.

Then I went up to my sister and I motioned her to move up a little. She got up and began to move. I went to the bed where she was and pointed the feathers at the spider where I saw it. I crossed the feathers at it, and something kind of streaked out. Then I pointed the feathers at it and I saw it was dead. From these feathers, when I pointed them at it, I saw fire come out the way it does when you shoot a gun, and I could feel the shaking of the feathers too.[68]

[68] The crossed feathers are here being used as a weapon with which to "shoot" the objects of witchcraft. The contest between a shaman and a witch is once more couched in terms of battle psychology.

Neck said, "Don't do anything to it. Come back." So I went around as the sun goes and came back to him.

I was still holding the feathers in my hand, and one of the feathers spoke right to me. It said, "Ask for me, and I will be at your pillow tonight."[69]

[69] The narrator has become much impressed by the ceremony and Neck's interest in teaching it to him. He now feels that supernatural power is going to approach him and urge him to continue Neck's ceremonial work. Such a vision experience would be considered by him a validation of his right to learn and practice the ceremony.

I asked this man, "Did you hear what was said?"

He answered, "No." Then he said, "Yes, it is all right. Go ahead." He said this without my telling him. The sun was shining bright, and it was like daylight to me, though it was night.

Then I thought, "It's best now to find out what else there is for me to do." Then he said to look around among us. I never turned my head but I saw them all without turning. I saw the power of all before me. I could see my father, I could see Jack Marsh, I could see Edwin Bird, and those on either side. I looked and I saw that spears were pointing towards us. The feather said, "All these things are sickness and suffering, they are sent by witches."

Then I asked, "Who are the witches?" I looked and before me stood a woman who, when she was not being looked at by supernatural power, claimed that she was very kind to everybody. Now she was standing before me, one of the worst, half naked. I looked carefully, for she was a woman I never thought was a witch.[70]

[70] This is, of course, the woman whom Neck has described. There is a conceptual link between the idea of witchcraft and wantonness, sexual aberration, and incest. It is assumed that no one but a witch would be likely to be a sexual deviant or commit incest. Witches are described as carrying on their practices in a naked or half-naked condition and indulging in lewd gestures or acts.

The feather said, "That's the woman who did this terrible thing that your sister is suffering from. It is witchcraft."

Then I could see the rays of the sun hit the woman who was sick, and every time they hit, they would go right through, and she would twist around. She felt pain, she doubled up and made faces. And I said to the feather, "Why don't you stop that?" And it told me, "You're not the one to say that to me. It's only the man who is owner of my power who can say it."[71]

[71] Since the narrator has not yet obtained this ceremony and supernatural power, he should not criticize or appeal to the supernatural source. Such

privileges and intimate exchanges are properly open only to an individual through whom the power source is carrying on its ceremony on earth—that is, to the shaman of the rite.

And then I looked toward the place where this witch was living, and I saw that her daughter was a witch too. Then the feathers pointed out another one to me, and then came a bunch of witches, there must have been fifty in that bunch, and some of those are still living.[72]

[72] Ceremonies for beneficial purposes tend to be passed along in families. The relationship tie is so strong that a shaman, when he is seeking someone to continue his work, normally tries to interest a son, nephew, or grandson in learning his rite. If his own relatives are not interested in it or if he has no relatives of the proper age and generation, he seeks an associate outside the family circle. It is believed that witches perpetuate their lore according to much the same pattern and that therefore witchcraft, too, tends to be passed along in families. The period the narrator is describing was one of great disillusionment, frustration, sickness, and humiliation for the Mescalero. Consequently, as has been mentioned, family feuds, antagonisms, and charges of witchcraft were common. This circumstance is reflected in the large number of witches the narrator sees in his vision.

Then came the other half of the ceremony. I just kept what I saw to myself. I could see that my sister was going to be well at the end of the autumn. But the ceremony would have to be carried on two or three times until she got well. It was shown me that the shaman could cure her any time he wanted to.[73] She could gain her strength in two or three days. I did not speak up to him the way I am speaking to you, but every time I thought this way I could hear the feathers talk. Power was talking through these two feathers, and this man heard it, and I heard it too. And so we kept it up for half the night.

[73] The repetition of ceremonies to insure continual improvement is not uncommon. The impatience of the young man with the predicted slow course of the cure of his relative is apparent.

Neck said to me, "Be careful about what you say. Don't tell anybody till I call for you or come to your tent, which will be not tonight but tomorrow. So take these eagle feathers and put them above your bed or on your hat tonight."

Lots of things were shown me all during the ceremony for four nights. At the end of the fourth night, the shaman took some of the spider webs off her heart. She was just nothing but spider web. At the end of the third night he called me to his camp. He said, "Tomorrow I want you." We stayed up till morning.[74] In advance I saw the killing of those spiders and also the taking of the spider webs off the body and even off the inside, off the heart and lungs. There's nothing can hide from you when you've got a real power like this.

[74] The implication is that the two stayed up praying and singing.

I had shot everything that was in the body of that woman the second night, and she said she was very, very tired. Then we were to rest for two nights and then finish in two nights. That is just what was done.

When we began the third time the shaman handed me the feathers as he had done on the first two nights. Then he put pollen on me and marked himself. The others were marked but in a different way.[75] The feather was getting me so interested that I didn't pay much attention to the marking. Every time he sang of his killing of witchcraft, I could see fire come out of the feathers. I could see the spider try to come back, but every time it tried, I could feel the feathers turn me to it and the sparks or arrows fly. I was interested in the feathers because they talked.

[75] To mark the witnesses to a rite with pollen is to involve them in the purposes of the rite. Usually the shaman marks those who are present with pollen, and they reciprocate. Their marking of the shaman with pollen is a demonstration of their faith in him and his power source and of their willingness to aid the rite by a prayerful and affirmative attitude. It is believed that power is pleased by evidence of unanimity of faith and good will on the part of all those present at a ceremony and lends its help more speedily and effectively when such conditions prevail.

The shaman said, "That power surely likes you!" And I could see all those men and women they call witches talking against us.

This time the shooting with the feathers was deadly all right, because I could feel it through my arm; they were shooting harder. They were killing something different. Something yellow came out of them. Every time they shot an evil thing in that woman I could see the smoke and smell the smoke, but that woman didn't feel anything at all, because the power made it so that she would not feel it, I guess.

There was just one thing I had overlooked when I started to sit down. But the shaman made me stand up again and aim the feathers, and I saw there was an even more ugly-looking thing than the spider. This thing was lying right at the back of her head. The feathers said, "Cross me before you shoot." I went up to her with everybody looking on and crossed the feathers and shot. I saw smoke come out. Only my father and Neck knew what I got up there for. And then I smelled something pretty bad. I had killed a big black tip beetle. You know how dangerous it would be to use these feathers out in the open. But only men with power use them, and they say the witches use them in the same way too.

Now came the killing of the last one. This was the vinegarroon. They say that he's one of the worst things that could be shot into your body, worse than lizards, snakes, or anything else.[76] The feathers had told me to go back and sit down. But the man helped me up and didn't want me to sit down. I asked the feathers why. "We missed something. It's still kicking." I looked again. It was not in her body but in her bed.

[76] Reptiles, beetles, crickets, and stinging insects such as the vinegarroon are among the favorite "arrows" of witches. They have to be "killed" and extracted by shamans if the victims are to survive.

He said, "Do to her bed as you did to her body."

I went to the bed and crossed the feathers. I said, "Let's be done with it. This thing is tiresome."

So I killed lots of things on the bed that I thought were nothing, but they were all living things and disease. We did the bed and under the bed and on the pole and outside. Outside I saw lots of things. Even the marking on the pole we had to shoot. The feathers said, "Now I am with you."

I was sure we had everything. The feathers told me, "We have done everything." I came back and sat by the old man, and he kept singing. I looked to be sure I had everything. I asked the feathers if we had got it all. The feathers moved me around and led me to look in her eyes, her head, her body, all over. All the evil things were dead.

Now the birds were singing, and it was getting toward morning. The shaman said, "Now be ready and at sunup I'll take the spiders and the spider webs out. Build a fire outside, and we'll burn them there."

And so that morning we had a big time. We were all sleepy, but we had gained what we were after. Neck said, "We have turned that witch woman loose without anything. All of her witchcraft is killed, and she herself is going to be killed also."

Then the patient came up close to the fire and she looked at the fire, and from her, from all over her head came different things—oak leaves, herbs, grasshoppers, vinegarroons, a cricket, a beetle, and thousands of little spiders, and the one big spider which had been raising the young which were wrapping this woman up. Even the webs had life in them, because they moved around like snakes, and they could bite too. Just think of it! There were some places where she was not wrapped up yet, but she was wrapped over most of her body. The webs were in balls and knots in some places.

The shaman said she had a crescent at her neck. "It's got to be taken out. She may faint, but she is strong yet, and it won't harm her. And the vinegarroon has to come out too; it is another strong one, and she may faint, but it has to come out. They are all dead."[77]

[77] The objects of witchcraft had been shot with the crossed feathers and were "dead," but they were still within the woman's body and had to be sucked out in order to prevent future complications.

Lots of the neighbors were invited to see this taking out of the witchcraft objects on the last morning.[78] Edwin Bird was told to notify the people and tell them to come and see that there was really such a thing as witchcraft and to learn how things had been shot into the body of this poor woman.[79]

[78] Though ceremonies are described as lasting four nights, the final events often take place on the fifth morning, at sunrise.

[79] Shamans often lectured their audiences on their scepticism concerning witchcraft and their lack of faith in the ability of supernatural power to cope with witches. These harangues are not unlike those of Christian evangelical preachers to their flocks on the subject of the need for more faith and conviction.

Then the feathers spoke up. They said, "It's just about sunrise." The neighbors poured in. And among them there were three that I had seen were witches. I didn't have to look at them. I knew they were there, for the power of those feathers shows you everything.

I spoke to the shaman. "The rays of the sun are just climbing over us." Then he told me to ask for a little water, and Jack got the pollen and the water when I spoke to my father about it. He placed it before us. Then the sun began to rise just a little. The feather said, "All is ready." And the shaman moved up to the fire.

He marked her in every way with pollen. Then he put the water and the pollen on her head, made a cross with it over her head, and made a cross at her breast also.[80] "Now," he said, "everything is ready." The feathers told me just what to do. He put the pollen on his hands and rubbed it between his hands, and I could see the smoke come out of his hands. Then I could see that the woman was sitting in nothing but pollen, which is a good sign of relief.[81]

[80] The cross of pollen or other coloring material appears frequently in Mescalero ceremonialism.

[81] A vision or dream of pollen is a good omen.

He was kneeling before her and he motioned his arms and hands up and down before her with palms up. The daughter of the woman and my mother were holding her up. Her dress was tied around her breast, and he told her to untie that. He made four steps toward her, and he was right in front of her. He motioned from the bottom of her body to the top four times. Then he put pollen in her mouth four times, then in his own four times. Now he was ready. The white sheet was there.

The feathers said, "First point to her neck." I alone heard it.

The shaman first took pollen and then said he wanted specular iron.[82] He put specular iron on his hand and tried to pull out the crescent. He could move it, but he couldn't pull it out. Every time he moved it, the woman turned because she felt it.

[82] Specular iron (hematite) is another important Mescalero sacred substance.

Then the feathers I had in my hand said, "The downy feather is better than anything. It will take it out in no time." I was going to tell him, but I just thought it and he knew it. He said, "Give me a downy feather." I took it out of his pouch, made a cross of pollen on it, and gave it to him.

I saw the sparks fly out of the downy feather because he was shooting. He was working again. He made motions toward the crescent four times.[83] He said, "I'm going to get it out, and in a hurry." He put the feather up to the crescent, then put his mouth to it and pulled. He came near pulling it out, but it slipped away into the woman again. It got away from him three times. Then he put specular iron on it and tried again. I saw the sparks fly from the downy feather, and the crescent cried out. It jerked him and it jerked me, just like a gun kicking. And the fourth time it was shot, it yelled out. Then he moved up to it and, by George, he pulled it out!

[83] This was a crescent-shaped piece of human bone, one of the weapons or "arrows" of the witch. The use of human bone in witchcraft, because it is

associated with death and violation of a grave and corpse, is particularly horrifying and enraging to the Mescalero.

He put it on the white cloth, and you could see it moving around. It kicked around for a time and then lay still. Then he went to the back of her head. The tip beetle got away from him once, but he got it the second time. The rest was easy. It was easy because he had the leaders now. He caught the cricket too. Then came the leaves and the herbs, and then the bone arrows that were shot into her body. Then the spiders were taken out, and then all the webs of the spiders.

I forgot to tell you that she fainted when the crescent was taken out, but they put water and pollen on her head and she came to. She hollered once, "It hurts!" She came near fainting when he took out the vinegarroon too.[84]

[84] The attitude, comments, and expectations of the shaman and the onlookers have a marked influence on the reactions of the patient, of course.

Then he took all the wrapping off her lungs and out of her lungs and off the windpipe too. Then her heart; he was a little afraid of the heart, but the eagle feathers said, "It's all right; she won't feel it." And sure enough, she didn't. Then he took things from her legs and feet, intestines and stomach, and every place. She was in pretty bad shape. I don't see why it didn't kill her, for they claim these are killing things.

Now they saw right before their eyes proof of witchcraft. Edwin had the fire going outside. The feathers said, "Be careful, those women back there see their own weapons; see what they will do."

We knew every word the witches were saying in themselves. But all the others were thinking and saying, "Oh, oh, we are poor people, and look at all the things for killing that are lying before us!"

Now he took all this and poured it right in the fire, cloth and all. When it started to burn, it made a sizzling noise, then it went "bing, bang!" four times. It made a loud explosion like a cannon going off.

After we had killed all the little spiders and after he had taken out all the witch weapons from the woman, I was just about to quit. Then he said, "I forgot something."

Then the feathers spoke; I heard it. "There's a big one under the bed yet." It was the big mother spider who was making all the little ones. "It's the worst one," the feather said.

So I crossed the feathers again, straightened them up, and shot it. The old man took it out from under the bed. It was a big one. The fire was blazing, and he put it in. The legs burned just as if there was oil on them. Then it made a big explosion like a cannon. It blew the fire all over.

The woman got well, and this man gave her a cure so that no witch could shoot her again, they say.[85] In the morning he gave her some medicine that he made himself. This was to keep away witches.

[85] Sometimes a shaman claims that the patient whom he has cured can never again succumb to the same malady or evil influence from which he has been rescued.

He said, "Do not give me a pinto horse, that is, if you want to give me a horse. Give me a one-color horse." They gave him a horse with a saddle. They gave him money and the buckskin. The buckskin was required by his power. The curing had taken place at this man's camp.[86]

[86] A shaman may impress his clientele by making unusual and peculiar requests. This is part of the individuality that goes with shamanism and parallels the underlying similarity of pattern in all shamanistic rites. By making it known that he wants a horse of solid color instead of a spotted horse, the shaman fairly certainly insures that the payment will include a horse. A rite usually takes place at the home of a sick person, but sometimes a shaman will request that a special structure be built or suggest that the ceremony be held at his own living quarters. A good deal depends on the condition of the patient and whether he can travel or can be moved.

Afterwards I held the feathers like this for several other men at different times. Once I did it for Old Jim, and I did it for Tall Raider. This was after the Chiricahua came here.[87] When Cloud had a broken rib, he hired Tall Raider. I helped Tall Raider. We came to Cloud's camp at Rock Quarry. Tall Raider helped him by means of the power of Water's Child. He put an herb on the bone. He said the herb would do the work, and it did. I just sang for him, for I knew his songs. The helper usually knows the songs as well as the shaman himself.

[87] The Chiricahua Apache were held as prisoners of war at Fort Sill, Oklahoma, until 1913. Then they were given the choice of taking up allotments of land in Oklahoma or of moving to the Mescalero reservation. About two-thirds of them did come to Mescalero in 1913, and they and their decendants now share the Mescalero reservation with the Mescalero and the Lipan Apache.

Ramon Tcikito's wife had an infected arm. At the hospital they wanted to cut the arm off, but she wouldn't let them. She hired Tall Raider. Her arm was badly swollen. Tall Raider sang for her and used eagle feathers to suck the poison out. He saved her arm. The only thing that happened was that the fingers of that hand shrank a little, but she could use the hand and arm all right.

Of Bears and Horses

During my school days here a bear was killed by Chief Peso. It was a big black bear and it came up to Peso and started to fight as Peso was butchering a deer. Peso took a rifle and killed it. Then he dressed the bear and laid it on a log. He took the deer into his camp and then got helpers and a wagon and loaded the bear on it and brought it in to the school. One of the employees bought it. Most of the employees had a little piece of it and some outsiders did too.

There was a peddler who came around and sold fruit, peanuts, and such things, for we had no store at that time. He got a piece and roasted it at his fire. Some

Indian boys came up and one of them wanted some. Other boys told this one i
no use to eat it, for it was likely to make him sick. The boy was crippled in th
and said the bear might help straighten his leg out.

So the boy asked this fellow for a little piece to see what it tasted like. He ____
it was very good and told others to try it. The peddler asked if he wanted more, and
he ate a little more, and then we started back to school.

About midnight we heard this boy crying. The bear was after him; he saw it go
out the door.[88] The boys tried to keep him quiet but they couldn't. And so he kept
crying till morning and also vomited. He said the bear was coming in and putting
its paws down his throat, trying to catch something. He was very sick all that day.
They didn't know just what to do. The doctor gave him some medicine, but it
didn't help him. The relatives of the boy were told, and they went to Swinging-
Lance, who was a chief now that San Juan was gone.[89] Swinging-Lance talked to
the agent, who was his friend, and got the boy out of school, for that boy saw the
bear every night, and every night it put its paws in and out of his mouth, and he
cried. It certainly scared the boy pretty bad and made him sick too.

[88] Bear meat served ritually by a shaman who "knows Bear" or who has a
power grant from Bear is thought to be efficacious in correcting deformities,
but the boy should not have eaten bear meat without ritual safeguards.
Undoubtedly he was reproached for his carelessness and presumption and
warned of the danger he had invited. His reaction was the hysterical one that
is described.

[89] San Juan died in 1886.

The boy was taken to Nogal Canyon, and a shaman was hired who knew Bear
pretty well. He told the men at Nogal, if they had a chance to kill a bear, to do it,
for he needed it. Someone killed three, so they kept an old one and sold the young
ones to white people.

The shaman asked for some bear meat, and they smoked it and hung it up. Then
that night they held a ceremony for this boy who was suffering from the sickness
of Bear. The boy foamed at the mouth and acted as though he was tired and coming
in from some place, trying to get his breath but not able to make it.[90]

[90] These are some of the classical symptoms of sickness from Bear according to
Mescalero symptomatology.

The shaman held a ceremony four days straight without resting. At the end of
four days, the bear hide was given him. He took this bear hide and laid it on the
ground with the head towards the sunrise. He took the boy out and walked him
around the hide four times and took him from the south to the head of the hide.
Then he put a buckskin over the bear hide, put the boy on it, and with two eagle
feathers started to work on the boy from the head down. He also took eagle feathers
and motioned from the boy's mouth to his throat and down his body to his feet.
He had some roasted bear ribs. The boy seemed to be coming along very nicely.
There was a big crowd, but they didn't come up close; they sat in a circle where

they wouldn't smell the bear. These people were afraid of getting sick, like the boy, from the bear smell.[91]

91 Sickness from an evil animal can enter the body of a person as a result of seeing the animal, smelling it, tasting its flesh, touching it or its excreta, being frightened by it, crossing its path, or coming in contact with a spot where it has lain.

The shaman asked for pollen and marked the bearskin and the crowd and told the crowd to move in. He asked for oak branches which were laid at the head of the bearskin. Then he took one coal and then some bear meat and held them in his hand, praying, and went around to the four directions. He said if the people wanted bear meat, now was their chance; it would be given to them ceremonially and then they could eat it any time.

So those who wanted to eat bear came up close, and he handed it in small pieces to men, women, and children, and to the boy. He said the boy was well now, nothing was wrong with him. After all who wanted to had eaten, the shaman also ate the bear meat.

The white doctor said that the boy just had an upset stomach, that there was nothing wrong with him. But the Mescalero said he had Bear sickness and would have died if it weren't for them. This boy could eat bear after that and was well all the way through, but he was still crippled and is now an old man.[92]

92 Again the opinions and tactics of the agency doctor and the shaman are contrasted, to the advantage of the Apache practitioner.

The shaman told this boy that some day he would have horses and be a good rider, and this came out just the way he told him, for in spite of being a cripple, he became a good horseman, a trick performer on a tame horse or a bronco. He also raised the best horses to run down wild horses with. His horses knew how to dodge trees at full speed and jump fences and ditches and stop short. Every horse he trained knew him well and knew how to cut out and run the wild horses. He'd just whistle or fire a shot, and his horse would come. I wanted to buy one of his horses, but he wouldn't sell. When they got old, he didn't ride them; he just let them run and die on the range. He had four horses he trained to bring in wild horses. He'd take one, lead it out into the mountains, and when this bunch of wild horses would get used to it, it would begin to lead them. It looked like the horse had forgotten after two days, but the horse never forgot. Then this fellow would whistle twice, and the horse would run in, trying to get in the lead, and the others would follow. All these four horses he trained would avoid traps, even the sure ones. He'd take a horse to the tie-ropes, the hardest for a bronc to miss. A horse is easily caught in a snare. But these trained horses could avoid this and all snares. He taught his horses to enter a corral, stop wild horses at the entrance, kick at them, and wait till he came up. That is the best thing I ever saw in training horses.

I saw him break a very nice horse and train it to put its front feet on a table and walk plumb around it. I didn't think he'd ever get it to do what he wanted, but he sure did. It was a pretty animal. He taught it to lie down and count with its head. One time some men were coming through when the horse was performing and he was offered a good price for this young pretty little horse. He was with me once. We didn't have quite enough to go to the circus. I had only fifty cents. So he decided to sell his horse. I said the horse was worth a hundred and fifty dollars. And he got it for the horse. He had intended to ask only sixty dollars, and so he wanted to give me the rest, but I took only fifty dollars of it. We took the mail and went to town and then went to the circus.

This man says he has given up horses now, and just has mules. He had power from Horse so they could understand him.[93] That's why he had good horses and well-trained horses. And this bear shaman told him what was going to happen, and it did. I've killed bear, and he's eaten it.

[93] There is the expectation that a person who has power from some source will know a great deal about this source and what it represents. This relationship between ideas of supernatural power and practical matters is a circular and self-reinforcing matter. An individual who is greatly interested in horses is likely, when he acquires power, to obtain supernatural help in taming, riding, and training horses. The acquisition of the ceremony then further feeds his interest and leads to greater confidence and proficiency in his handling of horses. Through beliefs in supernatural help, hunting prowess and many other activities were similarly advanced for particular individuals.

Animal Trainer

There was a boy in school called Walter Kakas. He went to Fort Lewis Industrial Training School with some of the boys. He's dead now. His father knew many things. His father was a man they used to call a witch and they were afraid of him. He gave this boy power from the green-backed tree swallow. The swallow showed this boy how it was to be used for charming, for luck with horses, for finding out things, and so on. After he came back from Fort Lewis he was bigger and he knew a lot of things. He was a horse charmer more than anything else.

One day he showed off. A raccoon kept coming in the dining room at school, and they were trying to capture it. The raccoon was breaking dishes. We had a time with that raccoon. Finally this boy told us to keep away and see what it would do. That night he was out alone. The next day he had the raccoon in a box. It was a big coon. He tamed it in that one night. In the morning he was carrying it around.

The disciplinarian carried it around too. He tied it outside. This coon was to become the mascot of the school. He was a great pet. He bit me once by mistake. I was giving him a live gopher to fight, and the coon jumped for it and bit me on the hand. He was sorry too. He licked my hand. The boy said to let him lick it and it would get better.

This boy carried the back of the green swallow and the wings. "I'll show you," he said.

One time we drowned out a big squirrel by pouring water in the hole. He rubbed it with these feathers. Then this big old rock squirrel ran up his shoulder and ate there. He tamed it. It was a pet of the agency after that too. He was a great tamer, that boy.

Once we thought the agent was coming after us. This boy said we could go anywhere we pleased, and we did. We didn't have any trouble. The agent told us we could go off and play that day.[94] In those days there were no days off. He made me believe many things, that boy. This same boy told them to catch a wild dog and he'd tame it. But they couldn't catch one.

[94] Note that this boy's ability to tame and influence recalcitrant animals included control over the white man!

He was young then. I never knew him to cure with the green-backed tree swallow. He died at Elk Springs when he was about twenty-five years old. His father had showed him about the bird. His father knew a lot of things.

His father used the golden-crowned kinglet too. He tried it for healing together with the tarantula. He worked on Tony Lewis when Tony was shot by Edwin Bird. He used the feathers of this bird then. And he cured him in no time. Tony was shot through the leg. They sent for Kakas and he worked on him in the day for four days. The spider came and worked on the leg right in front of everybody. Kakas sang and prayed, and the spider came and walked right into the wound.[95] Kakas sucked the wound, using something he held in his hand. He used the feathers of this bird to see what was the matter, how bad it was. "It just missed the blood vessel," he said. "The blood vessel has a blue spot on it." Then he put the feathers away, and the tarantula came and healed it.

[95] Probably these were ceremonial songs which drew a word picture of a tarantula entering the wound and healing it. A believer does not feel the need of distinguishing between the works of power which are visible to all and those which can be seen by the shaman alone or which are merely described in the songs and prayers.

Help from the Towhee

While we were yet in school at Mescalero there was a boy who thought much of the towhee. He used to tie the feathers to his bed. At night he used to say he wished to see the bird so that it might show him something.

So one night the towhee came in and slept under his pillow. He spoke to the bird that night, and the bird stayed right there. Early in the morning the boy got up, and the towhee flew out. Others tried to catch it, but it came to this boy, and he held it in his hand. Others asked for it, but the towhee told the boy to turn it loose, and he did. It came for the next three nights too. But no one but the boy saw it these other times. He learned supernatural power from it.

He didn't want to go away from the reservation to school. But he was picked out to go. He got the help of the towhee, and he didn't go. He stayed right where he was. It did that much good for him. The towhee showed him where he could go to learn more. "What good will school do me? I can't be like a white man."[96] That's what the boy said.

[96] Note that a good many of the anxieties of the youths of school age had to do with separation from their families and worry over being sent away to off-reservation educational institutions. One of the incentives for seeking supernatural power was to cope with these difficulties. The usefulness of the education they receive under white auspices has been a topic debated by the Indians from these early days until now.

This boy was hard to scare because of the towhee. He went to every dangerous place and found no danger. Once they asked him if he could walk to the graveyard.[97] Three others tried but were afraid. He walked around it and came back.

[97] When a graveyard was established at Mescalero, it was at first sedulously avoided by the Indians. A test of bravery was to get reasonably close to it.

Another time he ran away from school and we thought he was going to be punished for it, but he was not punished in any way. He was told to go back where he belonged.

Assisting Father

When I was about seventeen years old, Carlos was sick. He hired my father to sing for him, and my father took me along.

When we got there, my father and I faced the sunrise. Carlos was lying before my father. My father marked my hand with pollen, my right hand, and tied turquoise on my middle finger with buckskin. I just sat there and smoked. Then my father said, "You see it." I looked.

I saw light. I could see everything. All around me I could see nothing but flat country, beautiful country. There was not a tree in sight. It was nothing but prairie. The grass was waving back and forth. I saw the patient. He was there laughing. I saw him mount a white horse and ride toward the east. He came back and sat down. He put pollen on me. I could see his future. I could see his children and his wives. He's always got a woman there.[98] I started to tell my father. Then everything went away.

[98] During a ceremony power often indicates that the patient will get well by vouchsafing the shaman or his assistant a vision of the future. If the patient appears well and active in this vision, it is a demonstration that he will recover from the present affliction. The patient of this ceremony has had two wives who are sisters, for the Mescalero permitted polygyny and, in cases of plural wives, favored sororal polygyny.

In the course of discussions with the writer Carlos gave added details of the ceremony conducted over him by the narrator's father. He said that a stick or cane decorated with colored designs and referred to in the songs and prayers as the "age stick" was used by the shaman. This is presumably the "staff" described in the account of the acquisition of power by the narrator's father. (See p. 46). A buckskin shirt decorated with the same designs was also part of the ceremonial paraphernalia. These objects were held up to the directions during prayers. The shaman retained the "age stick," the symbol of the long life the patient would live to enjoy, but at the conclusion of the ceremony the patient was given the shirt to wear during convalescence. Carlos gave as the purpose of the rite the restoration of health, the determination of the source of the sickness, and the foretelling of the future. Of the narrator Carlos said, "His father used this ceremony; maybe he knows it. I think he has power from Coyote and Wolf because his father did. He is a good trapper. People who specialize in this kind of power are usually daredevils."

My father said, "Don't say anything." Then he touched me on the leg and said, "Tend to business; don't think those things." I could feel the turquoise on my hand move all over. My father said, "Don't tell."

I tried to tell Carlos about this years later, but it was at a party where everyone was drinking corn beer and he didn't listen.

I Throw My Elder

Jack Marsh, Tom, George Kos, Julio, and I went hunting deer. I was seventeen years old then. Jack killed a deer, and George and I ran for it. We both touched it at the same time. So the others told us to wrestle to see who would get the hide. We wrestled and wrestled.[99] Neither could throw the other. While we were wrestling he told me to let him win because he needed the hide, but I wouldn't do it; I needed it too. So at last I threw him. He was an older man and I was young. Afterward I was looking for the skin, and there Julio had it. I said, "Nothing doing! I won that and I'm going to keep it." He had to give it back. When you come alone with the man who kills a deer, you don't have to race and touch it. This is just done if two other men are along and both want the hide.

[99] This follows Mescalero hunting customs. If a person is out with another and kills game, his companion is entitled to the hide and as much as one half of the meat. If a person is hunting with two companions and brings down an animal, his companions are entitled to a share of the meat, and the one of them who first touches the fallen animal is entitled to the hide. Should the two companions race to the animal and touch it simultaneously, they wrestle to determine who is entitled to the hide. The man whom the narrator bested in the wrestling was an adult in his prime. This bespeaks the physical hardihood of the narrator.

Greed for Power

Natsili talked about seeing this red bird, the cardinal, in peyote meeting. This bird was not his power. He saw it there and tried to catch it. It belonged to another man. He did catch it, and it spoke to him.

It said, "Why do you catch me when you have other things and that poor man won't have anything if you take me away from him?"

He tried to hold it. He tried to put his hand around it, but it was so slippery, just like grease was on it, that he couldn't hold it. He tried to put ashes on it, but it was just as slippery. This showed that the bird was stronger than he. This happened in Natsili's last days, before he died.

The bird told him this was no way to do in peyote meetings. If he wanted a decent peyote meeting, it was best to leave it alone, or else he might cause trouble and upset the whole peyote meeting. Natsili tried four times in every way to catch the bird, but it always kept above his head, or, if he touched it, it was just as if his hands were covered with grease. This is the story Natsili told us himself of how he tried to steal someone else's power. But he couldn't do it. He was not strong enough. This shows that the supernatural power of this bird is pretty strong. The man whose power he was after was the one killed with his wife after finding the cave with the gold bullets in it.[100]

[100] Indians in the Southwest made bullets of any malleable metal they could acquire. Gold bullets were obtained from Indians of the Gila River area as early as 1853. See Aubry 1942.

This bird told Natsili that he didn't like him at all. He said, "You are doing wrong. There is a man who is chief of this meeting, and you are not listening to him. Because of this I do not want you. I will stay with this other man. And for what you have done, I tell you this: whatever you eat will kill you."

They choose one man to be the peyote chief. His power may not be the strongest but they choose him anyway. He is supposed to watch over the meeting, to see that they help each other and keep even and that no witching goes on. He knows what is happening. He just sits there and watches these things.

This time the peyote chief knew what was happening, even though this was all inside Natsili's head, between him and the bird. The peyote chief said, "This man is doing wrong. We might as well break up the peyote camp."

But the others told him to let Natsili go ahead. "If he loses and doesn't get what he wants, it's his own fault."

Right after that peyote meeting they went around and asked if it couldn't be fixed up, this struggle between the two men, so that it would be even and as if nothing had happened. The other men asked the peyote chief about this. But Natsili wouldn't do it. He tried every way to fix it himself with all the supernatural power he had, but he wasn't strong enough. He lost out.

About a week after the meeting, Natsili died. He got to the agency after the meeting. He was eating some mesquite gravy, when some of the mesquite went up his nose and in his head. The doctor got some seeds out, but not all of them.

Natsili said, "I'll barely make it over to where I live." This was a place below Elk where the spring is named after him. He just got there and died.

He knew he was going to die. The bird had told him, and he told lots of other people. I heard it at the time. He was a stepfather to my half sister and was staying with her. I was there often too. I stayed there sometimes but not all the time. I told him, "I can just be sorry for you."

Hazards of the Water

There was a boy at the agency who always monkeyed around these dipper birds. He hunted for the eggs and ate them. One day he was hunting for these eggs and found a bunch of them under the bank of the stream. As he was about to set his hand on them, the water ouzel came up, big as a goose.

"What in the world are you doing?"

"I'm hunting eggs."

"Why do you do that? They are not enough to feed you. If you leave the eggs alone, I'll show you how to go around the water like a fish and I'll show you all the things in the water that are good for you. And I'll show you power that's the best thing for a boy like you."

And so one day when everything was finished he left the place, and he became a fine swimmer.

I was swimming with him once. He dove down and came out with something that looked like a big black beetle. He gave me a leg and told me to eat it. "Eat it and you will be just like a fish." He took the shell off and ate the body. He wanted me to eat some, but it looked too bad. I couldn't do it. He laughed at me. He ate it all himself. But I ate the leg, and a little later I turned just like a fish; I could swim under water and everything. I could see pretty well under water too.

One time my brother Edgar was nearly drowned. He had the green stuff of the water in his mouth and he was just about choked. Two other boys were there swimming too. They all nearly drowned. We pulled them all out. My brother was the worst. But this boy who knew the dipper worked on him and brought him to life. This boy said that the dipper had taken the water out of him and brought him to life. Since then I have never shot a dipper.

One boy was bucked off a burro, and they said it had killed him. The others came back crying and told us. We went to see. We told the others to stay back and we went up, that boy who knew the dipper and I. It surely looked like the boy was dead. The boy who knew the dipper told me to go and he worked on him and brought him to life. He was using his power from the dipper. He cured lots of things with that bird—diarrhea, sore throat, and colds.

I have seen him take the white stuff from the feathers of this bird. It is like dandruff. He always kept this. He showed me lots of things about the water. He was just a young lad then. He is still living and uses it.

Ceremony and Departure

Walking Along got her songs and her ceremony at the time when the Mescalero were captured and guarded by the white soldiers.[101] Along in the fall they were allowed to go out because the yucca fruit, pine nuts, and such things were beginning to ripen.[102]

[101] In 1880 General John Pope, in order to prevent the Mescalero from giving assistance to Victorio, ordered Colonel Edward Hatch to disarm them. Three hundred Mescalero were rounded up, deprived of their mounts, and confined in a stockade that had been used as a cattle corral. They were closely guarded from April 16 until September, so these events must have occurred in the fall of 1880. The Mescalero have not even today forgotten or forgiven their confinement in a corral in which the ground was covered by a thick layer of manure.

In 1934 a Mescalero who was being interviewed said with obvious bitterness: "When Geronimo and Victorio were out, my mother was a young woman. They brought all the Mescalero together. They made a line they couldn't go over. They took them to a place near Uncus' old house, then to a corral. They had to dig for ground for fires; it was all manure. Then they took them to where the hospital is now. Lots of the men had run away. Now they began to come back. The white commander told Ramon Tcikito, Muchacho Negro, and others that they were going to take them away to prison. Muchacho Negro knocked him down, kicked him, and started to run. He was shot in the leg and captured. The whites had Navaho scouts. The Apache had buffalo hides, Navaho blankets, and such things in their camps. They were driven out of their camps and not allowed to take anything. The Navaho scouts got all these things. The government should pay for this."

The historical background of the confinement of the Mescalero during this period has been summarized in Opler and Opler 1950: 28–30, as follows:

Attempts had been made in the past two years to abolish the reservation that had been set aside for the Chiricahua bands and to remove the Indians living upon them to San Carlos, Arizona. These forced removals met with great resistance, and the Indians who refused to cooperate were termed renegades. Pursued by the military, they would be captured and taken to San Carlos only to break out and flee again to the mountains. It was finally decided to remove one of these renegade bands under Victorio to the Mescalero reserve, but Victorio was not willing to come.

However, in June of 1879, Victorio and his men did come to the reservation and began arranging to have their wives and children brought from San Carlos. In July, Victorio was indicted for horse stealing and murder. When, a few days later, a judge and a prosecuting attorney visited the reservation, presumably on a hunting trip, Victorio believed that he and his band would shortly be arrested. Accordingly, the band left the reservation immediately. During the next few months, they were successful in a good many skirmishes with the troops who had been sent after them. Russell reported that by April of 1880 two hundred or more Mescalero had joined Victorio and added that the fifty or sixty men involved "were of course of the worst Indians belonging to this agency."

Now, to the great alarm of the Mescalero, who thought that perhaps they too were to be sent to San Carlos, Colonel Hatch arrived with 1,000 troops and Indian scouts. The Indians were induced to come together, and Colonel Hatch had a talk with Chief Natsile on the evening of April 12, 1880. Afterward, he informed the agent that he intended to disarm the Mescalero and seize their stock. Since the Indians had assembled in good faith, Russell protested, but Colonel Hatch was acting under orders from General Pope and was not to be dissuaded.

The next morning, over two hundred horses belonging to the Mescalero were seized, and men, women, and children, after being searched, were confined in a corral where the old manure was three to five inches deep. In all, fourteen persons were shot and of those who were killed, one was the father of Natsile. These events were doubly tragic in that they occurred after the agent "had repeatedly assured them that those who remained faithful and did as requested would be well treated, and their horses put in my hands." For the next four months the Mescalero were under guard and were treated as prisoners. During that time, they constantly questioned their agent as to why they were held, how long they would be confined, and whether they would be paid for their horses. . . .

The three hundred or so Mescalero who were confined as prisoners of war on their reservation were allowed, in September, 1880, freedom of movement within a radius of eight miles of the agency. Others were brought in through military pressure and through promises that they would be protected and would be given arms for hunting and stock. Individuals who objected too strongly to these plans were threatened with confinement at Leavenworth.

[102] The roasted fruits of the "Yucca bacchata" were a Mescalero food staple. The pine nuts mentioned were probably those of the piñon pine, "Pinus edulis."

Walking Along went into the hills. She was a healer and was looking for herbs. Coming back she saw some grackles. She prayed; the grackles answered her. She looked around. At the foot of the cattle corral lay a big mountain lion, and it was looking right in her eyes. Then from across the hill a fox yelped four times and ran towards the corral where it began eating juniper berries.

The woman had a load. She put it down. She thought it was the end of her right there. She was pretty sure she had seen her last days. The mountain lion began to wave his tail and lick his mouth. His big orange eyes with the black spots in them gleamed, and he looked just as if he was about to jump on her. That woman was shaking. She was going to yell when she saw the mountain lion get up on its feet and begin to come four steps towards her. This was in broad daylight.

Then it opened its mouth and said, in her own language, "I come to you for a good purpose. Don't be afraid. I've come to give you help, for you need my help. That grackle up there is not just a bird; he also comes to assist you in every way. And there is another who will speak for himself. Here he is."

Then came the fox, trotting. It yelped four times and said, "I've come to help those who need me and are run around as slaves."[103]

[103] The indignation of the Mescalero over their confinement and their resentment at the white man are evident in this passage.

Then the bird began to speak too. Grackle said, "If you want me I will talk to you for myself also. I have also come to help. You will receive strength from us. You will receive many things you have never heard of." Then the rest of the grackles began to call and sat on the fence.

She knew a little power which had been shown to her by her relatives. She had some pollen in a pouch tied to her belt, and with it she marked the two animals and the bird. They were glad of this, for it was their way. A pile of rocks can still be seen at the place where this woman was shown the power of these three.

They spoke of her brother. He was already killed, and she was very sorry to learn of it.[104] The mountain lion said, "We are doing good for you. It's no use to think of the one you have lost. He would have suffered for you now if he had lived."

[104] The implication is that this was the first knowledge the woman had of her brother's death.

Grackle reminded the mountain lion, "I was here first."

"No, I was here first," the mountain lion said. "I am just as strong as any of you."

So they gave the first chance to the mountain lion. "I'll give you my power now," he said, "I'm going to help you to take your burden back."

The fox also said, "I will do the best I can." And the grackle made the same promise and said, "I can do more than you think I can."

Then the mountain lion took something from a bag. Two eagle feathers were tied to it. He gave it to her. She touched her body with it, and the feathers disappeared. The fox gave her a bag, too, with downy eagle feathers on it. It, too, disappeared. The eagle was not present, but his power was given to her, too, in this manner.[105] She marked them all with pollen. She had a great load of prickly pears and other cactus fruit and herbs.

[105] The implication is that these gifts and aids from the supernaturals entered her body.

Then the grackle, in his turn, came down and sat on the head of the mountain lion. "I also give you what is worth having. This will help you till the time you are called." And he handed her something. She marked it with pollen and thanked them all. She was told she could use her power at once. She looked at her basket. There were four baskets instead of one.[106]

[106] These were large burden baskets of the kind which the Mescalero women carry on their backs by means of a tumpline which crosses the forehead or chest.

Now the blackbird, the fox, and the eagle turned to men. And, as for the mountain lion, she rode on it with a burden basket in front. The others came behind, each carrying a basket. There were the stalks of narrow yucca in the baskets too.[107]

[107] The fruit of the prickly pear cactus and the stalks of narrow yucca with which the baskets were filled are Mescalero food staples. Yucca stalks were roasted and peeled, and the inner part was eaten. See Castetter and Opler 1936: 38.

The sentries were going up and down near the military camp, so the others put the baskets close and went back. She went in with one basket. Then she came back with some of her relatives, and they brought the others in. They wondered how she got it all and asked her.

She said, "I worked hard and carried them in, one by one." But she didn't seem tired. They couldn't believe it.

Lots of old men, like Luntso and Tomas, were there. They knew power and they thought about it. So they questioned her. Finally when the people needed help they said, "It's best to hire this woman as a shaman." Then she told everything, and she was the one who prepared Black One. She could sing for masked dancers and Black One. They say she could see through the earth and the mountains in those days. They didn't like it when grackles came during her ceremonies, but she said, "Leave them alone.[108] They are helping us."

[108] Black birds, particularly ravens, are considered birds of ill omen by those who do not have supernatural power from them.

Later they had peace with the whites and she cured a white soldier. She did many things with the help of the mountain lion, fox, eagle, and the grackle.

Walking Along sang for me when I was to go off to school.[109] She had beautiful songs. She said, "You'll be back here well. All your family will be living and well. From that time on I do not know, for I have not looked at that part. If you see an antelope on your way, do as you please about it." And on the way, crossing the San Andres Mountains, I did see an antelope and shot at it.

[109] This indicates that more than one ceremony was held on behalf of the narrator when he was about to go to school in order to provide him with supernatural protection and to discover what the future held in store for him.

Albuquerque School

In those days we used to go off to school and stay for three to five years before seeing our families. Arthur Web and I and another fellow went off for five years. But the third boy got sick after three years and went back, and he wrote Arthur that his father was sick and told the family they ought to see Arthur at Albuquerque.

In those days we didn't have much money. Train fares were high, and we didn't have enough money for our parents to come and see us.

A shaman with power from the fool quail was hired by Arthur's relatives, and he told the sick man that it was best to come to Albuquerque and see us. So they waited till early summer. They started about the middle of May, and it took them four days to reach our school. We were all glad to see them. That shaman had told them we would be glad to see them and that it was the father's last chance to see the boy because he [the father] would not get back to the reservation alive from Albuquerque.

During that visit I could see that the man's eyes were in very bad shape. He had told my father that he was witched during a peyote meeting at Mescalero. He said that his eyes hurt and he was going blind, but he was glad to hear his boy's voice and mine.

Well, they started back. On their way, while they were passing through some mountains, this man dropped dead. He died on the way as he had been told he would by that shaman.

After his relatives left, Arthur was worried, and this same shaman began to sing for him so that the agent might let him come back to the reservation at the expense of the government.[110] And the agent did; everything turned out the way this shaman had seen that it would through the power of this quail. On the way back the boy got sick too. And he also died right after he came back. Only two sisters were left. Both have families and live here.

[110] Note how many Mescalero ceremonies are held in order to influence white government officials.

Old Man Web was killed there where the gate was witched. He said that he knew he was witched when he was in peyote meeting with another man, Besh. He said that Besh came around behind him, took out his heart, and lifted it up four times. Then he knew he was witched. He told us that at Albuquerque when he came to see his boy.[111] Then he died on the way back. I hate to say it. They say lots of bad things about Old Besh. One man lost his power in peyote meeting. He saw Besh standing right behind him taking it away. After that he was no good.

[111] This is something he saw in the visions induced by his eating of peyote.

It seems that during these days there was a lot of witching going on. Back on the reservation a Lipan suspected a certain Mescalero of witchcraft. Then he saw him with something from the bear that he used in his ceremony. He said, "You must be a witch, for you have the real thing that kills. You must have killed my brother."

The Mescalero said, "No, I didn't kill anyone. I just have this for my own purpose, to get long life with it."

"Yes, but you pay out others for your long life. You ought to die yourself." And he shot him.[112]

[112] It was believed by a number of Apache tribes that when his time comes to die, a shaman with evil inclinations might prolong his own life by allowing or encouraging supernatural power to substitute another person instead. Substitution of this order is considered a form of witchcraft.

This happened while I was still in school. It led to lots of trouble. They had court in Las Cruces over it. Choneska's brother was shot at La Luz on the way back from the trial. A servant, a captive who had grown up among the Mescalero Apache, was shot and killed too, but this was never found out.[113]

[113] It was the obligation of a family to avenge the murder of one of its members. Blood feuds stemming from past murders or charges of murder have continued for generations and have taken a considerable toll over the years.

They claim that the power of the fool quail is pretty strong. It is used in curing and in other ways. Its power is used a lot in the moccasin game, because when Quail hides, he's hard to find. When a man knows the power of this bird, he can hide out and can't be found.[114] The Mescalero didn't eat this bird until the Chiricahua Apache came from Fort Sill, Oklahoma. Some are still afraid of it.

[114] Note that the shaman is credited with sharing the abilities and attributes of his power source.

The man who knew this bird used it for healing too. They say he could pull out its feathers from any place. When a child is sick, this power is used to find out what the child is sick from and where. The child can't talk and tell what's the matter, so this bird walks inside the child, they say, and finds out what the trouble is. In this way this bird helps in the sickness of the little baby.

One time this man who knew the fool quail was called to Three Rivers by an old woman. Nothing was wrong with her but worry. She asked him to sing for her and get her well and keep these worries away from her. He did sing for her for four nights and showed her signs for good luck.

She told him she was worrying about a boy who was in school. She was afraid she would not see him any more. But he told her that the boy was coming back that summer and she would see him. "He will be bit and will stay and not go back to school any more." If she was a little younger he would go back, but because of her he would stay and marry a little early, and things would be a little different for him, this man told her. And it came out that way. She saw her boy healthy and strong and stayed with him till he married.[115]

[115] Because of the rule of matrilocal residence, at marriage her son joined his wife's extended family.

One time while I was in the Albuquerque Indian School, I got in a little trouble. I was out alone shooting birds and had my bow and arrow in my hand. Another fellow came along and asked me to carry two watermelons. I was carrying them, holding my bow and arrow under my arm. I thought they were his, that he had bought them. All of a sudden this boy and some others began running. And I looked around and saw a farmer running in back of us. I stood still because I hadn't done anything. Then he came up and tried to grab me. Then I started to run. I was crossing a bridge, and he was right behind me. I dropped one of the melons over the side, and the other one slipped out of my hand and broke to pieces just in time for him to step in it. He took a big spill, kicking me in the leg as he went down. I walked on. He was knocked out. Pretty soon some other people came along, and I saw him get up and point at me. I went around in back of some houses and came to the school.

That day they lined up all the boys, and out of that whole line I was the only one picked out for stealing watermelons. I got put in jail and got a good licking too.[116]

[116] Tales of arbitrary treatment and injustice are often related by Mescalero who went to the off-reservation boarding schools during this period.

3

Unsettled Years

Return to Fear

I WAS JUST OUT OF SCHOOL. We were all at Turkey Springs around Bill Sotol's place. I went around doing nothing but hunting. There was no work for any-body in those days. I used to like the country around Indian Springs and Pajarito. There was no fence around to bother you, no people, no cattle. I camped out alone on those plains. Coming back one day I heard about the killing of Giye.[1] We were all scared, and I went back to camp.

[1] In his annual report, published as a part of the Annual Report of the Com-missioner of Indian Affairs for 1902, the agent at Mescalero mentioned that two Indians had been sentenced to five years in the penitentiary for this homicide.

There a performance of power was being held by the sister of my mother. She looked over the country. "From the gate on down east of the reservation it is witched," she said. "This was done by a man I do not know very well. He's already dead. That's why this place is being cleaned out. The witching was done because of the killing of the Indians of Indian Springs. His people were killed; that's why he witched the place."[2]

[2] The sorcery is again conveniently attributed to someone already dead. In the fight at Indian Springs to which reference is made, seven Indians, including a prominent Lipan Apache, were killed.

The father of the Sotols died there, Old Leggings, Old Juan, and all the Nitsigane family but Louis died there. He moved out and this saved him. I was also taken sick but was moved out of there and brought to the agency. I got well and went back.

138

She said, "The witch weapon is not hung up anywhere. But the gate is marked, and at the foot of the gate, under a rock, is the deadliest weapon of feathers a witch could use. But it's dead now and you can go tomorrow and burn it."[3]

[3] The implication is that she has already "killed" or neutralized the evil objects with her ceremony and that they may now be touched and disposed of with impunity.

The ones that touched the gate were supposed to die. Louis' mother and his brothers had all leaned against the gate. Ceremonies were held for many of them, and in these ceremonies it was seen that they had leaned against a gate. "Nothing can be done for you. It is too late. There is one woman who could have saved you, but now it is too late; she is dead," they were told.

They wanted to know who witched them. "They are all gone, all dead." It was too late. There was nothing but death. It all came true. They all died. The ceremony through which they found this out had been performed for Louis' brother. He's the one who killed Giye. It was a Lipan who witched that gate. Louis' mother knew a power herself. She tried to hold her ceremony, but she could do nothing. It showed that her power had already run out. It was the same with Bill Nitsigane and Natsili, who had tried to help them before his death. They could not do anything. Jicarilla performed many ceremonies too. But it was too late. They were barely walking around. The best things in them were already dead.

When my aunt was performing her ceremony, she said, "Now some of our own people stepped pretty close to it and that's what made them lose." And she looked at me.

A couple of weeks later I went out to defecate. When I was through I reached for a stick to help myself up. I couldn't get up.[4] The stick broke right in my hand, and I went down in all that mess. I couldn't move my hind end. I called for my father and mother. My sister came running. I said, "Sister, you better get back. Something terrible is wrong."[5]

[4] With the stories of sorcery fresh in mind the narrator was psychologically prepared to interpret a temporary stiffness as paralysis due to supernatural attack and became hysterical.

[5] There is a strict restraint relationship between siblings and cousins of opposite sex who have reached mature years. One of its terms is that they must avoid seeing each other in embarrassing or intimate situations. The girl the narrator had presence of mind enough to warn to stay away was his half sister, the daughter of his father's first Mescalero wife.

She ran back crying. Then my brothers came running up and they pulled me out. They were crying too. My mother came and carried me on her back like a little baby, smelling and dirty. Think of it! She took me to a tent and cleaned me up. Then my father performed a ceremony over me and sucked out lots of things from my knees, heel, and leg. After that I got better.

We cleaned up the gate. Tom, the Sotol family, and some others went up with us. His mother told Tom to go from the east side towards it. She told him he should kick the turf four times toward it and then go up to the rock at the foot of the gate. "There is a lightning mark on the rock and it's used in the witching. You dig below the rock and build a fire around the rock."

We got the rock in the middle and then turned it over. Under it was a staff with lots of feathers on it, and the handle was made pretty. The buckskin at the end of the handle was cut in four ways. Another wrapping which looked like hair was on it. There were four strands of it; two were white and two were black. My aunt said it was hair from the lap of a dead woman or man and that it is a deadly weapon used against anyone to make him lame.[6]

[6] The implication is that this is pubic hair. Again unconventional sexual elements or lewdness and witchcraft are associated.

The staff was marked very beautifully. She said, "Look at it carefully and know for yourself." The staff was about one inch in diameter, six inches in length. The feathers were of all kinds. I'm even afraid to talk about it now. Hear that ball socket? It makes my hip ache now.[7] Along the handle were all sorts of markings, pictures of the claws of animals, heads of animals, sun, moon. The hair was wrapped all the way down the handle. The buckskin work was very fine. You saw many feathers on it. It was beautifully decorated, but it was a deadly weapon.

[7] The narrator shifted his position uneasily at this point with the results described.

She said to me, "That's what made you sit in the excrement. Look at it!" She said there were four circles around that rock, and anyone who stepped inside the circles got sick. I had stepped in the first one only, but I got it anyway.

Tom dug it out and we discussed it. While we were looking at it we turned blind. We knew something in the side of our faces was shaking.[8] Bill Sotol felt it too. Then we said, "It's no good! Throw it in the fire!" And we marked the gate with four crosses of ashes from the fire. Even the rock burned, burned like wood, and you know rock won't burn. The feathers went off four times like rifle shots.

[8] The Mescalero—and other Apache groups as well—believe that involuntary muscular tremors are warning signals of good or evil events to come. Some of the interpretations are generally accepted. There is tribal-wide agreement that a muscular tremor under the eye symbolizes misfortune and tears. This probably was the sign that was experienced by the protagonists of this story. Various other tremors are open to individual interpretation. An individual will attempt to remember what befalls him after he notices a muscular tremor in some part of his body, and he makes up his mind, on the basis of experience, whether this is a good or bad omen. Interest in muscular tremor and dependence on it vary greatly. A few individuals depend upon it to the point where they consider it their guardian spirit or source of supernatural help. As we shall see, such persons may be called upon to use their knowledge of muscular tremor to predict or guide the fate of others.

Many had died because of that witching. Louis' mother—she was good to me, she helped me when I had typhoid fever—was one. I tried every way to get my mother and others to cure her, but they said, "No, it's too late."[9] Louis' brother said he remembered that when he touched the gate he felt something go into his hand. He looked at it but couldn't see anything. Then his hand began to ache and it swelled all the way up. Running Water died around there too. He saw four bears at that gate, he said.

[9] Shamans are often well able to recognize a hopeless case and seldom claim that their power can cure it. Instead, as here, they say that the patient has waited too long before consulting them or give some other reason why they cannot accept the case.

The place is all right now. Natsili, Louis' brother, all of his children except one, died though. Kakas was called to help those sick from the gate. I went and got him. But he didn't do any good. He didn't even tell them anything.[10]

[10] There is small faith in a shaman who cannot convincingly explain the cause or background of sickness or trouble. The popularity of shamanism can be accounted for to a large extent by the practitioner's ability to give substance to vague and amorphous fears so that the alleged causes may be dealt with and a feeling may prevail that something positive is being attempted.

Swinging-Lance

After his father died Swinging-Lance got to be chief. He was only about nineteen years old then. He didn't get to be chief by doing things like Natsili did, or by meeting the enemy. He just took his father's place.[11] He was made a policeman here and captured children who were to be put in school. He talked to the families to say that education was good and that young people had to be educated because we needed interpreters and that we would have to pick up the white man's ways. He was a good leader. He said, "We have to learn to hold ploughs, picks, and shovels and build houses and have farms and stock of our own."

[11] Before the reservation period leadership always had to be earned or validated by ability, effort, and success. There was some tendency for leadership to run in families, but the Mescalero explanation for this was that the children of leaders had good examples to follow and received more careful instruction. If, in spite of his greater opportunities, a leader's son showed no marked talents, he was given no special responsibilities and had merely the status of an ordinary member of the tribe. Yet it was assumed by white officials that chieftainship was hereditary, and favors and opportunities were given the sons of "chiefs." Consequently, experiences with the white man tended to over-formalize and enlarge Apache concepts of chieftainship.

He was a great church member. He never missed church after he learned what church was. He said, "We must follow the white men as they have churches to lead us in the right road." He asked me about this white man's religion because I lived near his family after I came out of school. He asked me how to plant fruit trees and I showed him what I knew. I also showed him how to raise vines and how to set out cabbages. I always helped him with farming and he showed me how to rope and ride horses.

Swinging-Lance tried to lead his people and show them the best way to live, but he talked against the whites who tried to keep all the Indians on the reservation. He spoke very little English.

Before he joined the church, he had power from Yusn.[12] I was present at his ceremony many times. He marked with pollen, had prayers and songs, and held it for four nights or even for four days. He was like all other Mescalero, afraid of different kinds of animals; he said there was sickness from them and his power wouldn't permit him to touch them. He was afraid to eat fish and at first wouldn't eat bacon, but he finally got so that he could eat this.[13] He was never present at the peyote meetings; he didn't like it. Through his prayers he did his part against the white man.

[12] The word "Yus" or "Yusn" ("he who is Yus") is a corruption of the Spanish term "Dios" (God). In the absorption of the concept into Mescalero Apache religious ideology, "Dios" or "Yusn" becomes just one more source of supernatural power.

[13] A number of Indian tribes of the Southwest, including the Mescalero, placed a taboo on the eating of fish. At the time this life history was recorded a good many of the older Mescalero and even some of the middle-aged people still would not eat fish. Formerly there was a feeling against the eating of pork, too.

Once I asked him to teach me his ceremony. He said it was not to be shown to anybody. I asked him why he didn't want to show it to me. He told me that even if he taught me the songs I wouldn't have any power.[14] So I didn't learn anything from him. Once when I rode out in the mountains with him he told me, "To get power like mine you have to go without food and pray all the time. Then Yusn will pity you when you're starving and give you power."[15]

[14] The implication is that power did not want to "work through" anyone besides the shaman and that, even if someone else learned the songs, prayers, and ritual round mechanically, this would not be effective since power would not cooperate or lend its presence to accomplish whatever was desired.

[15] Although it occasionally happens, such an obvious, active, and persistent quest for supernatural power until it is obtained is not the usual Mescalero pattern. When he becomes adult, has responsibilities of his own, and is less protected by the efforts of others, a Mescalero does feel the need to have "something by which to live." He is then sensitive to any hints that a source of power is seeking him out, and he is receptive to dreams and visions that

would bear this out. The vision experience usually occurs at a time of crisis, when the individual is exhausted, worried, or in danger, for this is when he is psychologically prepared to welcome any additional help and needs to feel that he has the backing of a supernatural monitor and partner. As the stories of the acquisition of ceremonies indicate, however, power is prevailingly represented as seeking and needing the human channel, too. The individual is frequently pictured as requiring some persuasion to accept a particular power and often does some shrewd bargaining and extracts some attractive promises before assenting. Yet, however obtained, power is considered necessary to a full and fortunate life; and, in the aboriginal pattern of thought, the few individuals who were too prosaic to acquire supernatural help considered themselves unlucky and were deemed unfortunate and vulnerable by others.

That time when we were in the hills he said, "I'm going to ask my power to let us see a bear and I'm going to shake hands with it." A big sandstorm came and dust settled on everything. On the way back, in a steep canyon where there was no way out, a bear stood in front of us. The bear kept coming closer. Swinging-Lance said, "I've turned coward. I'm going to tell the bear to go away. I can't shake hands with him." But I wanted to take the bear's paw. Swinging-Lance had jumped off his horse. He said, "No, let's not do it." So I said, "Tell him to move out and we'll go on."

So he got on his horse, rode a little ways toward the bear, and started to talk to his power. Then he said to the bear, "Be kind enough to move away." Bear looked and moved three steps. So Swinging-Lance said, "Couldn't you move a little more? Be kind enough to move; we're in a hurry." Then the bear walked down to the trail and sat close to it. Swinging-Lance told it to move again, and the bear moved slowly and looked at us till it got in the bushes. Swinging-Lance was saying prayers. The hairs of my head seemed to stand up. He told me not to look at the bear but to keep on. We hurried on till we came to a spring. He told me to wash my face. I did, took a drink of water, and felt better.[16] He told me not to tell anyone of this for a long time. Swinging-Lance never mentioned whether he got his power from his father or not.

[16] An encounter with an evil animal like a bear is unnerving and usually causes physical symptoms.

Once Swinging-Lance told me, "Tomorrow I'm going to say a few prayers and then I'll show you what Yusn can do. I will go up to the wildest horse without any rope."

The next day he marked his hand with pollen and started walking up to a wild horse which raised its head as though it was going to run. He was saying something. He stopped at the fourth step. He did this four times. The horse looked at him instead of trying to run. He walked around the horse once, the way the sun goes, and then he walked toward the horse from the east. I heard the horse snort; it turned the way the sun goes and raised its head four times. Swinging-Lance touched it on the forehead and petted it as if it was a gentle horse in pasture. He came away toward me. "Let's see how you'd do it," he said.

"I'd go on a horse and corral him," I told him.

Once we corralled a big bunch of horses. Swinging-Lance said to run the biggest and wildest past him as he stood in the corral and he would show what could be done with the strength of Yusn. He said just a few words before I started to run the big horse by him. He threw his rope and caught the big horse around the neck. Just as the rope began to tighten he pulled on it and the big horse swung around as though it was a little colt. He threw that horse on its back and didn't even move from the spot where he was standing. He jerked and threw him four times. Then the horse stood still, shaking all over.

Swinging-Lance said to me, "Take hold of that rope and see if you can do what I did." I told him I couldn't do it, for it would take a good horse to hold the wild one. So he pulled the rope toward himself four times and the horse started to walk toward him, though it had never been roped before. It shook its head four times and rubbed its head against him. Swinging-Lance said, unloosing the rope, "Now you can go," and the horse jumped and raised dust.

Afterwards I tried to hold this same horse. I was on a horse trained for roping. We were dragged around until the rope snapped in two. I told some cowboys about Swinging-Lance and the horse. They didn't believe it. They laughed and said, "Swinging-Lance must be a great cowboy!"

I stayed with Swinging-Lance quite a bit. Once he came to me and said, "I've got a horse at Three Rivers. Will you help me get it?" It was a long trip from Nogal to Three Rivers on horseback. It took us all day. When we got there we stayed with Nishchee, who lived there. Nishchee had seen this white horse the day before and told us where it was. We circled and headed it off. Swinging-Lance was in front of the horse and I was in the rear. I noticed he was saying something. The horse followed him and then trotted faster and caught up to him. Swinging-Lance held the rope up with his hand, and the horse just put his head in.

We came on to Nogal that night without stopping. Swinging-Lance was afraid of owls. We shot at every one of them we saw with our .22s.[17]

[17] The spirits of dead witches are thought to linger in owls, and the hoot of the owl is heard as some gloomy or threatening message in the Mescalero language. Consequently, attempts are made to keep owls at a distance. If they hover about a camp, firebrands may be thrown in their direction.

Swinging-Lance showed me another good power, the power of a gun. "This gun speaks," he said, lifting a rifle. "If you handle it right and do the right thing, it will do whatever you say. Put a rock way off on the side of that hill."

I rode up there and did it. I heard him say, "Gun, we want to show how to hit the right mark." He took aim and shot and knocked the rock off.

Then he said, "Make a mark on that tree." The tree was a hundred and fifty yards away from him, and I made a mark you could barely see. He said the same thing he had said before and shot. He told me to go and look at the tree. Where I had marked it there was a bullet hole. He said to me, "Sometime you will see me shoot a deer that is so far off it looks like an ant. I can tell the gun to hit the heart or break the back, and it will do what I say."[18]

[18] The bow, and later its substitute, the gun, was thought of as something that could become animate and personified, that could receive messages and give them and thus could become a source of advice and power. The conception is that supernatural power can reach man by "working through" any channel, animate or inanimate. The inanimate object becomes animate while power is suffusing or using it. Thus we are told of power from the gun, from rock crystal, from the knife, and so on. The gun became so valuable and important that, in terms of the system, it was almost inevitable that it would become a "channel" or source of supernatural power for the Mescalero. Cf. 2[7].

One time when we were out hunting we saw a deer. The deer was far away, running across a canyon. Swinging-Lance was talking to his gun. He took aim and fired. He hit the deer. "You are a good shot," I said. "I told the gun to hit the back," he told me. We had a hard time reaching the deer. We found that its back was broken. It was a good-sized deer and we packed it up Indian style on a horse.

The Food of the Raven

Old Elk is still living. He claims he has known Buzzard, Raven, Owl, and Snow.[19] He also knows Fog and Light Rain and something about Horse. He has the best breed of horses on the reservation. That's all we know about it; we don't know how he gets them.

[19] To "know" in this sense is to have ceremonial knowledge or aid from some animal, bird, or other potential power source.

First he used the buzzard. He had known it for some time. Then Buzzard told him one time he was through. "What for? What have I done?" Buzzard said, "You've got to pay now if you want to keep me. You will have to pay the life of one of your children or of one of your relatives; or you can throw me away."[20]

[20] Because the supernatural helper sometimes demands the life of a kinsman of the shaman as a price of his continued success in ceremonies, there is frequently an uneasy feeling toward relatives who are very active ritualists. Elsewhere I have suggested that this fear of the ceremonial power of a relative is indicative of repressed conflicts and resentments between persons who are required by the culture to cooperate amicably regardless of personal feelings. See Opler 1936b and 1938a.

Old Elk said, "Then I don't want you. I thought you were good, and you said you were good, but now you want me to do something that I will not do."

Before this he knew the buzzard and the ways of the buzzard. But when Buzzard asked him for a relative to make his power a little stronger and make his life a little longer, he gave it up. He told this right before a big crowd. His power from

Buzzard had been good in lots of ways, in healing and in raising children. And he said the buzzard, when it left him, went home. He meant it went to the mountain in Mexico where he first got it. He mentioned the mountain, but I don't remember which one it was.[21]

[21] Power, when inactive, is described as being in its "home," the place, usually a cave in a mountain, where the shaman learns a ceremony in his vision experience.

His next one was the raven. He started to work with the raven. It worked very nicely with him. It had power against witches and for healing his children. When the raven came to him, Elk was a young man and he wanted to marry. He asked the raven if it could help him get the woman he wanted to marry. The raven said to him, "Getting a woman for you is nothing. I can do anything. I went to that woman. She will be yours pretty soon. You take my power and I'll show you what to do." Elk said this woman was the prettiest in the crowd. That's the way it looks to you when you like a woman.

His power said, "If you think you like this woman, make your ceremony the way I tell you." So he held his ceremony in the way of the raven. He bought a looking-glass, but he was not to touch it or look in it till he was told. He worked and finished the ceremony of the first night.

The second time he saw her going by, his power told him to touch her in some way or to let her just touch his shirt, and then she would be his friend. After this he did touch her, at the store, just as they got in the doorway. And from there on it wasn't long before they were talking to each other.[22]

[22] Love magic usually involves some behavior which is certain to attract the attention of the target of the efforts. The person for whom the ceremony is held is instructed to brush against the person he is trying to influence, to throw a beam of light from a mirror upon him, to play a flute in the vicinity of his camp, and so forth. Since the general pattern of love magic is well known, the target of the ceremony is very likely to guess what is going on and, if he is at all interested in the person trying to influence him, will be flattered and excited by this evidence of devotion. These are circumstances well adapted to break down bashfulness and reticence.

They were young and were bashful, and so they set a date to meet one night outside the camp. After that they always selected some place to meet out in the woods. And then he paid for his girl, he gave the old lady a horse and saddle and a gun.[23] He said that was his first marriage, and they slipped out of camp and went in the woods without anything to eat for a week. This was never the way. I don't know why he did it. Other people asked him why he did it. "Oh," he said, "I just wanted to be out in the woods with my woman."

[23] Traditionally the initiative in Mescalero marriage was taken by a man and his family. Usually, in the case of a first marriage, a go-between known to be a

persuasive speaker was asked by the boy's family to approach the family of the girl. The go-between was usually authorized to describe presents that would be given to the girl's family when the arrangements were settled and even to deliver these presents if the answer was affirmative. In a strict sense it is doubtful that these presents can be called payment or bride price, for they gave the man no proprietary rights over his wife and were not returned at separation, divorce, or in the event of the death of the wife. In fact, regardless of the magnitude of these gifts, the married man was obligated to work for his relatives-in-law and to show them honor and deference. This so-called payment, therefore, is best interpreted as an indication on the part of the young man of the economic aid and service the girl's family could expect from him if they consented to the union. The presents varied in amount according to the wealth and status of the girl's family and the opulence of the boy and his family. The bride herself received little besides prestige from the gift-giving. Even the girl's father and mother ordinarily retained little of these goods. It was customary to distribute them among all the relatives of the girl who had cooperated to protect, sponsor, and train her.

So he got his woman through the raven, and this raven, they claim, is a great charmer.

Then he began to raise his children. The raven saw it and was jealous of the children. So Raven asked him for pay. Raven said he had given him long life and had got a woman for him and had helped him heal lots of children, and now he was hungry and wanted something to eat. Raven meant that Elk had to pay one of his children, one of his family, or himself. That's what Raven told him.

Old Elk was very angry. He said, "That's not right! Your power is not good if you have to have something to eat."[24]

[24] The Mescalero conception of supernatural power is complicated by the belief that power may be beneficent, neutral, or basically evil. Beneficent power seeks only to cure and protect the Mescalero and searches for individuals of comparable lofty ideals through whom to operate. If it should misjudge its human vehicle and become associated with someone who seeks to do harm through it, beneficent power will rebel and desert the religious practitioner. Thus power is sometimes confronted by the evil in man. Power that is neutral or amoral, that simply seeks to exert its influence in human affairs for either good or evil, is manipulated according to the character of the human being who uses it. It consequently can be either a source of curative rites and protection or a source of witchcraft. The Mescalero call power that is used for beneficial purposes and a shaman who so uses it by one term. They call witchcraft or the person who manipulates supernatural power for evil by another term. Besides helpful supernatural power and power which may become either beneficent or evil, there is supernatural power that is always completely evil in intent and thus without question witchcraft. The difficulty is that evil may pose as beneficial supernatural power in order to enlist the services and association of an estimable Mescalero. The evil power may even

assist this Mescalero to perform cures and build for himself a reputation as a good-hearted, eminently respectable shaman. Then, when the evil supernatural power feels that the Mescalero is sufficiently involved with him or obligated to him, it reveals its true colors by making some unprincipled request. For instance, it may suggest that the religious practitioner "pay out" one of his patients; that is, allow the patient to die. Or it may suggest to an ailing or elderly practitioner that he can prolong his own life by allowing one of his children or some other relative to die in his stead. If the practitioner refuses to acquiesce, his power may turn against him, and his life may be endangered. At the very least he will no longer be able to use this ceremony and will have the embarrassment of explaining its unavailability to those who seek his aid. Some of the most serious tensions and anxieties in Mescalero ceremonialism and, indeed, in Mescalero life arise from conflicts between a religious practitioner and a source of power which he thought to be beneficial but has discovered is evil. The psychological study of these shifting attitudes and relationships is most intriguing. There is evidence that shamans who fail repeatedly and sense public censure begin to "suspect" their power and finally slough off their ceremony with the explanation that they have discovered it is witchcraft. Also shamans who are moved to hate and anger and who are tempted to think of the possibility of making a supernatural attack on their foes probably relieve their guilt and suppress their unrighteous tendencies by blaming their unpalatable urges upon their power.

Note that to attack and destroy someone through evil supernatural power is here phrased in gustatory terms. The victim is sacrificed to appease the hunger and appetite of power.

But the raven said, "You will have long life if you give whatever I ask."

He didn't like it. "Take your power and leave me alone. You're going to ask me that! I thought you were good power." So they had trouble.

But he also knew the owl. Then he started to use the power of the owl. The raven didn't like that much. He said, "You give me back my power, and everything will be free.[25] Don't use it any more."

[25] That is, "There will be no retaliation."

Elk said, "Take your power! I don't want it any more."

The raven told him, "It will cost you your life if you use my power any more." And he quit him. And the raven flew back to his home where Old Elk had got the ceremony.

The power of the owl had told him to quit the raven, and he did. Now he started to use the power of the owl, and he said he got along better with Owl than with Raven or Buzzard. He put it along with the horse and it was still better, he said. He used both in healing and both were pretty good. And after it was shown him that everything was good about Owl, he kept it.

A Ceremony Overheard

One time Old Elk's wife was very sick. The doctor tried his best but he said there was no hope. Then Elk started in his own way to see if he could heal her. He used the power of the owl.

We were camped close to them, but he did not invite us to the ceremony, so I did not go. He invited other people. I wanted to go, but lots of people told me he was a witch, and so they cut me off from going to see the ceremony of the owl which he knew.[26]

[26] Relations between Old Elk's family and that of the narrator were not cordial during this period. As so often happened, these ill feelings spilled over into mutterings about witchcraft. Another informant gave an account of the activities of Old Elk which also contains charges of sorcery. "A witch can send a ghost to bother a person. This is one way of witching. A certain man suspected Old Elk of witching his son. After his son died, he shot at the witch but only hit his arm. Carlos, who was on the police force then, went down to see the wounded man. This man said, 'It's true, I witched this man's son and he shot and nearly killed me, but now I'm going to witch him and he will go crazy.' And the man did go crazy. Nothing could be done for him. They took him to the crazy house and he died there in the hospital. I don't know if this was ghost sickness that he sent, but it looked like it, for those who have ghost sickness usually go crazy."

In all these sessions he was doing pretty well. He said, "She's going to get well. I'm not the one who's going to make her well, but it's going to be someone else." And he said he had got a good sign to show the people so that they would believe. I could hear him because we were living close to him, and he was a loud talker. And he told those people, "Tonight, close to morning, there's a sign that I'm going to show you that shows she's going to get well. Owl and I are going to have a talk. He will come on that hill over there. You'll hear me talk from this tent. When I sing a song, you'll hear in it the words of the owl. That will be me calling the owl. You'll hear me hoot, and the owl will hoot, and then we'll have a talk about this sickness. But when I'm going to talk to him, I'll step outside, and you stay where you are in here and don't move away."

He finished his song, then he hooted like an owl. After his hooting you could hear the owl a long way off, just once. But it was too far away. He told them, "The owl says he'll be here in a few minutes."

Then, just as he spoke, the owl hooted from on top of the hill. I heard him, for I was listening; I was not asleep at all. Then Old Elk stepped outside. I was inside. I heard the wings of something outside. But I kept still. Then in a few minutes he was back inside. He did not say anything but started to sing another song. When he finished, the owl hooted outside close by. Everybody was pretty scared.[27]

27 It will be noted that power is obtained from birds and animals such as the owl, snake, wolf, coyote, and bear, which are considered evil and dangerous. In the total Mescalero ceremonial and curative system such power is quite essential. There is a strong homeopathic element in ideas about healing, and it is considered that the animal that caused sickness is the one which, under shamanistic supervision, can best repair the damage. Yet, in spite of the need for them and their apparent good works, shamans who have ceremonies from dangerous and sickening birds and animals are always under some suspicion. Inevitably there are some who wonder whether these ceremonies are not being surreptitiously used for evil.

When he heard the hoot, he told them not to be frightened, because the owl was killing the disease that was sent upon this woman. He said, "This is the only one I care for, and I'm going to cure her. I'm not parting with her yet. Among all the good-looking women I picked her out as the best looking."

I heard him sing the song of the horse too. And when he put his head up to his wife's head, he made a noise like a stallion. He used his mouth on her head four times and then said he'd sucked out the disease. He threw it in the fire, and a funny thing happened. The fire blew out but was not entirely out. Then it smelled kind of queer, like a candle or some grease was burning. It smelled real strong. In a little while the fire started to blaze again. Then he poked wood in the ashes, and the fire came near going out again. He wanted all that disease to burn up.

They say that every night for four nights he did this. Everything was the same. Even the hooting of the owl came at the right time. At the end of the four nights the woman asked for something to eat.

She wanted venison, and they asked me to go out and hunt for her. The old man wanted to go out with me. This happened in Carrizo. There's many I know who were present there. I used the man's horse to show that I was willing to help them. I took the gun that was loaned to me by Patricio. I went out with Old Elk, and while we were riding along he told me the story of Water's Child and of the times of the killing of the monsters. Pablo was with us.28

28 The myth referred to is the Mescalero "origin story," the account of the birth of the culture hero and of his exploits in ridding the earth of the monsters that once preyed on man and prevented his increase.

All at once I told him to be still. I got off and went behind him, and there was a deer with its head behind a tree. I did not know whether it was a buck or a doe. I aimed to break its back. It was along in September, and the horn was in velvet yet and nearly ready to shed. At the crack of the rifle the deer came down, and then another jumped up. I shot that one, and he kicked. I killed two on the spot. With my third shot I hit another one, and it ran down the canyon. A fourth jumped up, but I had shot all the cartridges that were in the gun. By the time I was loaded again, it was gone.

Some people in camp had said, "They won't get deer; they'll get wild beef."29

[29] The reservation was surrounded by large ranches at this time, and there were a good many stray steers in Mescalero hunting territory. There was also a good deal of unauthorized use of the Mescalero range, and the Indians felt entitled to benefit from this to some extent.

There were lots of those then. But by noon we were back, all loaded down pretty good.

They took their choice of the hides, Old Elk and Pablo. I had to stay away, and what they left I took. The old man took the first deer, hide and all. He built a fire while Pablo and I were getting the others, and we ate the liver right there. He was a good butcher, the old man; he was used to it, and we were not. He didn't even lose the blood of that deer, he got it in the big gut. And me, too, I finished butchering mine before Pablo, and we both helped him then. Pablo took the second one I shot, hide and all, because he saw it had big horns. I got the third one I shot, the one that ran down the canyon. But they were all good ones, nice and fat.

When we came into camp, the sick woman ate some of the meat and said she felt better. Within the next few days we saw her walking around.

Just then they sent for me from the agency and said that I was to help put the sawmill in at Water Canyon. That was the first year the sawmill was put up.

Feud

The first year I was out of school was the year Tobacco was killed.[30] We heard about the killing and the moving of the prisoners to Silver Springs. They had trouble there in trying to move them. They kept them under guard for a few months and then took them for trial—Muchacho, Sam, Dana, and all those in the fight. All but Muchacho and Dana were turned loose. They served five years in the penitentiary. The fight was between Muchacho Negro's side and Tobacco's side. The two had a fight. Sam and Dana were there on Muchacho's side. Muchacho was related to that bunch some way. Tobacco's son was fighting from the side of the hill with his father. Muchacho was in a ditch, without his gun, and Tobacco's son was pouring it on him. Just about sundown, Tobacco was shot and killed from the back by Dana. Then the police came.

[30] This homicide occurred in 1902.

Old Nishchee didn't have a chance to get in it. He was Tobacco's son-in-law. He didn't know about it till it was all over. Nishchee was tough when he was young.

They had these feuds all right, that's one thing. You might be the brother of a man who gets in a fight. You have nothing to do with it when it starts but you get drawn into it. You take sides with your brother. After that the families can't get along. Lots of families are against each other and hate each other because of this. The Mason family have had a long feud with another family and it is still going on. Long ago some of the Masons were witched by some of this family, they say, and the feud has been going on since then. Not long ago there was a fight right in front of the agency buildings on account of this. Roberto Carlos, whose mother is a Mason, started fighting Tony, and Tony's wife started to fight with Roberto's sister.

Not long ago one of the Mason family, an old woman, died. Before she died she called Dick Mason to her and said, "You know what they did to our people. Get your revenge on them if it takes you all your life and costs you your own life."[31] Ted Mason has tried in every way to find out who did the witching. He knows I was at a ceremony where the shaman told who did it. He tried to get me drunk so I'd tell him who it was. But I'm careful. The shaman, when he told me who did the killing, said that there would be more trouble and that I'd be mixed up in it if I told.

[31] The bitterness involved in these feuds between families can be gauged from the old woman's instructions to the young men of her family, though she was virtually on her deathbed.

Diego's Power

Diego was a peyote man. He knew the power of Summer and Fox and Coyote too. He also had power from Night, Ghost, Lightning, and Horse.[32]

[32] Diego is a good example of a shaman "loaded up with powers." He had an unsavory reputation and was considered by many to be a witch; there was also gossip about incestuous relations between him and a daughter.

"There's one good thing I know in the way of power," he said.

"What?"

"I can stretch a man's penis."

"That's a hell of a power!"

"Well, women like it that way. Don't you want one like this?" He took his out, and the old thing hung down like this. He was a champion. He used his power for two men that I knew of.

I saw him use his ceremony for one of these, a young fellow about seventeen years old whose penis was hardly developed at all. He wanted Diego to help him. I was passing by a field with this boy, and Diego was out there. He called the boy to him and they talked.

Diego took a stick and measured it off and gave it to him. "We'll make it that big," he said. "Take this stick with you and keep measuring it and see it grow, then come back and see me again." He told him to come back at a certain time.

That boy had to come back four times altogether. He gave Diego ten dollars for using this power. That's all Diego did while the boy was around. No one knows what he did for him when he was alone. But anyway the boy's penis began to get big, and before Diego stopped working for him, it was as big as that stick.

We once asked Diego how children come. "It all begins with intercourse," he said.

I saw Diego examine one of my chums who was sick. The worms were little ones. You could hardly see them. There were millions of them.

Diego said to him, "I can't help you. You monkeyed around women too early."[33]

[33] Since the tribal community was small and concentrated at this time, it did not take too much supernatural help to obtain information about the private lives of others.

Frank speech and banter about intimate matters is not unusual between Apache of the same sex. The narrator described a verbal exchange he had recently had with an old Chiricahua as follows:

"Hunter met me and asked, 'Chris, do you know where I can get a woman for tonight?'

"I said, 'How much money you got?'

"He fumbled around and finally brought out a one-dollar bill.

" 'That's not enough,' I told him.

" 'I've got it for that before.'

" 'Well, then you better go back to where you got it before.'

" 'No, it's no use. I was only fooling. I'm no good now. I went to a woman and stayed on top of her a long time. I was wild for it, but I couldn't get a hard on. Pretty soon I got ashamed and got off and went home.'

" 'Why didn't you put your finger up and smell it? That would have helped.'

" 'That's just what I did do but it didn't help any. You'll be like I am some day. When I was your age I was as good as at eighteen.' "

He had too. He was only seventeen. He died shortly after. This was Edwin Bird's youngest brother.

Mescalero Fears

I killed an osprey in 1902. Lots of people wanted it. I said, "No, I know a ceremony of this bird."[34] They laughed at me.

[34] The narrator has constantly told his fellow tribesmen that he has no ceremony. He is obviously poking fun at them for their persistence in believing he has supernatural power.

Old Man Nogal came and said, "I'll give you a dollar for the two middle tail feathers. I want it for a ceremonial purpose. I know this bird." I gave him the whole thing. He stuffed it.

The osprey is used in ceremonies, and its feathers are used for arrows. It is classed with the hawk. While I was carrying it they said, "What are you carrying that for? It'll make you sick." Many won't touch it. They are afraid to touch its feet.[35] This is just one of a good many things they don't like to handle.

³⁵ The claws of eagles and hawks are avoided because in their hunting these
birds sink their talons into snakes and "dirty things."

Most people here are afraid to touch a wolf.³⁶ Seven wolves were killed while my
father was living. He got fifteen dollars' bounty on each of them because no one else
would touch them. He scalped every one of the seven; the other people left the
place where they were. He skinned five of them and then quit. He knew Wolf and
wasn't afraid.³⁷ He used to use the power of Wolf for strength and for speed in
running.

³⁶ The wolf and fox are classified in a general way with the coyote ,and are
thought capable of causing sickness, too. Even the dog is viewed with a certain
amount of suspicion because of its general similarity to the coyote.
³⁷ That is, he "knew" the ceremony of Wolf.

Another thing: The Mescalero never touch the kill dropped by an eagle. I have
seen rabbits and antelopes dropped, even deer. They are never touched. I saw a big
white-tailed deer killed by an eagle at Whitetail. "Someone is riding that deer," said
one of the fellows when he saw the deer run. We went and found that an eagle
had killed the deer. It was just about dead. It was an eight- or ten-point buck. It
had good meat on it, but they wouldn't let me touch it.³⁸

³⁸ Note that the narrator, who has small patience with these restrictions on the
touching or utilizing of animals that others fear, was willing to eat the meat
from this deer.

The Mescalero also believe that if you eat during a storm you are going to lose
your teeth before old age or else your stomach is going to be mouldy. The food
goes in your stomach and moulds there, and you die of a big stomach, or you get
rheumatism and become all crippled up and no good for anything. So every time
lightning flashes they stop eating. If you have food in your mouth at the time, you
spit it out. They watch me when I eat during a lightning storm. "That fellow
thinks he's a white man," they say. "He's going to have rotten teeth."³⁹

³⁹ This is another instance of the narrator's unorthodox conduct and the censure
to which it gives rise.

Love Magic

Old Juan knew love magic well. He used the deer, the lazuli bunting, and the
butterfly. There was a woman who was a charmer too. She knew Peyote and Moth.
These two had it out. She said he couldn't make her come to him. He took her
up on it. She went out and before she got very far, he said some words. Pretty soon
she walked right back and came to him. He slapped her four times with the back

of his hand and sent her away then. The back of the hand always means that you don't want the thing, that you are getting rid of it.

Then there was an old fellow about sixty-seven and bowlegged. He came to Old Juan. Juan gave him something and told him, "All you have to do is go to the east of her with this." Right away he went out with it. The fourth morning after that he married the woman he wanted. I was interpreter for him when he went to get his license. He laughed and said, "Why don't you use it? Look how old I am and what a young woman I got."

Old Juan also did it for a white man. He wanted to marry the woman who was the girls' matron at the school. He didn't know her well at all. Juan gave him something to rub on himself. He told him to go to the windward side of her with it. A little while later the two met going into the store. She turned around and smiled, and they started talking and walking off together. They never even went into the store. A week later she resigned and soon they were married. He gave Old Juan a hundred dollars for this. Juan gave me some of it for a new saddle. "I can get more any time I want it," he said.

There was a Mexican woman who laughed at him. "Why does everyone say he can influence women? He can't do anything to me." They warned her not to talk like that. They told her that she would have to follow him wherever he went if she didn't look out. But she wouldn't listen.

Old Juan went off to a friend's place and stayed there for the night. Pretty soon the friend was surprised to see a woman come up to his place. "Is that Indian here?" she asked.

"Yes."

Juan came out. He wouldn't have anything to do with her. He slapped her four times with the back of his hand and sent her away.[40]

[40] See also p. 175 for an instance of this gesture of rejection.

There was a Mexican boy, Pedro Gomez, who wanted to marry an Indian girl. He came to Old Juan. I was out hunting deer when he came and got in with a deer just when he was trying to make Juan understand what he wanted him to do. They called me over and I acted as interpreter for him. I told the old man, "He wants you to help him get the girl. He will give you ten dollars; it's all the money he's got."

The old man said, "I don't know if it's the right thing to do."

I told him, "Why not? You've done it for plenty of others. What if he is a Mexican? Do it and he will always be a friend of the Indians."

The old man answered, "Ask him if he'll be my friend and cut wood for me and fix my house and fence."[41]

[41] For evidence that the Mexican became a helpful "friend" of the Indian see p. 205.

I asked and the boy said he would. So Old Juan gave him something and told him to rub it on and go to the east of the girl. A couple of days later I came to the agency. He was there getting his license. I cut the wedding cake.

Old Juan finally lost all his power in peyote meeting. Only the deer was given back to him. If Muchacho had been there it wouldn't have happened.

The butterfly is used as a charmer with other things, with the caterpillar, or with a rope. For instance, if it gets in your bed, you're a goner, you are charmed. I have heard that the hummingbird, which has strong power for making people and horses run fast, is also used ceremonially to make a person love you.

One time I paid a fellow six dollars. I just wanted to see if it worked. He used Butterfly and a mirror.[42] I had my chance, but I got cold feet. The girl even came up to me at the store and said, "Will you carry things home for me?" But I got cold feet.

[42] The butterfly is associated with love magic because it seems to flutter irreso-lutely hither and yon. The love ceremony is used to destroy the resistance of the victim and to make him willing to go anywhere or do anything at the command of the one who seeks his affection. Again, a colorful bird is men-tioned in connection with the love ceremony, as is the deer.

The man got after me. I used to say to him, kidding, "You owe me six dollars." He'd get mad and say, "It's all your own foolishness!"

Once, a few years later, when Tall Raider's wife was drinking corn beer, she promised to show me what she knew. She sang one of the butterfly songs to me. I couldn't get on to it, for I heard it only once. In the morning, when she was sober, she changed her mind and wouldn't show me more. I heard Tall Raider sing too. Another woman, now dead, also used the butterfly.

An Aunt, Famous as a Healer

Tom's mother was my mother's sister. She never mentioned how she got this power; all I know is that she healed, and they knew she was one who had power from Rock Wren and from White Painted Woman. She also helped at the girl's puberty rite.[43] The women who do this are supposed to know White Painted Woman. She didn't tell in the beginning of her ceremony from where she got her power; they usually do. She always held her ceremony four days: two nights, four nights' rest, two nights again. She had to be sure she knew what her patient had. She allowed very few people at her ceremony.[44]

[43] The family of the pubescent girl hires three principal ceremonialists whose combined efforts are required for carrying out the girl's adolescence rite. One is a male singer to whose songs the girl dances for four nights in the conical ceremonial structure or "big tipi." The second is a woman ceremonialist called "She Who Trots Them Off," who ritually dresses, massages, and feeds the girl, advises her, looks after her when she is not in the custody of the singer, and who supervises ritual runs to the east which the girl makes at certain points in the ceremony. The third ceremonialist whose services must be obtained is a shaman who has the right to costume the masked dancers and sing for these impersonators of the Mountain Spirits during their performance. During the

early part of each evening of the rite this ceremonialist's set of masked dancers, who have been prepared in the foothills away from the "big tipi," approach a large fire that is kindled immediately to the east of the "tipi" and perform their animated dances. There are some religious overtones to their exhibition, but it is carried on mainly for the entertainment of the onlookers. Meanwhile the more serious aspect of the rite is being conducted inside the ceremonial structure under the guidance of the singer. The primary functions of the masked dancers in the general Mescalero religious system are to cope with enemies in Mescalero territory and to keep epidemic disease away. It is not possible to say for certain how this separate ceremony became associated with the girl's puberty rite and why the presence of the masked dancers at the puberty rite is considered today as important as any other element of it. The girl's puberty rite is an occasion when a large number of people gather and camp together. It may be conjectured that the masked dancers were first involved in order to bless and protect the gathering and that this association grew to be considered useful and important and was continued until it became an expected and integral part of the rite.

44 Some ceremonialists, for fear of courting interference or failure because of the presence of witches or sceptics, confine the audience to the close relatives of the sick person.

She was once treating a woman who had a bad case of tuberculosis. There were not many present, because the sick woman didn't have many relatives. She had a son-in-law and a daughter, that's all. The daughter had come to ask for help for her mother.

Tom's mother came. She held a ceremony. She put pollen on the head and on the bridge of the nose of the sick woman just as the adolescent girl is painted in the big tipi. The woman was very sick. Her face was yellow. Her mouth was dry, and her teeth too.

Tom's mother knew what the matter was. At the beginning she looked at the sick woman and put pollen in her mouth and began to pray. At the first prayer she got up. She was kneeling toward the east. In her prayer she was saying that she wanted to know what was ailing this poor woman. She finished her four prayers and marked everybody. Then she sang four songs. She knelt toward the south. Her hand was marked with pollen. She prayed and sang as before. Then she did it towards the west. Then she knelt to the north and did as before.

She came back and sat down. A cigarette and pollen were put before her. She took the pollen and threw it into the mouth of the sick woman four times. She stopped and said, "She's got a hard case of what they call 'worms' in her lungs. The herb that is shown to me to use is what they call 'slim medicine.'45 I've got it at my tipi."

45 "Slim medicine" is probably "Perezia wrightii."

She directed the son-in-law of the sick woman to go out and kill turkeys or fat deer.46 She also sang a song of the deer and said a prayer of the deer for him. She showed him the way to go, towards the sunrise. He got out in the morning, early, and came in that night with a big load. He had two deer and four turkeys. The patient was to eat the turkey roasted.

[46] Note the assumption that it is the woman's son-in-law who should be sent out to hunt. The term for son-in-law is literally "he who carries burdens."

The second day the ceremony began again. It started the same way as in the beginning. When she finished, out before her lay this "slim medicine." She had a ritual for the medicine. She lifted it and marked it four times with pollen, and she marked the mouth of the bowl four times with pollen. She prayed to White Painted Woman, kneeling with it to the east. She said that this medicine was made in the home of White Painted Woman and was put here on earth for different purposes and for tuberculosis. Then she sang of the medicine, and the song was very beautiful. It began with the song of White Painted Woman, about her home. The medicine came from there, it said. And the medicine was placed on earth for those who were sick. She did that to all the directions. There were four ceremonies of this kind for the medicine and four for the woman. The ceremony for the medicine was held from the second day to the fourth day.

At the end of the fourth day the patient was pretty well fed with the meat. Then they quit feeding her. The next day she was not given a bite to eat. The next morning she had her hair washed.[47] Then they gave her a big bowl of "slim medicine" to drink, after marking it, putting it to the directions, and to her mouth four times.[48] She drank it. The healer told them not to feed her till they were told to. The same day, a little later, they gave her the same thing. She was given, in all, four bowls of medicine before noon. Then they moved her out to the hill and left her alone. No one bothered her.

[47] The washing of the hair, especially of women, is common as an act of purification in connection with ceremonies.

[48] What is meant is that there were three "ritual feints" toward the mouth; on the fourth occasion the vessel was put to the woman's lips and she was allowed to drink.

She lay out there. About mid-afternoon, she yelled for her people.[49] My aunt went herself. She took a bowl of water with her. White Painted Woman had given her a root of some kind. She gave the sick one this to chew on four times. Then she told them to give her a big dinner of turkey. She told her to wash with the water that she had brought. The patient was well cleaned out now and was feeling good.

[49] She was to call when she had had a bowel movement. The medicine, among other things, has laxative qualities.

They brought her back to camp and fed her pretty well. She ate turkey and soup. Then in a little while they gave her venison and she ate it. In the evening she felt pretty good. She thought she was well all the way around.

Then Tom's mother held a ceremony by herself. Her power directed her to use another herb, a strong one. The woman drank the medicine made from this herb, and they didn't have to give her anything else. She was very happy, and they saw her walking around.

Tom's mother was regarded as one of the best doctors. She cured many other diseases which were killing her people. She once worked on her own granddaughter, who had pneumonia. The doctor said the girl had no chance. The girl was out of her head. My aunt performed the same ceremony, but the herb medicine that she gave this girl was used in a different way. She made a mixture of four herbs that I did not know and washed the body of the girl. Then she put some kind of herb into her mouth too. No one knows what it was, not even I myself, though I was there while they were doctoring this poor girl.

They were out in a little cabin where the lodge is now.[50] I was working in the sawmill at that time. Tom phoned to me and let me know how the girl was getting along. I was interested in the ceremony and I tried my best to find out all about it. It was snowing very hard. I went to the phone and asked how the girl was getting along, and the voice told me that the girl was now getting along very nicely. At the end of the week I was told I could come back and see her again. The next week I rode down and found the girl as well as she could be. My aunt danced before me.[51] The girl spoke up to me. I sat close to her and took her hand. "I'm glad," I said.

[50] The "lodge" referred to is a meeting place and recreation center maintained by the Protestant church near the agency headquarters.

[51] In Mescalero religious contexts dancing is a symbol of joy, affirmation, or approval.

That night I told Tom's mother to hold the ceremony for us. I wanted it while I was present. She didn't want to. "Going to pay me?" she asked.

"Sure."

"I didn't mean it. You don't have to."

She did it. She used her power and her four prayers and songs. Then she held out the medicine too, and she showed me the medicine and the marking with the pollen. I caught on right away. She went all through it.

She said, "What makes you take this interest in it?"

"I think some day I'll learn it."

"You could if you stay around me."

I know this ceremony of my aunt pretty well. I've never used it though. She taught me the ceremony for woman's disease too. I use this but not the other.[52]

[52] This is another instance in which the narrator paid close attention to a ceremony, aroused the interest of the shaman in him as a possible candidate to carry on the rite, and then allowed the matter to drop. However, as will appear, he has made good use of the treatment for venereal disease which he learned from his aunt. See pp. 239–245.

When she held her ceremony that time she saw that four or five days later there would be trouble. Four days afterwards a man and his wife were shot.[53]

[53] Though a ceremonialist concentrates on finding the cause and cure of his patient's ills, he often impresses his audience by relaying unrelated miscellaneous information that his power source reveals to him.

Another time I was at a ceremony being conducted by my aunt for a woman who had been told she had tuberculosis down in her throat and that her throat was in bad shape. That's what the doctor said. But the rock wren saw it differently. It said, "You can be healed." My aunt took great care in giving the medicine Rock Wren directed. She gave it just as directed and enough of it too. And the sick woman got well and she lived to be old. She was young when the ceremony was held.[54]

[54] Here again there is evident satisfaction in demonstrating the superior knowledge of the Mescalero healer when compared to the American medical practitioner.

I never knew my aunt to fail. I have a brother she treated. The doctor had to turn him out of school and said he wouldn't last two weeks. He had tuberculosis. He was just nothing but a skeleton. They took him to her, and she held a ceremony and said to break camp and go to the mountains. So they moved up towards Head Springs and lived up on Peso's ranch. There she doctored him. After they had stayed there long enough, they moved to Turkey Springs. She kept giving him different herbs. While she was holding a ceremony for him, she told of a big hailstorm that was coming. She said they would have to use rawhide instead of canvas. The day they finished putting up the rawhide, the hail would come, she said. They got to work sewing rawhide, using any kind of hide that was thick enough.

The next day after all the hides were up, they had the biggest storm they had ever seen. Rain came first, then little hail, then hail as big as stones, then the biggest hail began to drop. You could hear it coming a long way through the air. She picked up four hailstones and told my brother to eat them. He chewed on them and then asked for a cup of hailstones. After the hail was over, some old people went out and found prairie dogs, rabbits, and snakes killed by the hail. Old people who liked prairie dog meat brought in plenty. Those who ate pigs and chickens went to the farms below them and got plenty.

Now my aunt started with the strongest herbs and gave them to the boy to drink, and he kept getting stronger and stronger. The next spring the doctor sent for him, for he had heard he was well, and they took him back into the school. From that time until now he has had hardly any sickness at all. Of course, he has had colds and headaches, but he says his lungs don't bother him at all, and he's done lots of heavy work.

Illness from Civet

They used to say the civet cat was a poisonous animal. I was told that if its bite didn't kill you right away, you'd die later. The first time I trapped one, I just picked it up and carried it in. They have pretty fur, black in wavy lines or buck color on white. It's a member of the skunk family. People made me go away from camp after I trapped it. They said I smelled bad.

One time one of these little animals had bitten a man. This cat is known to be something like a mad dog. When it bites a dog, the dog goes mad. If it bites cattle, they die from running and falling over. Quite a while after this man had been bitten, though he seemed to be in perfect shape, he went from place to place asking to be cured, trying to find the best cure for this bite. He felt kind of sick over this all the time, but he was not losing flesh and looked all right. He told them what was the matter. He said that at night these cats bit him all the time, bit his hands, and he felt them crawl in bed and bite him all over, and he could smell them too.[55]

[55] The accepted symptoms of a particular sickness are well known, and the fear or conviction that one has been in a position to contract the sickness is often enough to induce the symptoms.

Thinking of different powers that might help him, he came to a man who knew the power of Bear. He told him what had happened, how he was bitten, just what kind of a day it was when it happened, and the kind of sickness that came upon him. He said that all the time he had been pretty healthy but he couldn't get his rest. He asked for a ceremony to find out who could cure him.

After holding a ceremony for one night, the shaman saw he couldn't do anything for this man and that the man might soon come to his death, but he saw something good too, a woman who had power, who knew herbs and animals, and he told him to go to my aunt who knew Rock Wren power.[56]

[56] Sometimes shamans act as diagnosticians and use their ceremony to find out who will be able to cure the patient, rather than to attempt the cure themselves. Or, if they learn through their ceremony that their power is not adequate to cure the sickness, they attempt to find out for the patient who can cope with it.

So the sick man came to my aunt. Through her power she had heard herself talked about and knew he was coming that day. Towards noon, as she was serving the meal, she saw a wagon and said, "Here are the people coming now," and the others went out and saw that it was the man they had heard about who had been bitten by a civet cat.

He put up his tent near where my aunt was camped, and before sundown he came to her and, without saying a word, marked her with pollen and gave her a cigarette crossed with a match.[57] Then he told her his purpose in coming.

[57] This was a ritualized request, of course. The match, a product of the white man's culture, was firmly fixed in Apache ceremonialism by this time.

She said, "All right, I'll do my best for you. But first we must wait four days, no matter how urgent this is."

"I wish to have it as quickly as possible, because the man who told me about you said my time was close, and I might die in those four days of waiting."

"Not when you come to me. I must do it the way the power tells me, and in those four days you're not going to die."

So he had to wait, but those four days seemed like four years to him. At the end of the four days, during the last night, he dreamed about the civet cat with pollen in his hand coming to mark him. When Civet Cat came to him, it started to raise pollen in the four directions and was talking to itself, and the man could hear it plainly, talking of Water's Child, Life-Giver, and White Painted Woman. The pollen was in the hand of the little cat, and he began to bend down and mark the man, and after the cat had marked him, the man seemed to feel a hand moving over his face, and he seemed to feel very good; and he woke up, seeing nothing at all, just the night. He got up and woke up his wife and told her what had happened in the dream. So she got up and began to cook his breakfast. He felt like eating for the first time in a long while.

My aunt was out looking for herbs, asking her power what ones were best to help this man. She was going towards the hills, praying, and her power led her to where a rock wren was sitting on a rock. The little wren began to flap its wings and flew towards her and showed her an herb. It showed her three other things to mix with it. It said to use juniper needles from a tree that was pointing towards the sunrise as one of these. After bringing these herbs back to camp, she pounded them and began to boil them and made a stronger and a weaker brew; the stronger for the man to wash in and the weaker for him to drink. He was to do this four times before moving away.

He washed himself four times that day. People heard about it and began to come for the ceremony. Before it started, my aunt told of her power and how it seemed to help everybody, but she said she had never before tried to cure anything like this man had. She might fail and she might not, she said she didn't know. By the end of sixteen songs she would know just what to do, she told them. She marked everyone present with piñon pollen. Next she marked the patient and placed pollen in his mouth four times and told him to swallow it. Then she took juniper needles and told him to chew them and swallow them and to rub a little of the juice on his nose. She said, "I do this to you to take away all the smell you have in your nose since the civet cat bit you; for that's why you can't eat."

Then she lifted up the bowl and began to pray and marked it. Then she went to the patient, put it to his head four times, and held it toward his lips four times and prayed. She crossed it, marked it on the side he was to drink from, and told him to drink it. After he drank it he was saying his own prayers that this herb might help him. My aunt said eight prayers without stopping, then she held up pollen, marked the people and was marked by them, smoked a cigarette, and sang eight songs and stopped.

She held the tail feathers of this little wren. She said, "There is no answer yet," and put it down, smoked, and sang again. At the end of four songs, she stopped and began to roll a cigarette. She took a downy eagle feather and began to move it around the place on the body of the man where he had been bitten. She placed the feather in front of him. She told the people to watch this feather during the third verse of the second song.

Saying a few prayers first, she sang the first song. At the second song the feather began to rise, and from the quill end poured something yellow. The feather moved up towards the man. Nobody touched it, and she kept on singing. Four times the feather moved to the place where the man had been bitten. It stopped. It looked as if something was pouring out of it. Then it looked as if earth had formed itself into a cup and dumped this stuff in the fire. It burned like oil. They saw this thing, and some moved back, for the fire was too hot. She told them not to move outside. Then she sang her last song and opened her eyes wide and looked at the people, very happy. She looked as if she was going to fly.[58] Finally she quieted down, finished the last verse, marked everyone, and was marked. She started to roll a cigarette and kept very still, said a few prayers, and finished her cigarette.

[58] Shamans often imitate the actions or calls of animals and birds from which they obtain their power. This is expected to attract the attention of the power source to its ceremony and the shaman's need. This ceremonialist was obviously imitating the wren.

She looked up and began to speak. "My people, I have good news for you. I do not know if it is really going to be true, but I've said these things many times before and they've always been true. This man was on the point of death. But now we've held a ceremony for him, and the power that is in the ceremony has fought and overcome this civet cat that bit the man. The man is going to get well."

She said to the patient, "You don't have to be afraid. You were going to die, but the power of Water's Child, Life-Giver, and White Painted Woman has saved you. The power is not mine; you know who has all the power; it is Life-Giver."

She told them, "We're going to hold another ceremony, the last, tomorrow, and all those present can come back. We will start earlier." The first ceremony had lasted only sixteen songs and eight prayers. All the people went home. And they sent a man out to hunt for deer for the next day, as it was time for them to eat meat instead of fruit. But fruit should be there also. This man went hunting and the rest began to gather fruit, and they brought it all to camp.[59]

[59] Note the emphasis upon herbalism and dietary measures in the ceremonies of this woman.

The next day the ones who didn't want to miss anything began to come early. Quite early she marked the patient, and he marked her with pollen. She marked the medicine, and he took it. Then she marked the visitors, and they marked her until she was almost covered with pollen. She said four prayers, then four more, then told them to rest and smoke. So they all smoked and talked. The patient furnishes tobacco and papers; the visitors can smoke their own if they want to, but so long as it's free they take it.

Finally she told them to be quiet and sang four songs, then four more. She said,

"I must stop. That's the end of the ceremony. Power won't let me go any further, for that man is well." She marked all the people, and they, in turn, marked her, and the ceremony was over.

They had a big feast for the people because they were glad to see one of their men healed again. After everything was cooked, they called my aunt and spread a big sheet on the ground and spread the feast. Many people came. Some came who had not been at the ceremony, so she marked them, and they marked her. Then she prayed and marked the food with a cross of pollen. She raised fruit in a bowl and marked it and raised it up and down and placed it on the ground, praying. She sang two songs, and after that the patient was given the first of the marked food.[60] Then she took two children, a boy and a girl, and she did this to them, too, before the people. The children started to eat. They wanted to know why she did this. She told them to stop eating so she could tell why. She said she did it that all children might be like that, so that there would be no trouble to raise them, and so that there might be more children and more people. She said also it was so that they all might have more power, and that Life-Giver and Water's Child and White Painted Woman might be kind enough to give power to cure the sick and help these people. She said she wished them good luck and that there might be stronger power for younger people some of these days. Then she told the people to eat. The man who had been sick had a big appetite, for he had not been eating much.

[60] Medicine or food consumed as part of a ritual is usually marked with pollen and given to the patient or spectators on the fourth time, after three ritual feints.

She also told them, "There is a cure for this. If any man gets the bezoar of the male or female deer, it is a sure cure for the bite of the civet cat."[61] She saw this through her ceremony. "If anyone finds one of these, he should not throw it away, for it is good for bites from different animals."

[61] A bezoar or "madstone" is a concretion occasionally found in the alimentary organs of certain ruminants.

From that time on I looked for the madstone of the deer; she said it is usually in older deer. She said you wouldn't have to go to a doctor if you had this. I got one along in 1909, on White Mountain. A bunch of engineers from the Rock Island Railroad came in. They used to let them hunt on the reservation. One asked me about it; I showed it to him, and he bought it from me. There was a white boy at Carrizozo who was bitten by a dog and had hydrophobia. The doctors said there was no hope for him. The boy heard about this stone, and they wrote to me for it. I had to get hold of the white man and get it and take it up there. It cured the boy too.

When I got that bezoar out, everyone wanted it. There were old Indians with me. Yet they couldn't ask for it. They claim that this stone is a man's luck and should be kept by the man who kills the deer. Sometimes it is black, sometimes it is white. It's in the stomach. Mine was about a half inch across. It is the only one I ever got.

Finding the Hidden, Lost, Strayed, and Stolen

My mother and this same aunt who knew Rock Wren were the best ones at finding things I ever saw. At one time they wanted to find some shells that they needed badly. My aunt went and found them. Nothing could hide from Rock Wren. It could see through rock, dirt, and through the world, they say.

One time Short Man just about gave up trying to find a good mule of his. He had been looking for it for five years. He came to Tom's mother. She sang two songs, using Rock Wren. Then she stood up. Her arm was straight out before her, and she faced the sunrise. Power moved her hand to the south. She said, "Don't worry about that mule. Tomorrow morning he will come right to you from the sunrise."

The next morning Short Man got up very early and stood outside his camp. Just about sunrise he saw that mule come to him from the east. We were camping near there, and I saw it. He slapped his knees and brought his right hand down on his left palm, and then clapped his right hand over his mouth.[62] That's the way we do at a time like this, you know. And he said, "A great thing has been done for me!"

[62] The hand clapped over the mouth is a gesture of pleased astonishment.

Another time she helped Peso find his horses. He lost his work team, six horses, for three years. Everybody looked for them; he hired outsiders; and he finally came to her. She said, "I might fail." He said, "You never fail." So they held a ceremony for one night. She told him to go out alone, and he went. Something was driving him; he'd go off one way and come back to the trail, go the other way, and come back. He got up White Mountain and sat down to smoke. While he was thinking about his lunch, he saw his horses right close, all of them. He was sure glad to see them.

Still another time she got back a good horse for Tom. We had been looking all over for it for two years. Finally Tom said, "Mother, why don't you try?" She said, "I'm afraid; I don't want to lie." Tom said, "You won't lie, Mother; just try it anyway." So she said she would. She sang to Rock Wren. All at once power lifted her up. Her hand was pointing in this direction and then it moved slowly this way. She said, "That horse will come back all right. I see two men who are going to find it, and they are going to bring it to you tomorrow." Then Tom was glad.

The next day she told him, "Get ready and go and meet them. They're coming with that horse right now." So Tom went over to my horse and threw a saddle on and started off. I hollered to him, "Hey, where are you going with that horse? You've got no business going off with him like that." He said, "It's all right. I'm going over to meet my horse. I'll be right back." And sure enough, he rode over and there came the two men his mother had seen and they had the horse. They had been going along, and all at once that horse came out of the woods and stood before them. He was neighing as if he felt good. Nobody but those in our camp knew anything about this ceremony.

One day we were all away from camp. When we came back we found a lot of things missing, buckskins and money and several other things. We didn't know who could have stolen them. Tom's people lost a lot of things too.[63] So Tom's mother made her ceremony. She sang two songs and said, "You won't have to go far to get the things back. I see who took them. You remember that woman you met?" and she told us where we had met her. "Well, after she met you, she came around the hills and came into our camp from the opposite direction. It was just as the shadows were getting long. She took that stuff and she has hidden most of it. Right now she is on her way to the store to spend the money. If you go now, you'll meet her just about at the store."

[63] Tom's mother is the narrator's mother's sister. It is evident that both women lost property in the theft at the same time because they lived in adjoining camps; that is, matrilocal residence was being practiced.

So we started out just as fast as we could go. On the way we picked up Muchacho Negro and Short Man, who were policemen then. Just about the time we got down to the trader's we saw that woman going in. We waited until she was inside and was buying. Then we went in. When she saw us come in with the policemen, she was afraid, and she didn't want to look at us. We asked the trader what she was doing in there. He said, "Spending money." We asked to see the money. One of the bills had been torn in two and pasted together with paper, and we traced it by this.

Then I remembered what my aunt had said about the rest being buried and hidden away. I was a great tracker then. I just tracked that woman from where she had come out in the hills. Pretty soon I came to the kind of a tree my aunt had described. There, right in the crotch, were some of the things, and right at the bottom, buried under some rocks, was the rest. We got everything back, and that woman nearly went to jail for it.

Another time I lost my gun. I looked all over for it. Finally I said, "Mother, I can't find that gun anywhere.[64] I don't know what I'm going to do." So she marked her hand in some way. I didn't notice how she marked it; I didn't pay much attention to those things then. Pretty soon her hand moved in a certain direction. Then she said, "You remember that Mexican you were talking to? That's where your gun is. You lost it, and he picked it up; he's got it right there by his sheep camp up in a tree. You can go and get it now."

[64] Note that the narrator calls his maternal aunt "mother." Matrilocal residence, sororal polygyny, the sororate, and child training practices encouraged the classification of the mother's sister with the mother.

I jumped on my horse just as fast as I could and rode to that sheep camp. And right where I had been talking with him, hung up in the tree, was my gun.

Cold's Friend

Boneska, a great player of the hoop and pole game, had power from the snow bunting. He said the snow bunting has power toward the hoop because where he

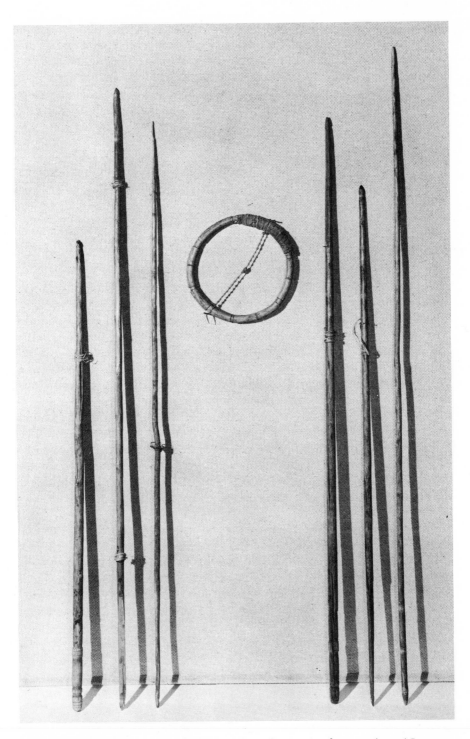

Equipment of the hoop and pole game. The poles are in three sections (Courtesy, the American Museum of Natural History).

plays in the snow it is just like the grounds for hoop and pole; the mounds he makes are the same.[65] When the hoop game was going on Boneska always had something of this bird and used it. He always had a way of touching the red pole with the feathers, and then this was the one for him all the time.[66] He used it all the time when he was old and couldn't do anything but just play that hoop game. He cleaned up on many good hoop players.[67] He loved the game and couldn't stay away from it.

[65] The mounds at the hoop and pole grounds are for the purpose of guiding the hoop that is rolled in the game.

[66] One of the two poles used in the game is marked with red. This is the one used by the player who is ahead in the scoring. If he should fall behind, he has to relinquish it to his opponent.

[67] The hoop and pole game was the most prominent gambling game of the men.

Once, when the snow was deep, he said he could walk to Elk Springs without clothes or moccasins. They came near taking him up on that bet, and then they backed out on it.

He did do it later. Ammunition and guns were valuable in those days; five cartridges for a horse, three for a mule, two for a head of cattle, one for a sheep, and one for a goat was what they paid. That was the money among us. The best horse was never worth more than five, and there were different prices between. They bet horses and ammunition against him. He was bet ten cartridges and two horses that he couldn't do it. He needed those things.

He tied his clothes up. The snow was deep and cold and the wind was blowing when everything was ready. After he was gone they were to follow his tracks. He had only a gee string around his waist. His clothes were tied in a bundle on his back. He started from Whitetail. Two men rode after him. He came down the road to the Summit. From there he cut down to Fence Canyon. He went on the side of the hill from Windmill down. He didn't go on the road, for he didn't want to be seen.

At my place he stopped. He went out and relieved himself there. When the horsemen came up trailing him, what he had done was frozen as hard as a rock.

He met some people. They asked him why he had his clothes off. He told them not to talk until he finished his walk. He rubbed snow on himself every couple of miles. He said he got too hot. This was in January, after New Year's.

He came down to the agency. There was ice all over his head. He had a little goatee, and it was covered with ice. He shook it and said, "It's a bell." He sat down by the fire and put his clothes on and told of his trip. It was sundown. The men came after him and got there at dark.

He went back to Whitetail and laughed at them. He said, "The cold is my friend. I would rather be in it than have it hot." After that they gave him the name of "Cold's Friend."

Some were afraid he would get sick, but he did not feel it at all. He said the snow bunting gave him clothing and that he had covering all over but they didn't know it.

Once he told Old Elk, his "brother," "You don't know things, but you think you know everything. You say you are going to the agency, but I don't want you to go. There is going to be a big storm tomorrow. Stay here and kill deer. We need more deer to keep us till spring." Elk said he was going anyway. Boneska held his ceremony that night.

The next morning Old Elk started out and was caught in one of the worst storms he had ever been in. It took him till noon to make the Summit, and he couldn't get farther. The horse couldn't stand it. The horse just turned his tail to the wind. So Elk had to turn back and had a hard time making it to camp.

He came in and cursed his "brother." "Why do you do such a thing?" Boneska had done it too; they say he really brought that storm.

So they had a big argument. Boneska said, "My whiskers stand for the Mexicans I have killed."

Old Elk said, "You mean that's the number of white women you killed because they couldn't fight."

"I heard you were out in the hills hiding and there was pitch on your gun so you could hold it."

After their quarrel they were all right. Boneska was the only man I knew who didn't drink corn beer or whiskey. He said, "I like women and all other things, but drinking I don't care for." He never went to the parties. I never have heard that the snow bunting was used in any other way except for snow and weather and in the hoop game by this one man. He never told how he knew it or where he learned it. Boneska was a good swimmer. He said once he had walked across the bottom of a lake. He said there were many who saw him.

The Varied Uses of Raccoon

There is one woman who never said much about her power but she sang and prayed like the rest and used pollen. She used her power for charming and against charming too, I heard.

She said, "The supernatural power from Raccoon is pretty strong. If you do it right, say it right, and do what it tells you, you will never be in danger of witchcraft or anything else. It is best to be on the good side of it."

She cured one man whose mule got mad at him and nearly chewed him up. She sang over him only two nights. At this ceremony she used the bridle in the way some use pollen. She raised the bridle from all sides to his head. She got some saliva of the mule, mixed it with some kind of medicine from her bag, and lifted it in the four directions, and marked his sores and swellings with it.[68] He came through.

[68] Here the trappings and saliva of the mule are being used to undo the mischief for which this animal is responsible.

She cured another man who was in a bad way from some kind of a sore. He smelled pretty bad and was rotting alive. Some could have got him well but they would rather see him die. She took pity on him and performed her ceremony of the raccoon, and the power told her, "Do not do anything but put pollen on him. Put pollen in his mouth four times. Put water on his head four times." The man faced the east. She threw water on him from the four sides. The fourth time his sores were just about healed. Everybody remembers this and they always talk about it.

Peso was shot in the leg. There were bone splinters in the wound that were hard to take out. When they moved he was in great pain. So he asked this woman to come and take the bones out. This was performed at Rinconada. She came to his camp. He killed a fat sheep for her and gave it all to her. She was very glad. I was at Peso's camp when his leg was bothering him. I was helping him herd. I took turns with his son. I stayed till the ceremony was over.[69]

[69] The implication is that the narrator, who had such a strong interest in watching ceremonies, purposely lengthened his stay in order to witness this one.

She took out her bag and marked it. "You're not going to suffer long, for I'm going to take it out right at the start," she told Peso.

So the first night she gave him pollen in his mouth four times and put some in her own mouth. Then she sucked out four splinters of bone and spit them out on the cloth. These had been moving around in his leg. She worked on him two nights, and he told her his leg was all right. So he was let go. She stayed there a few days longer and then left.

She's living here yet; she's not so old. She's helped many a man here. During the Spanish influenza epidemic she found out through her power that piñon and juniper needles were the best thing for it. And every time they feel a bone ache they chew it and use it for tea now. She not only knows Raccoon alone but also knows Peyote. Harold Nitsigane was in trouble with the Sanchez girl and he hired her. She saw it wouldn't amount to anything and that she was not to hold any ceremony. It was going to come to nothing. So he went to the agent and was turned loose at Alamogordo. The trial amounted to nothing.

Of Insects and Field Glasses

Old Man Felix, the singer for the girl's puberty ceremony, also knew the child-of-earth well. He knew it with the centipede. These two insects are a pretty good combination. He and his wife knew it. His nephew is living and knows it now.

This man used this thing in many ways. Early in the morning I'd hear him sing the song of the rising star, and he would sing it in a good way. I heard him do it many times in Rinconada during that time I was there herding with young Peso. This man also had a song about the sun, its rays, and one about the rainbow. He sang that the rays of the sun were something like gold and silver. Then he sang of the child-of-earth. I still remember it. He had a prayer about how Child-of-Earth and Centipede started on their crawling, how they stopped many other things, and of a fight with the lizard. But it was told that Lizard won. He always sang about the highest, thinnest clouds. He said they were the manes of horses. He talked about the colors on the child-of-earth. The colors of its back were the colors of the horses. The sky represented the blue horse. He knew Horse too. He knew it in a different way, with Centipede and this other insect, Child-of-Earth. The rays of the sun were ropes to rope the horses with. He could rope the wildest horse with it. He would say, "I'll go to White Mountain and catch any horse you point out in a bunch." And he could do it.

One time we were going along. He stopped and looked in the distance. He said, "I'll show you I speak the truth; you'll see when we get there. I see a head of a deer behind that dead log. It's chewing its cud."

I had field glasses. I looked through the field glasses. The deer were there, four of them. I told him, "I've got more power than you have. I see four." But I never could have seen them if he hadn't said they were there.

Child-of-Earth is not used alone. Old Felix carried the body of it and used it against bites of the tarantula and insects. And he even used it against the vinegar-roon. He mixed it up in herbs to put on the bites. He carried a looking-glass around with him all the time.

Conflict and Doubt

I had trouble with Bronco once. Bronco and his father-in-law, Swinging-Lance, were drunk and fighting it out.[70] My father and mother were there, my brothers too. Then Tom came in. Bronco had a gun and held them all prisoners in the house. I heard three shots and women crying. I came over to see what was the matter. Bronco had hit his mother-in-law with a stick and just about scalped her.

[70] The son-in-law is supposed to obey and respect his father-in-law and has to use a special third-person form of the verb in speaking to him. In ordinary life it is very difficult for a son-in-law to voice any complaints or give expression to any grievances about his father-in-law. But when inhibitions are relaxed, as in this case, pent-up antagonisms may come to the surface.

I had a sling.[71] I kept coming for him slowly. He was backing up. Pretty soon he backed into a hole and lost his balance. That was what I was waiting for. I was on him before he knew it. I dragged him over to a puddle and soaked his head in it good. I had him by the throat and held him under till he was still. I said to them, "That man drowned himself."

[71] The Mescalero were very skillful in the use of the sling. The sling was not only used by boys in play but served in hunting small mammals and in fighting, as well. The Mescalero sling is a diamond-shaped piece of rawhide, perforated down the center so that it will fold over on itself to hold the missile securely. It is carried and swung by two end straps, one of them looped, the other not. When the sling is swung around the head and slung forward, the unlooped strap is released and the stone is propelled ahead for a considerable distance with much force.

They all started to cry. "You killed him!" While I was choking him they tried to pull me off.[72]

[72] Note that, despite the reprehensible behavior of the son-in-law, his wife and relatives-in-law rally to his side as soon as he is in danger.

Later he came to and shot at my camp. I went back. They wouldn't let me touch him. I slapped his face good for him though.

The next day he came over. He was trying to make up. I paid no attention to him. After a while he said, "You nearly killed me yesterday."

"Yes, and if I did, I'd be glad. I would make a big fire and do a Mountain Spirit dance all night."[73]

[73] The narrator is here referring to the air of celebration with which the Mountain Spirit or masked dancer performance is carried on at the girl's puberty rite.

Then he apologized. He told me he was drunk and didn't know what he was doing. He asked me to go hunting with him. I went, and he killed a big deer for me.

When he hurt his mother-in-law, she came over to our place, and my people sewed it up for her.

Once Bronco had tuberculosis and was very sick. Tom's mother sang for him. Her ceremony was for four nights. She used no drum. She sang and prayed. She sang of a beautiful home in each of the four directions. It was the home of the plant called "slim medicine." In her ceremony, if a patient was very sick, she did not give him "slim medicine" right away but some other things first. She used "slim medicine" in this ceremony; it was her power. She got some ready for him to drink and she told him that the medicine was going right to his lungs.

I was there and thought to myself, "How can it go to his lungs? When he drinks it, it will go to his stomach."[74]

[74] This is an indication of the fund of practical knowledge which the narrator has and of his naturalistic bent, aspects of his training and personality which have made it difficult for him to enter into the Mescalero ceremonial round in the fullest sense.

She knew what I was thinking. She turned to me and said, "I know what you are thinking. But will you believe me when I tell you that if you believe in this plant in the right way, power is strong enough to make the medicine go to the lungs and cure this poor man?" And she did cure him too.

The White Man's Nemesis

There is one man here who is a powerful charmer. He can be a friend to white men any time he wants and get a job any time he wants. He can show you the image in a mirror of the woman you desire. He did it with one fellow. This man is Kenneth Swinging-Lance, nephew of old Swinging-Lance. Right now he's going with a white school teacher. She wants to marry him, but he says he's too old.[75] I don't know how many women he's had. The young fellows all hate him. He gets mad when I talk of his ceremony and kid him about it now, but I remind him of how he used to tease me when I was young. He knows several things. He learned his crow ceremony from Old Man Nogal.

[75] Mescalero girls are supposed to be extremely diffident in their relations with men. Any forwardness by a woman toward a man is assumed to mean that she has a romantic interest in him. Thus the innocent but open friendliness of a white woman toward an Apache man is likely to be misconstrued. To judge from what the writer observed of this relationship, it is very unlikely that the woman in question had a romantic interest in this man.

I have seen him do many wonderful things. Once he said, "You don't believe in me. Now I want someone to go over to that woodpile." Someone started for it, but every time he'd go for it, the rattling of a snake was heard.[76] No one could get near it. No one dared. Once there was a big white horse on White Mountain that no one could get near. This man went and had no trouble at all getting it. It was just as gentle as the gentlest saddle horse for him. He can charm anything. He sometimes works with a mirror. He worked on Tom this way. In the mirror he showed the faces of witches. If their faces were down, they were the strong ones.

[76] The rattlesnake is one of the creatures most feared by the Mescalero. Its supernatural power and the sickness associated with it are dreaded as much as its bite.

He got his ceremony from a Ute.[77] While he was away at school he went off one summer to visit a Ute boy who was his friend at school. He used peyote and took some with him. He heard that the Ute had ceremonies that he didn't know, so he asked his friend to take him around to the old men. He was more interested in power than in school. He wanted to know all about the plants and asked about them. Some of the plants used by the Ute people were the same as those used by the Mescalero, some were different. Some plants tasted funny and some were very strong. He tried to find out about their uses as medicine.

[77] Ceremonies performed by visitors from other tribes or ceremonies obtained from different tribes have a particular aura. The fact that they involve language and elements that are not entirely familiar makes it possible for exaggerated claims to be made on their behalf and to be accepted.

Purposely he cut his hand and rubbed it with a plant that would make him sick. Then he went to a healer. This man tried some kind of herb that hurt and burned. He washed this off with another kind. Kenneth learned that these were plants that are found in this part of the country. His hands were swollen, and they were using juniper pitch, boiled and distilled. He thought it was turpentine. It soothed. They used wool instead of cotton to wrap the wound. He said that some of that medicine made it hurt and some made it feel good. This last one he liked best and later used it for wounds, bites, and wire cuts.

While he was there, a real old Ute offered to teach him the ceremony. He paid for it and learned it. He learned it through Peyote. When he came back, everyone was his friend.

When he first came back to the reservation he stayed with me at the dormitory. I didn't know him well at all then. After he was there a few days, he borrowed money from me. He said he wanted to get married and needed a new suit of clothes and other things. I gave him the money. He said, "Some day I'll help you." I asked what he meant. He said that he could help me get married within a week if I ever wanted to.

He never paid the money back. So one time I decided to go and stay with him. I came to his place. "I've come to stay with you for a long time. Now it's your turn to take care of me."

He said, "All right, come and stay with us."

He was pretty good to me. He gave me two horses. His wife didn't like that. She said, "Why do you give those horses away? We need them."

He answered, "This man is my friend."

Then she said that I was trying to charm her. She said, "You give our things to that man and all he is here for is to charm me!"

The pine grosbeak is what Kenneth uses in his charming ceremony. This bird is a charmer. When he's flying, other birds, like the pine siskin, the Rocky Mountain bluebird, or the bluebird, fly with him. They go around with this bird because he always wants company.

Kenneth has used that bird to make friends against the biggest white men, like Fall or the superintendent.[78] All the employees like him. I saw him fired out of his job and he came back and held it again in less than three or four days because he knew this bird. It was on the fourth of July that he lost his job as policeman. He knew they were working to get me in there. I did not want the job because I was doing something else. I was a special policeman there for a few days, but I handed back the badge. He used his power to influence the agent and got the job back in a little while. He gets positions any time he wants them. He always carries something from this bird.

[78] Albert B. Fall, Secretary of the Interior during the administration of President Warren Harding, is the man to whom reference is made. He owned land adjoining the Mescalero reservation and was constantly suspected by the Mescalero of plotting to add to it at the expense of the Indians. Another persistent rumor which greatly alarmed the Indians was that he intended to turn the reservation or a part of it into a national park. Note the element of sympathetic magic in the choice of a bird whose power will aid in making friends.

Everyone likes him. When there was a little trouble between the Indians and the outsiders, he worked to bring about friendship between them. They sent one family into the reservation to keep peace, and one family from the reservation was sent out to live among the outsiders. Then there was peace. Those who had formerly been enemies and were now friends looked up to him. He foretold hard times, mostly outside the reservation, but said the people would be helped by the President.[79]

[79] The depression and the New Deal, with its aid and development programs for the Indians, are the events allegedly foretold.

An Apache is very careful about hitting anything with the back of the hand. It means getting rid of the thing, selling it, or giving it away. If you are selling or giving away a horse, you slap it with the back of the hand before it goes.

When I was living with them for a while, I saw Kenneth Swinging-Lance get rid of his wife this way. They couldn't get along. I saw them in many fights and watched close, but he never used the back of his hand till this one time. This time they had an awful fight. He started to walk off. She picked up a rock and threw it at him. It brought him down, hit him on the leg. He got up and said, "I've tried in every way to get along with you but it's no use." He walked up to her and hit her four times with the back of his hand. "'Now you can go."

In a little while that woman got sick, and in twelve days she was dead. They had a ceremony for her while she was sick, and Kenneth was there. She said, "I don't want that man around. He told me he didn't want me, and now I'm going. I don't want him to act sorry." Kenneth just had his head down; he didn't say a thing.

Not long ago a group of people were together. Kenneth was there. One man told stories like this. He didn't mention names, but Kenneth knew what he meant. After a while he got up. "You mean only me," he said, "and some day we're going to have it out."

Power Learned from the Ute Used in Curing

Kenneth Swinging-Lance has also used his power to help many who are hurt or sick. One man was bitten by a rattlesnake. The doctor said he couldn't live. Kenneth treated the bite with something that was poison, washed that off, used something else, and then used the pitch. The man lived. The doctor asked who had healed him. But he told nothing, he just said the bite had healed itself.

Another of Kenneth's patients was a schoolboy who came home sick with tuberculosis. One lung was all gone, the other was very bad. Kenneth sang for him, and finally we caught on that he was singing about a plant. He used peyote and some kind of pollen. The next year the boy was well enough to enter school again. The doctor examined him and found he was all right, but he had just one lung. The doctor asked all about who had cured him and how. Then the doctor went to Kenneth and asked about the herbs that had been used. Everything was shown him, but he didn't recognize the herbs. He tried it out on himself. He boiled the plants, drank the medicine, and saw that it wasn't poison. He had it distilled, he used it in grease, he let it settle in water. He said it was strongest distilled, a little weaker when it settled in the water, and weakest when it was boiled. He thought he had something good. He tried it on white people. Sometimes it worked and some-times not. But he said it would cure an early case of tuberculosis. The doctor also used this medicine for the boys here and for his own people when they had colds.[80]

[80] Whether the doctor's interest in Mescalero medicine is being misinterpreted or exaggerated is hard to say. Some reservation doctors of the period were not greatly superior in technique to Apache practitioners and were almost as credulous.

Swinging-Lance was now using both Mescalero and Ute ceremonies and power. Everyone understood the peyote part—that is the same for Mescalero and Ute— but many people tried to find out what songs he was singing, for they were in the Ute language and sounded like dance songs. But he just let people wonder and went on healing the sick. He said that many times when he was using peyote in the Ute way, he could see the Ute people up there in their country, and he could talk to them through peyote. The Ute who taught this man is now dead, and he has all the power the Ute once used.

One time I was cutting wheat with a sickle and putting the wheat in my left arm in a bundle. I was doing that and talking to Tom back there. I looked back at him and then turned my head around quick again, and one of those wheat stalks that was broken off stuck right in my eye, right in the black circle next to the white part. It broke off and the splinter stuck in there. I thought I was blind for life all right. I just ached from the top of my head to my little toe. I knew something was still in that eye; I could feel it scratch on my eyelid.

Well, I went to the doctor, and he took me to El Paso to an eye specialist. The doctor put something in my eye to hold the lids open and then he looked at it. He said, "It's a wonder your eye didn't burst. I'm afraid to pull that splinter out."

I said, "All right, let it go. If you're afraid to pull it out I don't want you to." I knew Kenneth could get that out without pulling or anything like that.

So I came back here and went to him. He just worked around it for a while. I don't know what he did. Then he said, "Here's your splinter." And there it was, lying in front of me. My eye got all right again after that.

Another time Edwin Bird's wife was cutting meat. She looked around and went on cutting. She cut her hand where that big vein is on the back. The blood just spurted out. They got Kenneth. The doctor was there too. Kenneth said, "This is how I stop that blood." And he just rubbed around it a little. I don't know what else he did. But it stopped bleeding right away.

Then one time Don Nitsigane was chopping wood. He was holding the piece of wood with his foot. He brought that axe down and hit his ankle. It made a big deep gash, and the blood just came out all around him. They thought sure he was going to die.

Kenneth said, "He won't die. He's got plenty of blood yet." Kenneth put pollen on it and worked around that leg. I never saw him use pollen any other time. It stopped bleeding. He said, "Now don't go to the doctor for two days."

After two days the boy went to the doctor. The doctor began washing that cut and washing that pollen all out. Then it began to bleed again as bad as ever. The doctor sent for Kenneth. He said, "Run, get Kenneth Swinging-Lance. This man is going to die for sure in a little while."

They ran to the store and got Kenneth. He came and worked on it again. And he got it stopped again. The doctor and the nurses couldn't understand it. They said he must use magic. That man got well. He isn't even lame now.

The Hunt

It happened in snow time, in November when the deer were fat. Diego, Mrs. Diego, Juan Tomas, and his family were present. I was there. Diego called me. I said, "I've been hunting day after day. I've seen hundreds of tracks, but I haven't seen a deer yet."

"You're as bad as I am," he said, "I've been trying and I haven't killed a deer yet."

This happened at Nogal, right at the place they call Ice Cave at Dripping Springs. Diego said he would make it easier for us to find the deer. We were having a little party, drinking corn beer. Our corn beer is not as bad as regular beer anyway, and we were all drinking.[81]

[81] The corn beer used by the Mescalero is called "tiswin" or "tesvino" by the Americans and Mexicans and "grey water" by the Mescalero. To make it, corn kernels are dampened and allowed to sprout. Next they are ground and placed in water. The water is then boiled and allowed to stand. At a certain point in the fermentation process the beer is ready. It is a rather weak beer but is drunk in large quantities. The Mescalero claim that it is nourishing and that it purifies the body.

Diego said then, "We'll have a big snow, and then it'll be easy to see the deer. It will rain right now and then after you all go to bed there will be snow on top of it." And he sang his song. Swinging-Lance sang too. He sang of the summer.[82] Diego sang of the cloud and the thunder. He beat his drum, and you could hear thunder in it. He was that kind of a shaman. You could see sparks of lightning on top of his drum too. That's the way it seemed to me.

[82] Summer is often thought of in a personified sense, and a person who knows the songs and ceremony of Summer can control the weather and make the wild harvests and game animals abundant. Cf. 1 [70].

They got together and sang, and it was raining in no time. This was not a real ceremony, he said, but just a little performance of power. But it was plenty, because there were two of them singing for one thing.

"If it is needed, I can make it big," he said, "and then you'll see rain and snow, but this is plenty."

We didn't pay much attention to the rain because we were pretty full by this time, some of us.

He said, "Tomorrow we'll go out after deer and see who's the best hunter."
I said, "I want to go."

Diego sang the ceremony of Deer and of the way that he hunted with the power of the wolf. But it was different with Swinging-Lance. He sang of the ceremony of the deer but mentioned the mountain lion to be sure to make a certain kill. And Bronco knew the power of the deer too, but he sang only of the deer; also Juan Tomas sang only about the deer. But I didn't sing of anything. I just listened to these songs, because I didn't know this power. They claim I know lots of things, but I didn't know this. Even my father didn't know the power of the deer.[83]

[83] Yet on another occasion the narrator asserted that he once knew Deer power but surrendered it because he was tempted to try to use it as love magic. See p. 180.

It rained first, and in the morning the snow was about six inches deep. Bronco and I went the same way, south; Swinging-Lance and Juan went towards the sunrise; and Diego went towards the north. And so we were pretty well scattered, far apart and each one out of the range of the others.

Very early, while it was still dark, Bronco left me. He hit for the hills. I kept to the canyon about two miles above him. I climbed on top. I knew just where to look for the deer. Pretty soon I ran into a bunch, about fifteen deer. I shot, and down came a deer, a little buck. I shot a second time, and down came a doe. I shot a third time, and down came a doe. Then a fourth. At every shot, down fell a deer. I killed five bucks that morning and two does. It was quite a load. It took me some time to cut up the deer, but it was before sunrise, and by sunrise I had them all butchered and in small pieces so I could carry them on the horse.

There was hardly any room for me to ride. So I tied a rope around the meat and led the horse. I dropped into the canyon. I got back to camp. There was nobody there yet when I got back.

Then I caught another horse and I said, "I'm going to shoot a big buck this time." I hit for the mountains again. It was getting late and by now the snow was frozen. It had been noon when I got back to camp before, and now I had hunted all afternoon. I was just about to quit when I caught sight of a very fresh track. It had been made just a few minutes ahead of me. So I jumped off and left the horse, took my gun, and started to trail. I walked a little ways to the canyon, and up he jumped, twenty-five yards ahead of me. I didn't try to shoot him while he was climbing the hill. I waited till he was on a flat place. Then I shouldered my gun and shot. I saw him drop. He was a big deer, big antlers on him.

I walked back to the horse instead of going at once to the deer. I then rode as fast as I could to the deer. It was a big fat one with heavy antlers. The sun was already down, and I had to hurry.

When the moon was up, I was done. I loaded my horse as quickly as I could. All I had to do was drop into the canyon, and I was on my way to camp. But it was getting late; my feet were wet; I was wet through, and I felt it. But I sat on my horse and went on anyhow.

Bronco also tried to make a second kill. He had killed a big one that morning.

Swinging-Lance, Juan Tomas, and Diego were still out. That morning they had brought in one deer apiece. And I brought in seven that morning and got eight that day.

Then the policeman came to me and brought me a note that I was to bring fifteen turkeys to the agency. I got them the next few days. I didn't use a shotgun then for turkey. All I used was a .30-.30 rifle. But I was a shot those days! I could always shoot where I could hit it and not hurt the turkey much. When the turkey is standing with head toward me I always shoot just enough to take the guts out of him, or I could hit it in the head or the neck. And I did bring about nineteen turkeys to the school that time, and the school took all of them; the employees didn't have any. I started the next day and killed fifteen more in the next few days. Swinging-Lance killed four, and I took them in, for he never ate turkey at all in those days.[84]

[84] Because turkeys were said to eat snakes, worms, and "nasty things," the older Mescalero were reluctant to use them for food.

That was the hunt. That showed that the power of Diego was just as strong as that of Natsili.

Shorty, an old Mescalero, also performed a ceremony for us when we were going hunting. He spoke of the white-breasted nuthatch as being pretty strong and he used this bird in his ceremony for luck with deer. Then he told us that the next day would be the lucky day to get the biggest deer. He sang and said a prayer too. The ceremony ended in a little while. In the morning we all had high hopes of killing deer. We sure worked hard! Shorty, Tom, Cloud, Kenneth Swinging-Lance, George Kos, and I were in the bunch. Cloud got two deer, and Shorty, George, and I had one each. We were loaded on our way back.

Temptation

A man who knows Deer can be a real woman charmer. But if he uses the power of Deer for this, he has not a darn thing but his gee string; that's what they say. He will get horses, and the next day they'll be bony. They say that's how you can tell he has power from Deer. He can get deer with this power, but if he uses his power to get the women, he loses power to get deer.[85]

[85] The deer ceremony is linked ideologically with love magic because in both cases an attempt is being made to bring a resisting or fleeing being under control. In fact, as indicated here, the deer ceremony can be used as a love ceremony; but in that case it will not again be effective for hunting game, and the shaman, though lucky in love and even seemingly fortunate in the hunt, will always be poor. See 1 [104].

Old Juan was very strong with power from Deer. One day he was down at the hoop and pole grounds. All the best hunters were there. He had an argument with one of the men who said he was the best hunter. "All right," Old Juan said, "can you go out just a little way and get a deer at once as I can?"

Nobody believed he could do it. He told them to put something up and he would do it. They put up two horses, a saddle, and a gun. Then he said it was enough. "Tie these horses over there for me, and build a fire for the deer meat," he told them.

Then he rode a little way out near an arroyo. They could all see him. He got off his horse and motioned around with his gun as if he was hunting. He was using his power. All of a sudden he shot. No one thought he was really shooting at a deer. He went down the arroyo and came up with a two-point buck.

Old Juan's Apache name means "Bringing in Horses." He was known for his influence over the women. George Kos's mother-in-law thought she was pretty strong. She told him, "You can't make me come to you."

He got pretty mad. He told her, "You are going to beg me to do it. You will beg before a big crowd."

And she did. Two weeks later they were at a party drinking corn beer. After she got a little drink in her, she asked him right before the whole crowd. He went with her and had plenty. He was stronger than all of them. He was always poor too; he went from woman to woman.

He used the lazuli bunting with the deer for charming. When you use one of them for charming and the woman is stronger, put both together and you're sure to get her. She'll just come by herself. Old Juan had about forty women. White girls used to chase him. He used it on white men too. It makes a man your best friend, the best you ever had. But Deer and this bird are a bad combination; your pecker is getting plenty, but it is not good for stock. A man who has this is poor always.

Old Juan showed me Deer power but in a different way. It was just for luck, so I knew where to find the deer. I had it for a while, but I gave it up. It didn't take me long to learn the songs. When the power likes you, the songs just come to you in no time. It was that way with me. I'd sing before I went hunting, and I'd be talking to the power in my mind when I was out hunting. I had it for a number of years, and it worked very well; but I gave it up and I'll tell you why.

This power from Deer could be used to charm women. I was a young man then. It was before I was married, and this power kept tempting me. I'd see a young woman over there that I wanted and another over there. I nearly got in trouble with it. You see these women, and you want them, and you feel as if you've got to have them. They belong to somebody else, and it's a temptation when you know you could make them come to you. So I made up my mind to give up the Deer power.[86]

[86] This is an excellent example of an instance in which desire and weakness are attributed to temptations offered by supernatural power and an attempt is made to reduce tension by relinquishing supernatural power. Cf. 3 [24].

Deer power came to me. "I hear you're going to turn me loose."

"Yes, I'm not going to use you any more."

"Going home," was all that power said, and he left me. I never tried to use it again. About a year after that I got married.

Now I've got power for hunting in the white man's way. Do you know it? A white hunter showed it to me. It's not anything I carry. It's some words I say, and it works just as well. I've not had this for long. But after I had given up Deer power and even before I had learned the white man's way, I had just as good luck with deer. It didn't seem to make much difference.[87]

[87] The narrator's experimental attitude toward many things and his willingness to make matter-of-fact comparisons in regard to subjects involving belief—attributes that are incompatible with complete faith—are here in evidence.

A certain man wanted to know what my power is. I told him I didn't have any. He said, "You have it in your hands. You are strong. Nothing can work against you." He was thinking of the way I can catch animals with my hands, I guess. I told him, "I don't know what you mean." I know many songs and prayers and movements, but I have no power.[88]

[88] The narrator again goes out of his way to assert that, in spite of his interest in ceremonial matters and contrary to the opinion of a good many of his fellow tribesmen, he does not possess supernatural power.

Old Jicarilla

They have a belief about the horned toad. It has to be a small one. It is caught. Then anyone, man, woman, or child, can rub it in the palms of both hands and after that he or she will be a good hand at anything—painting, beadwork, arrow-making, anything. It is still going on. I see children walking around looking for the little horned toad.

Once I put a big horned toad in my shirt. I asked the children what they were doing. "We are looking for a little horned toad." "Why?" "We want to be good workers, good at everything."

"Here's a little one." I took out the big toad, and they ran away. "You're a witch! You're a witch!" they hollered at me.[89] They wouldn't let me come near them. It sure made me laugh.

[89] In spite of the provocation, it is doubtful that the children would have called the narrator a witch unless they had heard their elders talk about him in this vein.

The old people say the horned toad is poison and a great witch. They won't touch it. But it is used in many ways. Jicarilla used it. He was the man who performed the girl's adolescence ceremony and he knew it with other things. He knew Water, the girl's rite, and Horned Toad.

He had a funny idea about the Indian ways, but it may be the Jicarilla Apache way. Max and Jicarilla had a discussion about where the Indians came from. Max said that the Mescalero were always here. Jicarilla said that all Indians came from a hole in the ground.[90]

90 As his name suggests, Jicarilla was part Jicarilla Apache Indian. It will be
remembered that the Jicarilla and Mescalero were stationed together from
1883 to 1887. The Jicarilla origin story is a myth of emergence, and according
to Jicarilla Apache belief mankind was created in an underworld. See Opler
1938c: 1–10.

Jicarilla knew the horned toad pretty well. He knew it in the way of sucking out
disease or witch weapons. He used pollen like the rest, but he had a turquoise tied
to the middle finger of the right hand, and on his left hand he had abalone tied
with a buckskin. It was on the inside of his finger. I never saw a Mescalero do this.[91]
I noticed these when he was holding his ceremony for Mary Nastane, for I used to
stay with them sometimes. My mother was there all the time. She was related to
them.

91 Actually these objects appear in Mescalero ceremonies frequently, too.

Mary had taken sick somehow one time. This happened where the Catholic
church is now. We were camped there. He stayed there with us during the ceremony. He went at it in a different way. He marked her as in the girl's adolescence
rite, across the nose, and he put pollen on her head and a cross of pollen on her
back and then one on her breast last. Then he took abalone and held it with his
right hand. He looked for the cause of her illness. "I can get you well if you mind
what I tell you in these four ceremonies I'm going to perform for you."
The first day it didn't last long. He prayed and then sang. His motions were
very funny. He blew himself up like that horned toad does, and he raised up his
knees. He went to Mary's head, sucked, and blew it away. Then everybody spit.[92]

92 The spitting is a ritual purification and a symbolic way of ridding the body of
evil.

The second night he came in the same way, and then he put pollen at the
door.[93] He walked around the fire and stopped. He marked himself. He got up
later and marked Mary, from her left shoulder to her back, and from her right
shoulder to her back, and then the breast. He walked around towards her and began
to raise her hair from the back. He sucked and spit. He prayed and sang, and then
it was all over for the second night.

93 The pollen was put at the door as a barrier against evil.

The third night was different. He tied the abalone on her forehead. He moved
his right hand before her face, palm up, with the turquoise before her. He prayed.
He said, "My water movement says it's all right. Tomorrow afternoon I'll finish
it."[94] This time he sucked above the ear on the left side.

94 The "water movement" to which Jicarilla refers is a feeling that water is lying
in the palm of his hand and moving in various directions. Its movements have
particular meanings for him.

The first three ceremonies were at night, the last in the afternoon. This fourth time he had white clay. He put it on his hands and face and marked her with it across the nose. He put it on top of her head too. He marked everybody there. He told me to move back of him and learn it. He took the turquoise from his own finger and put it on me. I tried as hard as I could, for I thought it might mean some good for me. I sat through the last ceremony. He prayed and moved his hand before her.

He said, "I'll pray, sing, and suck the last out." He did this. Then he said, "It is all right." Then he sang of the dream she was to dream that night. He tried to finish before sundown. He sucked from the top where the abalone was fastened. He spit it out. We all spit, and the ceremony was over.

Jicarilla went back to his camp that evening after curing Mary Nastane. The next day he went down to Max's. His boy was a brother-in-law to Max. He stayed down there for quite a good while, and there Julio practiced the songs of the girl's adolescence rite with him and learned them from him. Jicarilla had a way of learning when his life was not in danger. But this time it didn't show. His time was short, it meant. So he taught Julio all the ceremony.

Faith and the Wager

Marsh Hawk was another thing known by Old Elk. At horse races, to get the winning horse, he used its power with the power of Swift Fox.

Tcikito's horse had won many races and Ishbai's too. They matched them; they wanted to see whose was fastest. Elk spoiled it. He made Ishbai's horse win. He was paid for it. It nearly made trouble among those placing side bets, for they found out what he had done. He stood right in the track and made his ceremony. They knew that Tcikito's horse was the fastest.

Old Elk had asked me to ride Ishbai's horse. I did. He took my horse, saddle, gun, everything, and bet it on this horse. I didn't know it. I was to be paid twenty dollars. I didn't think the horse was going to win. I led the horse back after the race and found I'd won a sorrel horse.

I said to Old Elk, "Suppose I had lost?"

He said, "There's no losing while I'm here."

There was a race between Boneska's horse and another, and Old Elk did the same thing.

Family and Strife

In 1907 I got involved in a mix-up. Jake Bead and Leggings got in a quarrel at the hoop and pole grounds. It was at Pajarito, and many of them were drinking. I was sitting at my sister's camp. Someone came running in to me and said, "Your cousin is being killed!"

Tom had got in the quarrel and sided with Leggings. I ran out. Bead was coming for Tom. Leggings, who was on Tom's side, was coming up with a gun. He shot twice at Bead. I came with my gun. I aimed right at Jake Bead and pulled.[95] Something went wrong with the gun. I tore my hand on the sharp point of the hammer. Juan Tomas and Besh both yelled at Jake Bead and told him to run. Before I could fix the gun, Jake Bead had run off.

[95] This account indicates how family solidarity operates in family feuds and serves to perpetuate them. We learn that the narrator rushed to the defense of his cousin and narrowly avoided committing a homicide, even though he had no idea of the origin of the dispute or the part his cousin had played in it.

Bead and members of his family have been involved in violence a number of times. Bead was convicted of killing Running Water and another Mescalero in a quarrel over a card game and served time in the penitentiary for this. Many Mescalero believe that he killed his wife in the course of a quarrel, though officially the death was labeled accidental. His twenty-four-year-old son was slain by an older man, with whom he had been living, in a quarrel over a woman. When the writer knew Bead, he was quite old and much subdued.

My hand was badly torn, and they poured whiskey on it.

Father's Ceremonial Power

The bear is told of in many different ways, and its power is used in many different ways. It isn't the most important animal, though many are afraid to touch it or its tracks, and even if they only see mud on a tree and think it's a bear sign they won't go close to it or touch it. They won't take a chance of getting in any place where a bear may have been. I was watching five bears in the rain the other day. Most Mescalero wouldn't even pass if the wind blew from that way.

Raymond Belt asked me to sing a bear song once. He thought he was going to catch it with his Robin power, for a man who knows Robin can catch a song in no time and has a real voice. It was a cold night. The wind was blowing. I said it might shake the house. But he wanted to hear me so I started to sing. The house began to shake. He motioned to me, "Quit, my friend, quit!" He thought I did it. I laughed and laughed.[96]

[96] The narrator is amused at the readiness with which people are willing to believe he has supernatural power, particularly supernatural power from Bear.

At peyote meetings they have a bear song and in many other ceremonies. Bear has a girl's puberty ceremony song and a moccasin game song and many songs in other ceremonies besides bear ceremonies.

When the Mescalero are in the mountains and see his tracks they say, "Uncle has been here." But those who know him speak right out and say, "Bear is here."[97]

[97] Since relatives are expected to be helpful and kind to one another, dangerous animals and powerful forces are referred to by kinship terms by those who fear them or who seek to mollify them. Thus lightning and thunder are usually called "grandfather," and bears are addressed as "uncle" in order to prevent them from doing harm.

His ceremony is very interesting. He's good if he is used right. In his ceremony, everything is done through him and nothing else. In the mountain lion ceremony and some others, he is mentioned in the songs.

My father knew the bear well. He carried its power from the time when he was young till he was very old. To his last days he used it. I remember well how it was done; I've seen how it worked. He was using it during the time I was a policeman at the agency.

Whatever sign Bear gives, it comes true. If Bear said, "There is going to be a sandstorm tomorrow at a certain time," it would happen. And if it said that some kind of storm that had never happened before was going to come, such a storm would come. I saw these things, so I know it well. What it had said about the next day or the future, I saw happen. Bear never asked for anything, but he wanted his ceremony done in the right way.

In the old days those who knew Bear used to go around in the form of a bear. But since the white man has come they don't do it, for they are afraid of the gun.[98] The last time this happened was when one man who knew the ceremonies of the mountain lion and other animals came in the form of a bear, wolf, mountain lion, and horse at different times. He was the one who took Mrs. Jacinto captive. He knew all those animals and many other things besides. When he came to the end of his life they all deserted him. Then he knew his time was getting very short.

[98] The belief that a strong shaman can assume animal form, especially the form of the animal which is his power source, is accepted by some, but not by all, Mescalero.

My father said, "I could be like a bear if I wanted to, but that's not my way now." But he knew the bear, and he knew how to heal with the bear, how to hold a bear ceremony to control weather, how to tell things of the future and the hunt through it, and how to use it against the white man and against witches and evil things. He was very careful. He used it at peyote meetings but only with decent people, only with the best-known people who wouldn't take things away from others but who would work together and think together instead of trying to make someone blind or sick as they do nowadays. I've seen my father work in Three Rivers, Rinconada, Turkey Canyon, Elk Springs, and all over here. Also the Kiowa, the Comanche, the Navaho, and the Pima knew him. Even some Pueblos knew him.

They held a ceremony once for a man named Hiding. My father said, after looking him over, that Hiding knew many things but because he did not know enough, a small power ran against him and ran over him. He came near dying and would have if it hadn't been for my father who worked for him for four nights. Hiding had got sick from his own kind of supernatural power too. He thought he was strong, but he didn't have much power at all. That's what my father showed him.[99] Since then he doesn't show off any more.

[99] When a person who has a reputation as a powerful shaman becomes sick and has to hire another ceremonialist, it is a good opportunity for the second ritualist to demonstrate the superiority of his power over the supernatural helper of the sufferer.

When these things were told to Hiding, he begged my father to show him the ceremony of the bear plainly. My father said, "The bear is an awful thing to learn. If you know anything that is wrong, the bear will be after you and is likely to pull you to pieces. If you want to know Bear, it's best to put the other things away and just know the bear by itself. That's the best way."

My father said he could do anything with the bear. He said he would take any-body on who didn't believe him. And he took a horse and a saddle and a gun and led the horse out, and he showed a few of his own people what he could do. The horse was standing there with the saddle on. He went off and he turned his back and told them to turn their faces away. And there where the horse had been was a bear. They turned around again, got scared, and tried to run. He told them to turn and look again, and there was the horse again. He told them he could bring a bear from a certain spring, from the bottom. "If anybody doesn't believe me, I'll prove it." He wet a stone with his saliva four times. "Anyone who doesn't believe me can take this stone and throw it in there, and if a bear doesn't show himself, you can have your way." He was not taken up on it.

Long afterwards, Diego, Turquoise, Swinging-Lance, Bronco, Juan Tomas, and my father were all together. They were drinking wine, and my father had taken just a little too much. He spoke to Diego, and Diego took him on. Diego said he'd bet a can of corn beer it wouldn't work.

My mother told him not to do it, but he had had a little too much and wouldn't listen. He told Diego, "You are a pretty wise man. You think you know everything. Now stand over there and don't run."

Diego was drunk too. He went over there and stood. The others just looked on. My father asked Diego whether he was ready. Diego was praying. He said he was finished. My father gave him the stone. "Throw it in any direction you want."

He threw it towards the sunrise. There appeared a big dun bear there, bigger than Diego. I saw it. I was not drunk. Tom was not drunk, and he saw it.[100] Diego jumped. He was a speedy man, faster than a horse. He started to run. My father laughed. He said something and the bear disappeared. Diego looked back and it was gone.

[100] In spite of his denial, the narrator and Tom may very well have had enough to drink to kindle their imaginations and to heighten suggestibility.

A white man owned a place at Bent before it was called that. The adobe building was his store. Some Indians were there and they were very full. Diego and my father were both there. My father offered to bring a bear, and Diego offered to show what he could do too. The storekeeper looked at my father. "No bear for me," he said. He took on Diego. He gave Diego a feather and promised him four bottles of whiskey and eight dollars if he would make the feather disappear. Diego put it right down his throat and it disappeared. He pulled it out of the lower part of his shirt then.

Diego and my father talked. They said, "Let's not drink much. This fellow might get us drunk and killing each other." They took only one drink apiece there.

The white man broke a knife in small pieces and gave it to Diego. "You put that together." Diego said a few things. The knife pieces began to go together until the knife was whole. Diego pounded it. "You can't break it," he said.

The storekeeper yelled, "Get out of here! You're a devil! I don't want you around."

Both Diego and my father laughed and walked out.

Swinging-Lance was out riding in the hills when a meeting of the bear and the mountain lion took place before him. I was hunting with him. We were to meet at a certain place. He didn't show up. I tied the horse there and went out. He was not there when I got back. I killed two deer and butchered them, but he had not come yet.

Swinging-Lance had seen a very interesting sight; that's why he was late. A bear was coming through the quaking aspen, going south. The mountain lion was on the side of the hill trying to cross the canyon. They found each other out. They growled. They came towards each other till they were less than twenty feet apart and sat there. The mountain lion jumped at the bear. The bear fell over, and the mountain lion missed the bear. The bear tried to get up, but the mountain lion was quick and sat on his head.

The bear knocked him off with his paw, then grabbed him with one paw and threw him down. He tore the skin on the shoulder of the mountain lion, and it couldn't use that shoulder. The mountain lion ripped at the bear, and the bear ripped at him too. The fur flew and the blows poured out. The guts began to come out of both, but still they fought. The mountain lion finally fell over. But the bear kept at him, slapping him this way and that. He bit him on the neck and threw him around like a small thing. Then the bear began to walk off, wobbling. He'd go a little distance and lean against a tree. He walked about a hundred feet and he fell over too.

Swinging-Lance went over. He found that both were dead and he went to look for me. At the appointed place he found my horse with the meat piled up. I was out in another direction hunting. I came in just as he was coming up to my horse. He took one deer and I took the other, and we rode up to where the bear was. It was stone dead and so was the mountain lion.

We rode into camp and told the story. My father, Diego, and several others started out there. When we arrived at the place, the bear and the mountain lion were still there.

My father jumped off and cut the bear open and took the gall from the bear. He also took it from the mountain lion. And he took the paws of each. They went back. I didn't know he was going to take these galls, but it was shown that he had use for them in some way. I did not know how he used the galls, because it was the early part of my days.

He would hold a ceremony for the sick for four nights. That's as long as he would do it. He cured many different diseases through the bear. He used it on a case of pneumonia. It was right out in the hills. It was the worst case of pneumonia I ever saw. The girl had hemorrhages with it. I thought she was going to die. This was a schoolgirl, nineteen years old then. Jim Cholla and his sister are related to her.

The ceremony was through the bear, and it was found out what was to be done. A mixture of different kinds of herbs was given right at the beginning. That was to stop the hemorrhages right away. They got the strongest herb first. That was pointed out by the bear. My mother went and got it, and that night it was given in four doses to the girl.[101] It was given in pollen and lifted to her head four times and to her mouth four times, and the side of the cup from which she was to drink was marked, and then she drank it. My mother mixed the second dose and was ready for the hemorrhage. They thought it would stop at the second dose. They gave it to her with four motions again.

[101] Note the manner in which herbalism is woven into the ceremony.

The next thing was to get after the pneumonia. She was strong yet. The hemorrhage was stopped. My father took the right front paw of this bear and warmed it and put it on her chest where the pain was going through. He took a bowl and put it to her chest. Blood and pus and suds came out and were rising up. He did that four times. They had good medicine for pneumonia. It was the plant called blazing star.[102] It was ground fine, mixed with grease and water, and then they rubbed her with it and wrapped her up.

[102] The botanical name for blazing star is "Liatris punctata."

The first night they had given her four doses of the hemorrhage medicine and had sucked out the pneumonia. They tried to make the ceremony short because she was weak. The second night it went the same way. My father sang two songs. He marked her. He put pollen on the bear's paw before he used it. The pus was sucked out the second night by my father too. It just came out by itself. Diego was there and he saw it and he thought it was a wonderful thing.

My father waited two days, but my mother kept up the herb medicine. Then my father found that the girl was gaining and was getting well. "No use to suck. Let me look at her," he said. He said he thought it was all right. He told them, "I don't think it's necessary to suck again." There was just a little pus left. He asked the bear. The bear said he'd better take it out because that little bit might get bigger. So he marked her and put pollen in her mouth as before and sucked it out.

The girl said she could breathe much better. She said she wanted to get well quicker. She surely prayed all through that ceremony. That's why she got well so quickly.

The fourth night, there was a short ceremony. That girl was getting along nicely now. They just gave her the medicine.

The last night of the ceremony we got news that Besh was dead, shot through the heart. They mention two men who may have done it; it was one of those two. Tom's mother came over to tell us. Charlie Three-Fingers, Juan Tomas, and Raymond Belt were all present when Besh was killed. When he was hit he said, "Someone shot at us!" and he threw out his arms, hitting Raymond, and went over. It made Raymond's nose bleed. The women of the family thought they knew who did it. All were put in jail, but they turned them loose. This was about 1908.

The girl my father treated lived a long time after that and was married to Bob Eddy. Later she had a child that died while she was still nursing it. She died too. Bob stayed with us for a while. He went to Rockford to work in the beet patches and then to St. Louis, and then to Buffalo, New York, to work in the Ford plant.[103]

[103] This was one of the rare instances during this period when an Apache youth left the reservation for any length of time except to go to school.

I've seen my father treat horses. He used to use ground juniper charcoal mixed with water and salt for an eye medicine for horses. He used this medicine for a horse whose eye was all white.

I never knew how many things my father knew. Of some of his powers he said, "I can't tell you. I'd like you to know it all, but some things I cannot tell. I could take you where I went in the cave, where I got my power, but you might not make it," and he laughed. He knew Horse, Wolf, Lightning, and lots of things. My father never did eat peyote much. He said, "All it is used for is taking power away from other poor fellows."

Law and Order

Two of the first chiefs of police were Boneska and Peso. Peso was chief for a long time. Many others have held that job since then. Old Naiche and my father were policemen but were not chiefs of police. I was a policeman under Tom and another chief. They wanted me to be a policeman lately, but I didn't want to stay around the agency. I'd rather live out where I want to be. I'm only here at the agency when there is sickness. When everything's all right I'm out trapping. They say Tom and Carlos were pretty good. Carlos brought in whites and Mexicans too. In Tom's time they were tough customers, and there was much killing; also in Peso's time. They all did very well. Diego, though, got drunk and deserted the reservation and lived out in the hills with his whole family. They let him alone, and he finally came in and surrendered. He lived out for two or three years.

The police used to drill; they were taught to shoot from a horse. We used to watch them drill. The government furnished guns and ammunition. A lot of them didn't want to join the police force. It all seemed like trouble against their own people and they tried to talk others out of it, but the whites made them come in

Converts to the new Silas John Edwards religion at their Mescalero "church."

anyway. I think everyone who ever served as a policeman was forced to be one. The ones who were police would say to the others, "It's your turn, you've got to be a policeman now."

The police try to keep all behaving the way they should. They go after schoolboys who don't come to school. It's a good thing to have a policeman, but he always makes enemies.

A Song of Foreboding

Peso said that when the Western tanager sings, it means something for the ones who know its power; it always has a meaning about what is going to happen, good or bad. About 1908 they were having a feast. It was the last feast (girl's puberty rite) at Head Springs. During that time several men were sitting around the oak trees at Peso's place, and I was among them. Peso heard a bird singing and he looked up. He watched it and saw it was the Western tanager singing. Everybody knows the bird well, for it has a sweet song, something like a robin's.

Peso said, "My people, I hear a bird that is singing of danger. He is singing so because for the last time the feast is being held here. I hear the bird singing about our tipi chief who knows the songs." Then he turned and saw Old Felix coming. The bird flapped its wings and came back. Peso said, "It is doing this and singing of Felix. He will not be here at the next feast."

I was there and heard every word of it. And Peso told of Silas John too.[104] He said, "There is one man far away at San Carlos. From now on he will be among us, and his songs will be among us, and he will be a religious leader." And that all came true.

[104] Silas John Edwards was a member of the Western Apache tribe and was the originator of a religious cult which sought to reconcile Apache religious beliefs and Christianity. Later he visited the Mescalero reservation and founded a branch of his "church" there.

This was two years before Swinging-Lance died. And he foresaw that too. He said, "Our chiefs are going, and then the hard times will come."[105]

[105] It is interesting that a very general remark such as "Our chiefs are going" is accepted as a prophecy of the death of Swinging-Lance, who died two years later. With such faith and latitude the prophecies of shamans can seldom fail!

When the tanager stopped singing, Peso spoke in prayer to himself. "My brothers and sisters, the best one we ever had, our singer of this rite, will pass away." He was speaking of Old Felix.

He sat down. He called me. He said, "You're a strong man in every way. Why, I don't know. What I have is yours."[106] And he did mean it. He treated me like one of his own children.

[106] This was an invitation to the narrator to take an interest in his ceremonies and learn them.

"This bird that sang there is sent from the sky. It speaks; it can heal; it can do many things. What I've learned of it is not much, but it has done many good things for me. I have picked it up from some of my own people; but the bird did not show me much, and I know very little."[107]

[107] As has been pointed out in other contexts, the power grant obtained from a power source may vary greatly in scope and importance. By the statement, "I have picked it up from some of my own people. . . ," Peso means that he was taught the rite by relatives.

Old Nogal, Kakas, and other old men were there. That night they tried their own ceremonies to find out if what Peso said was true. And two of them said it was. And it was true. The hard times came, and no feast was held again at Head Springs.

Led by a Bird

I told you about a funny man, Iyeho. He always put a pine siskin feather on a brand new hat. When the hat got old, he would take it off and put it on a new one. Once when his hat fell off, I took the pine siskin tail feather from it. I didn't know that he knew this bird. I was looking at it. He came up.

"Where did you get that?" he asked me.

"I found it on the ground." He wanted to see it.

"It came off my hat."

I gave it back. "You must know some power from this bird."

"Yes, I learned it from some of my people when I was in the south," he said. "There were many times when this bird came to me. I didn't bother it. I didn't throw rocks at it. I was out on the hills where the sunflowers were dry, and the siskins were feeding on the sunflower seeds. I talked to them, and they began to talk to me. I was shaking the sunflower seeds out. I had a sack full. I started to carry it towards my camp. A siskin followed me and after a little way it began to talk my own language to me. 'You are a good boy. You have done me no harm.[108] Now I am going to give you power, and you will see many good things and have good times till you desert me.' "

[108] Apparently this power was acquired when Iyeho was quite young.

So he stopped and listened to this bird. He asked many things of it and was told "Yes" all the way through. "I will give you many good things if you will stay with me," the bird told him. He told me this when I found the feather. He did not tell me how he used it, and I was afraid to ask. But he was led by this bird till the white hair showed on his head.

Malice

Grasshopper has very strong power. It can get you anything in the way of power you want. That is what was told to us by a woman who knew it. She could always tell us if anything was wrong about a spring or a piece of land. She'd say, "The water is witched; the land is witched; stay away from it."

They claim this woman was a witch herself and used her Grasshopper power in the way of witchcraft. They claim she witched many a spring, that she said, "He who drinks this water shall get such a disease and die of it. If the sick one gets a shaman stronger than I am, he will get well, but if he hires a weaker one, one under me, he will die, and the shaman will be in danger of his own life for trying to conquer." This woman lived mostly at Nogal. She was never seen at Whitetail or Carrizo. But I have seen her at Elk and around the agency too.

A certain man performed his ceremony, and he is the one who saw this woman doing these evil things around water holes and fruit. This was shown and proved to us. When this man was holding his ceremony, he said, "Beware of this stream that comes out of there."

I was drinking it up to then. I told him so. "It was not meant for you," he said. "I look through you, and I see you know her well. You know what she did. You remember her daughter?"

"Yes," I said.

"Well, she paid the life of her daughter so she could live this far." That's what he told us, and Tom was there with us. "There is nothing against you," he said to me. "I don't know why. It is meant for Tom or for Ralph Thorn, or for any of Tom's boys."

She was sitting towards the sun and performing her witchcraft, and she did it in the form of a grasshopper. Tom was witched in that way. She shot the morning star into him, used it as a weapon four times. The blue one was in the lead, the black was second, then the yellow, and then the white.[109] That's the way it was taken out before Ramon Tcikito and a Chiricahua Apache man who knew the power too. And in the morning this ceremony went on for Tom. It was at a peyote meeting, and it was performed by the power of Raven.

[109] This is not the usual ceremonial color sequence. Possibly the sequence is altered to show that reference is being made to something unorthodox and dangerous. However, shamans are sometimes directed by beneficent power to use colors in other than the usual sequence of black, blue, yellow, and white.

The shaman would caw four times, then suck. He took out the four pointed stars. He put them into a handkerchief and it lay before him. "Every one of you watch me," he said. "What do you want me to do with them, burn them or swallow them?"

"Swallow them."

He put them in his mouth and chewed them. They shot off four times right in his mouth. The rest of the time his voice sounded as if he had a cold. He didn't say much. Later he said it hurt his throat.

He sucked out something red, a liquid, the second morning. "This is the menstrual blood of a woman," he told us. "I don't want to swallow it. I won't swallow it even if you tell me to."[110]

[110] Here, again, we have the association of sexual and abhorrent elements with witchcraft. Menstrual blood is considered polluting and dangerous, especially to men. Contact with it or even the smell of it will make a man weak and rheumatic.

He put pollen in his mouth and spit in the cup. Then he set fire to it. And it burned, cup and all. I thought the cup wouldn't burn and would have to be thrown to the west. You know metal can't burn. But it did this time.[111]

[111] It must be remembered that these extraordinary events were seen by persons under the influence of peyote!

The third morning he sucked out four hairs, human hairs. He burned them, and they popped. He did the burning inside the tipi. The fourth morning he sucked out all the rest of the disease, and it was burned too. Every morning when the ceremony was over, the ashes were taken out, taken sunwise around the camp to the west, and thrown away.[112]

[112] Dangerous or polluting substances are usually disposed of to the west or north.

The woman, while she was performing her witchcraft, saw a bird that came close to her and told her that her witching was known and her days were ended. When she got home, her power told her about this bird too, and it was true. She died of a disease. She tried to hire many shamans, but nothing could be done for her, for she had "shot" a man, and her witchcraft had come back to her. This man was stronger than she was. She died about a year after this ceremony.[113]

[113] One of the reputed dangers of dabbling in witchcraft is that, if unsuccessful, the witch will fall victim to the "arrow" he prepared for another and will suffer the fate he planned for his enemy.

She had lived at Nogal with Swinging-Lance. From there she rode out and witched four springs, each in a different direction. Then for four days she took the form of a grasshopper and did her witching. The shaman took us out to the spring. "Look under that rock," he said. We did, and there were feathers in the water there. "You think they are wet and won't burn, but build a fire." We did, and they popped and burned just as if they were wet with oil.

The shaman said that when this woman died, it would all go away, that she would take her witchcraft with her. But there are others who witch springs, lands, fruits, and it is as strong as ever. I can show you a chokeberry bush[114] in the next canyon that is witched. If you eat the berries from it you get tuberculosis.

[114] "Prunus calophylla."

Some of these witches even admit it themselves. Old Nogal was a witch; that's all he was. Once he got drunk and got out before a whole crowd. He talked right out. He said, "Now listen all you men and you good-looking women. I've killed many of your relatives. I've killed plenty of whites and Mexicans too with my witchcraft. The hairs on my chin and the marks on my arm stand for the number of people I've taken."

And right there he began to call off the names of those he had killed. He mentioned one of Buck's relatives. I was sitting right by Buck. He started to go for his gun, and I had to grab him and hold him down.[115]

[115] It is the duty of a relative to avenge the slaying of his kin. If it was believed that the murder had been effected by secret means or witchcraft, there were even stronger than normal revenge feelings. Before the reservation period and white control, anyone who boasted that he had practiced witchcraft would have been attacked sooner or later by the relatives of his victims. Whether or not overt witchcraft practices really have existed among the Mescalero is open to serious question. No one admits to witchcraft except in angry boasting when intoxicated, or under torture when being dealt with as a suspect. Though charges of witchcraft are rampant, in normal circum-

stances no one admits that he himself has practiced witchcraft or that he has sought the help of a witch in dealing with his enemies.

Some said Old Nogal was a shaman and some said he was a witch. He himself said he was a shaman until he was nearing the end of his days and then he admitted he was a witch. Before he died he admitted he used his power for evil, they say.[116]

[116] These occasional stories of last-moment confessions of witchcraft are affirmed by some witnesses and denied by others, depending upon their relationship to and feelings toward the alleged sorcerer. They have something of the flavor of stories which circulate in Western culture about the reputed death-bed confessions of erstwhile atheists and agnostics.

Trapper and Naturalist

I saw them often, trappers coming in to the reservation, saw them bringing in all kinds of skins of wild animals. I looked over the skins, and they seemed very pretty to me. I said to myself, "That is what I'll start out to do this coming season. I'll see if I can make myself into a trapper."

I talked to many a trapper and asked many a question about trapping all kinds of animals. I was interested in all that they told me but could get no advice about setting traps for catching the first animal that I was after. And this was the bear.

So I threw over all the information I got from trappers. I bought three traps and started to set them the way I thought I would catch one. I went where I thought there were bears and set the three traps. The next day I went to see my traps, and two were gone and one had a cat in it, a big lynx. So I killed my first trapped animal by clubbing him to death. Then I did the best I could to stretch and dry the skin.

I looked for the other traps, came to one of them, and found that there had been a bear caught in it. I trailed him fifty yards and I worked hard, but I couldn't see any more trace of him. I went back to camp, got my dog, and brought him back to the trail. I started him where I had left off. He also couldn't trail any farther but walked around a tree, but I never did think that bear could climb a tree with a trap on. Then the dog tried to climb the tree himself, and that's how I saw the trap up in the tree, hanging on a limb, but no bear in it. I climbed the tree, took the trap down and looked it over and saw much blood on it, with one paw in the trap which the bear had broken off. And that was my second catch.

The third trap was gone. I worked hard all that day with the dog, and the next morning early we came back to look for it again. I heard brush rattling up the mountain. The dog left me. Then I heard him howling up on the side, calling for help, and there I saw him tangled up with a big timber wolf. I didn't know how to kill that wolf; I didn't even have a gun. I went back to camp, leaving the wolf in the trap, brought back a .22-gun, and shot him in the back of the neck. And I thought that because these three traps all caught something I was really a trapper.

An Indian on the cattle range heard of my catch and came over and wanted to see the wolf skin. I showed him the skin and he wanted it. He told me that the scalp of the wolf was worth a twenty-dollar bounty. That is what the government was paying on wolves. He said he would give me the twenty-dollar bounty on it himself, give me five dollars for the hide, and also one-fifty for the cat hide. I thought I sure was going to make a pile of money after this!

With this money I bought six more traps and then started out to be a real trapper. I bought a gun and set all the traps around close where I could make a day's ride to them. The second day after I set them I found that I had done some damage to some poor animals. My first catch was a crippled bear. He was hung in the trap, caught pretty deep. I had caught him by the testicles. He had sat in it. He couldn't move. The Mescalero howl when they make a kill.[117] I do it. I did it when I got the bear. When I got that bear in, after shooting it, there was a big crowd around. Some asked where it had been caught; they couldn't find the mark. There were women around, and I didn't want to say. Later I told the men.

[117] This is a howl in imitation of the wolf.

I was using too big a trap and didn't know it. That was my first bear. It took me all day to skin that bear, and I had to let the other traps go till the next day. The first thing I did the next day was to stretch the hide. In the old days they used to stretch the hide in triangle shape, and so I stretched them in that way for market. Nowadays they have real stretchers just the shape of the animal. We clean them nicely now and take all the flesh off. We used to leave too much flesh on. They used to say that if you put salt on hides it would ruin them; and nowadays we find out that it's good for hides. Isn't it funny!

When the first season was over, I had quite a nice number of furs ready for sale: twenty-three coyote hides, twenty-five foxes, seven cats, five badgers, nine ermines or weasels, one mountain lion (I did not catch it; some other fellow lost it, and I found it with a trap), and one bear. I got one check for two hundred and ninety-five dollars and another for forty-five dollars. I had to work three months to get this; it was real money to me.

I was working all by myself at first with no outside help at all. I wasn't married then. I sold these hides to a buyer who was on the road and came to the reservation. Nowadays you can't make much. The prices on hides are too low. But it pays enough to make a living if there's nothing else a man can do.

There are lots of ways to trap an animal. It is not only the regular traps that catch them. I buy the wire and make my own snares. And you can make holes in the ground and make deadfalls on the trails. Catching them alive with wire netting on box traps is another good way. And setting out poison is another way, but you lose most of your furs this way. I'm not interested in poisoning the wild animals and so I've stopped that part. But there's still another way, that is tying a gun out there and letting the animal shoot himself. Another way is with a tree bent over the trail with a snare tied to the end of it. When the animal gets into the loop, it springs into the air. Or you can take a big fishhook and bait it and hang it so that the animal must have his front paws in the air to get it. I've tried all these ways and got good pelts out of them all.

At first I used to shoot them and club them when they were caught in the traps, but now I only have a choker and choke them. In this way I save the hide whole. For the choker I use bailing wire; for smaller animals, I use my hand. I just put the wire around and tie him up in the tree. If a coyote or a fox has his front paws caught in the trap, you pull the hind legs, step on the neck, and squeeze.

The easiest to catch are the bear, the raccoon, and the badger. They are always hungry and will come for any kind of food. The coyote, the fox, the mink, and the timber wolf are really the hardest to trap. You have to keep the traps well hid and keep as much human scent away as you can. You must keep the brush from rubbing on your clothes, leave very few tracks, keep your knee off the ground. When you make the rounds, always try to be on horseback. If you have no horse, you have to be as careful as possible and keep away from the trail. But when you know there's going to be rain or snow you don't have to take care, and the next morning you are sure to have a catch. I can set about thirty or forty traps in one day. I have over a hundred and fifty traps, all kinds.

When you have caught an animal in a trap, it's best to leave the trap where it is, for the scent of the animal will bring others in. Moving traps around too much will do no good. The scent of the last animal caught is the best bait for the next. Choosing the places to put the traps is something the trapper must learn. Now if there is a trail and you see one animal track, that often tempts the best trapper to set the trap. But he will find better places. He may find where they come together and scratch around and find one place where they do their wetting the ground and use for their toilet. These two places are the best to set by. That is when bait is not needed.

After one experience the fox can trip every one of a dozen steel traps without being caught. I tried half a dozen times for one fox. I made different kinds of sets and the last time I made an awkward set. I never believed I would catch him with it. I set it down instead of up. The next morning he was in the trap. Eagles are the easiest things to kill around dead carcasses. Some eagles I just turn loose if the feathers are no good. There is no season for eagles. It just depends on finding them in their right plumage. I turn animals loose too if their fur is no good. Traps will catch the eagle. If you find a dead carcass of a horse or a cow, not too dry, that's the place to set your traps.

For a long time I did my trapping alone. Then I got a couple of fellows, Andy Buck and his brother, Ralph, to help me with it. They got pretty good just from going around and watching me. At first they wouldn't touch a coyote, but then they saw that nothing happened to me. We had a hard time getting one coyote. He was a smart one. Ralph told me he had tried every way and couldn't get him. So I said, "We'll get him the Indian way." I noticed which way he always came in. Then I told Ralph to hang a loop from the top. In the morning we had him.

For a while the Bucks worked with me and then later they started working on their own.

I always dry my skins before I send them to market. If I don't they spoil. The railroad cars are too hot. Not long ago I got twelve dollars apiece for two badgers, but they were good ones, silver-tipped, and I worked hard on them. I would never have got it if I had shipped them off, but a buyer came. He kept coming as I worked on them and when I finished they were sure good ones. He said that he never saw an Indian who took as good care of skins as I did and he said they were worth the money.

I've never trapped any mountain lions. I tried for them but never got them. I shot one at Elk Springs and broke its leg. He was too hard to trail. The grass was deep and I had no dog. I'm pretty sure that there are some here still. There used to be several kinds of bears here. They used to have the grizzly bear, a big dun-grey-colored bear. They also had the silver-tip. They are gone. The last silver-tip was killed by me at my cabin at the foothills of White Mountain. It weighed at least eight or nine hundred pounds. A general at Fort Bliss got that hide from me. He carries it still. Then there was the little black bear. The Mescalero are afraid of it too. There is the little brown bear. There are lots of these now. This is the only kind left.

After I began trapping these things, George Kos and Shorty wouldn't eat with me. They said, "You might have had bear grease in that cup."

I told them, "No, don't be afraid. If anything happens I'll sing for you."[118]

[118] The narrator is again joking about the common belief that he has super-natural power from Bear.

Then I caught some silver badgers. These same two men were there. They wouldn't come near and they wouldn't touch them. I've got a coyote and two badgers down at my camp now. Lots of people here won't have anything to do with me because of it.[119]

[119] Note the consciousness of the narrator that he is isolated from others to a certain extent because he traps and handles animals that are considered dangerous and polluting. In the traditional economic system animals that were not used for food were seldom hunted. In the main, sufficient hides were obtained from the recognized game animals to provide skins for clothing and shelter.

Another time when I was at trapping camp, Shorty and George Kos came around. I shook out a coyote hide and they wouldn't get near. I had some coyote hides, pretty ones, so pretty that you wouldn't want to be afraid of them. But people wouldn't go up to them. They were afraid and said that even if they only smelled it, it would make them sick.

The Mescalero won't eat porcupine. They say it looks like a human being when it is skinned. The Western Apache sure like it, but the Jicarilla Apache are afraid of it too and so are the Navaho. I killed one in Ruidoso and skinned it. It certainly did look like a human. My folks were afraid of it and made me throw it away.

When the Bucks were working with me, Eugene Flint used to come around to our trapping camp and he always had something for us to do. He would want us to catch a horse for him or something. To get rid of him we said, "Well, we've got wildcat on the fire. You can eat it or go."

He said, "Just give me a cup of coffee and I'll go."

One day we gave him boiled meat. At the end we said, "That coyote tasted pretty good."

He said, "Ow, I feel sick right now!"

"You take some aspirin and you'll be all right," we told him.

Most of the Indians I've known won't eat jack rabbit. They claim the jack rabbit causes them bad luck of some kind. I've never found out why. I've been among them and tried to give jack rabbit to them, but they won't take it. It's the same for the Mescalero and Chiricahua Apache and Navaho and White Mountain Apache. But if it's a cottontail rabbit it's all right.

There is strong feeling against the snake. Once I saw a chameleon kill a snake. It was a big rattler, and I wanted the rattles. They got after me for it. They said, "You think you're a white man. You don't believe in anything."

I said, "When it's dead, it's dead. It's just an animal."[120]

[120] The constant criticism to which the narrator is subjected because of his commercial trapping and his own common-sense defense of his behavior on this score are evident in this exchange.

Once, long ago when I was trapping, old Joe Sanchez came along. He said, "You don't want to do this. Why do you want to monkey around with coyote, bear, wolf, and fox? They are all no good. They are the worst witches. One of these days one of them will witch you. Your head will be all twisted. You'll be walking one way and coming the other."

I laughed at him. He was part Mexican, you know. I said, "That's the Indian head in you. Get the white man's head working and you'll be better off."

He said, "You're no white man."

I said, "I'm no white man but I know these animals are put here to use; that's all they could be put here for."[121] He just laughed.

[121] The narrator is here voicing a familiar Mescalero conception, that animals are given by the supernaturals for mankind's use. He does not attempt to meet the argument that this is true of some animals only and that others are forbidden to man by these same supernaturals.

Accident

I was working on the round-up. The very first day, my horse fell with me on the side of a hill. The others came up to see if I was hurt. I didn't realize that I was hurt badly at first. I got up and walked over to my brother and stood leaning against his horse talking to him. All of a sudden I fell over. I had broken my ribs.

They sent for Muchacho Negro and he came at once. The first thing he asked was, "Did anyone touch him?" My brother, Edgar, had touched me. "Then you have to be at the ceremony too," Muchacho said.[122]

[122] It is considered that the ceremony carried on over someone who has had a mishap with a horse will be most effective if the victim is not moved but is treated where the accident occurred. It is necessary to have the horse present, and the ceremony inevitably includes an attempt to have the horse involved in the cure of the person it has injured.

He made all the others look away. Then he marked me with pollen and he marked my brother. He had the horse's bridle tied before me, to the east, and he marked that. Then he got some soft sod and kicked it four times towards me. He marked the turf and the horse too. Then he worked on me. I felt something cold all over my side and shoulder. I did not know what it was; I was too far gone.

Muchacho started to sing. "If the horse neighs when I sing," he told me, "you will get well." He sang and the horse neighed at every song. Then he sent my brother to get the horse. The horse was trying to find me and rubbed his nose on me. This all happened right there where I fell. They had a job to get me back to camp.

It took two months before I was all right. Tall Raider, a Chiricahua, was camped close by. He knew Horse too. He also sang for me. He said, "I see that a good strong one has already sung for you, but I want to help him." Each night he moved my arm up and down four times. He did this four nights. Muchacho didn't like this so well when he heard of it. He said I would have gotten well quicker if Tall Raider had not worked on me too.[123]

[123] It often happens that a sick or injured person has a succession of ceremonies carried on over him to insure complete recovery. This is particularly true if the convalescence proceeds slowly or if there are relapses. A shaman is sometimes less than pleased to learn that his ceremony has been closely followed by the rite of another religious practitioner.

The Ways of the White Man

Once they had me in jail. It was for forgery. You know in those days we didn't know what a check was. We thought you could just make out a check and the government would pay for it. We often had discussions on how it worked, but nobody seemed to know.[124] We were crazy young fellows when I got in that trouble. There was no need for it either, because I had money right at the office. I'll tell you how it happened.

[124] The mysterious ways of the white man have long been and continue to be a topic of discussion among Indians.

You know in those days a lot of the employees drank. Even the agent finally got fired for being drunk. Once I was going along with Bent-Arm, and we passed the agent. He started to swear and go for me. Bent-Arm got scared and began to run. I saw what was the matter and yelled, "Don't be afraid of him. He's just drunk."

The next morning the agent called me in and said, "I want to tell you I'm sorry for acting that way. I don't know what got into me."

Well, anyway, this time that I got in jail, I was a policeman. I went over to the club room, where the employees were and where they had their pool table, to tell the agent something. Right there on the table was one of those old square bottles of whiskey. Just as I came in, the agent had taken a little glass full and put it down just like you're putting that cup of coffee down now. I went right over to it and picked it up and poured it full and drank it. I did this three times as quickly as I could.[125] He said, "Hey, stop that! You better go home and go to bed." So I went out. I was as drunk as could be.

[125] It is likely that the drinking of the whiskey was an act of resentment and defiance. These white employees were at their place of recreation when they should have been in their offices. They were drinking whiskey, which was supposedly forbidden to them during working hours.

I went over to the hospital. This agent had got the hospital started. He tried to get people to go there, but most of them wouldn't have anything to do with it.[126] It was during his time, too, that the Catholics really got started here.

[126] Until very recently it was considered a virtual sentence of death to be taken to the hospital. The fact that former patients had died in the hospital was enough to make it a most dangerous place and a rendezvous of ghosts.

Tony Lewis and Millard Lake were at the doctor's desk. They had a blank check there. "Hey, sign this," they said to me. I didn't know what I was doing, and so I made it out for sixteen dollars and signed the chief clerk's name to it. He was over there at the club room too.

The electrician was driving the first model Ford out, the first one on the reservation. We got him to take us down to town. Tony cashed the check, and then Millard got a whole lot of drinks. Before we knew it we were all arrested, and the judge said I did it. So they put me in jail in Alamogordo.

While I was there Tony came down to see me. He said it was his fault and said he had tried to get me out. Back in my camp they tried to do everything they could for me. Tom's mother sang to see whether I'd be sent to a reform school. She saw that I was coming back. She said, "I see him coming to the door," when she was using her power. Charley Three-Fingers and Kenneth Swinging-Lance were singing for me too.

They fired the electrician on account of what had happened. They said he should have known better than to take us down there.

The day before the trial I had a strange dream. I dreamed I was right on top of a cloud, and that cloud was going straight to White Mountain. I was sleeping in my cell right in the daytime when that happened. I woke up and looked out, and it sure was clouding up, just starting to rain a little. It was about December.

When my trial came up they couldn't prove that it was my thumb print on the check, so the judge dismissed the case.

Major Llewellyn was the district attorney.[127] When I got out he gave me a dollar and said, "Go and get yourself something to eat and then get home."

[127] Major William H. H. Llewellyn had been agent at Mescalero from June 1881 to November 1885. He was one of the most understanding and effective of the agents and continued to take a friendly interest in the Mescalero for many years.

I got outside, and I met the sheriff. He was a good friend of mine. He said, "Look at you, you dirty, ragged prisoner. You come with me." And he bought me some clothes and took me to get something to eat. "Now," he said, "don't hang around here. Get out of town as fast as you can or I'll put you in jail again."

I said, "I've had enough of it. I'm getting out just as soon as I can catch a ride."

Just then I met a man who said, "I've come to get you. You want to ride back with me?" I said I did and we started. "Now you forget about the reservation. I'm going up to Cloudcroft, and you come with me for a while."

"No," I said, "I'll go as far with you as La Luz Canyon, and then I'll walk home."

Just before we hit La Luz we caught up with a wagon stuck with a load of lumber. We pulled it out, and the driver said to me, "I knew you were going to get out. I had a good dream about you last night. I dreamed that I was stuck just like this and you came along and met me." This is how a white man had a good dream about me too. He wanted me to come to his place, but I told him I was going to Tularosa for the night and then on to Mescalero. I was going to stay with an old cowpuncher I knew well.

I came in on him, and he said he'd fix me up for the night. He had a whole barrel of chaparral wine. He said, "If you want some of that, you can take all you want. But I think it's too strong. I drank some of it, and it made my head feel awful funny."

The chaparral berry is a kind of chokecherry.[128] Very few Indians eat it. They say it is poison. I said to him, "Don't you know that berry is poison and will get you sick if you eat it? That's what's the matter with you."

[128] This is apparently a local use of the word "chaparral." Chaparral usually refers to oak trees and is also used of any dense brush.

He said, "No, the berry's all right; I eat it lots of times. But the wine's too strong. It sure made my head feel funny. I got drunk on it about two months ago, and my head still ain't right."

I didn't drink any of it. He wanted me to stay there with him, but I left next morning. He tried to give me a horse to ride, but I said, "I don't want to have to lead that horse back. I'm too fat anyway. I want to walk it off." So I started for Mescalero.

While I was on the way, Kenneth Swinging-Lance was using his power for me. "That boy is going to be here pretty soon," he said. Nobody believed him. Then he saw me coming, a long way away. He jumped on his horse and came to meet me. "Come on, get on behind," he said.

I got on, and the first camp we came to was Muchacho Negro's. He was glad to see me and asked me to stay with him. But I said, "I guess I'd better not stay here. My father and mother are over there, and they will want to see me."

Just before I got to our camp, my mother stood up. "I feel that someone is coming from this way," she said, pointing. Just then I rode up. I had borrowed a horse from Muchacho Negro.

I saw Tony Lewis and Millard Lake. We were all pretty mad about it. I said, "Why do we let the agency people treat us like this? They're no better than we are. We can make lots of trouble for them. We saw them drinking." The other two backed out. But I went to the chief clerk anyway. I told him I was good and sore for his putting me in jail, and that I could make plenty of trouble for him.

He said, "I'm sorry for what has happened and I want to be friends with you. If you'll forget it and keep quiet about it, I'll tell you what I'll do. I've got a lot of whiskey up at my place; you go there and ask my wife for a bottle of it if I'm not there, and there'll be some money tied right to the neck of it. I'll tell her about it so she'll know."

So I did; I went to his house, and his wife answered the door. I said, "I came for that bottle of whiskey your husband promised me."

She said, "Come in." She gave it to me and said, "Now here it is. But promise not to tell where you got it and promise that you won't make any trouble for us and won't drink it around here."

I said, "Your husband and I have agreed on that part of it already, and I won't drink it till I'm twelve miles from your place."

So I started out on horseback for our camp. There was a big bunch camping there: Boneska, Tom's people, my people, Charley Sotol, and others.

In the excitement I forgot all about the money that was supposed to be tied to the bottle. My mother picked up the bottle and tore the top paper off. The money was there in an envelope, but she didn't know it and just threw the paper on the floor. Just then Muchacho Negro came in. He had been sent by the agent who said he wanted me back at the agency to ask me some questions about the chief clerk. The old man saw the envelope there and picked it up and opened it. He saw the money. With it was a note saying, "A present to show we are friends." Muchacho was a very honest old man. He called me and said, "Does this belong to you?"

"Yes," I said, "that's mine." And I gave it all to my mother.

Then we opened the whiskey and had a real drink. Tom had about a gallon of whiskey there too. Every man in the whole camp got dead drunk.

In the morning the agent called me up and asked if I could come to the agency. I said yes, but I'd have to get back the same day. So they came and got me with the Ford car. When I got to the agency, I found that they had fired the chief clerk.

The agent said, "Now if you want to make trouble for him, you can."

I said, "No, I'm young and I'm out of jail now. I'm willing to forget it. He's fired anyway, and there's no use doing anything more."

"All right," said the agent, "let's forget about it then. Come on in here." And he took me to his clothespress and gave me a big drink of the best whiskey I ever had. And I went back to camp. This was before prohibition.

After he got fired, this agent came back to visit once. He wanted to see me, and they came up to my camp and told me he was waiting at the agency for me. I wouldn't go to see him. I said, "Tell him he raised enough hell when he was here."[129] So they went back and told him just that and had a good laugh on him.

[129] Very few agency employees have been admired by the Mescalero or considered to be anything but parasites and a burden upon them. Some have had a mistaken notion that the Indians feel kindly toward them.

When I got back to camp, Tom was waiting there for me. He said, "There's no meat in camp and I've hunted all over but haven't got any deer. These children are hungry. So tomorrow you and I are going out." I said, "All right," and early next morning we started out.

We killed one deer, and Tom started to take that back. I stayed out hunting but didn't have much luck. Finally I sat under a tree, thinking. I was thinking, "I used to know a deer ceremony pretty well once. Why don't I use it now?" Then I thought, "Oh, I gave it up. I won't have anything to do with it anymore." Just then two deer walked right in the open in front of me. I got both of them, butchered them, and started back. Everybody in those camps had lots of meat that night.

I never was a policeman again. When Muchacho was a policeman they wanted me on again, but I wouldn't have anything to do with it.

Right after that hunt I received a notice from the agency that I was wanted to work at the sawmill again. I went to work there and was earning good money.

Charmed

One day at the sawmill I had a funny feeling. I had to quit working. When I first felt sick, I said, "I'll get out of this place." I washed my head but I only felt worse. I started out and got as far as Rattlesnake Tank. I got into the pines. I rested and went on. I was all in when I got to Pajarito. At noon I was around Encino. I had started in the morning. I was riding an agency employee's horse. I didn't think I could make it. I was blinded. Something would get in front of me; there was movement in front of me. I could see nothing but butterfly wings crossing in front of me.[130]

[130] It is evident from the symptoms and from the mention of butterfly wings that love magic was being used against the narrator.

I started to follow the wagon track down towards Red Lake. From there I went across to Number 3 Tank and from there straight across the canyon to Turkey Tank. I got there and saw Shorty. They fed me at his camp. Shorty knew what was the matter when he saw me.

I rode after Old Juan. At the rock cliff I caught up with him. He said, "Let's get out of sight here. You're in bad shape." He knew why I had come.

He worked on me just as soon as it got dark, for he never works in the day. He told me, "You are lucky you made it here in time. Two or three days longer and it would have made you crazy."

He worked on me two nights at this place. The second night I felt pretty good. I felt that I could eat the whole side of a deer.

He said, "You're feeling pretty good. We'll finish the other two days of the ceremony at the house that Pedro Gomez built on my ranch at Turkey Springs. Now you'll have to go out and get deer in the morning. I'm too old and can't shoot. You take the gun and go over to that big juniper. If you see two deer, kill one. If you see three, kill two, and if you see four, kill two."

I went up there very early and I put my head up. There stood the biggest buck I ever saw. I didn't see the others, but I aimed at this one and fired. When it fell, four others jumped out. I shot one more.

I called for Old Juan to bring the horses. I butchered the deer. He came up and gave me the blood of the deer, gave it to me hot. It gave me strength. He filled the stomach with blood. When we got back he put in cabbage, onions, salt, liver, kidney, and entrails and cooked it. It tasted good, maybe because I hadn't eaten in so long. I ate lots of meat.

We waited two days and we went back to Turkey Springs. Pedro Gomez had built a place for Old Juan and fixed all the fence too. He had kept his promise to Old Juan.

Old Juan started the ceremony. He said prayers and also sang. He said he was going to send back what the woman sent me that very night. He was going to send it by singing. It was going to be sent the fourth song. He sang, and at the last song it felt as if something was being pulled off me. He took it in his hand and sent it to the west. I saw something go. I couldn't tell what it was. "Maybe she'll be more careful next time," he said. He did this the beginning of the third night. The next time, the fourth, he sang that I should be well and things like that. He said I had to stay there four days more.

I stayed there a week. I hunted for them and killed about eight deer for them. I had money. I was single then and always had money, so I took them to the Elk store on the other side and bought them flour and calico and goods of all kinds. I thought it was worth it, what he had done for me, so I gave him all I could. When they had everything they needed, I told them I was leaving. He was very sorry, but I said I had to work. He said he was coming over to see me and he did later.

When he came I took his horses and watered them and hobbled them and turned them in the pasture for him. It was near the sawmill where I worked. There was no more ceremony after that.

He had told me right at the start who it was and where it happened. It happened at the store. She used the butterfly and something else, he wouldn't say what. He knew but didn't tell me much. She was after me. I didn't know it and paid no attention to her. I don't know what she did with it; she got it back though.

Old Juan had a special way in which he had to be asked to work for you. You had to give him the hide of a black-tailed buck. It's true of about all ceremonial men that they ask for black-tailed deer. Juan's had to have a turquoise tied between the ears of the buckskin. I didn't have it at the time. My mother gave it to him later.[131]

[131] The presents that are required by the supernatural power should properly be given before the rite begins. Sometimes when it is important to hold the rite at once and some of these objects are not immediately available, the ceremony is held with the understanding that these gifts will later be supplied.

They say I went out with Old Juan just to learn his ceremony; that's what Shorty said. He told it on me, I heard later. Can you imagine that! And they were sure afraid of me because they said that if I learned it I wouldn't respect anyone.[132]

[132] This passage mirrors the suspicion under which the narrator labors. The charge that the narrator sought love power and was likely to use it in a wanton and unbridled manner borders on an accusation of witchcraft proclivities. In fact, love magic, since its aim is to influence another rather than to cure or help another, is not really considered beneficial supernatural power. Yet most Mescalero are not willing to call it witchcraft either, for while its use is dangerous, ordinarily the intent is not to harm another individual. Rather, love magic stands on the somewhat ill-defined ground between the two more definite polar manifestations of supernatural power. The fact that the narrator traps and touches polluting animals leads many of his tribesmen to think that he would be likely to use any power entrusted to him in an unorthodox and dangerous manner.

4

Search Unended

Marriage, the White Man's Way

WITH THE MONEY I EARNED at the sawmill, I bought a lot of cattle and had a pretty good herd. But Tom drank it all up on me. Every once in a while he'd sell one to get money for some drink, or kill one and sell the meat just for drink. So I got pretty sick of it. Then he wanted me to buy some more cattle.[1]

[1] The precept of generosity and the inability to refuse economic goods to relatives and especially to relatives-in-law have made a good many difficulties for the Mescalero in the modern economy. This is particularly true when the funds for the purchase of stock or the improvement of housing are borrowed from the government on the reimbursable plan and a family head is held responsible for the debt incurred, although it is his various relatives who have received the benefits of the loan.

I said, "No, I'm tired of this. You've got your woman, you've got children, and it's time I find me a woman too and raise children instead of going on like this."
Tom said, "All right, all right! Don't get mad. Do what you want to."
I had been getting acquainted with a girl. When I saw her she used to motion to me. One time I began talking to her. And after that I saw her more and more. I didn't hide out. I went right to the agency to see her.[2] She was still in school and was about seventeen years old. I was about eleven years older. I did it the white man's way. Her father saw us. He asked her if she meant to marry me and she said yes. He said, "I've got nothing to say." I didn't give him presents. We just set a date to get married.

[2] In the traditional practice a man would not appear in public with a girl in whom he was interested until after his marriage to her. Contacts before

marriage were made to seem casual or unplanned. A boy might just happen to be passing a spring when the girl of his choice came for water. Meetings of lovers did occur but were nocturnal and secret. The only culturally approved opportunity for young people to have contact with those of the opposite sex to whom they were attracted was at large gatherings where social dancing took place. On these occasions the girl could ask a boy of her choice to be her partner. At the conclusion of the dancing the men gave presents to the women, and the magnitude of a young man's present was some indication of the seriousness of his intentions. Young marriageable people were taught that, if they particularly liked some eligible individual of the other sex, this should be confided to their older relatives. A family council would then decide whether this was a possible union and one in the best interests of the family. Marriage negotiations would be entered upon after this. It was considered appropriate for the family of the boy to take the initiative. Therefore, a girl who was attracted to a youth was helpless in the matter unless she could induce him to carry the matter to his relatives and persuade them to act. A girl was expected to heed the advice and directions of her parents and older relatives in marital matters; therefore girls who had no particular preference or who had not been able to attract boys of their own choosing often had to marry men whom they did not know or for whom they did not care because these men had been able to impress their families with presents or promises of economic cooperation. The marriage of the narrator occurred about 1908.

He said to me, "I've got nothing to say. In the old days we used to get twelve horses for this.[3] But you are learning the white man's ways and now you are doing the white man's way. I've got nothing to say."

[3] Twelve horses would be a handsome marriage present. The girl whom the narrator married is from a prominent family. Her father was Muchacho Negro, a well-known Mescalero leader.

I went out on the range and stayed there for quite a while. When I came in I found out that everything was arranged for my marriage, although I hadn't known anything about it. The girl and her father had everything all ready.[4] Just as soon as I got in everybody was saying, "I hear you're going to get married."

[4] In spite of his disclaimer it appears that the girl's father took a very active part in the marriage arrangements.

They told me that the matron at the school wanted to see me. I went down to see her. She said, "I hear you're a half-married man."
I said, "Well, a half-married man is a long ways from being a full-married man."
She said, "No, they tell me you're just as good as married now."
I said, "I guess I am, but I don't know anything about it."
Then she told me a lot about married life and things like that. She said, "Now

you're marrying a very young girl, and you've got to be very careful of her. I think she's almost too young for you."

I said, "Well, suppose your husband died and you wanted to marry a younger man. Then you wouldn't think that way."

Then she said, "This girl is graduating from school in January, and you'd better marry right after that."

They gave me permission to visit the girl right at the school. I'd go up and the old disciplinarian would open the book and say, "Oh yes, you're the fellow coming to see the girl you're going to marry."

When the girl got out of school, the priest had everything ready. He said to me, "I've got your suit ready for you, and tomorrow you've got to take a bath and get a haircut. And I'll go down to town and get a license for you." I gave him the money. I paid for everything. Then he asked me, "When do you want to be married?"

And I said, "Well, I think Friday would be best."

So we were married at the church, and there was a big crowd there.

As soon as I was married, I avoided my mother-in-law. I had to. The younger people don't like to and a few have stopped doing it. My mother-in-law thinks the white way is best, but it's too late now. She is camping up the hill near me now. I hid at once from one of my father-in-law's half sisters. To another I used the polite form of speech.[5]

[5] There are certain relatives of his wife whom the married man must completely avoid and others with whom he has a restraint relationship which includes speaking in a particular "polite" form of address. Some of the avoidance relationships are obligatory; for instance, the mother-in-law must always be avoided. In other cases the avoidance is optional. When it is optional, the initiative lies with the bride's relatives. What they request of the man depends on their former relations with him and their attitude toward their newly married relative. If they have been familiar and friendly with the man in the past, it would seem inappropriate now to demand total avoidance. If they have had little contact with him in the past, the more formal relationship is likely to be established. To call for an avoidance relationship where polite form would technically suffice or to call for polite form where no special formal relationship is absolutely necessary is considered a gesture of affection toward one's relative. Therefore a relative of the bride who feels very close and affectionate toward her will demonstrate this and honor her by requesting avoidance or polite form from her mate. Thus the course of action that is followed is based on the past contacts with the man who has married into the family and the feelings toward the relative through whose marriage the new tie is being established. The Mescalero network of avoidance and polite form is very extensive. Avoidance is obligatory between the son-in-law and his mother-in-law, his mother-in-law's mother, and his father-in-law's mother. His mother-in-law's sisters and female cousins, his father-in-law's sisters and female cousins, his wife's sisters and female cousins, and a number of other relatives of his wife may request either avoidance or polite form. Polite form is obligatory between son-in-law and father-in-law and is used in speaking

with brothers and male cousins of the father-in-law or mother-in-law who request it of the groom. A number of other relatives of the bride also may request polite form if they so desire. The Mescalero system of avoidances and restraints between affinal relatives is one of the most complex and extensive that has been described in anthropological literature. Cf. Opler 1933.

The narrator spoke in a matter-of-fact manner about several young persons who had recently begun to disregard avoidance obligations. However, he himself was punctilious about avoiding his mother-in-law and observing associated restraints. The following is a typical note I made which describes his behavior: "Chris and I were sitting by the road when his wife and his mother-in-law came along. They were on their way back from gathering piñon nuts. When son-in-law and mother-in-law caught sight of each other, Chris went far back in the woods and the old lady left the road and made a wide arc on the other side. The narrator would not pronounce his mother-in-law's name. When asked what her name was, he merely laughed in an embarrassed fashion and said, 'I don't know.' "

Experiences with Peyote

Diego, Charlie Three-Fingers, Gade, Old Man Nogal, and Kakas were the best-known leaders for peyote meetings when I was young. Bronco was always present but was not a leader.

A man who knew more about it than others usually gave the peyote meeting. He selected the place and they put up the biggest tipi they could find. This man did most of the singing and hired a young man to build the fire and one to beat the drum. He saw that everything went the way he wanted it and that no witching went on, and he saw to it that any man he was afraid of was below him. This means that he found this man out, that he knew more than this man all the time, and that he was always able to control him.[6]

[6] Another important function of the peyote "chief," not mentioned here, is the obtaining of a supply of the peyote "buttons." Note the overtones of rivalry and fear of witchcraft that mark the use of peyote among the Mescalero.

The first meetings I went to were one-night meetings; they were not for curing. One was just a special young men's meeting. This was to get more young men interested. That's the reason I went. The peyote leader feeds the peyote to those taking it the first time. He motions toward your mouth with the peyote on the two eagle feathers three times, and the fourth time it goes in your mouth. He did that to me. He asked first if I had eaten it before. I said, "No." He motioned three times, and the fourth time he didn't have to put it in; it just went in. He didn't come near my mouth. That's the way it is; it flies into your mouth, even from across the tipi.

I just took two peyote buttons the first time. That was sure enough! I couldn't stand any more. It's strong. The second time I took four.

When I was there the first time, the peyote chief made me sit by him and drum for him. If the shaman is not strong, his drummer may be witched and will vomit. They told me how witches make boys vomit. I said, "I'm not going to vomit!" I had never been in one of these meetings before, but I started right in singing.[7] When you eat peyote, you want to get up, sing, and learn songs right away. I sang four peyote songs. Then I began to sing smoking songs. I was told to stop. They said others wanted to sing peyote songs.

[7] The narrator is well known for his good singing voice and vigorous style of delivery.

If you see a vision of a girl when the ceremony starts, you'll see nothing but girls. You'll want all of them.[8] Whatever vision you start with in that ceremony, like walking with dead people or having a broken leg, that's what you'll see all through it.

[8] It is felt that the manner and spirit into which a ceremonial occasion is entered does much to influence the outcome and benefits.

They just sing and eat peyote; that's all they do. All during the night the head peyote man tells his visions. He stops and says, "I see a bad man in here. He wants to harm someone. I warn him not to try it. It will be too bad for him."
Once you get in, you must stay till morning. I wanted to get away; I got tired. But they wouldn't let me go. You are not supposed to go back to your own camp while you are under the influence of peyote. It begins to take effect in about twenty minutes. It takes it an hour or two to wear off.
You can't hide a thing in there. The chief sees every movement, he knows what you think. He says, "There's a man in here thinking of nothing but evil. We don't want that. Have nothing but fruits in your mind.[9] All right, go ahead if you want to! But after the next peyote meeting we'll fix you!" If you feel like it, you tell what you see. If you see anything bad, you are supposed to report it to the head peyote man. But he knows all about it; you don't have to tell him.

[9] Fruit connotes growth, fulfillment, and plenty and is therefore a symbol of the good in dreams, visions, and ritual references.

I saw a rainbow. I was standing in between the ends, in the middle of it. I looked back. I could see nothing but a little juniper tree standing there alone.[10] I listened to the singing. I started to talk, but they stopped me. You see everything when you eat peyote, eagle tail feathers, animals, all coming at once. They crowd in on you.

[10] The visions which the narrator obtains in the peyote meeting once more emphasize essential loneliness and isolation.

In the morning, about sunrise, after eating peyote all night, that's when you feel good. Everyone came out at sunrise. They had their shirts off and were dancing around and singing. Then, before breakfast, all were lying around. That's when you see visions. One man saw himself being killed by a burro. After a while they call you to eat breakfast. There are sunrise songs in the morning. The chief starts them; then all sing as they know them.

In the peyote meetings I saw things that later came true. I saw myself without a wife, with grey hair.[11] I saw my cousin fall from a horse, and I saw myself looking for Old Jim (who is now dead) and unable to find him.[12]

[11] The narrator's wife had died not very long before he gave this account.

[12] Again, isolation and separation from friends are suggested by this imagery.

About five years ago, I was at a peyote meeting in Kiowa country. There was one Kiowa there they were all afraid of. I could see he was looking at me, though I had a blanket over my head. The Mescalero cover themselves with a blanket and keep huddled up at a meeting unless they are singing or drumming. This Kiowa was looking sharp and thinking, "There's a new man; I wonder what ceremony he has." I felt his power come and search me and then go away. It never came back. I saw Mescalero country and White Mountain, and then the camps of the Mescalero people came into view.

You are supposed to sing your own songs first, then peyote songs or any that come to you, even someone else's. I sang this Kiowa's songs. Everyone was afraid. I sang four of them.

The man on the other side of me yelled out. I said, "Be quiet, you're at peyote meeting." Then I looked at him. I saw he was following trails. He came to the place where they crossed. He counted four and then took that trail. That's why he called out.

You can see more supernatural things in peyote meeting than any other place. At other places your power has to fix it so you can see, but here you just see; you sit and see it. I saw many awful-looking animals, fishes, and trees. But mostly I saw young boys and girls dancing. You don't know who they belong to unless you have power.

They tell you to come in to the peyote meeting for your own good and not to try to steal someone else's power. But they try to find everyone out. One man shouts, "I'm afraid to show myself!" Then they give him the drum. They want to hear his songs.[13] He gives himself away like this. The peyote meetings led to lots of trouble and lots of witching.

[13] The curiosity about the supernatural power of others is evident here.

Peyote is still used a little here. I have seen one woman who had lockjaw helped through it. Her trouble started at noon and soon she was helpless. She couldn't talk; she could just look around and see her relatives. They got Kenneth Swinging-Lance. He told them to give him four peyote buttons as ceremonial gifts. He used the power of a bird, the Maryland yellowthroat. All peyote men have to cure through something else; they can't just do it with peyote.[14]

[14] This suggests that when the use of peyote became part of the Mescalero religious system, it was subordinated to the on-going shamanistic practices.

Kenneth sang and prayed for her. He took a long flint, put pollen on it, and was about to put it to her jaw.[15] She spoke then and said, "No wonder they die without speaking! I couldn't open my mouth. I was getting weaker and weaker. It's a good thing you brought the right man." Everyone felt good when they heard her talk. She was just as strong again as she could be.

[15] Blades of flint and obsidian are much used in Mescalero ritual contexts.

This happened just a little while ago. They don't allow peyote meetings now on the reservation, so they didn't have a meeting.

Some of us got together at my camp in June.[16] We got some buttons from a Mexican in Texas. There were fourteen to twenty present. It was not a real meeting. We just got together to practice the songs. We had rawhide stretched over a bucket for the drum. This is not the right kind for peyote, but next time we are going to have the right type. We had gourd rattles.[17] The women didn't come in. They stayed in the next tent. We told some of them to come in. They said they didn't want to, that they just wanted to listen. We heard them talk. One said, "One of these men might want me and get me." We laughed and said, "No such thing. There's no power in it. We are just singing."

[16] This meeting was held on Saturday, June 13, 1935.
[17] The use of gourd rattles at peyote rituals is widespread.

Power and Peyote

Power from a plant that is used a good deal now was learned by a man who often went alone through this part of the country. He had a little power from some bird. He went into a peyote meeting with some of his family who knew Peyote well. When it was time for him to take the peyote on the eagle tail feather, he asked the peyote chief if he should take some of this plant along with the peyote. The leader of the meeting told him to take it after the peyote. So he took the peyote. And after that he pulverized the plant in his hand and asked for all the power in the plant with peyote. In his vision he could see this plant growing right in front of him, a beautiful big bush. Grass, moss, and wild strawberries grew all around it in the shade of a big spruce tree. The plant told him to pick it when it was found growing that way and not to take it from beneath oak trees or any other trees.[18]

[18] When plants are associated with ceremony or are a source of power, the rules for gathering and utilizing them are often more complex and stringent than is the case in simple herbalism.

The plant was swinging back and forth in the breeze, and he could hear a song being sung. He sang this same song but did not quite learn it and never heard it again. Now the plant spoke to him. "Why do you bring me here and chew me with peyote? Don't you believe in peyote alone?"

"Yes," the man said, "but I think highly of you too. I have been told that you and peyote are a good pair to know together."

The plant said, "I am thinking of you, for you have understood that I am a big thing. Now I'll show you that I can come to you in a form like yours and speak your language."

The man marked the plant with sunflower pollen which he was carrying, and the plant told him he would be given power from Water's Child and White Painted Woman. The plant said, "Before you use me, always use pollen, spruce pollen if you have it, for it makes the medicines stronger."[19]

[19] These pronouncements of power are not general cultural prescriptions but have to be understood and accepted in the context of the particular ceremony. In another power experience it might be quite a different kind of pollen that the healer is urged to use.

"That is just what I want. I want to be a healer and help the sick. I want to help even the animals which are hurt or sick."

The plant now started to teach him the songs and prayers of the ceremony. He was going to be able to use it at once. But he was not to let people know about his power. He must let them find it out for themselves. For this reason he was not too well known at first. But he was good at finding lost things, finding people who were missing, and locating the enemy. He cured diseases. They say he cured smallpox, using spruce pollen, this plant that had given him power, and peyote mixed together.

A Comanche, Quanah Parker, brought his son, who had been struck by lightning and who was paralyzed on one side, to this shaman. The shaman didn't want to show his power before a crowd, but Quanah Parker begged him to hold a ceremony. He said, "I will give you many things if you will save my son's life, for he is my oldest son and I depend on him more than I do on the rest of my children." So a tipi was put up back in the hills where there would not be such a big crowd, and a peyote ceremony was held for four nights.

The Mescalero shaman asked the Comanche, "Brother, do you know power of any kind? And if you do, how do you use it?"

The father said, "I know power and I used it while it was raining."

The Apache asked, "Do you know power from Lightning?"

"No."

"That is the mistake you have made then, to use power during lightning. My power showed me that but asked me to question you about it. Now you have told me the truth, and I will tell you the truth. Your boy will get well."[20]

[20] Sickness is said to occur when lightning strikes too close. Here the shaman is attributing the anger of Lightning to the use of ceremony by the sick boy's father at an inappropriate time. The Mescalero stop work, stop eating, and pray respectfully during a violent lightning storm.

"Do you mean it? Will my son get well?"

"I have already spoken. Why do you ask questions when I have already given you the answer?" Then he told him not to worry and not to think of anything else. He knew the father was thinking that no power on this earth could cure his boy.

The shaman was using the herb that had spoken to him but tried to keep this concealed. He was using it with things of the lightning. He used a strong-smelling plant to help hide it too. And he found spruce pollen, even though it was not the season for pollen. After he had collected these medicines, he held a ceremony alone with his family and used them. A hailstorm came up as he was doing this. He picked up the first four hailstones that hit the ground and mixed them with the herbs and marked them. Something seemed to hold the bowl of medicine up and move it around to the four directions and back to him. It touched his lips, and he sipped it four times, marked it with a pollen cross, and let it settle. Then he took this medicine and some more hailstones to the sick boy.

Now he asked for a large pan and poured medicine from the little bowl in it until it was half full; still there was medicine left in the small bowl.[21] He put four hailstones in the big bowl and set it outside. It was still raining. He was praying. They heard thunder, and the lightning hit a tree to the east, a second one nearer, a third one nearer still, and a fourth time very close. That time something fell into the pan, and the shaman went and got it and put it close to the sick boy. He marked the small bowl again. Now the contents of the big pan started to boil as if it was over a fire, but there was no fire. He stirred the medicine with two eagle feathers until it overflowed. He marked the liquid again, marked the patient, and then had them lift the boy and dip him four times in the big pan and wash him all over. Then they put a buckskin over the boy and laid him down again. The father was told to take the bath water and throw it to the west, and the others were to spit four times.[22]

[21] The "miraculously abundant" or "inexhaustible supply" theme is often encountered in ceremonialism involving the use of plants and decoctions.

[22] To spit or to make a spitting noise four times is symbolically to expel evil. Ritual spitting is particularly common in ceremonies having to do with lightning. The disease and evil were presumably washed off the boy and disposed of with the water.

Now lightning struck four times on the other side of the tipi, and it began to rain very hard. The whole tipi seemed to be on fire. When the lightning hit, the shaman yelled four times, took his shirt off, and shook his shirt and the boy's shirt. He had the boy's father hang the boy's shirt on the tipi pole toward the sunrise. They had seen sparks come from the shirt when he shook it, and he told them not to touch it for four days.[23]

[23] Sickness and evil were ritually shaken from the boy's clothing. Taboos and restraints of the kind enjoined upon the boy by the shaman involve a patient in the curing process and make him responsible, in part, for his own welfare and for the course of events.

More marking with pollen followed, and the boy, who was leaning against his mother, said he felt that his ills were leaving his body. Now the shaman marked the bowl, and, just as he had told them it would, the bowl rose, moved about, and went to the boy's lips so that he could take the medicine. Then the shaman worked on the boy with two eagle tail feathers. The shaman cleaned the larger pan with burned dirt from the four sides of the fire and clean water. Then he prepared more medicine.

That night after this part of the ceremony, they told stories of the old days, and the boy listened. They stayed up till the middle of the night because the boy liked to hear those stories.

The boy had a good sleep that night. He said he had the most beautiful dream, he dreamed of himself as a great man among the Comanche people. He told this to the shaman, who warned him, "If you have another dream, don't tell it until four days are up."

The ceremony went on the second and third days, and everything was done just as it had been the first day. There were more people present now, though. On the fourth day the boy began to have a little life. He could move his legs and the side that had been paralyzed. The boy was very grateful to the shaman for helping him so much.

He stayed there and rested four days. Then they held the ceremony for four more days with very few changes. This time the storm was very bad. The shaman told the people not to be frightened, that the lightning was taking away the lightning sickness of the boy. The children cried, but they told them to hush. The rain was so heavy that it washed away roads, and big logs drifted down the canyons. Horses, sheep, and cattle were drowned.

After that we had one of the best summers we had ever seen with fruits of all kinds, wild flowers, and tall grass. The cattle and sheep were fat. And the boy got well.[24] His father kept writing to the man who had cured him until that shaman finally died.

[24] Though ceremonies are carried on for specific purposes, successful rites have a generally beneficial effect, as these remarks indicate.

Before he died, this shaman gave his power to another man who used it for mumps, diphtheria, earaches, and all sorts of ailments. He cured many, but he said the plant never spoke to him as it had to the other man. He didn't have so much power as the first man either. He had to raise the bowl himself to the patient's lips. He had success using the power for hunting and in searching for things. He used it for the "flu" and for tuberculosis, but whether he did much good with it, I don't know.

I was present at this second man's ceremony the time he used it to find a man who didn't come home when they expected him to. This shaman found out the boy was hurt and was out Silver Springs way, sitting under a tree, unconscious. He said they should take a car out there to get him.

They found him there, badly hurt. He had been thrown by his horse. The shaman treated him, put him in the car, and brought him back. They took him to the hospital. He had a cracked rib but was able to see most of the ceremony that was held for him there in the hospital.

This shaman was really good at finding things. He could tell us where to find deer and turkeys. He had us put spruce twigs, pointing towards the sunrise, in our hats while we hunted. Once when we were having a hard time finding deer, he directed us to a place. I was to stand on a point of rock, and the others were to hunt towards me. Pretty soon there came two beautiful deer with the prettiest antlers I have ever seen. I showed him the kill when he came up. The two others that were with us came along, and we dressed the meat.

That night he talked about his power. He said to me, "If I was to hunt bear, I'd choose no one but you."

So I said, "I guess it's best for me to go look for bears," for I needed a bear for a friend.[25] He held a short ceremony, directing me where to find bears.

[25] Note that when an individual requires some flesh or body part of a bear for ceremonial purposes, he is likely to ask the narrator to shoot one for him. This is because the narrator is a good hunter and also because he is believed to have supernatural protection from the ordinary consequences of encountering the bear.

Back at the same spot where I killed the deer, I came to the biggest bear I ever saw. There were at least five grown bears there together, pretty close. The wind was in my favor, and I went forward quietly. When I got about two hundred yards from them, the biggest one stood up. I thought I was hidden pretty good, but he saw me. While he was standing there on his hind legs, I fired the one shot I had to fire. Then I climbed to a high place and watched because the others were circling around where I had killed the biggest one.

We stayed up till about ten that night, and he held another short ceremony. I asked him about lightning and thunder because I'd seen the other shaman use them, but he showed me that he had no power in rain or snow at all. I asked him a good many things and especially why his power didn't work as well for him as for the man he learned it from. He told me, "That man hid his best part from me and showed me the weakest part. At that time he wanted to keep the stronger part to take care of himself and help others."[26]

[26] It is alleged that a shaman who teaches another his ceremony often withholds part of it or part of his ritual knowledge. It is then necessary for the new practitioner to make up this deficiency by gaining additional information from the power source itself. Sometimes this is achieved, sometimes not. Therefore two shamans can perform the same basic ceremony with quite different results.

Swinging-Lance Loses Supernatural Power

Swinging-Lance used to have power from Life-Giver and also from Spruce before he gave it all up to become a Christian. He got power from Spruce in this way.

There was one spruce standing close to the top of a mountain. Down below there was an ice-cold spring of water. Swinging-Lance knew that tree was up there, and a Mexican also knew it was there. One time, just before high winds came from the east—the time we had a cyclone that blew trees down—that tree was acting funny. It moved like a masked dancer coming to the fire.[27] Swinging-Lance looked at the spring. There was this same tree growing at the spring. He looked up at the mountain where it had been. The tree was gone from there. Just oaks were growing up there. He drank from the spring. He thought and thought about it. He could not put it out of his mind. The tree was the same one. It looked the same, like a masked dancer's headdress waving to the east.

[27] The masked dancer shuffles toward the fire with a weaving or side-to-side motion.

Swinging-Lance came back a second time. The Mexican was there. Swinging-Lance said, "This tree was not here. It was way up at the top. How did it get here?"

The Mexican said, "I put it here." He was just fooling.

"No, it hasn't been pulled up. Look at it. It used to be up there."

They went up to the place where it used to be. There was no sign of roots pulled up, just oak brush was growing there. The Mexican thought he, too, remembered that the tree had been up there. Then they came back and looked at the tree. The third time he was there, Swinging-Lance was pretty sure, and the Mexican was too. The next morning they went there again. They climbed on top. They stopped. The tree was way up on top again.

"Do you remember that tree?" Swinging-Lance said. "It's the one. That tree came down to water and was there for four days. Now it has gone back."

"I can't believe it."

"You remember it was at the spring yesterday. The water was going under its roots."

They went to the spring. The tree was gone. A Mexican and an Indian saw this with their own eyes. They couldn't believe it. The Mexican didn't know what to say. "It might be Diablo. I'm going home. I'm not going to stay around here." He went home.

The Indian stayed there and bowed his head. He thought about it for a long while. Something touched him on the head. He looked up. He couldn't see anything. He was blinded. He wanted to see whether it was true. He rode into camp. He was touched four times before he got into camp. He thought and thought about it. Finally he slept. Then something told him to get up. "Come outside." He did. "Look towards the spring." He did. He knew he was being raised from the ground, which way he didn't know. He was taken into a forest of nothing but spruce trees.

"Do you believe now?"

"I believe. I must believe my own eyes. I have been seeing it for four days."

"What do you think about it?"

"I think that tree wanted water and went down and got all the water it wanted."

"Come to the spring."

He went. The spring was gone. He went where the spruce was. There was the spring running under the roots of the spruce.

"Now what do you think of it? Do you think that the water went up to water the spruce?"

"No, I don't think that at all. I don't know what to say. First you moved the spruce down by the water, and now the water is up there."

"Now I'll tell you. These trees have all kinds of movements, these bushes too, but you do not know it." It was just a voice speaking. Nothing showed yet. The tree shook and pollen fell heavily into his hand. "Put that in a bag." This was done a second, third, fourth time. "Can you do that? Can you shake a tree and get pollen like that?"

"No."

Four branches were pulled off. "Take these. You have everything you want. Everything is shown to you now." And before he knew it he was back on his own bed.[28]

[28] It is obvious from this phrasing that this was a dream or, as the Mescalero interpret it, a vision experience, in which power from the spruce tree was granted.

The Mexican thought differently (about the tree). He came back and asked, "What did that witch tree do for you?"[29]

[29] The implication is that the Mexican was incapable of perceiving that the tree was a potential source of beneficial power and could only react negatively to the unusual occurrences involving the tree.

"Many things, and I believe it's good for me."

"Oh, that's nothing! It's no good."

"All right. You're a white man, and I'm an Indian."

The Mexican wouldn't go near the tree. "I won't drink any more of the water of that spring," he said.

Swinging-Lance kept still about this; he said nothing for quite a while. But one time they were talking. Then he said to many of his people camping with him, "Will you believe that a tree will move?"

They said, "A tree stays where it is; don't tell lies."

"I can't make you believe it if you won't, but I have seen this thing, and a Mexican knows about it and he calls the tree a witch." Finally he told it as best he could to make them understand.

Someone had a very bad cold. He gave the fellow just four needles from the four branches he had. The fellow said, "Oh, that won't help me!" but he chewed them. Before he knew it he was all right. He said, "It tasted like spruce and smelled like spruce, but it can't be spruce."[30] He thought about it. Another time some people from Fort Sill (Chiricahua Apache) were here. One had a bad cold and took it, and it cured the cold. Then came two Mescalero boys. He cured them. They tried to find out what he was giving.

[30] The person who was cured could not believe that so common a tree could have such extraordinary curing powers. The implication is that the ceremony significantly added to the worth of the remedy.

"It's easy to tell by the smell and the taste. What do you think it is?"

"It's pretty good, but it just tastes like a spruce needle."

"That's what it is. When you get a cold just go to a spruce and eat the needles like this."

But finally Swinging-Lance joined the church of the white man. He didn't want any more power. He made a great mistake, he told me, when he joined the church and let his power go. He said, "Power has left me, and I have no power now. The only holy thing I have now is my church. My power told me I won't live long now that I have left it." He knew very well what was going to happen and he couldn't get his power back. He tried several times, but his power had left and there was no coming back.

A few years later he got very sick with pneumonia. The doctor said there was no hope for him, so they sent for an Indian shaman. It was still dark when they left to get him, I understand. They came, but it was too late. Then this sick man talked about the spruce. He tried to speak to it. The spruce told him to get the four branches that had been given to him. "That's the only way you can get well."

"But I burned them up."

"Then it's your own life."[31]

[31] The destruction, especially by fire, of the symbols of ceremony originally given him by his power makes it certain that this shaman can never successfully use the rite again. Some Mescalero, when converted to Christianity, destroyed their symbols of supernatural power in their early zeal. Later, if their faith in Christianity ebbed or interest in power reasserted itself, they were much worried about the consequences of their act.

They tried other spruces, but they wouldn't work. So it cost him his own life for not practicing. The spruce told him he would have been all right if he had just tied the twigs to a tree or hidden them.[32] "But now it's too late, and you can't do anything." Swinging-Lance seemed young even when he died.

[32] If a shaman loses confidence or interest in a power and wishes to sever working relationships with this particular source of supernatural help, he ties the material symbols of power to a tree. Their disintegration is considered evidence that the supernatural power is retrieving them. But to mutilate or destroy ceremonial objects prevents their return to their source and their home and is an insult and affront to the power for which proper amends can never be made.

Power is still among us, but some are dropping it. Some who know power quit using it to get along with the white man. Some think it's wrong to join a church and use a curing ceremony too, so they give their power to the priest or preacher when they join. They might know the songs afterward but the power has gone away. They throw it away. Many say that when power is leaving, they see it go toward the sunrise.

Some are throwing their power away and some try to learn the ways of power. Some, even if they try, can't get a ceremony of any kind. Cloud is a man who has not got any ceremony and can't get any. He tried to get some power, a man tried to show him a ceremony.[33] But it didn't work; he never got it. Others are trying right now.

[33] Though many Mescalero claim some supernatural power—perhaps nothing more than a minor rite that is used privately or within the family circle—there are members of the tribe who never succeed in obtaining supernatural help, as this passage indicates.

Anthony's First Moccasins Ceremony

When my oldest son, Anthony, first began to walk he had a good first moccasins ceremony.[34] Tall Raider and Old Man Dan did it. They knew power from Water's Child. Many came up where I lived, and we had plenty of food with which to treat them. They had a big hoop and pole game going on there too. Dja and others were playing while they waited for the big dinner.

[34] When a Mescalero child begins to take his first steps, a suit of clothes is made ritually for him, and a first moccasins ceremony is performed on his behalf. The Chiricahua Apache practice a first moccasins ceremony, too, and the two men who performed the ceremony for the boy were Chiricahua. This is one of a number of life cycle ceremonies or rites of passage which are believed to be essential to the development of the child and which are designed to bring him safely to adulthood.

The boy wore buckskin with different markings on it, a crescent and stars and other things, and a metal cross on the shoulder. Old Dan had directed my wife how to make the buckskin outfit. It has to be from a black-tailed buck for boys. For girls it has to be from a black-tailed doe. In Old Man Dan's ceremony just a top shirt was used for the boys and low moccasins.

They start just as early as they can. Many prayers are said to Water's Child and White Painted Woman. The songs tell of how Water's Child was raised. I was very much interested in it. After the prayers, Tall Raider marked everyone the way they do at the girl's adolescence rite, on the head and across the nose, men and women too. This was just before sunrise. It lasted till the sun was up. He took the boy just at sunrise and lifted him towards the sunrise and shook him four times, then to the south in the same way, and then to the west and north.

He made marks [resembling the footprints of a child] on a piece of white cloth just as White Painted Woman made them in the story of the killing of the monsters.[35] Then he took the boy and said a prayer about Water's Child and his first step just as Anthony took the first step; then another prayer for the second step, and so on till four prayers and four steps were over. I was holding Anthony on one side and Tall Raider was on the other. Then the boy took four steps by himself. Tall Raider prayed and sang. Then we turned the boy sunwise and brought him back, and he made the four steps in the same way again. Four times we walked him. Then we took him in a circle sunwise four times. After the four prayers Tall Raider sang his four songs. All those who knew his songs helped with the singing.

> [35] In the story of the killing of the monsters, White Painted Woman tries to hide her boy, Water's Child, from a giant who devours human beings and who has a special liking for the flesh of children. The giant sees the child's footprints around the camp and accuses White Painted Woman of concealing a baby from him. White Painted Woman assures the giant that she has no baby and that she made the footprints herself because she was lonesome for a child. She demonstrates how she did this by clenching her hand, striking the soft earth with the side of it, and adding marks for the toes. The giant is temporarily satisfied, and Water's Child is spared. In the first moccasins ceremony the footprints through which the child is led are made in this manner.

We sat down. Then everyone, Tall Raider first, marked that little boy as they mark the adolescent girl. We certainly had a good ceremony. The people were dancing, women and men, boys and girls. They danced in place. The women gave the cry of applause when Water's Child and White Painted Woman were mentioned.[36]

> [36] The cry of applause is a high-pitched, ululating call which sounds to the white man's ears like a cry of mourning and is often so interpreted by him. This call is heard at the time of the girl's puberty rite when "She Who Trots Them Off," the girl's female ritual attendant, sends the pubescent girl on ritual runs to the east and also on some other ceremonial occasions. The call, which indicates reverent approval, is uttered when important supernaturals or sacred substances are named in songs and prayers.

At the third set of songs, they made me sit in the center with the boy, and all danced around. They were drumming and singing. Anthony was not bashful. He danced there up and down and looked around. He was only about one year and nine months old.

Then Old Man Dan and Tall Raider stood by as this was finished and said the last set of four prayers. The others marched around us.

When the people playing the hoop game heard about this, they all came up because we had presents there to give. Bill Sotol had helped me to buy them because he wanted the ceremony held. He is a relative on my wife's side. My father-in-law bought some of the stuff and our sisters helped also. My wife's sisters helped with the cooking.[37]

> [37] Matrilocal residence and the importance of the maternal kin in the life of the Mescalero child are reflected in this passage.

They kept marching. Then they started to sing the last set of four songs, and the end of the ceremony was near. They sang and sang and they told me many things. We had a good time all through the ceremony.

Everybody kept quiet at the end of the singing. At the end of the last four songs, Old Man Dan picked up the moccasins. He put pollen on them and lifted them to the directions. He put pollen on the boy's foot and put the right moccasin on first, then the left. "Now you can run," he said.

Anthony put his foot right in; he was glad to do it. Everybody said, "He's just like his daddy."

Then the presents were blessed. Old Man Dan and Tall Raider put pollen all over the baskets of fruit and presents, and the man just passed it among the people. They offered Dan and Tall Raider some first; they gave them tobacco. Then the candy was given out for the children, then the bananas, oranges, and nuts. After that the big dinner began. They feasted that one day. This ceremony is held because Water's Child, when he started to walk, had a ceremony like this one.[38]

[38] The Mescalero life cycle ceremonies are associated largely with the culture hero and culture heroine and events in their lives.

Wrongs That Were Never Made Right

When General Scott came back to visit this part of the country, I stayed with him at Ruidoso.[39] We talked of the times when he was a soldier here. In those days there was a lot of killing and trouble. Choneska came in from the wilds once and was accused of killing the trader's hired man, who had really been shot by another Apache. Mariaboy was in jail for another killing at this same time. Ramon Tcikito was there too. He was a big chief at this time. The reason he was there was that he had a brother who was crazy and ran around wild in the mountains. They were always bringing him in, and he'd run away again. Some friendly Mexicans were shoeing horses for Ramon, and this brother shot one of them, for no reason at all. So this brother was accused of murder, and Ramon was sent to bring him in. He wouldn't do it, and so they put him in prison for it.[40] Choneska was a foxy old fellow. He got them all out; he helped them escape. Bloodhounds were sent after them, but they got away somehow. Mariaboy was not blind then. They say he was a good runner and fast even though he is so heavy-built. They all got back to the reservation. They were not bothered after that, though the whites knew they were back.

[39] The reference is to General Hugh L. Scott, well known for his campaigns against Plains and Western Indians. As a captain, Hugh Scott was the first supervisor of the Chiricahua prisoners of war at Ft. Sill, Oklahoma. He became Chief of Staff of the United States Army when this country entered World War I.

[40] One of the great embarrassments of the Mescalero "chiefs" and police was to be ordered to arrest close relatives. Often leaders or family heads were held as hostages until relatives or followers surrendered or obeyed some

order. To judge by these tactics, the conception of collective responsibility held by the white military leaders seems to have exceeded that of the Indians.

General Scott asked me about a lot of old killings, and I told him a little of it. He said that these stories ought to be written up in a book. Then I told him what the soldiers did, what he did, and said that would have to be written too. He didn't like that so much. I told him of the time they shot down three children and a real old man just above where the agency is now. I said, "You didn't have to do that."[41]

[41] The Mescalero, as is the case with many other American Indian groups, are well aware that the Western history that the white man has written has much to say about Indian "atrocities" but has passed very lightly over the cruelties suffered by the Indians at the hands of their white antagonists.

There were lots of officers there when I told him this, and some of them began to get mad. He said to them, "There's no use denying it; we did those things. We did anything in those days just because we were soldiers." Then he said to me, "Well, it's all past now, and we are friends. We'll make it all up to you people now."

They never made anything up. But Scott was a good man. He liked the Indians. Later he tried his best for us, but he couldn't do anything. He's dead now.

Finding-Out Ceremonies

I heard of power from Star being used and I tried my best to get around to see it. I stayed with Alfred, the man who knew it, and was just like one of the family, but he never used it for a long time. Then his girl got sick. I said, "Why don't you use supernatural power if you know it? If you know Star, use it; that's what it's for, for your own children." I wanted him to do it so I could see it.[42]

[42] This is another indication of the avid interest of the narrator in seeing and assessing all kinds of ceremonies.

So he used it when his third daughter was sick. He knew Morning Star. He used it in the form of healing. He carried glass beads which represented the morning star. He took the girl out of school and started his ceremony.[43]

[43] During this period teachers at the school were baffled by the frequency with which parents insisted on taking their children out of school for short intervals. Often, as in this case, it was to permit a curing ceremony to be carried out for some ailment about which the child had complained to his relatives.

He used ashes. He used Star in the way of shooting to the east, south, west, and north. Then he went to the head of the child, sucked, made a noise like a buffalo, and spit into the fire. All present spit too. He did this four times and then he sang songs. He sang sixteen different songs representing stars. Also he had many prayers. That's what made it very long. He had his hand up with ashes and the beads on it, and you could see it sparkle and see the shafts of light fly. The girl was all right in a few days and she went back to school.

Then he was sick himself with pneumonia; he had a hard case of it. The doctor said he was going to die. He begged for his life.

There was another man whose power I wanted to know about, so I went to him.[44] Julio and I got Jicarilla, and Jicarilla cured Alfred. Jicarilla used the power of Water. Water gave him motion. He said, "I learned it in my younger days, not tonight, and this man will be well." And Alfred did get well. Alfred gave me a note to the trader. I went and got twenty-five silver dollars, and those were handed to Jicarilla. He laughed and said, "That's the way to do it. Don't promise and then never give it. Hand it out like this and then there is that much more power."[45]

[44] The narrator is candid enough to admit that his choice of a shaman was at least in part dictated by his desire to see the person perform his ceremony.

[45] Shamans often say that supernatural power takes pleasure in seeing its representative well paid. This is one of the strands of mutual interest between a shaman and his supernatural source.

When a man knows Water, he doesn't hear a voice, but by feeling he knows what is being told by the power. Jicarilla blew to the directions. He shut his eyes and motioned with his hand. "You have only two days to live. I'll stretch it for you."[46] He talked about the water then. "I know he's going to be cured. The water moved. It showed me. I've got the feeling in my hand." He held the ceremony for four days and four nights. "This is not the only time the water has given me the feeling," he told us.

[46] It is a frequent boast of shamans that their ceremony has altered the course of events and prevented catastrophe.

When a man who knows Water dreams of water, that is his long life, his luck. It's just as it is when a man who knows Snake dreams of snakes; it's his long life, it's a good sign.

Jicarilla sang of big waters in his songs. He told Alfred of his whole life. "You've done many bad things, but that's not the cause of it. It's just a disease and therefore easy to cure."[47]

[47] In the aboriginal Mescalero thought system ethics and religion were quite distinct aspects of the culture, with relatively little overlap. A kindly and respected person, if he touched a polluting animal or substance, would be sure to get sick and require ceremonial help. An unruly and unpleasant person, as long as he obeyed all necessary precautions in respect to food and behavior, might escape such difficulties. It was only when a person of vile disposition endeavored to use supernatural power to implement his aims—

that is, became a witch—that religious forces were mustered in defense of morality. Note the implication that ordinary sickness, uncomplicated by witchcraft, is not too difficult to cure.

Alfred told me to kill a pig. I went and killed one. I got a Mexican woman and her husband to clean it. We gave them the entrails, liver, and feet, and they were glad to get them. We had a good feast and Alfred began to get well.

When he was nearly well, he held a ceremony for himself. I sat up with him. He told me many things. He said, "I see terrible things.[48] This is a dangerous place. Those who can't see don't know it. I see colored things pointed against us. We'll always have hard times among ourselves. That's what pretty near got me," he said.

[48] The "terrible things" referred to are, of course, witches and witchcraft.

He took the beads out. He commenced with his prayers. He used four prayers and four songs. Then he turned to me. "Brother, these are terrible times. I'm doing my best to get rid of those who have run over me."

He kept up the ceremony for the second set of prayers. Then he sang four short songs. He went on to a third set of four prayers and then started four songs without saying anything. After the fourth set of prayers and songs, he held his beads in the four directions and began prayers of the star he knew.

That's the way he went through his ceremony. He pointed his beads to a place and said, "That's where the things that nearly killed me are." I saw sparks fly from the beads four times. Then he moved up to the west side of his camp, then to the north, and then to the east.

"Now we are pretty well off. Nothing can hurt us. I feel pretty well. Let's go out and work."

The next week we finished cutting ten cords of wood.

A Serious Illness

In 1918 I was in a bad way. I had high blood pressure, and the doctor gave me up for dead. All the family was crying over me. I told my folks to try the blanket flower. The top and root are boiled. This makes a red liquid which is used for blood trouble or high blood pressure.[49] Peso once used this blanket flower medicine for a wound when he was shot, and it helped him. For wounds, the root is powdered and put raw in the sore; the liquid from the boiled root is drunk too.

[49] The scientific name for blanket flower is "Gaillardia pulchella." There is often an obvious magical connection between a medicinal plant and the purpose for which it is used. In this instance a root which yields a red liquid when boiled is considered efficacious for blood disease.

I took six doses a day. After the first six doses I sat up and laughed. I had been in bed from May to October. I got well quickly after using this. I went to work. Then I caught the "flu" the next day after I went back to work.

Epidemic

We Mescalero say that there are people who live in the mountains and we call them Mountain People. These people paint masked dancers just as we do, but the masked dancers that they paint are the real Mountain Spirits, the ones who show ceremonies to people and the ones our masked-dancer makers imitate. Very often someone will go near a mountain and hear drumming from within. Sometimes men are led in there and see these people and the Mountain Spirits.

Just about a week ago I saw Sanchez at Rinconada. He told me that at a cliff near Beaver Springs he heard a sound. He looked up and saw a human figure there. It looked like the clown of the masked dancers to him. He said he had a feeling as if something was going from his foot to his head. His hair was just standing up. I went there with him. I didn't see anything. But I heard a sound like an eagle's cry.

I used to act as a masked dancer. The first time I put the mask on I could hardly breathe. But the second night I felt light and wanted to fly. It gives you lots of life to wear that outfit.[50]

[50] The young man who impersonates a Mountain Spirit is said to receive added strength from the real Mountain Spirits to carry on his vigorous dance. The Mescalero point out that the mask worn is hot and close-fitting, with very small holes at the eyes and nose. They say a dancer would soon become exhausted unless he were buoyed up by supernatural help.

During the first World War, when the Spanish influenza was first coming this way, Old Man Dan called all the people together. He was going to keep it away. He made masked dancers and Black One.[51] He wanted to pick out the best man for Black One. He tried to get me, but I said, "I don't know the ways of Black One. I might make a mistake, and everything might not turn out well." So I was one of his regular masked dancers instead. I was leader and Steve followed me. Robert's boy was Black One. Dan used only one Black One; they always make only one. We had a good clown, that old man named Hunter. Hunter said afterward, "You fellows certainly put on a good dance."

[51] The protection of the Mescalero and their territory from epidemics and general disaster was considered the proper function of the Mountain Spirits and was the purpose of the ceremony in which they were worshipped.

The people were very quiet when this was going on. Black One said he saw nothing but fruit and flowers around the fire, so Dan said, "All is well." He asked me if I saw anything, but I did not.

Old Man Dan told the people then, "Don't say anything bad about this sickness. Don't mention it, or it will come back."

For a while no one did. Then someone mentioned it, and the sickness began to come again.[52] Old Man Dan took us up on a high hill. The wind was blowing dust from the east. Dan pointed to it. "That wind is bringing the sickness back. I'm sure

sorry, but I can't help it. I told you about it. I warned you of it. Now it's too late."
And it was true. The sickness came back and many died. Sos made his masked
dancers, but it did no good.

[52] At the conclusion of a rite a shaman usually lays some taboos or restrictions
upon the patient or those for whom he has performed the ceremony. If matters
go amiss or there is a recurrence of the sickness, it is always possible to claim
that someone must have violated the taboo, perhaps unwittingly, and angered
supernatural power.

The second time it came, Old Man Dan did not hold his ceremony with dancers.
He said, "All of you were safe. There was no sickness. I helped you. I told you
what to do. But now it's coming back. I can't stop it."

I went over to Dan's camp. Many were camping around his place. He had his
masks there, and the people stayed around the masks and marked them with pollen.
All these people kept well.

The first time Old Man Dan hadn't told what to do for the disease. Now he sang
the songs of the medicines. He sang of one herb and then another. None helped.
Then he started on trees. He got to juniper. Then he stopped. Power showed him
that juniper was good. "What kind of juniper?" Power told him to name the
junipers. "Alligator-bark juniper?"[53] he said. "No." "Rock juniper?"[54] It was not
right either. "One-seeded juniper?" "You've got it," said the power.

[53] "Juniperus pachyphloea."
[54] "Juniperus scopulorum."

He started another song. Right at the beginning he stopped. He nodded. "There
are four," he said, " 'slim medicine,' sumac,[55] the whole plant can be used, and the
needles of piñon and juniper."

[55] "Rhus microcarpa."

But there was death already, and he didn't sing any more.

My family got busy. We pounded up a whole sack of juniper needles. And others
did too.

Now we heard of death. There was Hiding's family. For four nights we heard
him pray, "Let my children live. Let me die." The fourth night he died. It seems
that every woman with child who had it died. Pablo's whole family was wiped out.

A woman who knew a ceremony from the wildcat used her power for the Pablo
family. She tried her best to find out something for the "flu." She failed at first.
Then she tried it in a different way and tried to find out which way was best. She
got angry because she was losing relatives.

Her power said, "You've got to wait till a certain day."

"No," she said, "you must show me now!"

The power finally showed her a woman who knew what to do. This woman was
using juniper and piñon; she saw that these were to be used. But it was too late by

this time. The Pablo family was wiped out. She was mad because she was told so late.

But her power said, "Their appointed time had come. That's why they died." That's the only time she failed. It was shown her too late.

Besides the Pablos, Charlie and others died. Julio's father died, and Jicarilla and Lester, one of Short Man's relatives, and many others too. I'm sure sorry to call their names.[56]

[56] It is dangerous to mention the names of the dead, for this is thought to anger and "draw" the ghosts of the departed.

Dan was a kind man. Every day he walked around to all the camps and helped the sick. He always came to my camp. He said, "My power likes you best of all the people here. You will be a shaman just like me some day."

I said, "I wouldn't want to be a shaman."[57]

[57] The narrator's ambivalent attitude toward acquisition of supernatural power is again in evidence here.

Dan showed me lots of herbs, Tall Raider also. They were shaman partners. During this "flu" epidemic these two came to me. Some didn't have the sickness yet. They said to me, "Bear is your power. Kill a bear. Feed it to the people. It might help."

I told them I could kill a bear all right but that I didn't know Bear the way they meant.[58]

[58] Once more the narrator affirms that he does not know the bear ceremony of his father.

They didn't believe me. Dan said, "Talk to the bear before you kill it. You know what to say. Don't just give it as food."

Then Edgar, my younger brother, came to me and said, "Let's kill a bear and give it to the people to eat."

So I took some pollen, used it when I saw a bear, and killed a male bear.

The Davis family, then Louis Nitsigane, and then Chester East were down with the "flu." I gave them some. I helped East a whole lot. I gave him entrails with pollen. When a person is sick it's best to give him the gut. I gave him one dose close to morning, one at noon, and one when he went to bed. He said he felt something working inside him that made him feel like a different man. I gave him an herb too. Valerian was the herb I gave him.[59]

[59] The scientific name of valerian is "Valeriana trachycarpa."

He wanted to give me something. I said, "Just give me a package of smokes."
He said, "I know by your words who I should come to when I am sick."

I gave him a rib of the bear. He stayed at my place till he got well. Lots of them did.

The next morning I went to the hospital. I had a sack of bear meat and I handed it out to all the sick ones who wanted it. The doctor asked me, "What are you giving out?"

"Real 'flu' medicine."

Everyone who was able to eat it got well. The ones who threw it up all died. One I did my best for. He tried it four times and couldn't get it down. This was Lester. Pete, his brother, sure swallowed it. He thought he was gone too, but he got all right. Web couldn't swallow it. His mother was there and got scared. I gave it to him four times. She cried and cried. I said, "I've done my best for you but he was down too far."[60]

[60] Despite his denials that he had supernatural power from Bear, the narrator nevertheless feels justified in feeding bear meat ritually to those afflicted with influenza.

My mother's brother died of "flu"; he tried to get in from Rinconada but couldn't make it. He died on the way.

During the time when I was impersonating the Mountain Spirits I sure had queer dreams, dreams about clouds, rains, sickness, and things like that. And some of them came true. I dreamed that some of my children were dying, and then I said I'd quit dancing and all that Mountain Spirit business.[61] I heard that my mother was burned up through one of these dreams; and she was. I never saw her again. My brother wouldn't even tell me what happened.[62] After that I just looked on when the masked dancers were made and helped sing sometimes.

[61] When a shaman of the Mountain Spirit ceremony paints and costumes a set of dancers and sends them out to dance in a rite to cure the sick or to combat epidemics, he tells the young men of his dance group that they may receive messages from the Mountain Spirits and that they should report all visions, extraordinary feelings, or tidings to him. Consequently, while they are in the midst of their exertions and busy driving sickness and evil away with their wands, dancers sometimes believe they have received signs and knowledge which should be communicated to the shaman. They usually dance for four nights, and they are expected to report all dreams and visions that come to them any time during the whole ritual period. Apparently the suggestion of the shaman that he might very well receive dreams and visions from the Mountain Spirits bore fruit in the case of the narrator, but the messages he received were so negative and disturbing to him that he refused to perform longer as a masked dancer.

Some additional background material describing the narrator's difficulties as a masked dancer were obtained from the Chiricahua Indian named Steve. The episode that Steve relates is said to have occurred on the first occasion when the narrator performed as a masked dancer. Steve's account is as follows:

One time I was dancing for Old Man Dan. Chris, Robert's boy, and I were dancing. It was Chris's first time. Chris was speaking in English, cussing while they were painting him. You know Chris is just like a mockingbird, doesn't respect anything.

The old man said, "Look here, that kind of talk doesn't go here. You men should be praying in your hearts. Pray for all the good things. Be saying, 'Let me be a reliable masked dancer. Let me be reliable in life.' That's what you should be doing while you're in this brush hut."

Just as soon as the old man stopped talking, there was Chris cussing in English again. Well, we went out, the three of us. We came toward the fire. The last minute Chris was putting on the headdress. He couldn't get it on. "I can't get this damn thing on! How does this damn thing work?"

I told him in Apache, talking softly, "Don't talk that way. You can't talk loud in that mask. Have some manners. You shouldn't speak English or talk loud in that mask."

The old man said, "Hey, what are you doing? Now if anything happens to you, you'll say you are witched, but I warned you."

Chris said, "Oh, I always forget."

We went out to the fire. The first time we went to the fire, he bumped up against me. I heard him cussing in English and laughing. Every time we went around and started toward the fire he bumped into me. I said softly in Apache, "Keep your distance and be careful. Don't be talking English." I was the leader. Chris was right behind me.

All of a sudden I noticed Chris was putting his hands to his head. He just took his sticks and pressed them to his head. Then I saw him break out of line and run away from the fire. He ran right to his camp, pulling off the mask. His camp was just a little way from the grounds. They found him there crying and hollering. He threw himself on his bunk and held his head and groaned.

Pretty soon they sent a message to Old Man Dan. "That man who danced for you is pretty sick," they told him.

The next time we came out from the fire, Dan came to us. "We'll have to go right over and see that boy," he said.

So we went over. Chris was just like out of his head. He was rolling around, trying to stand on his head. They couldn't hold him down.

Dan told me to work on him, because I was the leader. Robert's boy came behind me dancing, but I was the only one that touched Chris. First I came toward him from the east. The fourth time I crossed my wands over his head. Then I grabbed his head in both hands and shook it, shook it hard. You can't be gentle with them. Besides I was angry at missing the dancing over there at the grounds all because of his foolish talk. Chris hollered, but I pulled him around good. I did this from the south, west, and north. Each time I shook him we made the masked dancer call and then I blew his sickness away to the four directions beginning with the east.

After I finished, Dan said, "Now you're all right, nothing the matter with you. Get up, no matter how you feel, and follow these men." So Chris followed us, and we went around once and then toward the east.

"All right," said Dan, "you fellows go back and dance. He'll get better now. He'll be over there at the feast pretty soon."

So we went back. While we were dancing I watched for Chris. I looked around every once in a while to see if he was there.

Pretty soon I saw him there, sure enough. He was laughing and hollering and clapping his hands, having a good time. It was just about an hour after we worked on him.

I don't know what made that fellow well. I didn't do it. I just followed Dan's directions. It wasn't from me, but it was Dan's "medicine" that did it. The old man knew what was wrong with Chris and how to cure him. Dan was singing his songs and praying while I was working on Chris, of course.

Compare, also, the version of his masked dancer experience given by the narrator on p. 227.

[62] The closer the relative, the less likely it is that the death can be freely discussed. Fires that resulted in injuries and even fatalities were not uncommon. Many of the Mescalero were living in tents and preferred to remain in them even after log cabins or small frame houses were available. Even if a wooden house was initially occupied, it would often be abandoned after a death had occurred in it, and its owners could be found living in a tent close by. The tents were heated by wood and kerosene stoves which were all too adequate for the space involved, and the interiors often became uncomfortably warm. As a result of hot stovepipes and embers which fell back on the roof of the tent there was constant danger of fire.

I was usually present at all the ceremonies held by Kenneth Swinging-Lance. He always showed me ways to handle things in his ceremonies. That's why he always had me in there with him. During the "flu" epidemic, while I was still sick with it myself and was just up and walking around, Kenneth came to see me. People didn't know what to do to help each other, and the doctor didn't know what to do, and often whole families went. Many came to Swinging-Lance and asked him what was killing them and what was best to be done. He left for the hills all alone. He asked his power what this was that was happening and what was best to use against it. Out there alone, praying for his people, he found out what was best for all these things. Also by this time the doctor knew what was good to use for these people.

Instead of going back to his family, Swinging-Lance came where I was and asked me if I was able to move. I said "Yes" but that I was very weak. So we went first to a family near us and showed them what was best to use for their sickness. We went from one to another, and many families were saved. Even Mexicans and whites came to him. They lost one man they depended on for this same curing; the "flu" got him. But before he went, he told others to go to Kenneth Swinging-Lance.

Swinging-Lance held no ceremony; there wasn't time. He just gave out his herbs. He told people not to move outside the reservation until the doctors outside had checked the "flu." He told them that those who stayed on the reservation were the only ones who were going to live. Outside it was terrible. Houses were left standing with many whole families dead and no time to bury them. A man would be all right one day, digging graves, and be gone by the next day. Many left out in camps were hunted up and found dead. They had to pick up many bodies along the trails. Kenneth said that if he had had a chance to save them, he could have saved these people.

What the herbs he mixed up were he wouldn't show anybody, even me. They were hard to find out by the taste. Kenneth stayed out and treated those who lived off in the mountains. The ones who lived closer to the hospital came to the doctor there.

Kenneth Swinging-Lance said, "In these days when there's death going on, there's no ceremony to be held for anybody." The only ceremony he held was the one he performed out in the hills all alone to find out what to use. He did use markings for the sick, using pollen and white clay when he gave the medicine.

A Girl Bewitched

Kenneth Swinging-Lance is also the one who treated a girl who was witched. She had a black cricket in the back of her head and lay in the hospital for four months, getting awfully thin. Many of us who knew this shaman spoke to her people and told them to get him for her. I told them I'd do my best to talk him into it because he always let me come to his ceremonies. Her family agreed, but we had a hard time getting her out of the hospital. The doctor had taken her to Fort Stanton to be X-rayed, but they couldn't see a thing. Yet she was losing strength. We came near having a fight taking her out. I spoke to the doctor privately and told him what we wanted to do. We sent for the police and the agent, and we talked him into it. We told him things he didn't believe.[63]

[63] One of the points of conflict between the Mescalero and agency personnel during the early years of the hospital was the frequent demand of the Indians that they be allowed to take a patient from the hospital to a camp for a ceremony. Sometimes when the case was considered hopeless or when they became very insistent, the Indians gained their point.

First Kenneth had to get the girl strong enough for the ceremony. He told them not to feed her too heavily, as she was weak. When it was agreed that she was to go, we drove up and he handed me a long black silk shawl. I put it over her, covering her head, and carried her out the back door. The nurses hated to see the girl leave, to die they thought. While they were still having trouble with the doctor and nurses inside, I put her in a car and took her to her people.

The place was all fixed up. It was going to be a four-night ceremony. The ceremony went well all the way through. Everybody was quiet and listened. Kenneth Swinging-Lance used a mixture of peyote and herbs he had learned from the Ute. He marked it with pollen and made a cross on the liquid to be given to her. After it was given to her she always felt good and wanted to sit up.

After four nights, I was very tired. He said, "The girl will want something to eat, wild turkey or deer." So I was hired to get it. He told me just where to go to find them, and I went there although I was so tired I didn't want to go anywhere.

As soon as the ceremony was over that fourth night, I started out. I was supposed to camp at the place he had told me about, but I didn't camp. He said it would rain and the deer would be moving. I passed the place where I was supposed to camp and came around from the other side. It started to rain. I went back to the place where he had told me to camp. In the distance I saw deer standing on a hillside where the brush was thick. I got up close and started to shoot. At the first shot I killed one; the second one I shot twice. Two deer, and it was only four o'clock in the morning! I cut them up. It was a big load. The two deer were very fat, both horns were in velvet.

I came in before noon. Everybody was sound asleep. I had to wake them up. Then I went back to camp and rested till late the next day.

Now the ceremony began again. The place was full of people. Two of the agency employees came and two of the Indian police were there. Kenneth asked me for a buckskin.[64] I asked no one for it but got one from my own camp and laid it before him.

[64] This buckskin was a ceremonial gift required by the power before the rite could begin.

He marked the medicine, the girl, and all those present. He prayed and I followed him the best I could. It was a hard thing to do as he spoke fast. He sang, and everyone who had heard these songs before helped keep the singing going. We prayed four times, sang four sets of songs four times, and morning came. The last two songs I finished myself while he seated the girl on the buckskin, facing the east. He turned her to each of the four directions. There was a cup of water in front of her. I knew just what it meant. I held the water up to the four directions and sprinkled the girl's head and Kenneth's head, and he sprinkled mine.[65] A white handkerchief was placed before him. The girl knelt and the people walked around to the four directions while I sang.

[65] This sprinkling has the same ritual meaning as reciprocal marking with pollen.

Before the last song was finished, a live cricket was dangling from the eagle feathers in his right hand. When the girl saw it, she fainted. He motioned to me, and I sprinkled water to the four directions and put it before him. He motioned toward the girl, and I sprinkled her head four times. Then I sprinkled Kenneth again. He said the girl was safe; the poison was out.

The employees examined the cricket. There was flesh on its mouth and legs, and it was still moving.[66] These two men said if there was anything wrong with them they would come to this shaman instead of going to the doctor.[67] One of them did come to him to be treated later.

[66] The flesh on its mouth and legs was that of its victim whom it had been consuming and destroying.

[67] The Mescalero seize upon any evidence that the white personnel approve of their ceremonies and cures. They know that their techniques have been widely ridiculed, censured, and opposed and have something of an inferiority complex about their methods of combatting disease. As a result, they make capital of any endorsement from the outside to which they can point. How seriously the employees meant what they said is hard to judge. Actually there were many persons of limited background and meager attainment in the Indian Service at this time.

General Practitioner

The man who is now my son-in-law was once shot in the leg; the bleeding was hard to stop. I was working out with some white man and they telephoned me to come. The white man brought me in, picking up Kenneth Swinging-Lance on the way.

When we came in, the boy was in very bad shape, bleeding, becoming unconscious. Kenneth gave him plenty of pure spring water, marked him, and then stopped the bleeding. The bullet was in the foot. He gave the boy a strengthening herb which brought him to his senses. He recognized me, so I stayed on. Kenneth just sucked that .38-caliber bullet out with his mouth. After that I showed the boy how to use some herbs on his wound. He used them the way I told him to and in a little while he was all right. His foot never swelled. Kenneth can heal better than any doctor.

When one of my daughters who is grown now was a baby, she had a bead in her ear. The ear ached and swelled. The doctor couldn't do anything. I took her to Kenneth, and it didn't take a minute to get it out. There was no ceremony. He just got it out, a bead that we had lost.

Another time a little boy swallowed a needle. They were afraid to take him to the doctor and they called Kenneth. But he was afraid they had already taken the child to the doctor, and he didn't want to be found out.[68] I just happened along and saw that there was something wrong. The boy was crying, and they called me in. They told Kenneth they hadn't been to the doctor. He asked for eagle tail feathers and was given one with beadwork at the end. He removed the beadwork and used it plain. He motioned four times towards the boy's throat, and there was the needle. He also looked into the throat, and there was just a scratch. The boy stopped crying and ran out to play just as if nothing had happened.

[68] That is, he didn't wish to compete with the doctor by treating the same case at the same time and consequently run the risk of bringing the white practitioner's ire down upon him.

One man went up against Kenneth Swinging-Lance with his power and tried many things against him, but Kenneth's power told him about it. He told the man he might as well go home. On the way, this man got very sick with pneumonia.

The doctor came after me. I was skinning birds.[69] I left with the doctor and came in quickly. Kenneth was already working on the sick man, right in the hospital before the nurses and doctor. He showed me what pneumonia can do. In this man's lungs I could see suds and blood; there was no room for him to breathe. All one side was filled up; the other lung was half full. I knew what Kenneth was going to do.

[69] The narrator was working for a naturalist from an Eastern museum at this time.

He took a hollow piece of horn out of his bag. He wiped the sick man's face with eagle feathers and put them up to the lung and asked for a basin. He put the horn up to the breast and blood came into it like into a cup. I saw it. I was watching. It was done several times, and the basin was overflowing. When the full lung was emptied, it started to have life again. He looked at it. "To take all the blood out would mean death to this man." So he did the other side and left some blood in. The man came to and moved his eyes.

I saw that Kenneth was praying. Out of his pocket he brought a black silk handkerchief and put it on the man's face and then on his breast. He took a yellow handkerchief and spread it over the man's face. The doctor and I helped him pour a teaspoon of medicine into the man's mouth. He was not to take the doctor's medicine until he was told to.

We had showed the doctor that Indians could cure, and he thanked us. He said, "I think he will be all right. You can go back to work. If I need you, I'll come for you myself." And we said we would come, rain or shine, unless our car broke down.[70]

[70] There were occasions when the doctor, in order to prevent a patient from being taken out of the hospital, had to permit a ceremony to be performed over him at the hospital. Later this would be interpreted by the Indians as a demonstration of the inability of the white doctor to cure the patient without the help of the shaman.

The sick man's strength came back after eating, but he became unconscious again after we left him. When a night and a day were up, he was coming back to life again. But we left the rest to the doctor, and he got him through.

Four days after Kenneth Swinging-Lance treated that man, there was another case of the same disease. The doctor said we'd better save a child who had pneumonia. This child belonged to my close relative, to a man who was a great friend of mine. I had just moved into another section of the reservation, and they had quite a time finding me, but they finally found me.

The child was in very bad shape. It had taken no food for eight days and was unconscious. This poor man, his father, said to me, "I might as well dig a grave for my child."

The doctor and I and two nurses and the mother were there, and the father was sitting outside crying. Something told me the child would live without the ceremony. Kenneth showed me the child's lungs. Just the lower part had suds in it. I was tired and I wanted to rest. He gave the child medicine. I thought it would be all right to rub tule pollen on the chest and leave it there.

I said, "If he wants milk, give it to him. Tomorrow morning he will be all right."

"How can that be?" asked the doctor.

"You wait and see. Hasn't it turned out all right before?" I said.

The little boy got up at midnight. Here they had a grave dug!

The next morning the brother and sister and father woke me up very early and offered me money. "I don't need it," I said.

"It's for your children," they said.

"Keep it, or give it to Kenneth Swinging-Lance. You're my relatives, and I won't take it." Kenneth wouldn't take it either.

"Take that boy out in the fresh air," I told them.

The doctor sure thought a lot of Kenneth. The doctor agreed with us now that the boy would be all right.

A Visit Across the Border

One time I went with Tule to Old Mexico. He was going to tell me about plants down there.[71]

[71] These were plants with medicinal properties which had been used in the past by the Mescalero but which were not available in their present territories.

He knew of a place where there was money, American dollars with heads on them that had long flowing hair. Geronimo and his people had this money once. They were gambling there when they saw the Fort Apache scouts coming.[72]

[72] These were Apache scouts recruited by the United States armed forces to locate and force the surrender of Apache who had fled the reserve.

The money was dumped in a sack and hidden.[73] Tule said, "We'll look for the money in Mexico."

[73] There have been constant rumors and reports that during the Indian wars of the 1870s and 1880s Apache groups which were being pursued had to abandon valuable booty, including gold and money, in caves or mountain hiding places. A number of expeditions have traveled to Mexico to seek these lost treasures.

But we went right by it. Tule was scared to get it. He said, "If a Mexican sees one dollar, he will kill you." Tule used to fight with the Mexicans and he thinks they are just like they used to be.[74] Anyway, we went mostly after herbs, not money. Tule had some kind of power, but I don't know where it was from.[75] I used to see him singing for lots of children and men and women.

[74] The long and bitter strife between the Mexicans and the Apache is mirrored in these statements.
[75] That is, the narrator is trying to convey that he does not know the source of Tule's power or the holy home where it was granted.

Mexico is a beautiful country with grass as high as this ceiling and cattle and horses fat even in winter. Indians couldn't starve there. We picked mountain laurel berries.[76] There are peccaries and quails as tame as chickens. You find springs in every mountain. Cactus grows as high as trees. I sure liked that country! A rich country! A white man wouldn't know how to handle it and he might starve, but not an Indian.[77] There is plenty of food there that the Apache like, juniper berries and prickly pears of all kinds.

[76] "Sophora secundiflora."
[77] This is an interesting reversal of the assertion often heard from white men about the Indian's inability properly to exploit a region.

Doctor's Assistant

Lots of sick people come to me. I was the white doctor's assistant for five years. He's an eye specialist in Chicago now. They say of me, "He was with that white doctor for five years; he's as good as a doctor."[78]

[78] The fact that the narrator's mother and mother's sister were well-known Indian herbalists and that he spent five years as an "assistant" at the hospital has brought many Mescalero to him for treatment of their ailments.

Dick Mason's daughter came here. Her tongue was coated all right. I had her stay here four days with my mother-in-law. Then she was all right. It was just her stomach. If you don't have the right food you can get rheumatism in this damp weather. A woman came up with her boy. It was just some little sickness. I said, "That boy will be all right," and he did get better.

There are many different ways to help people who are sick or who hurt themselves. One time Howard Day was thrown from a horse at Pajarito, and Tule performed a horse ceremony for him. They were not sure he was all right though. They told me to watch him. I rode with him six miles to Tank 2. At noon we got in. I was going to leave, but he called me back. He said to the boss, "I want this man with me. I'm not very well." We went under a tree.

I said, "Now you sleep." I put my hands over his face four times. Then he slept. Later I put my hand over his face four times, and he woke up.

He said, "Oh, what's happened? I feel as if I just got up from a good sleep." He said he didn't remember one thing that happened after the horse fell with him.

My father told me to motion over the face four times. I've done this many times. It helps every time. The man comes to his senses better.[79] I did it to Pete the time he and Ralph Thorn ran against each other full speed on horseback and Pete was knocked out.

[79] This magical act is not associated with any particular power and therefore does not have the status of a ceremony.

There is a sickness from eating too much fat. To cure it, you put the gut fat, you know how thick it is and wide, over you and dance for the one who is sick, and if he laughs he will be all right. If not, he's going to be very sick. There are buzzard songs for it too. The buzzard eats fat without getting sick.[80]

[80] This is another instance of sympathetic magic, so prominent in Mescalero Apache curative practices.

I killed an old deer that was too fat to run. It was at the Silver Springs station. Short-Leg, Hugh Giye, Old Jim, Edgar, and Robert Carlos were there. Short-Leg ate too much of the fat meat and got sick. Old Jim said he knew Buzzard and would fix him up.

He said something over him and motioned toward him with a stick. Then he said, "Now you go like this all night," and he made a noise with his mouth like someone farting.

And Short-Leg did. He nearly blew up that night. In the morning I got up early. I wanted to see what Old Jim would do. Jim went over to him and sang two buzzard songs. And Short-Leg got all right. He got up and ate with the rest of us.

You shouldn't urinate in an ant hill; you get stones in you from that. We had a boy who couldn't urinate. I was helping in the hospital then and took him there. I said to the doctor, "That boy's been urinating in an ant hill. He has stones in there."[81]

[81] As punishment for one who molests it, the ant, whose hill is of small stones, magically sickens its victim with bladder stones.

"What funny ideas you fellows have!" the doctor said.

But he used an instrument with a curved end and he got out four stones. He said, "That's bladder trouble."

I said, "All right, but who put them there?"

He said, "That's all I can tell you."

I said, "Well, it comes out according to the old stories."

Diego had two wives, but he never had enough. He was always chasing another woman. One killed him finally.

I was in the hospital working, helping the doctor, then. They brought Diego in. He was in awful shape. His penis was pulled out; the nerves and tissues were torn. The doctor couldn't do anything for him. It had happened over a week before that. Another week and he died. He wouldn't tell who did it, but he said that a woman did it. She promised him everything and then she got mad when he was on top of her and did this to him. Later Harvey Young's mother-in-law said she was the one.

Curing "Woman's Disease"

The two sisters, Tom's mother and my mother, were the real Indian doctors for woman's disease. Tom and I learned how to treat it from them. Last Saturday the Indians were talking about how much there was of it. They were talking down at the store. Some told us we should not try to cure them but make them go to the hospital so there's a record of it. We are not supposed to tell on them when they tell us who they got the disease from.

You can't get a venereal disease if you have intercourse with a woman only once, no matter if she has a disease.[82] A fellow came to me not long ago. He admitted he did it to a woman six times and to a sorry kind of a woman too. Nine days later he had clap. I didn't want to treat him so I sent him to Tom.

[82] It is also believed by the Mescalero that a woman cannot be impregnated by having intercourse with a man only once.

They have "blue balls," chancres, clap, and syphilis here. It was not so bad till the Chiricahua came.[83] Now even the old people have it. There are about ten women on the reservation who have a disease of this kind and more men.[84] Most don't go to the hospital. Indian medicine cures it.

[83] Note that the prevalence of venereal disease is blamed on the presence of members of another tribe, the Chiricahua Apache, who came to Mescalero in 1913. The narrator repeats the Mescalero charge about the Chiricahua even though his father is a Chiricahua. In this he reveals his own cultural and tribal orientation and commitment. By chancres the narrator is referring to chancroid. "Blue balls" is probably a stage of one of the venereal diseases.

[84] In 1935 the health services of the reservation had a record of fifteen cases of syphilis, four cases of cured or arrested syphilis, and five cases of gonorrhea. As the narrator indicates, relatively few victims of gonorrhea sought the help of the agency doctor during this period.

One fellow went to Tom. He didn't tell the name of the girl he got it from. He didn't give what he promised. Then he came to me. He said it was a new case. I told him it was old. I made him tell where he got it. "Don't lie to me," I told him. He didn't. I gave him the first doses. It cleaned him out good. He said he was all right. I told him no; I made him take a whole lot of the medicine and use it right along for a good while. He's all right now.

The patient has to tell the name of the one he got it from or I can't help. I've tried it and it won't work. After they have the medicine they can't get the disease again. Or if you have the medicine when you are young, before you have anything to do with women, you can't catch it. That's what was done with John Cloud and he never got anything, although he's been with some of the worst women. Women come to me. I have to look at their genitals. I've seen it before.

One time my wife got tired of having all these people come around and said, "Let's get away from here."

We packed, but just as we were ready to go, two women came. I told them, "No, I don't do that work any more. I'm all packed up and ready to move." They begged and pleaded. They offered money and everything.

My wife took pity on them. "You stay and help the poor things. I'm going on," she said.

I stayed and cured the one who was sick. "Why don't you stay true to your man?" I asked her.

The doctor here doesn't know that others are working along with him. We try everything. We are working on the various diseases, trying to find out what will cure them. Sometimes we have to perform operations to cure. Tom and I did once. It was a case of "blue balls." We wanted to use a razor. It was too dull. So we used a knife and glass and drained all the pus out. The man is all right now.

Alfonso Tomas had some sickness that made him bleed from the penis. Tom's mother cured him. She gave him bulbous panic-grass in a medicine to drink, and it cured him.[85]

[85] This is "Panicum bulbosum."

A tea made from the leaves or flowers of chickweed with wild gourd seeds added is used to wash the penis for chordee.[86] For chancres, the leaves of "wart medicine" are dried, ground, and put on wet. This is used in bad cases. I have used it on chancres, and my mother did too.

[86] Chickweed is "Stellaria sp.," and the wild gourd mentioned is probably "Cucurbita foetidissima" or wild pumpkin.

One Mexican came to me. He was like an old man; he couldn't do anything with his wife. I gave him some of this plant called osha to use.[87] The next time I saw him I asked him how he was getting along. He said, "That's good medicine. I'm bad, big as this," and he doubled up his fist to show me.

[87] Osha is "Ligusticum porteri."

One time we were waked up in the middle of the night, and there was an old woman with her daughter. The old woman was scolding the girl, telling her she ought to die. I came out with my wife. I knew what the matter was. The girl had clap. They were far-away relatives of mine, so I didn't want anything to do with it.[88] I said, "No, I've given up working on cases like that. Why don't you go to the hospital?"

[88] Since she was his female relative, a restraint relationship obtained between them in regard to intimate matters.

The girl just cried and said she'd rather die than tell the doctor. I didn't want to do it, but my wife took pity on them. She said, "Poor thing! Help her, my husband. They're some of your own people." So I said, "All right."

The old lady was still hollering at her. I told her, "Now stop that! It's just by your mouth that you have no son-in-law."

Then I told the girl, "Now tell me who you got it from or I can't help you."

She told me. Then she said, "Do something for me quick. I can't hold out much longer. I feel like I'm going to faint. I haven't urinated for two days."

Her belly was as big as if she was going to have a baby. I told her, "Now hold on and don't faint," and I quickly gave her some medicine to help her keep her head.

Then I took my flashlight and went out and looked for some shadscale.[89] I found it and dug it up. I came back and told her, "I'm not going to look at it. I'm just going to give you this to drink, and then you go off by yourself."

[89] "Atriplex canescens."

I gave it to her, and she went off and just fell over and urinated and fainted. She lay out there for an hour and a half. It was pretty cold, and so my wife went out and built a big fire. Finally she sat up and came back to camp. She was an awful sight. She had dirtied herself from both ends. She couldn't help it, for she didn't know what she was doing while she was lying there; she was unconscious and didn't know. And flesh kept coming out.

"I wish I were dead," she said.

"You ought to be. This is a nice way for a young girl to be! You just give your mother hard feelings."

I wanted her to go home then, but she wouldn't. "I'll stay here till I'm cured. If I go home, my mother will only get after me."

I told her it was no place for her to be, where there were children around, but she said she'd stay way off. She stayed around, made herself a little camp nearby, and I gave her the medicine. By the third dose she was all right. Then she said to me, "There's no use being ashamed before you now; you know everything about me, you know every part of me."

"Well, I don't think much of you for it," I told her.

"I couldn't help it. I just had to have a man. I went and got one, and that fellow gave me the clap."

I shouldn't have done it, but I told John Cloud about her. You know he doesn't care what he says. The next time he saw her he said something to her about it. He says she got after him so fast he had just about strength enough to get away. She put her finger down there and then put it up to his nose and said, "Smell that!" And he says it smelled awful too.[90]

[90] There is an insulting gesture which women use in heated arguments and which stands for this act. However, here the woman was so angry that she resorted to the act itself instead of the gesture.

It's a queer thing about this girl. Before this she had children right along. Since this she hasn't had any more.[91]

[91] Apparently the narrator is unaware of the part that gonorrhea can play in sterility.

Two sisters came to me with it too. They are relatives and I didn't want to do it. So I sent them to another, to a woman. Old Hunter had clap, and I cured him. I just smoked him with juniper and told him to wash his clothes with coal oil and gasoline. There are men going around with it right now. I know who they are. When they start to come around my camp, I always lead them off some place, get them away from my camp. They claim that your hand gets sore if it touches the pus. I put the medicine on with a stick and rag or with a skunk tail.

If the penis hurts when you hit it, it's chordee.[92] When a man has this, it just doubles up till he can't urinate and he has to have an operation. One man here has his cut off. He's ashamed when he sees me. An El Paso doctor cut it off. I said to him, "Why didn't you come to me in the first place? I could have cured you."

[92] Chordee is a phase of gonorrhea.

Then there is the kind that causes the pointed rough pimples. You can't touch the pointed ones. The least little touch drives you crazy. One boy had it. He's dead now. I had my first experience of curing this sickness with this boy. He said, "I got it from monkeying around an old woman." He nearly went crazy with the pain. I got the aster plant and put it with warm grease. I told him to let it drip on. "Don't mind how it hurts; stay with it." The first dose cured him.

Two years later he got chordee and came to me again.[93] He couldn't urinate and I had to straighten it. I made something different for him. I took giant hyssop,[94] a tall plant that grows at Three Rivers, and I took the plant called virgin's bower, the one with purple flowers.[95] I put these two together, pounded them up, boiled them down. I added salt and water later. You can add tobacco too. I tried it on myself first. You tell when it is ready to use by touching it. When it burns it is strong.

[93] In all probability this man was never cured but suffered an intensification of the venereal infection.

[94] "Agastache greenei."

[95] "Atragene pseudo-alpina."

I said to him, "I've got to burn you out. It's going to hurt a little."

He didn't want me to. I made him hold a stick while I put it on. He grunted like you were killing something. He scratched himself, his head and his legs.[96]

[96] See 4 [102].

Then I told him, "Lie down. I'm going to do something to you, one more thing to stop the pain."

I had something soothing made from mint, the one with purple flowers on top which grows along the water, and other things. The leaves are pounded together and boiled down to a strong taste. After that it is strained and put in bottles. You can drink it or put it on the outside. It kills nerves in the intestines. You can put it on your hand and put a needle in and you won't feel it. This soothing medicine is good for injecting too, I find. I got a needle from the doctor when I worked at the hospital. A dog was shot and I gave him an injection of this. In a week he was well. What all goes into this, I can't tell you. I put this all over this boy, and it cooled him. After a while he shook his penis and said it was all right.

One boy came to us with something we never saw before. It was in smooth lumps all over his penis and testicles. He got it from a whore. We didn't know what to call it.

I said, "I think I can burn it off."

Tom said, "No."

I said, "I'd like to try."

"All right, I'll give you a chance."

I put that strong medicine on with a skunk's tail. He reared up. "You're killing me!" Then I put my soothing medicine on. I put a hot stone on his belly and covered him. When I came back the lumps were gone, burned off. I asked him if it hurt much.

"I ache from the tip of my toes to my head." But it cured him. "I'm all right. I'm going now," he said.

Andy Buck died of clap. He got it from his wife. She had it and he didn't wait till she was all cured. I wanted him to go out fishing with me. I sent word over but they said he couldn't come. I went to his place and he was lying down. We always fooled with each other. I smelled something funny. I said, "What have you got under your bed, a skunk?" When I said this, the woman went out and I knew right away what the matter was.[97]

[97] It is improper for Mescalero men to discuss sexual matters before women.

I told him, "I know what is the matter with you. You've got disease from woman."

"No, I'm just a little sick. I'll be up in a little while." He was ashamed. He wouldn't talk about it. This was in the summer of 1932.

In the fall I waited for him to go hunting with me. He never got up from that bed. I came to his wife. I asked her, "What are you doing for that man?"

"We've got an Indian doctor."

"Who?"

She named a woman I knew.

"She doesn't know anything about it. You're going to be a widow."

I could have cured him. I told them to come to me but they never did and he died.

About six months ago I cured another man. It was not a bad case. He went out to urinate and couldn't. Then he noticed it felt wet. He didn't want his wife to know it and came right over to me. It usually comes on the ninth day, and he said he had the woman nine days ago. He said, "I've got a terrible case." But it wasn't bad at all. He didn't want to go back home, so I took him out in the woods with me and treated him out there. I just gave him medicine to drink. I fixed him up in no time. He paid me well too. He said, "I must admit that I like to do it!"

Tom had a white boy from town over to his place till today. He's turning him loose today. The boy has been staying there three weeks. He's well now. He was singing out under the trees today. A man with a gold tooth brought him up. He's a rich boy. He said, "My folks have got lots of money; you cure me and I'll pay you well." He's from the East. He was staying down here for a while. He got living with an old whore and caught clap. He said he went to two white doctors and they nearly killed him and didn't do him any good either. I first knew of it when Tom came up to my place. He was out of some medicine and wanted some of mine. He told me about the case and said he'd go half and half with me on what he got. I told him never mind that, but I gave him the medicine. The boy sure had a bad case. Tom says that when he gave him the first dose, the matter ran out and went all over. He stayed right there at Tom's place. He had his own blankets and his own dishes. Tom was very careful. Tom made him tell who it was he got it from; that's always a part of it. He made him put money down in front of him each time he treated him too. He explained to him that power would see it and be glad, for power would know the ceremony was paid for and cure it faster. I do this too. With the last one I cured I didn't do it, but he paid well.[98]

[98] Although the narrator and his cousin Tom sometimes cooperated in curing with herbs, a certain amount of rivalry existed between the two. On one occasion the narrator told me, "Tom had clap himself. He came to me. He couldn't cure himself." Once Tom looked over some plants Chris and I had gathered. Of one of them he said, "That's my medicine. What are you going to do with it?" When Chris left on an errand, Tom told me, "You better not let him fix any of that for you. He doesn't know what to do with it and how to handle it. It's my medicine. It might do you harm."

Again we find something close to an admission on the part of the narrator that he sometimes crosses the thin line between herbalism and ceremonialism.

I was down at Tom's today. The boy was under the tree. He didn't see me coming. I said, "How's the clap?"

He looked around quick. "Oh, it's only you! I'm all ready for another dame."

I looked it over. It was all right. I hit it. It didn't hurt. "Boy, now you're ready for business. You can do it all you want and it won't hurt you."

He went over to the store and bought me a big watermelon.

When he was being treated, he put down five dollars the first day. The next day he put down ten dollars. The day after that Tom turned back a five-dollar bill to him and told him it was too much and to save it for the next day. He told him to put down a silver dollar or two each time after that.

He had a sore on his leg. I asked Tom if he was doing anything for it.

"Not for that damn fool!"

"He's paying you well," I said. I put some stuff that burns on it and cured him of that sore. He said he had had it since he was nineteen and had had all kinds of treatments for it. It had cost him about a thousand dollars. He was putting all kinds of salve on it.

He said, "I've got a good word for your people after this. I came to you sick. You didn't scalp me but cured me."

One girl here has such a bad case of syphilis that she'll never get well. She got it from an old man.[99] She is a young girl and was pretty. Lots of the young fellows liked her. Instead she gave herself to that old man. Now her life is ruined. No one would have her. She said to me, "I like to have a man, but it has brought me lots of trouble."

[99] As this and other remarks indicate, a person is considered more likely to contract a venereal disease or a more severe venereal disease than otherwise would afflict him if his sexual partner is much older than he is.

Of Medicinal Plants

For my work with all these sick people I've had to learn a lot about the herbs. Cinquefoil[100] is good for weak kidneys. But it is too strong for a child; it is just for grownups. The root is pounded and boiled to make the medicine. It is good for gallstones too. That Oklahoma Indian with the braids who was here during the

girl's puberty ceremony came to me. He is a Kiowa Apache. I gave him some of
this for kidney trouble and the swelling all went down. He said, "Such a little fellow
and you know medicine!" The doctor asked me about this medicine. He says he is
going to see if he can bottle it and make it stronger. Mexicans and white people
come about this one.

[100] "Potentilla thurberi."

Dock[101] is good for diarrhea. Even the Navaho know this. A Navaho who was
staying here was curing a child who had diarrhea and was looking for this plant.
He came to my camp and I found it for him. A long time ago I found out that this
plant is good in another way. One time my boy sucked a centipede. They told me
to give this plant with sugar and another herb to make him vomit. I gave it to him
and it did make him vomit.

[101] "Rumex sp."

Through my own experience I found out that a certain sage is good for a wound
of the eye. I had bought some watermelons for a bunch of boys. They gave me half
of one to eat. So I picked up the half watermelon. I had the knife I used in cutting
them in my hand, pointing toward my face. When I lifted the melon to eat it, the
knife hit my eye. I felt the blood pouring down the side of my face and I just
threw that melon away. That night my eye began to swell and hurt. There was a
Navaho here and I met him. He said he had something for a sore eye. He took this
plant, crushed it, and strained it four times. Then there was no dirt in the water.
Then he put it in my eye. It sure did smart, but it healed the eye up in no time.
Then my boy, Anthony, ran into a branch and hurt his eye. It began to swell. I
told him, "Your eye is getting pretty bad; you'd better let me fix it. What I do will
make you scratch your head for a few minutes, but it will help."[102] I fixed medicine
from this plant for him, and his eye got better right away.

[102] The Mescalero reaction to pain is to start a counterirritation. The head and
body are scratched or the hair of the head is pulled while the pain is acute.

I use sage in another way too. If I have a pain from witchcraft I take sage and
burn it. It turns to ash which is easy to light again. Then I put it on my body
where the pain is and light it.[103]

[103] The use of a moxa to cope with persistent, localized pain is common.

I know a way to use one-seeded juniper[104] because I saw Old Lady Yube use it
on Tall Raider. This was during my younger days. Tall Raider was hit between
the eyes by a skunk that squirted at him. He fell like a dead man. The doctor was
there and couldn't do anything. He gave up in two minutes. They pushed him
away, and this old woman came out. She burned one-seeded juniper in front of Tall
Raider. He opened his eyes and got up.

[104] "Juniperus monosperma."

The doctor asked her what she had used. "That's my business," she said. "You pay me, and I'll tell you."

This old woman said she had learned it from an old man who had a ceremony from the juniper.[105]

[105] The implication is that ceremonial procedures as well as the plant were used.

A man was using power from the toad for children that were burned. One girl was burned pretty bad. The medicine that was shown is a wonderful thing. This man came to a chokecherry bush. Toad told him, "You can boil and strain the fruit and use the juice on the burned parts. It's a sure cure. It's better to keep the sores open; don't cover them." The toad hopped around some more. Then it said, "Use bark, the aspen bark or the poplar; burn it and use the ashes on the sore parts. Once they dry up there will be no more sores. Burn old leather and use the ashes."

The man who knows the power of the toad can throw hot coals in his own mouth, and they won't burn him at all.[106] I've seen that done. Many Indians can do it. You can put hot coals out and let the man walk on it with his bare feet, and he will put the fire out that way and yet won't be burned. That I've seen done. It's the power of the toad that makes this possible.

[106] In all likelihood the toad's coolness to the touch has given rise to its association with the healing of burns.

One time one of my daughters fell and got her hand in boiling coffee up to the first joint. We used chokecherry[107] to heal it. It is a good medicine for burns; it keeps the matter down and makes good skin come again. It keeps the soreness out also. It took only a week to cure my daughter, though lots of skin came off her hand. She's a big girl now.

[107] "Prunus calophylla."

Some of these same plants can be used for our animals too. To cure a dog which has been bitten by a mad dog, I take juniper needles, osha, eagle feathers, and the hairs from the tail of a skunk and burn them together. This is put up to the nose of the dog.[108] I do this instead of killing the dog. I saved my dogs twice by doing this.

[108] Incensing with the smoke of various materials is widely employed in Mescalero curing practices and is considered effective in the treatment of animals as well as man. It is also used in other contexts, such as to make a dog a good hunter. It is most often used, however, to prevent ghost sickness after death and to deal with colds and respiratory disorders. The materials burned and inhaled vary according to the malady or difficulty; for instance, sage or "ghost medicine" is always burned after a death.

I have my own way of curing my horses too. When a horse's eye is getting white I cut a vein near the nose. They used any sharp rock or flint in the old days. Now

I use a knife. I put the sharp point on the vein and hit it. After a while the blood flow stops by itself. You have to know the right vein to hit; if you hit the wrong one the horse will bleed to death. About two minutes is all it will bleed, and the eye turns black again. I saw the old people do this. I learned it from them.

We have many good doctors here in the Indian way. Once I had an awful nosebleed. It started in the night. Then it stopped. Then it started again. It kept this up till morning. I was so weak I hardly knew what was going on. A friend came up. He got Tony Lewis's mother, who belongs to some of my wife's people; she is a long-ways relation. I was about to faint. I could just about hear. I don't know all that she did. I wanted to know but I was too far gone. I know she gave me some herb and told me to drink it. It tasted like a plant I know. There was a big crowd there, my wife's people and my people. I felt the blood go back then, go back from my nose. When I felt better I got up in front of all of them and said, "Well, I went to the underworld." They all laughed.[109]

[109] It is believed that at death the soul goes on a four-day journey to the edge of the underworld. Persons who have recovered from very serious sicknesses occasionally claim that they were led to the very threshold of the land of the dead but managed to return and recover. See Opler 1946b.

The woman who worked on me told me to try to eat and drink a lot. She said, "Your blood is almost gone. You have to eat and drink a lot to get your strength back." So I ate and ate and drank and drank. The nurse from the agency called at my camp late that day to ask me to get a wild turkey for her. I told her I was too weak and couldn't go out.

"Why didn't you call the doctor?" she asked.

"I had a better doctor."

My wife had just started to tan buckskin when this happened. It dried up because I couldn't help.[110]

[110] The Mescalero man sometimes helps the woman in the initial stages of tanning or preparing large hides.

Even the children are interested in these plants and in finding new ways to use them. I told Anthony that the leaves of squaw weed are good for the feet.[111] He used the root on his corn and it helped. So then I used the root in this way on my own ingrown toenail. I pounded it up, put it with water, and boiled it down to make it strong. It softened the nail up when I soaked the foot and the nail became just like rubber.

[111] "Senecio fendleri."

Choosing among Beliefs

A good many Mescalero are very careful about everything they do because they have some belief or rule about it. I saw a boy, now dead, shoot a bird, a flycatcher.

He carried it around in his pocket. His people got after him for it. Some say this bird has good power; some say it is bad and brings sickness. Anyway they didn't like it. So he took the arrow, washed it in water, and shoved it in a red ant hill and let it stay there for four days. He said that maybe he would have bad luck otherwise and this would take it off him and give it to the red ants. He rubbed some of the dirt from the ant hill on his hands too.

I've often heard that the spider web is not to be broken. If you have something coming to you, it is in that spider web, they say. To break it is to break your luck. The youngsters are told to remember this and do not break webs. If they go through a web and break it, though they didn't mean to do it, they say, "There goes my luck."

I was riding with two other fellows, coming along last on the trail. The first man ducked under a spider web. I called to warn the second, but his head was turned to talk to me, and he didn't see it. It broke across his face. He said, "There goes my luck. I may have lost sheep or cattle or something that I don't know about now."

A Mescalero won't kill a spider. If he does happen to do it, he calls the name of a man he hates and says, "He killed you." Then the bad luck goes to that fellow. This is not done for the spider alone. A person says this when he kills any other insect that is dangerous and also if he kills a coyote or any other animal people fear. Even when you kill a dog you do this.

Some of these things seem to turn out as they say they will, all right. For example, they say that a pregnant woman should not ride in a wagon or an automobile. This may either kill the baby inside, or when it gets outside, it will make it dizzy or faint.[112] Most of the women keep this custom today. It is all right for a pregnant woman to ride a horse; it is good for her.

[112] What is meant is that a child born of a woman who rides in a wagon or automobile while she is carrying him will be prone to attacks of faintness or dizziness. There is an association between the turning of wheels and dizziness.

They told Bent-Arm's third wife not to ride in a wagon but to travel on a horse in her condition. She was about to have her baby. That's why they were coming in to the agency. But Bent-Arm made her drive the wagon and he rode the horse. They started from Elk Springs. She drove only six miles, to Rock Tank, and she got very dizzy. She tried to get off the wagon and jumped. We watched her. We saw her go around as if she was going to fall and then we saw her fall. A number of us saw this. We got up to her and knew what was wrong. She was dying. She died right there.

Bent-Arm was afraid they'd say he killed her. "Now remember, you are all witnesses," he told us. So we were witnesses for him, and they called it an accident.[113]

[113] The Mescalero were well aware that some white agency officials and regional court officers considered them to be undisciplined savages and invariably drew the most damaging conclusions about any episode involving a Mescalero in which an injury or death occurred.

If you are stingy you always get warts, especially on your hands. Even Mexicans believe in that. I had nine warts on my hands. Sanchez, the Mexican, counted them and said, "Give me fifty cents." I gave it to him, and he told me to come back in nine days. I came back in the nine days, and they were all gone. After that all the boys went to him. The Mescalero women get rid of warts with a basket. They put a basket on their backs. They pick at the warts and motion over the shoulder, making believe they are throwing them in the basket. I saw Mary Seco do this for a boy. In two weeks his warts were gone.

Another thing that I have seen come true is the shooting of thunder flints from the sky. Out at Elk Springs I found one of these black flints which are shot by lightning.[114] Big Hat and a bunch of fellows were out there when lightning struck a pine tree. Just when that lightning struck, they saw a piece of flint stuck in the tree, about half way in. They didn't stay around then, but later they came back and I came with them. We wanted to see how that flint got in that tree. It couldn't have come from the ground! We got there and the flint was gone.

[114] It is believed that when Lightning strikes in anger, it shoots flints. Pieces of flint which are found in a lightning-scored area are considered to be Lightning's "arrows." These "arrows" of Lightning are much used in ceremonies. Thunder and Lightning are related concepts and are expressed by one Mescalero term, Thunder being the "voice" of Lightning. Lightning is thought of in a personified sense and is, of course, a potent source of supernatural power.

Later I was walking along alone, thinking of arrow points. All at once I saw a black flint sticking out of the ground. A few days later there was a business meeting and the Indians were talking about the tree that was struck by the flint. I pulled the flint out of my pocket and said, "This is what you are talking about." They passed it around. Many of them wanted to buy it from me, but I wouldn't sell it.[115] It is worth a lot to the Indians.

[115] The Indians were called together on this occasion to discuss modern economic problems.

If a man is out on a hunt or raid and sees that a lizard or horned toad is trying to get in bed with him, he knows that his wife is unfaithful to him. Even today, if a lizard or horned toad runs toward you it means that. I was playing a game of pitching rocks with Ernest Chico, my cousin Henry, and his brother-in-law, Arthur Largo. A big old horned toad began running toward Ernest. Ernest is Chiricahua, but he knew what it meant. He said to me, "Ah, did you see that?"

"Yes."

"I'd better go home."

The others asked, "What's the matter?"

"Oh, you young fellows don't know anything! Don't tell them," he said to me.[116] I didn't say anything. Ernest said, "Oh, even if my wife was here it would have happened."

116 The older Apache of the reservation are keenly conscious of the degree to which interest in and knowledge of aboriginal beliefs and practices have fallen away under changed conditions and the supervision of the white man.

Some people are so careful that they won't let you do this and that. I found some masked dancer headdresses in a cave in the mountains. I wanted to take them, but my mother-in-law was afraid that the children would get sick. These were different from most, they had some red on top. The red on the headdress is dangerous, she said. I hadn't thought much about it, but I thought I'd better let it alone.117

117 It is considered very dangerous to handle or disturb the ceremonial paraphernalia of others, for the uninitiated person is certain to make mistakes that may anger the source of power and result in retaliation. An added reason for not disturbing this particular cache was the likelihood that the ritual objects had been placed in the cave following the death of the shaman who had made and used them. To violate the cave might result in ghost sickness as well as punishment at the hands of the Mountain Spirits.

Another account from the narrator dealing with the discovery gives some added detail: "I found some masked dancer headresses, one skirt [kilt worn by the dancers], and a bundle of things in a cave about two and a half miles in the mountains back of Sos's place. I don't know whose they were. They were hanging on a bush inside. They looked old. I tried to take a picture but it didn't come out. [When asked why he didn't take the objects out into the open for the photograph, he did not reply.] They have different markings from the Mountain Spirits being made now. There is a red circle at the top of the buckskin where the uprights are attached. I tried to remember back to who made this kind. I asked Sos and all the old men. They wouldn't say anything but 'You'd better let it alone.' I danced for Old Man Dan. I don't think it's his, though some say it sounds from the description like some he made."

I was out hunting with my boy Anthony. We came to a place where I wanted to stay for a while. Anthony said, "I don't want to stay here. I dreamed that this place was all on fire and I was here."118

118 Note that the narrator's son has the standard Mescalero attitude toward a dream of fire.

I said to him, "Why didn't you tell me about that dream, and I wouldn't have brought you here."

Every once in a while a person says he doesn't believe in some of these things, and then he is shown that many of them are true. Ernest Chico was with a bunch who were talking about ceremonies. After a while Ernest said, "I don't believe in that power stuff. Those men just say it."

Old Jim was there and he got very angry. "Ernest, come here," he said. Ernest came. "You will see it for your own good," Jim said, and he marked Ernest's hand with pollen. "I am going to sing four songs for you."

Jim began to sing. Ernest sat looking at his hand. At the beginning of the fourth song Ernest's hand began to move. Then he began to dance, watching his hand all the time.[119]

[119] Ernest's scepticism was obviously only skin deep. When put to the test, he quickly showed standard Mescalero reactions of the believer. The narrator thus described another episode in which Old Jim vindicated ceremonialism: "I remember one case at Whitetail [when a shaman assisted at childbirth]. The doctor couldn't help so Preacher Arthur went for Old Jim. He came. He sang two songs and said the baby would come in just a little while. At the third song the child came. Mrs. Arthur was saying, 'Sing, sing.' The doctor had given up. He wanted to cut her open. He said it was the only chance for her life. She wouldn't let him. She asked who a good Indian doctor was. Ernest Chico was there and said that Old Jim was. Mrs. Arthur grabbed the baby on the third song and it came easily. Old Jim told me about it."

I thought to myself, "I wonder what he is seeing. I wish I was the one seeing these things."

Jim knew what I was thinking. He said to me, "Don't think that way. Your turn will come." Jim was never afraid to speak up, even to whites.

When the song was finished Ernest said, "Brothers and sisters, I thought that it was just for fun. But now I know different. Now I believe with my whole heart. I see everything. I see lots of things but I'm not going to tell. I'll keep that to myself. But this is a real man. Everything he says is true. Whenever this man sings I'm going to be there."

Old Jim was like that. He showed his power plain. But some of these fellows around here won't tell you anything. They are afraid you are going to get their ceremony, become more powerful than they are, and witch them. They just tell you that they require certain ceremonial gifts and then carry on their ceremony. But they don't tell you much about it. When I hire a shaman I make him tell me all about his ceremony. Lots of them try to hide it. I say, "That's what I hired you for; tell me about it." And I make them say where they got it, who they got it from, how long ago they learned it, and how long it's going to stay.[120]

[120] This is a further indication of the narrator's curiosity about the power and ceremonies of others.

The Western Apache are just like doctors. They sure have some pretty strong shamans! They tell everything. They tell you just where they got their ceremonies, when, just what they do, when they have to sing for you, whether they have to sing in the morning, in the evening, or when. They tell you about yourself too. They trace you back to when you were a little child; they don't have to ask you about yourself. The Jicarilla Apache tell you everything, too.[121]

121 It is not uncommon among American Indian tribes to find this kind of exaggerated respect for shamanistic practices which belong to the generally accepted pattern but which are different enough to be exotic.

Shorty, a Mescalero, was a peyote camp leader. His wife ate peyote too. I tried to get on to where his power was from. I asked him when he was drunk. He told me, "I know what you're after. You're not going to learn my ceremony." He found me out right there.

I said, "Old man, if I were old and you were young, I wouldn't talk like that to you." I'll catch him at it some day.

Some of these Chiricahua are pretty jealous of their power too. Sos saw me paint a sun on something I was making. It was one where the sun is setting. He pointed to it and said, "That's my power." I told him, "It was the power of many of the Mescalero too. I am doing it the way my people did it." Many people around here don't like Sos and call him a witch. To tell the truth I'm a little afraid of him too. Once I had a fight with Alfred, and Sos got pretty angry at me. He wanted to butt in. Howard Sage wouldn't let him and he nearly shot Sage.

There are different kinds of sickness which the Mescalero claim are from animals. Cramps in the hand or fingers or muscles, foaming at the mouth, red eyes, snapping your teeth at somebody, scratching somebody—it all comes from animals. They say that if you handle coyotes you get cramps in the hand or wrist and you can't open your hand. I have handled all the animals that the Apache are afraid of and even the insects, the vinegarroon, the scorpion, the black beetle of the plains, grasshoppers, but I have not been sick. I've just been bitten sometimes. All kinds of animals have bitten me, the bear, the wildcat, the coyote, the snake, the tarantula, and the badger. Only the badger made me very sick. I've tried everything. I guess I'm the only Indian who has. Lots call me a witch.122 The Mescalero claim that if a bat bites you, you can't eat anything that a horse has carried. I have been bit by a bat and I do it, but an old Mescalero wouldn't. The white froth left by insects on juniper and pine is called "spit on pine or juniper." The Mescalero are afraid to touch it. They say it gives you sores. But I've touched it and it never hurt me.

122 The narrator shows that he is aware of the whispering that goes on about him because of his unconventional practices.

I have a ruler that Old Jim gave me. When he died they tried to make me throw it away. They said, "Do you want him to come back and choke you?"123

123 Anciently the Mescalero destroyed all of a person's property at his death. It was believed that, if this were not done, the ghost of the dead person would return to claim his property and persecute the selfish relative. This conception was associated to some extent with the belief that the dead needed their property for use in the underworld, a land in which much the same activities prevail as are carried out on earth.

I said, "Old Jim was a good man when he was alive and he won't bother me now."

Then there is the plant called "crazy cactus" by the Mescalero.[124] The berries get ripe in the latter part of July and are gone by September. The berries are eaten by birds and animals, and they don't seem to hurt them, but the Indians are afraid of them. They say that if you eat the berries they will make you crazy, and they won't eat or touch them. But I have eaten them and they never hurt me at all.[125]

[124] The plant referred to is tomatillo. Its scientific name is "Lycium pallidum."

[125] The narrator is a keen observer and has had enough contact with the white doctor, the American scientist, and others to give his thinking a naturalistic bent. This sometimes collides with Mescalero belief, and not infrequently it is the belief which suffers.

They say that sometimes you get a ball of flesh in the fingers from handling certain plants, mice, or gophers. Raymond Belt's first wife played with a baby gopher. They say it got right in her hands. The mark on her palm looked like a little gopher, about that size and shape. They had to cut her hand off at the wrist. Once I was skinning a gopher. Muchacho Negro came in. He said it was a bad thing to monkey around it. He told me how he once went to sleep with his head on a gopher hill, and the next day his face was all swollen on that side. But it has never given me any trouble.

Some of these things that you hear are pretty hard to believe. The Mescalero say that the Milky Way comes only in summer. I see it all the year. It's just a matter of belief.[126]

[126] Again, the narrator opposes his observations to certain Mescalero beliefs.

Sobering Thoughts about the Cardinal

There was a man here, a Mescalero, who knew the cardinal. They said that he was carrying it around mounted. I never saw it, but I believed he did. Once when I was at his camp I saw something that was wrapped up in a cloth that looked like a mounted bird or mouse. He went out, and I felt of it, and it felt like a bird.

One day he asked me for whiskey, and I brought him some. His son and his grandson were with me. This time I did drink some with him to find out about the power of this bird. He had come down to meet us right at the gate at Silver Springs. The other fellows drank a lot. They were so drunk they were helpless. But I was careful. When the old man got pretty full, I asked him what that was wrapped up at his tent the day I was there.

And he told me it was a cardinal. Then I found out what he had, and I asked him lots of questions. He was not too drunk, so he just answered a few questions, but when he got real full I asked him to go through the ceremony of that bird for me.[127]

[127] The narrator is trying once more to learn the details of someone else's ceremony.

He told me that it is good when a man is drunk. It is the enemy of drink. It can make you get over it. He had the two tail feathers of the bird with him. He went and dipped the tip of those feathers four times in water and put something on it. It was some kind of a powder. He put it to his mouth four times, then swallowed this powder. Then he drank the water. In less than ten minutes he was sober. Then he started to talk up like a man.

He said, "This bird is good in many ways but also is bad in many ways. It works both ways, but I use it only in the good way.[128] I don't use it to make enemies. So I have showed you about this bird, and you can think about it. But don't tell anybody."

[128] This is an acknowledgement by the shaman that the power can be used for either good or evil. He asserts, of course, that he is using it for good purposes only.

Since then I have thought about this thing, and two or three times I have seen a cardinal and tried my best to get close to him, but they are hard to come near to, even near enough to shoot. And so after trying I gave it up. The only two I got were killed by a white man. I skinned them.

I dreamed that this cardinal was talking to me. He told me lots of things. Then he was gone.[129]

[129] During this period when the narrator was trying to obtain a skin of the cardinal and was thinking a good deal about the bird, he dreamed that the bird was making revelations to him. This promising prologue was apparently never followed up, for the narrator does not claim to have power from this bird.

There are some Indians below Las Cruces, the Tortugas, who are now just about like Mexicans. I was among them. I can't understand a word of their language but I saw the cardinal used by one of them. He had a drum like ours, cowhide stretched over a hoop. On the drumstick this bird's skin was wrapped. It had downy feathers of some kind tied to it too. The drumstick had a ball on the end. I asked what he was doing and found out he was singing to bring rain. It wasn't raining, but the next day it was cloudy. I had to go away, so I don't know whether it rained.

Owls usually come around, but they didn't come last night. The coyotes were pretty close though, raising a lot of noise.

I told Tom I was talking about Cardinal. He said, "Say, why do you mention such a bird? It's one of the worst to talk about." They claim it is a witch and can witch other birds and start trouble between man and man.

Testing a White Man

There was a young white boy who was talking all the time about how he could outwalk any Indian. I thought I'd have some fun with him. He wanted to go hunting with me, and we started off early in the morning. I purposely stayed away from where the deer were. I thought I'd give him a good walking. He was going good, keeping ahead of me and going fast. He carried a lighter rifle than mine, and I had a big belt of cartridges on besides. I just walked behind him, going easy. I took him over four ridges and around and up again. I must have walked him about twenty miles. We'd go up a ridge in a different place, and he'd never know the difference. We circled around about four times.

Finally I said, "Now we're coming pretty close to where the deer are. Have your gun ready and look close." He was getting pretty tired by this time, so I said, "We'll just go up this ridge, over the other side, and up another ridge, and we'll find plenty of deer there."

He started up the hill, going pretty slow now. Finally he sat right down on the hill. "I've got to have a smoke," he said.

"Hell," I said, "what do you need a smoke for? Now every animal will smell it, and we won't get near them."

"Well, I've got to have it," he said. So I let him have his smoke, and we started out again. After a while he said, "God damn it! What do you think I am, a horse? I bet I've walked a hundred miles. I can't go any farther."

"I thought you could outwalk anybody, and here you are tired already!"

"Aren't you tired?"

"No, I'm just as fresh as when we started."

So he said, "All right, I'll go on."

It was getting a little dark by this time. Just then he said, "What's that?" I looked up and there was a bear on the ridge.

I said, "Now you go straight up here, and I'll go around the other way and head him off." I knew I'd never see him again that day.

I went on a little way and waited. Then I thought, "Hell, I shouldn't have done that. I'm liable to lose that poor boy." So I shot in the air so that he'd know where I was. But he was pretty mixed up by this time. It got dark, so I went back to camp. I knew he was all right and thought he could build a fire and go to sleep there.

The next day I started out to find him. I brought a horse along because I knew he couldn't walk back. I was pretty stiff and lame myself. Pretty soon I came on him. He was tired and hungry.

He said, "This is one time you have walked the legs off a good white man. I've been walking all night while I've been sitting here. I was so tired and lame I couldn't go to sleep."

"All right," I said, "take this horse and get back to camp." He took the horse and started off.

I went up to the place where we had seen the bear. Sure enough, he was there getting some grubs from under the rocks. I came pretty close to make sure it was a bear. He smelled me and he turned around and came toward me slowly. He was showing his teeth, and I could see the hair on his shoulders begin to stand up. Bang! I let him have it, and he went down with a bullet right through the face and out the opposite side of the head. I didn't know how I could get him back, for I had no horse. I began to drag him down the hill to the canyon.

The boy heard the shot and ran his horse back just as I got it down to the bottom. He said, "Oh, look what you've got!"

"It's lucky you came back with that horse, because I don't know how I'd get him back to camp."

"Well," he said, "what do you say we cut off some of the meat and have some, and then we'll take it back."

"All right."

So we built a fire, cut off a rib, and were eating it when along comes Carlos, Alfred, and a Mexican. They stood about a hundred yards off looking at us and wouldn't come any closer.

Alfred said, "See that fellow eat bear! He must know Bear."[130]

[130] It is assumed that any Apache who dares to eat bear meat must know the ceremony of Bear or at least must have been fed the meat of the bear ceremonially.

The white boy asked the Mexican to have some, and he said, "Sure, I like bear." And he came over and began to eat with us. But the others stood there talking and watching. After we finished, Alfred and Carlos wouldn't let that Mexican come close to them. Every time he came near them, they put their hands over their noses so they wouldn't smell the bear.[131]

[131] Note the reluctance of these Apache, one a Mescalero and the other a Chiricahua, to expose themselves to the odor of the bear.

The white boy said, "Well, let's load the bear on the horse, and I'll ride a little way, and then you ride the rest. I feel better now."

I knew he couldn't make it, but I didn't say anything. So we started off. The boy rode along with the Mexican right behind him, and I walked behind them. Carlos and Alfred came along far in the rear. They didn't want to get too close.

We came to the place where the boy said I was to ride. So we changed places. There was still a long way to go, so I rode along and kept my eye on him. He was getting weaker and weaker. Pretty soon he said, "Say, are you going to make me walk all the way to camp? I'm pretty nearly dead."

I said, "You told me to ride. You said it yourself. I walked all the way back to camp yesterday after I left you, and I walked as much as you did yesterday too."

"Yes, but you had a good sleep last night, and I didn't sleep at all. You better get off that horse and let me ride."

So I thought he had had enough, and I let him get on the horse. I told the Mexican to let me ride with him. He said the horse would buck, so I said, "Aw shucks, I don't care about that." I got on behind him. The horse did try to throw me, but we got into camp all right.

I played a trick on another white man once too. I filled a whiskey bottle with coffee. The man sneaked out to drink it and I heard plenty of French words as he threw the bottle away.[132]

[132] The normally high spirits of the narrator and his tendency to play the practical joker are evident in these accounts.

Some white men get along pretty well with these Indians. One white stockman here liked Indian food. He lived right with us in camp. He liked the way we fixed different kinds of meat.

I knew the old trader pretty well and got along with him. I don't trade much with the present white trader now though. I had some trouble with him. I got a little behind because I had to take care of my wife's sister, and he cut off my credit.[133] Since then I don't have much to do with him.

[133] Note that the narrator's credit trouble stems from his obligation to give financial aid to relatives-in-law.

The Hunt as a Test of Character

Once when I was hunting, I heard a shot and came upon Alfred butchering a buck. I thought I'd scare him, so I began to come up, keeping behind trees. I was a long ways from him, but that fellow has eyes like an eagle. He was stooping down there, butchering his deer, and he saw me through his legs. I got close and began to come around in front, and he hollered, "Hey there! I know who you are. Come on out here. What are you trying to do?" So I came out. He said, "Come on, cousin, help yourself."[134]

[134] Alfred is no relative of the narrator. The "cousin" term is purely honorific here.

But I know Alfred too well. He knows I'm a good hunter. So I said, "No, I can't take any of this meat. I'm out hunting myself. I can get my own deer." He tried to argue with me, but I wouldn't do it. So he packed up his deer and we went along. Pretty soon I said, "I'm going off now." And I started out hunting again.

After a while I came on two deer. I got them both and started to butcher them. Alfred heard the shots and came over and watched from a distance. But he didn't ask me for a piece.

Just then Max came up. He said, "Give me some of that fat meat. I just killed a little fawn, but I don't like lean meat."

So I said, "Help yourself."

He took a shoulder and a rib and thanked me. Alfred gave him the same too.

Once Ralph Thorn, Tom, and I were hunting. We saw a deer. They wouldn't shoot,[135] so finally I said, "All right!", took aim, and fired, and the deer dropped. Those fellows raced for it, and Tom touched it first. He got the hide. They gave me some of the meat.

[135] These hunters were reluctant to shoot because the person who makes the kill has to surrender the hide if one of his companions wants it.

Our custom is to be generous like this about the meat and hide, but some are selfish. Ed Hoosh is very stingy. He killed some deer and would hardly give any of the meat away. They all came around, old people like Hunter and others, but he didn't give them any. His own father got after him for it. He hardly gave any to his own father-in-law![136] Wait until he wants a gun or something of mine to use! Just about the same time I killed two deer and gave some to everyone. Even before I got back they were lined up, about seven of them. I didn't have much left for myself. Yesterday Nango asked me if I was going out to hunt turkey today.

[136] Note that the crowning proof of avarice is that Hoosh is ungenerous to his father-in-law.

Strength

Once Alfred jumped on me right outside the store. There was a whole bunch of Indians looking on. At first I thought he was just fooling with me. I said, "What's the matter? What are you doing this for?"[137]

[137] Rough horseplay is not uncommon among a group of Apache men, especially younger men.

He said, "I'll show you. Come on and fight if you're a man."

"I'm ashamed to hit you. I don't want to fight. Just leave me alone."

He kept hitting me. He hit me twice and I didn't do anything. Then he hit me a third time, and his finger caught me right below the eye and scratched me. I got real mad. I was so mad I could hardly see. I said, "All right, it looks like you mean business!" And I hit him twice. The first punch wasn't so hard, but the second time I landed solid, and he went down.

He got up and came for me again. I just pushed him aside and said, "I'm ashamed to hit you again with all these people around."

But he wouldn't stop. He came after me and said, "I'll make you taste it!"[138] So I hit him again and he went down again. He picked himself up and walked toward the office.

[138] The implication is that he would make his antagonist taste blood.

Then he came to me. He said, "I thought I was a man, but I see you're a better man. I thought a big fellow like myself could handle you easy, but I see you're a better man than I am. Let's shake. Come on in and have a smoke with me." So he took me in and bought me a cigar.

I said, "All right, I'm willing to be friends. You started it, and I'm willing to quit it now."

Another time I was lying out in the sun by the store. That sun sure felt good. Pretty soon Ernest Chico came along. He got on top of me and said, "Now, what are you going to do?"

I said, "Oh, go on and let me rest. I'm tired."

"No," he said, "let's see what you can do if you're a man."

I didn't want to do anything, but he kept sitting there and thumping me and pulling me around, until at last I said, "All right, now we'll see what I can do!"

Just then my cousin Henry came up and started to pull Ernest from me. I said, "No, leave him alone. I'll show him something." My cousin laughed and went back, because he knew what I'd do.

I got to my feet with Ernest hanging on me. I tried to reach him, but he was on my back and had a pretty good hold. So I jumped right in the air with him, turned, and came down full force on him. That finished him. He just lay there.

When he got up he said, "Well, I didn't think any man could get up when I had an advantage like that and had him down. I thought I was a man."[139]

[139] Although he was not a particularly large man, the narrator was extremely strong and muscular. Moreover, his hunting, trapping, and outdoor life kept him in excellent physical condition. I have personally seen him accomplish rather amazing feats of strength.

Another time Roger Gish tried to fool with me just to see how strong I was. He got hold of my arm and said, "I guess I'll break this."

I said, "No, don't break it. I need it for a lot of things. I have to go and skin some hides with it right now." But he kept on twisting my arm.

My cousin was there that time too, and he told Roger, "You'd better not bother that fellow."

Then I just pulled my arm free of Roger Gish and wound his own arm around his head so that he couldn't do anything. Since that time nobody has bothered me. I never bother a man unless he jumps on me.

Mad Dog and Madstone

We caught a wild dog. It was foaming at the mouth. I thought it best to shoot it, but the fellow who was with me said, "Don't waste a bullet on it."

Before I knew it I got too close, and it bit me on the hand. Then I shot it and left it lying there. I went to the hospital. I showed the doctor my hand and told him about the dog. He sent someone right over for the body and he sent it away. The answer came right back by wire that the dog was mad. They kept me in the hospital and started to give me shots. I didn't think these would do much good. I had a madstone from the stomach of a deer that I used. I'd take it out and rub it on when no one was looking. The doctor caught me at it and took it away.

I got angry. I said, "That's my property and you've got no business taking it." I walked right out of the hospital and went to my camp. They sent the police after me, and so I had to come back. But he had to give me my stone back. And when no one was around I'd take it out and rub it on.

My arm had begun to swell up and then I used the madstone. It was swollen up to the elbow when I rubbed it on, and it never went any farther. It was the stone that cured me.[140]

140 This is an example of the dual medical treatment which persons who stand partly in each of two cultural worlds often deem necessary. The narrator knew the consequences of being bitten by a mad dog and reported to the hospital for the treatment which undoubtedly saved his life. But he was not completely convinced of the efficacy of the white man's medicine and insisted upon using the madstone, too. When the madstone was taken from him, he became greatly upset and hostile. In the end he gives credit for the cure to the use of the madstone. See p. 164 for another reference to the madstone or bezoar.

The only other time I had trouble with a bite was when I was bitten by a badger. It got infected. My arm and neck and ear were all infected. I went to the doctor but it got worse. I said to the doctor, "If you're trying to do the best you can, why doesn't my arm get well?" I finally left the hospital and treated the arm myself, and it got all right.

A Cure with Power from White Painted Woman

I won't mention names: there was a boy who was very sick but didn't know it. I was out at sheep camp. I had some money to get and was coming to the agency. I found this boy on the road. As he was riding past me he fell off his horse. I did everything for him I could. It did no good. I got him to a spring. A woman was at the spring. I said, "Could you do anything for us? This boy is very sick."

She said, "All right, I'll do my best. Stay here." She went to her camp and came back.

She brought pollen and put it on his head and in his mouth. Then in prayer she told how White Painted Woman got Water's Child from the water and how she reared him. She talked right out, not hiding anything. She prayed and led the boy to the spring in four steps. She did this four times. I was holding him up on one side; she was holding him on the other. I had my hat off and so did this boy.

The boy was told to kneel to the east. Then she reached her right hand out with pollen on and put water on his head four times.

Then the boy said, "Where am I?" He had come to. He could see again. I told him where he was.

The woman laughed. "The boy is all right now. It's just a little sickness, something like hay fever that the wind is blowing around. You're all right now," she told him.

When he got to the agency, the doctor said he had nearly caught typhoid fever. But he didn't stay at the hospital and he was all right. He went down to the store, bought a big chunk of meat, some stockings, and some flour and different things and brought them to the old lady. She hadn't asked for anything, but he did it, and she felt very glad.141

141 Again the feeling is evident that the religious practitioner should be paid and gratitude for his efforts should be expressed.

So I found out that this woman knew White Painted Woman. Just those four drops of water on his head and the pollen in his mouth, that's all she did. This same woman helps the girls during the adolescence rite.[142]

[142] This woman is one of those who are known as "She Who Trots Them Off" and who is hired to dress, feed, and advise the pubescent girl during her adolescence ceremony. In this instance she used ideas and procedures associated with the myth of the culture heroine, White Painted Woman, and the origin of the girl's adolescence ceremony, to aid the stricken man.

Power Rebuffed

There was an old Kiowa Apache woman here from Oklahoma. She knew the power of the great horned owl. She called it the chief of owls. She told Mrs. Gish, "I know power you ought to know. It gives money. It is a charmer of men. If you want a man, he comes to you. I will give you all this because I'm going to die. You'll not see where I die." She gave her all of it. She told her, "Owl's going to come to you from the north and is going to call your name."

One night Mrs. Gish was alone. My family was the only one close to her. That night we heard an owl. I listened. It seemed to say one word, her name. It said, "I'm coming. Be ready. I'm coming to see you." It came closer and closer.

She spoiled it. She got scared. She ran out, ran to our camp. She said, "Owl's calling my name, he says he's coming to see me!"[143]

[143] The hoot or appearance of an owl is usually taken to mean that the ghost of a dead witch is seeking revenge on the living. An owl which is not a ghost can also appear and offer a ceremony which is useful in curing sickness, especially sickness due to encounters with ghosts. This woman was assured that Owl would visit her for the second purpose but became fearful that its real purpose was to persecute her. A person who does not show courage and steadfastness at the approach of supernatural power cannot be chosen for a power grant; power is thought to favor determined representatives who will carry out its ceremony despite threat and difficulties.

I said, "Go back. You always said you were so strong."
"I don't want any devil around me."
I said, "I wish I had it. I'd like to go back to your camp."[144]

[144] Here the narrator seems pleased and excited at the prospect of a power experience.

My wife made fun of me. She wouldn't let me go.
That young woman never got it. She spoiled it by running away. The old lady had died. They found her out in the wilds, dead, under a spruce tree.

There is another story of Owl which Charlie Three-Fingers used to tell. But I can't remember it. Every time I nearly get it, Owl takes it away.[145]

145 The implication is that Owl does not want him to remember or repeat Charlie Three-Fingers' story.

I had a chance to get a real ceremony but I turned it down. I considered it too dangerous. The loggerhead shrike is a killer; the man who knows it is a killer. Jake Bead said he knew power from this bird. He said the bird saved his life many a time. This bird took him through terrible places, such as punishment in the penitentiary, and he got out of it. He was always a trusty in jail. The bird told him he would get back and see the reservation, and he did. He got back here and has another woman. He asked me if I wanted his power.

I said, "No, I don't want to kill."

He said, "It's a bad thing to kill, but when you have to kill, you have to."

During the time he was drunk and killed two men, he says he had to do it to save himself. The bird told him to. It told him to go if he didn't want to have to kill. He got ready but didn't get away fast enough. The bird told him to say nothing but to go at once. But he started to talk instead.

Ishbai knew the shrike better than all the rest. It told him, "You're going to be old. You are going to live through till a long life." But now he's suffering. He's out there all alone, and his people don't pay much attention to him.[146]

146 The reference is to a very old man whose face was partly paralyzed and whose speech was consequently impaired.

The Market for Ceremonial Goods

People around here, and even visitors from other tribes, come to me and ask me to get birds or animals or plants that they want to use in ceremonies or for medicine.

One bird that is used for ceremonial purposes is the evening grosbeak, and his feathers are hard to get. This bird lives in the mountains only in the summer; in the winter it comes to the lowlands. The Mescalero say that when you eat the meat it makes you strong and healthy. But they say the brain is bad and can't be used, for it will make you sick and weak. Then the best cure is to eat the meat, raw, roasted, or boiled. People get strong power from this bird, too, because he drifts around in all parts of the world, they say. Wherever he goes, he is left alone; not even a hawk bothers him. They say that the man who knows power from this bird can see every part of the world and that sometimes the bird lifts him up so that he can see far parts of the world. The Comanche pay a big price for this bird, even for one leg. They want the feathers and a little of the meat. Every year I used to get a letter from some Comanche fellow asking for one of these birds. I got some for the museum man when I worked for him, but I never got any for anyone else.

One time when there were visitors here from different places, one Cheyenne sold a wing of the evening grosbeak to a Tonkawa for two hundred dollars. I asked him why he paid so much and why he didn't buy it from me. He told me, "If you send me a whole bird skin and a little meat, I'll give you eight hundred dollars."

I was collecting museum specimens then, and I got one but had to throw the meat away because it was poisoned. I tried to hide one skin to send to this Tonkawa but I finally gave it up and let the museum man have it.

People from many tribes are anxious to get the black hawk. Some come all the way from Oklahoma to get them or to buy the tail feathers. We use the middle tail feathers and the end wing feathers for ceremonies here.

Two Osage Indians came here, one named John and one named Russell. Both together paid seventy-five dollars for the tail feathers of two of these hawks I had shot. I had them because two Comanche fellows had asked me to get some for them. As soon as they saw those birds hanging up, these Osage wanted them. I would have asked only about fifty cents apiece for them. But John was an honest man; he said, "We'll give you seventy-five dollars for those."

I said, "No."

My wife was afraid I wouldn't sell them and said, "Let them have them."

So I said, "All right, I'll let them go."

Russell paid a dollar for each of the wing feathers. John came back here and said he got his money back for just the four tail feathers among his people. They asked me for other things, for weasels, bears, beavers.

I have a black hawk tail feather now. Nahakus offered me five dollars for it. This one's a little too young; it has a little greyish color on it. The older the bird is, the better the tail feathers are, for they get coal black. The Mescalero never touch the claws or the kill of this bird. Lots of them won't touch it at all. During the horse round-up I killed one. The boys said, "Take your choice of the feathers." They said this because it isn't like deer; you can give it away or not as you please. So I kept the tail and let them have the wings. I got a dollar apiece for the tail feathers.

The penis of a badger is used for toothache. They warm it and put it up to the cheek. John Cloud had a bad toothache and asked me for one. Mrs. Tomas always asks me for badger grease; her brother, Kenneth Swinging-Lance, asks me for it too. I don't know how they use it. I've never seen that woman's ceremony, but I know she doctors a lot of people.

Some of the richest Mexicans use the red-tailed hawk. They say it is a cure for the blood, gives you strength and health. I picked this up from a Mexican who came from Mexico and camped near us during the girl's adolescence rite one year. They eat the meat of this hawk, and they pay a good price for it. A Mexican who runs a saloon at the end of the bridge in Juarez brought his sick child here. I killed six red-tailed hawks for him. He gave me six dollars for every hawk. They just ate the hawks and threw the feathers away. But I got the feathers. The boy got well.

Dja asked me for a weasel. It is supposed to heal, is good for training horses, and is used to make runners long-winded. Itsine wanted me to give him some bear meat. He said, "You give it to me to eat and then I'll always be able to eat it any time."[147] I shot a skunk the other day. Tom just took it with him.

[147] Itsine, like so many others, is convinced that the narrator has power from
Bear.

Lungwort[148] is used here for an upset stomach and diarrhea. But the Comanche
use it for a ceremony. They put it on their bodies when they go out to war. A
Comanche preacher who was here asked me for some. He said he would pay me
for it.

[148] "Mertensia pratensis."

A Use for Everything

In some ceremonies the right paw of the badger is used. The right front paw of
the porcupine is used too. Shorty told me this the other day. It's a new thing that
I picked up.

George Kos, Shorty, and I were talking about the use of skunk and badger
grease against disease. When Shorty wasn't looking George would motion towards
him with his mouth to let me know that he had had such a ceremony performed
over him.[149] So I asked Shorty about it and he told me. As he explained it, grease
from the skunk and badger is put together when disease is approaching. The person
who knows it puts it on children. He marks their faces with white clay and uses
pollen. He puts a heavy coat of grease all over the hair and body. He carries on this
ceremony and does this for four days. They can't take the grease off until the
fourth day and then they can't wash it off but must wipe it off. After that they can
wash. They are supposed to stay around camp while the grease is on. This can be
done to adults too.

[149] Pointing is often done by the Mescalero with the lips, especially when the
hands are occupied or when one quietly wants to indicate something to a
person who is looking at him. The lips of a Mescalero develop a wonderful
mobility for this purpose. Women at the trader's store point unerringly at
goods on the shelves without raising a finger.

The power of the squirrel, they claim, is something like the power of Coyote. It
heals in coyote disease; the coyote tail used with the squirrel tail is a good cure
against coyote disease itself. That is one of the truest things I found out. A Lipan
showed me this when there was a girl they say was sick from Coyote. He took the
squirrel tail and burned it so that she could inhale the smoke.[150] He did this about
four times and she was cured. The doctor said she was paralyzed, but she wasn't.
Everybody felt very sorry for her. Every once in a while she would open and close
her hands and then she'd put her hand in her mouth and cause soreness on her
fingers. Or she would make her mouth go like a coyote. And she would put her arm
behind her back and move it sideways too. She was just a young girl in school. He
gave her some herb. She drank some of it and put some on her fingers too.

[150] There is a good deal of reliance upon incensing in Mescalero curative practices. Cf. 4 [108].

I wanted to go to a ceremony that the Navaho who was here was holding, to see what he uses. The Navaho wouldn't let me in. He told Nalade that if I came I would take the power out with me. I just laughed. I wanted to see what that fellow's ceremony was like, so I told him I was sick. He said, "There's nothing wrong with you!" If they are good, they know.[151]

[151] The Navaho had undoubtedly heard about the narrator's willingness to handle unclean animals and his excessive interest in the ceremonies of others, and he was suspicious and even afraid of him.

An Imported Ceremony

I never saw a Pueblo curing ceremony till I was at Three Rivers. An Isleta friend of Nishchee was there. One of Nishchee's girls got sick. The Pueblo man was going to sing that night. I asked if I could come. They said all right, so I came.

I got terribly sleepy and began to doze off. They woke me up every time. Nishchee explained that the power would get sleepy if I did. I laughed and the Pueblo Indian got mad.[152] Then I wanted to go. They wouldn't let me. I had to stay there all night. This man from Isleta told where he got power from.

[152] Again we see evidence of the mixture of hardheadedness and credulity which characterizes the narrator.

He said in his ceremony that the snakes would be thick the next day. And they were! I never saw so many at Three Rivers. I killed about ten. He said it was all right to kill them.

The cat brought back one and put it under the bed. We didn't know how the snake got there. It was dead, of course, for it was one I had killed and put out on the rock pile. I took it back to the rock pile again, and after a while it was under the bed again. I said it must be a ghost, and the kids all laughed; they are like me.[153] This time we watched and saw the cat bring it.

[153] The narrator prides himself on his good common sense. Here he assumes that there must be a simple explanation for this phenomenon. He suggests that he has turned his children away from unreasonable fears and apprehensions, too.

I wanted to skin the biggest snake. The Protestant missionary offered me twenty dollars for the skin.[154] But my wife wouldn't let me skin it. "You stop that!" she told me. "You're going to poison the children."

[154] This missionary was not getting along too well with the Indians. Here we obtain some hint of practices on his part which would be sure to encourage members of his congregation to keep their distance from him.

Meningitis Strikes the Reservation

A boy had been in school. Vacation came and his parents took him home. At that time he had a picture of Water's Child above his head on the wall.[155] He had been looking at all the stories about Jesus during the day. He went to sleep thinking about them. Then this picture showed him that Water's Child really was living and was everywhere, but he was afraid to say anything. The holy one came to him the first night as you see Christ in the pictures with a robe and long hair. The second night it came for the second time. It touched him on the head and he woke up. There was a bright light. He couldn't see Water's Child very well. Then he wanted to look at him. He looked.

[155] Since both Water's Child and Jesus were supernaturals miraculously born of a divine woman and came on earth to save mankind and to combat evil, the Mescalero have found it possible to identify Water's Child with Jesus. The picture to which reference is made is, of course, a religious picture of Jesus.

In the Apache language the figure said, "Why are you afraid? Why are your eyes closed?"

"I do not know who you are."

"Do not be afraid but look at me."

Then before him stood this same man wearing a yellow hat, and his suit was yellow and his shoes were yellow. He came in the form of a white man. His face shone just like the sun; you couldn't get a good look at him, but his pink lips were moving. He asked the boy, "What do you like best?"

"There are many things I want but I do not know whether these things are the best things in this world for me."

"There are many good things to have."

"I want to be kind and help everybody. I like to help those who are sick."

"Yes, that's a good thing. Be kind and do good. To help the sick is very good. That's what I had in mind. I knew you were going to ask for it. I am the one you call Water's Child. Now I stand before you. I show you who I am." And he pointed to himself.[156]

[156] What follows is a recital of a typical Mescalero vision experience which ends in the acquisition of supernatural power.

The boy looked up to see. All he could see was strong light, and he heard the voice.

"Is that all you can ask of me?"

"What more can I ask for?"

"There are many other things I could give."

"I want the best you can give. Give me strength to do what you say and help me out when I need you."

"You speak the right way. I have it to give. It's only for this earth." Then he was gone.

The boy lay down again and slept till morning. The next day he thought about it. "Why didn't he come in the day?" he thought. He lay down under a vine. It was a hot summer day. The bushes behind him began to move, and he was moving too. He saw the clouds come down close to him. He could see very well this time. Water's Child was coming in the clouds from the east. The clouds moved around his body. You could see only his face.

The clouds came close to earth. Water's Child was standing on the clouds. He was in his white robes. He said, "Now you will believe," and he showed the boy the places where the nails pierced him.[157] "Not yet are you to use your power, not till you are told to go among your people. I have come because you needed help." So they had more talk. The boy had his head down and was praying. He called on everything that he might not be led wrong. Then he was alone again. This time he had been shown in the daytime.

[157] Note the amalgam of Christian and Mescalero Apache religious ideas.

The boy was very, very glad. He had high thoughts. He went back to his camp and lay down. Nothing came to him that night. So the next day he went to a spring.

He drank and lay in the oak leaves. He went to sleep again. It was early morning. About nine o'clock the winds blew hard. Something moved before him. The trees moved. He felt the wind brush his face four times, and the fourth time Water's Child stood before him. His hair was cut and he wore a suit and clothes and shoes.[158] He was in the form of a white man.

[158] The completeness of the association that has been established between Water's Child, Jesus, and the white man for the purposes of this ceremony is evident here.

"You do not look like the one who came to me yesterday."

"I am the same one. Only my dress is different. Have you thought of anything else you need? And do you think I am the one who long ago gave to those in need?"

"You are the one I know."

And then his face shone bright and his clothes. He walked before the boy and stood there and looked square into his face. "I'm tired of this country but it cannot be helped. You must ask for what you want."

"I ask for the best part, and let it last till my time has come."

"I come to show you these things. Your life is long to you, but for me it's only a little way." He handed the boy pollen. "That and the water are all that are necessary. These are enough if you believe in them. Only believe what you see and that will guide you. But if you do not, I will not come to talk to you. It will show that you want something else. Keep these things in your mind and you'll have the best always; what I give is enough. That is all I will tell you." And he left, saying, "I have given it to you and have given you the best part. Now do as you please."

From that time on the boy never saw Water's Child till the day he was going to practice his ceremony.

It was a very dreadful disease that came now, one that will take your strength. It was spinal meningitis. A very little girl had it. She was able to talk and knew where the pain was. The boy felt very sorry when he saw the child. The tears came out from his eyes and rolled down his cheeks.

The father of the girl didn't believe much in this boy. But the boy said, "What shall I do for this child?"

The father said, "What power do you know and where did you get it, that you can cure this child?"

"I see through Water's Child and I talk through him. You give me the chance, my poor brother, and I will do what I can for you and this child. This child has a good chance yet. The illness is not too severe."

"I will remember and pray for you always if you cure this child." That's what the father said.

"I'd give my life for that child. I'd rather do my best for a little child like that than for an old person. I think I can heal her and she'll be back to you and keep you from being sorrowful in this world. You love to see your child strong and healthy. You love to see everything in good shape. I'm going to do it through the power that's given me. This is a most powerful thing I'm going to show you. I'm not ashamed to show you what I've learned. Just say, 'Help me,' and I'll help you."[159]

[159] In spite of his willingness and even his eagerness to perform his ceremony, the shaman makes it plain that the father of the sick child, in deference to his power and his ceremony, must approach him humbly as a supplicant.

"You give me your right hand. You speak like a man who has power. I want you to use your full power and save my child."

"That's all I ask. You've given me the chance and I'm sure the child will be all right in a few days. I do my work in broad daylight and before the eyes of spectators."

"All right, let's do it now."

The father went to the store and got all the food and candles that were needed. He came back. Everything was ready. They had a little bite and then gathered in the tent. There was a big crowd. I was present.

The shaman came up to me. "Sit by me. You're the one I want."[160] I sat by him. He marked my hand. Then he marked his hand. He said, "You look at the child."

[160] Once more the narrator emphasizes that shamans have often wanted him to be their assistant and to fall heir to their ceremonies.

I said, "I don't know how."

"If anything runs in the palm of your hand, it is the child.[161] If it is on the back of your hand, the child is going to die."

[161] A feeling of movement in the palm of the hand, interpreted as the running of the child, was to be considered a good omen, a sign of the future vitality and health of the patient. In Mescalero symbology, the back of the hand usually stands for rejection or bad luck and the palm of the hand for happier tidings.

I looked in my hand. I could see the child. She was talking to her mother and father. Everything was good. They were at sheep camp and she was healthy. He finished the first prayer. I said, "Poor child!"

He said, "Don't say anything. Wait." I looked to see further. He said, "Don't go too far. With the palm of your hand stroke the child from the head to the feet."[162]

[162] Note that the use of the palm of the hand in the healing rites is specified.

I said his prayer for the child and I stroked her. I was saying a prayer he taught me. The prayer says that this is Water's Child when he was a small boy and tells how he was raised by the water. I used water and pollen. I talked about the child's mouth and breathing and hearing and all things like that when I touched her head. Then I stroked the right shoulder and then the left, then from the breast on down, and the lungs and down to the foot on the right side, and then the left side from the waist down. The father held the child up. They all watched me. There was a big crowd looking on.

Then the shaman told someone to go to the spring and to bring water and dirt from the bottom.

Now he marked my hand again. I went over the body of the child four times before we were through. After the third marking of my hand I could see what was wrong. The child had a bubble on the brain on the right side at the neck. That's what was causing the jerking motion of the child. The bubble would expand and contract and every time it did, the wind would blow against the brain of the child, and the child would jerk. I saw all this plain. I could see right through the child. I wanted to tell him what I saw, but he said, "I know all that. Let us not stop."

The last time he marked my hand with pollen and with sand from the bottom of the spring. Then he marked me with pollen on the right foot, then up my leg and arm and to my right shoulder, then to my back, then to the left shoulder, then to the breast, and then from the left shoulder, left arm and leg and down to the left foot. There he made a cross. I did it to him the same way. We did it to each other four times. Then he marked the child the same way, except that he put a cross of pollen four times at the place where the sickness was and also at the lower part of the stomach. Then all marked him with a cross on the chest.

I told the people, "White Painted Woman comes first,[163] for we are working on a girl." All the young girls came first, then the middle-aged women, and then the old; then the young boys representing Water's Child, then the middle-aged and then the old men. I knew his pollen song very well, and he sang it with me twice. Then they started marking him, and I finished the song alone. He told me not to go too fast. I sang it two more times while they were marking him.

163 The women present are referred to as White Painted Woman, the mother of Water's Child.

He had already marked my hand. He sang again. I looked at the child. The bubble was in the bone yet, near the end. Then when he was all marked, it was outside altogether. It was gone. I looked at the bottom too. The same thing was there, but a bigger bubble. It was something I never saw before. At the beginning the child was very sick. Now she wanted something to eat.

The healer gave me a crucifix and marked it.164 He said, "Never have the head toward the child, only the feet." I looked at it. Her neck was well, but where she urinates there were lots of different little bubbles, and at the back end too. I showed it to him.

164 The Christian elements in this rite are underscored by this reference to a crucifix.

He said, "It's a good thing I got you. I'm glad you noticed it."

He gave me the sand and told me to rub it four times below the navel. I did and we covered up the child. Now she felt better and said, "Papa, give me some water." She behaved well through this ceremony, but she knew me well; that's the reason.

The healer said to me, "Now listen; this is the beginning of the ceremony where I'm curing all these things. We're doing a pretty good job of it. You like it. You sing and don't be ashamed. Keep it going." He started off with a song. I sang it with him. I didn't know the prayers. I placed spring water before him. He started another song. The child wanted to drink. "No, no water till I say so."165 We finished the second song. I sang the third song myself, the prayer parts and all. I did this with the fourth too.

165 Because of the involvement of the rite with Water's Child, who was miraculously conceived at a watering place, very specific directions concerning the use of water in the rite are given.

He put pollen in the water then and gave it to the girl. She drank all of it. We looked her over again. She was all right. It was just one ceremony.

The father offered everything. He told us to catch his horses and keep them. But the man who cured his child said, "No, that's not the way. When you want to give a man something, lead it up to him and hand him the rope."166 If you have anything to give a shaman you have to hand it to him right there. He won't go anywhere and take it.

[166] The shaman is emphasizing the doctrine that a ceremonialist should be paid generously and cheerfully at the conclusion of a rite to insure the future good will of power. He is also hinting that a horse would be an appropriate gift.

They all said it was a wonderful ceremony. And they believed in it all the way. Kenneth Swinging-Lance and others were present. Twenty to thirty people were there. The house was just plumb full. Even my whole family was there too. This happened in 1929 just before Muchacho passed away.[167] He was there.

[167] Muchacho Negro died in 1930 at the age of 70.

Later the father of the sick child had a horse led right up to my camp. I was away working for the man from the museum at the time. When I got back, it was waiting for me. They sent Nishchee's boy with it. They told him, "Put the rope right in his hand, don't just tie the horse there."[168] The boy was waiting for me and he put the rope in my hand.

[168] The members of the family of the cured girl are impressed by the shaman's directions, for they see to it that a horse is led in the proper way to the assistant as well as to the principal ceremonialist.

Family Trials and Tragedy

I always try to help my mother-in-law and get along with all my relatives through marriage. I got several deer for my mother-in-law this season.[169] This year I got a mule deer that weighed two hundred and forty pounds. It was an eight-pointer, an old deer. He had a hoof on him like a calf.

[169] The narrator is obeying the Mescalero injunction that a married man should support and hunt for his parents-in-law. Though he was a widower at the time these biographical details were recorded, he was continuing his economic assistance to the mother of his deceased wife.

Once in a while you are bound to run into a little family trouble. I had one fight with Will Sos. His first wife was my wife's sister, so I had to live near him. He still hides from my mother-in-law, though his first wife is dead.[170] Once he beat his wife and I interfered. He came after me and we had it out. After that we never had any trouble.

[170] Avoidance relationships, once begun, continue throughout the lives of those between whom they have been established, even though the person because of whom avoidance was initiated has died. Note the indirect reference to matrilocal residence in the narrator's remark that he "had to live near" his wife's sister's husband.

Another time we were camped right near John Cloud. He is my relative by marriage too, though not a very close one. John was drunk and beat his wife and cursed his father-in-law, Dja, when he tried to interfere. The old man sat there and cried.

I came in and threw the bottle out. I bawled him out good. "What did you marry for? You started it," I told him.[171]

[171] The physical abuse of the father-in-law, to whom the son-in-law owes complete respect and obedience, was a grave breach of custom and etiquette which could not be allowed to go unchallenged.

The next morning he came up to me. I told him I was going to move away from him. He gave me a good kind of talk, so I stayed.

My wife's sister, Cora, is married to Paul Yahi. They have a little boy. The father is no good; he always spends his money for booze and gets drunk. He never sees the child. Now he is staying with Ernest Chico, one of his relatives. My mother-in-law, the child's grandmother, is taking care of the little boy mostly. A while back Yahi came around dead drunk and wanted money. I sure got mad at him! "Look at that child," I said. "No pants, no shoes, and dirty. You never do anything to take care of him. Now get out." He hasn't been around since.

I do what I can to help another brother-in-law, Louis Nitsigane, who has been very poor. I gave him a car that he still has. I had two cars. The first one needed repairs, and James Benchee was going to take it to a fellow for me to have it fixed. After waiting a while I asked where the car was. Then James told me he had sold it to a fellow. I asked him why he didn't sell something that was his own. I was pretty mad at first and then I thought, "He's a poor fellow." So I didn't start any trouble for him. The second one I gave to Louis.

My two saddle horses are in very poor condition now. Louis wanted to use them. He used them too hard and ran them down. Another time I gave all my flour to his family. They got up in the morning, and there was nothing in their camp to eat. They all sat around looking at each other. So I gave it to them.[172]

[172] Note the relaxed manner in which the narrator accepts and discusses the disappearance of both of his automobiles. Note also the amount of economic help the narrator constantly extends to his relatives-in-law.

My own family has had great sorrows too. One boy of mine seven years old was run over and killed near the agency buildings. He was run over by one of the Indians; it was carelessness and fast driving. The agent turned the whole thing over; he let the whole thing go. I told the agent and the chief clerk, "I'll take your word for it now and I'll think it over. Maybe I won't do anything for two or three years and then maybe I'll act."[173]

[173] There is a suggestion here of a feeling for the right of the individual or of an aggrieved family to reopen an issue at an opportune time. For this reason feuds and conflicts which are apparently over or long dormant tend to flare up unexpectedly.

Signs and Portents

If your right ear itches someone is talking about you or thinking about you. I saw two girls. One asked the other for a stick. She peeled the bark off it, scratched her ear with it, and then threw it on the ground. She said, "Oh, it points to White-tail! He's still thinking about me." Up to then they didn't see me. When I came out they were ashamed. I picked up a stick and did the same. My ear didn't itch; I was just kidding them. I threw it and said, "Well, she is still thinking of me, but I left her a long time ago." They both laughed. I've seen lots of people toss a stick that way. It's the way the tip falls that counts. If the left ear itches, someone is talking bad about you or cursing you.

Some say they get dreams that tell them what is going to happen. If you go to a bear shaman and, during the nights of the ceremony you dream of bears, that's good. It means long life. If it's a snake shaman you go to and you dream of snakes, it's long life, and so on.[174] To dream of a house is good luck. To dream of fruit is good luck. It is good to dream of all growing things. A dream of pollen covering the ground is good luck too.

[174] Ordinarily for a person who does not have a power grant from Bear or Snake to dream of these dangerous animals would be unfortunate and frightening. But to dream about them after a protective ceremony which stems from them has been performed is a benign omen. It is assumed that the ceremony will protect the dreamer from harm and that the appearance of the animal at this time bespeaks its interest in the dreamer.

But if you dream of fire it is bad. Nothing is boss of fire. Or if you dream of losing a tooth it's bad. Then one of your relatives is going to die or someone of the encampment. But when you have such a dream, if you chew corn or put a rock in your mouth and throw it the way the sun goes down, the death won't happen.

Nango came in the store when a whole bunch of us were there. He told us, "I feel pretty bad. Last night I dreamed I had sexual relations with my old mother who has been dead these many years. Now what do you suppose made me dream a thing like that?"

The men tried to cheer him up. They told him, "It's nothing; it's just a dream. It doesn't mean that a thing like that happened. Don't think of it."

Then I said to him, "I know what that means. That means that you're planning to run with some nice widow woman. Who is she?" Then he got very much ashamed and walked out of the store.

This man was so worried because an Apache will feel sick all the next day if he dreams about a dead person. I have put a knife under my pillow many times when I had a bad dream.[175] I've tried everything. When a person is afraid of ghosts or bad dreams at night he puts a cross of ashes on his head and a cross of spit on his forehead. He puts ashes around his bed too. It keeps everything bad away.

[175] It is noteworthy that the narrator saw some sexually linked projection in this dream. It is also interesting that the dreamer was less disturbed about the

bizarre content of the dream or the incest motif than he was that he had dreamed about a dead person. Today a black-handled knife (formerly it was a piece of black flint) is considered a safeguard against unpleasant dreams involving ghosts.

Sometimes in my dream I have heard a voice or someone coughing. That is a sign of sickness in the family. Sometimes you feel as though someone is touching you. You can't move. You try to cry out in your sleep and you can't, but there is a funny noise in your throat. Then you say, "They found me last night," and you mean ghosts.

One time I dreamed that an old rattler with four rattles came to me. I said to it, "Why do you bite and make people afraid of you?"

It said, "I'm always getting stepped on. I get mad like you too sometimes." Then two snakes came to me. I told them to tell me something in the way of power the next time they came, but they never came again.[176]

[176] Here the narrator claims to have urged a power source to pay him a return visit and teach him a ceremony. He again ends by asserting that the power grant never materialized.

Another time I dreamed of a skunk. In the morning there were tracks of a skunk around my camp.

Just recently I dreamed that I saw my mother and sister. Then there were two white men there. There were four beds there too. I lay down on one of them. A snake came, a big rattler. He said to me, "I'm going home. It's all right, don't hold back. Tell all you know."[177] Then I woke up scared. I thought of the time there was a big rattler under my bed. I stayed awake for a while. After a while my arm went to sleep. In a little while I fell asleep again. Then the snake came back and put his mouth over my finger. I caught him by the neck and choked him. Then I was working for you. The man from the museum came. He was fleshing a hide. He kept saying, "I can't get this off at all; it's too thin; it's getting torn to pieces." I told him I was working for you and couldn't stop to help him.[178]

[177] The narrator had evidently been troubled about the wisdom of discussing some subjects fully with me.
[178] Once more cooperating with white men is associated with dangerous and suspected creatures such as the snake.

The Mescalero have a good many beliefs about muscular tremors and their meanings. Just this morning before breakfast I felt one on the right arm. I said, "Look here, I'm not the killer, but there's death. I feel sorry for someone."[179] In a little while we heard that Harvey Young's child was dead. The old woman, my mother-in-law, started down there, saying, "I must talk in a good way to them."[180]

[179] For further details of the meanings of muscular tremor see 3 [8].
[180] In Mescalero society, as in our own, there are always those who feel that it is their duty to help and comfort the bereaved at a time of death.

I don't know who causes this sign. It just hits you at certain times. One night I was lying down. It hit me under one foot. I knew I was going to have a visitor. A little while later two missionaries came up to see me. The sign under the foot means a visitor from around here. If it's over the eye, someone from far off is coming to visit.

When I am hunting and get this quivering in the right knee, I'm going to have something to butcher. If I feel it in the palm of my right hand, I'm going to shake hands; if it's the palm of the left hand, I'm going to get money. If it twitches under the eye, someone is passing away or there will be heavy rain or snow. In the lip, it means someone is going to curse me, or I will curse him. If it is felt in the elbow of either arm, it means death. A tremor in the biceps of either arm means hard work or a fight, or maybe I'm going to see a fight. To feel it at the shoulder means I'm going to shoot. In the back, it means sickness; in the belly, hunger. A tremor on the outside of the right leg means good luck, but above the hip, either side, something wrong. If it is felt in the buttocks, it means a long ride or that someone is going to give me a horse. Once I felt it on the outside of my left arm, and soon afterward a mule kicked me; then that arm was bandaged.

I have had these signs for a long time. I didn't pay much attention to them at first; I didn't care what was going to happen. But after I came back from school and was grown up, I paid attention. I guess it's the only power I know, but you wouldn't call that a ceremony; it's just a little quivering of the muscles.[181] The meaning of such tremors differs with different people. If I feel it in the index finger of my right hand, I'm going to shoot, but even these signs in the fingers mean different things to different people.

[181] Again the narrator takes the occasion to assure me that, despite these minor ritual aids and warnings, he does not possess any full-blown ceremony.

When I get a ringing in my ears, it means there's going to be a shooting. I got it just before the Day boy shot himself. He shot himself while he was with his brother above the feast grounds. I heard the shot. I had seen both go there, and only one came back. They had an argument over whether they should have an exhaust put on the truck, I heard. They had been having trouble right along.

When the Leaves Came

Some shamans work with muscular tremor. Before my wife died, when she was very sick, I hired Dja for her.[182] He worked with muscular tremor. He didn't tell all the things right. He said she was going to get better. She did. Then she got worse. He didn't see that part. He knows Dreams and Water's Child too.

[182] It is likely that the narrator's wife had a number of ceremonies performed over her before she was taken to the hospital.

My wife complained that her stomach hurt her all the time. I asked the doctor if it couldn't be tuberculosis of the stomach. We took her to El Paso. They operated on her, and I saw the operation. The inside of the stomach was all eaten away. When they got finished with it, it was just a very thin wall.

The doctor came out and said, "We did our best. I think she will live."

"Yes, she's strong now. You'd have to give her poison to kill her now. But when the leaves come I will be sad." I knew it would break through.

When my wife came back from the hospital, I tried to build her up. I gave her herbs and she got much better. Then the museum man came and I went to work for him. I had to go away, and while I was gone she didn't take them. I came back and she was much worse. She was too far gone.

While she was sick there I told her before everyone, "You know I have always done you good. But you wouldn't listen. You wanted others to work on you."[183]

[183] The narrator's remark, "You wanted others to work on you," suggests that a number of ceremonies were performed for the woman.

"It's all right, my husband," she said. "We've been together a long time. You have the children. You'll come to the same place. I'd rather die quick than suffer a long time."

She was in the hospital, and I was with her when it burst. I wanted to call the doctor. She said to me, "I'm so tired. Let me go, my husband."

"Look at your children," I told her.

"The pain is so great. It will be better to be at peace."

So I motioned them not to call the doctor, and she passed away. It was the fifteenth of May.

Widower

They are holding a little ceremony for my brother Edgar's daughter. It is just the little feast that they have when a girl becomes a woman. Later on they will put her through the full girl's puberty rite.[184] I have to be there or they'll get after me. These feasts are not much fun for me now. I always used to sing round dance songs, but the people know I don't want to sing or dance now because my wife died,[185] and so they don't bother me. The people always respect you if you have had trouble.

[184] Because the full puberty rite does not take place now when a girl first menstruates but is delayed until the first four days of July, a token rite is often performed to mark the time of her entrance into womanhood. One of the narrator's daughters came of age while she was attending school in Santa Fe. Upon learning of this, he sponsored a celebration and feast. In explanation he said to me, "They [the friends of the family] wanted to eat and have a good time and have a celebration, so we gave it to them."

[185] The round dance is a social dance in which men and women form a circle, facing inward, and shuffle sideways to the musical accompaniment of a knot of male drummers and singers.

They had a little ceremony for Yutsine's oldest girl. She is my "grandchild" in the Apache way of relationship.[186] There was a feast and social dancing. When she ran around the basket the last time, fruit and cigarettes were thrown in the air. I got cigarettes out of it.

[186] The girl is his male cousin's daughter's daughter.

My own daughter was ready to go through the girl's puberty rite this year. The old people wanted her to do it. I said not this year. I didn't want to be bothered because of the death of my wife. I guess I'll put her through next year. You know how the old people are. They did it for you and then you have to carry it on for them.

Some of these women are sure interested in me now that I am alone! I met one woman and she stopped to talk to me. She said, "All the women are chasing you now."

I said, "No, you talk foolishness. I don't see any women running after me. I guess you must mean that you would like to run after me yourself."

"Well," she said, "that's true. Ever since we were children together I have thought of you and have always liked you."

"Yes," I told her, "but I don't think much of you. I have been watching you too. You get mad and you holler and curse; I hear you. I see that you get drunk and have a mean mouth. I don't like that."

Then she got mad. "You mind your own business!"

"You are the one who started talking about such things." And I went on.

A few days ago another woman came to my camp. I was just beginning to eat. So I invited her to eat with me. While we were eating, she said, "I have been watching your camp. You are a good hunter; you always have fresh meat out to dry."[187]

[187] Because of his hunting abilities the narrator was considered a good provider and a desirable "catch." While young girls are expected to be shy and retiring, older, experienced women are allowed a good deal of frankness and freedom in relations between the sexes.

Afterwards I walked over to her camp with her. "You can come in and stay with me," she said.

"No, none of that," I told her. "You are too willing. I am not as hot as some people." And I went back to my camp.

She laughed. She said to others, "I invited that man to come and stay with me and he treated me as if I was a snake."

Assisting Kenneth Swinging-Lance

Kenneth Swinging-Lance doctored a man at Whitetail who had broken his leg. He asked for some yucca.[188] He used some of his medicine that burns, set the leg, and put long pieces of yucca on the inside of the leg, short pieces on the outside, and wrapped it all with buckskin. But the shattered bone was in the leg, and getting it out was pretty hard. I was there. I didn't think he could do it. Instead of operating, he just took a white silk handkerchief and placed it over the leg. This was early in the morning; it was the first day of a four-day ceremony. He had two eagle tail feathers in his hand. I moved in front so I could see with my own eyes, and I saw that he crossed those eagle feathers. He had the handkerchief, the buckskin, and the yucca over the leg, and I didn't understand how he could see what he was doing. He sucked it once and he brought poison out and spit it into a clean basin. The second time he got one piece of bone. The third time he got three pieces and some matter and spit it in the basin. The fourth time he took out all that was left in there. He had some of that medicine that he uses for tuberculosis, and now he took off the buckskin and poured the medicine over the leg. After a month that man was walking. If he had been in the doctor's care you can see how long it would have taken, six months probably, for the doctor would have had to cut the leg open to get the bone splinters out.

[188] "Yucca bacchata."

Kenneth takes a good many cases around here. For broken bones, or a child putting beads in its ear or nose or swallowing a dime, they all go to him. He says not to tell the doctor but to keep it to ourselves, so the doctor doesn't know much about what Kenneth is doing. He cured one old lady who had poison ivy sores that were hard to heal. It had started from a little spot and spread up to her arm and shoulder. This time it looked as if those two eagle tail feathers were all he was using. He just wiped it off four times and it was clean. He always gets paid, but his instructions from his power are that it must seem that he is not being paid.[189]

[189] That is, he must not demand specific payment. Older Mescalero often make an invidious comparison between an Indian shaman who accepts whatever payment is given him and a white doctor who demands specific fees. Actually, the putting of the burden of generosity upon the grateful patient often results in rewards that the shaman would have hesitated to demand.

Just recently a boy was out playing, not thinking anything was wrong with him, when his leg began to swell and get red. He was afraid to go to the doctor, for fear the doctor would operate on it. They brought him to me. I told him to lie on my bed, for his leg was in bad shape, blood poisoning up to his hip. I don't see how he walked at all. First he told me he fell down. Then he said it just happened. I said he must tell the truth and that we would know if he wasn't telling the truth. He was very sick and was throwing up. It was close to morning when we got hold of Kenneth Swinging-Lance.

We didn't want too big a crowd. I just let some of my family know. I sent my boy out to get spring water and sand and sulphur water; Kenneth had asked for these things. He started the ceremony in a quiet way, praying first and then singing. People came up, for they like to watch this man work. We couldn't stop them, for they heard the singing from my tent. He marked everyone there. After four sets of prayers and four sets of songs Kenneth used sand to hold the white stuff from the sulphur water up to the leg. He spread a yellow handkerchief over it and could see that part of the bone was turning blue. He sucked the poison out. Then he wrapped the leg in buckskin and told the boy to lie down and sleep, for the boy hadn't had a good sleep since this thing started. He gave the boy a piece of root to keep him from throwing up.

The boy slept soundly till daylight. Then he thought his leg was all right. He tried to walk but couldn't. Kenneth went off in the hills but came in again in the evening. During the day I went to the sulphur springs and got fresh sulphur water.

The boy said he had felt something burst open, so I asked Kenneth to let us take the buckskin off and look at the leg. He said it would be a good thing to see if the poison was coming out, so we took the buckskin off and found the pus running out. We washed the leg in sulphur water and wrapped it up again. Kenneth sang again that night. His songs are very hard; I tried my best to learn their meaning but couldn't get it at all.

It took six weeks in all to cure that boy. After two weeks we had the help of the doctor in opening the wound. Then the boy stayed in the hospital a month. Now that boy is working out on the road somewhere and has no trouble with the leg at all.[190]

[190] It is obvious that the boy did not respond too well to the shaman's treatment and had to be taken to the hospital for surgery and a month-long period of convalescence. Note how the narrator delicately suggests, however, that he and his companion "had the help of the doctor in opening the wound." As usual, the credit for the recovery is given to the shamanistic ceremony.

Another patient Kenneth had was a big fellow who fell off a bank back of the church. Instead of having his shoulder set when it was warm, he let it get cold before he came to us. His chest and neck were swelling. I was out at ECW camp; the phone rang.[191] I was reading. I felt my body going funny and prayed that all was well. The message was from Kenneth. He wanted me to come in by truck at once and bring some water from Elk Springs. He didn't mention sand, but I brought it anyway.[192]

[191] The Indian Emergency Conservation Work (ECW) was a federal public works program through which the Indians were helped to weather the depression. It was initiated in 1933 and continued until 1937. Telephone service was used by the Indians mainly for very urgent matters. Therefore the narrator had a feeling of foreboding when the telephone rang.

The narrator was familiar enough with the shaman's methods and requirements to bring the right substances.

I found the man who was hurt feeling pretty bad. He usually speaks to me, even
if he sees me in the distance, but this time he just looked and smiled. Swinging-
Lance told me to rub sand on my hands. The injured man said, "Your hands feel
good, as if they could heal." I took off his shirt. We had to cut his underclothing,
and it was a cold night too, with snow falling. Kenneth told me to mark him with
sand instead of pollen and asked me to get some sulphur. Though it was dark, I
went a little distance and got some in a pan with water. The warmer you make
sulphur, the faster it will work. After warming the sulphur, I put it on him. He
said it felt good. After his arm got warm, Kenneth put some kind of medicine on
him, I don't know what, but it killed the pain. He got his own brother and me
and another man to pull on the arm. We could hear it make a sound as if a door
slammed shut, and he fainted. When he came to, he moved his arm around and
said it was pretty good but it hurt. Kenneth had some wild mustard leaves[193] which
he used with sulphur and put it around the shoulder with white sheeting. There
were no songs or prayers.

[193] "Brassica sp."

The man wanted a ceremony though, so we gave him a two-night ceremony.[194]
This man said he never heard a prayer put up for him that sounded like our prayer.
He tried his best to sing the songs, but they were hard for him. I told him I had
been with Kenneth through all his ceremonies, and I knew only two of his songs.
I laughed and said that I ought to know more than two songs but that I was telling
the truth. I know his peyote songs; it's his Ute songs that I don't know, and he
depends on those more than on anything else. When he starts to forget his songs,
he eats peyote, and it brings all his songs back. The man with the injured shoulder
got well. Now he can go on a tough job like rounding up wild horses, and nothing
bothers him.

[194] Though he had had effective emergency treatment of a naturalistic order,
the patient wanted a ceremony performed just in case his mishap had occurred as a result of the malice of a witch or the anger of some supernatural.

One way Kenneth shows disease is in a glass. All disease is mostly germs, funny-
looking things big enough to see.[195] He showed me a lot of things in the glass, all
kinds of diseases, how they kill, and how to kill them. They can go freely about in
your body and do no harm. These germs come together in many ways. Every animal
has some but not enough to do harm. The doctor said this was true, that there are
always germs in yourself and in water and food.

[195] The Mescalero believe that much disease is caused by intrusive insects,
objects, or substances which have been shot into the body or which have
somehow made their way there. Consequently the germ theory of disease

seems quite reasonable to them, and, with some distortions and adjustments for size, they enthusiastically accept it.

When anything is going to happen, Kenneth Swinging-Lance tells me beforehand. I'm glad to hear him and know this, for then I warn others of danger that is coming. Once he was holding a ceremony. I was not at the ceremony but was singing a song over in Three Rivers. I had brought a drum to ECW camp. I came to this man's songs, and just then I had a queer feeling. I felt something coming up and I could see it spreading all over the country, disease, or rain, or wind.

The next morning I started to sing these songs again. All the camp woke up and asked why I was singing. "We're having a big wind with cold and maybe disease," I said. I said there would be a big snow at sundown. We had been having a dry spell. The boys kind of made fun of me. I always joked with them. We were a happy bunch, mostly Indians with an Indian boss. I also said we were going to work under a white man by the end of the month. They told me that I was always saying things I shouldn't, and I said they would find out for themselves whether I was telling the truth. Kenneth Swinging-Lance was telling me things through his power that others did not know.

Just before sundown we saw that dust had blown in and settled all over the country; also it was clouding up. When the boys were coming in at dusk, it turned very cold and there was a little snow. One of the boys said, "I feel awful bad." That same night there was such a heavy snow that we couldn't work the next day. One of the men came down with mumps and about half the men had colds.

I caught a cold too and had a fever. That night three of us sat up all night with a fire going. When we came in at the end of the week to get our pay, we found that the hospital was full; they were having colds and the measles.

Then we lost our boss, just as I had said we would. He left us, just beat it, and the next week we had a white boss. The boys didn't like it because there was one white man, and we were all working under him.[196]

[196] One of the constant complaints of the Mescalero during this period was that white men filled important and well-paid positions on the reservation which Indians could very well have occupied. Yet this account suggests the instability of Indian work habits that sometimes encouraged this.

After that some of the boys said I was Kenneth Swinging-Lance's partner and I should see what I could do for them from then on. They said I should be careful and not say anything about Kenneth while he was alive. But I told them I had no power except to take care of myself.[197]

[197] The narrator again has to combat the generally held notion that he exercises or shares important supernatural power that can be used on behalf of others. He does, however, hint that he has some supernatural help in protecting himself.

Let them say anything. The power will not be broken. It will last until it is thrown away or taken back to the home of all power.

Power and Policy

When a horse fell with one of the boys and hurt his leg, Bill Sotol, who knows the yellow-headed blackbird, came and worked for him. He also knows the red-winged blackbird and uses it in the same way. He carries the wings of both of these birds. The doctor had given it up, so Bill came and tried to set the leg better. It still sticks out on one side, but not as bad as when the doctor left it. Bill is still living.

He had a little party once. I asked him, when he was a little drunk on corn beer, if he would perform what he knew for us. He did a little. He told us it was good in healing. He said, "The power of this bird uses the water plants only and things that grow along the bank. The man who knows it is directed to use these things. The man who knows it makes few mistakes because there are very few water plants."[198]

[198] The red-winged blackbird is commonly found along watercourses.

I've seen him give some sweet grass for a sore throat.[199] He uses the seeds the same way. It never fails.

[199] "Savastana odorata."

He performed for us because he was a little full and was not afraid to use it. He got out the wing and feathers of this bird and placed them before the fire. Then he got out his pollen and began marking everyone who was in there. He spoke of many things in the future when he got started. He said there were many things he'd like to say, but he didn't like to say it because he was afraid it might be all wrong.

"But anyway we will have many things, and our Commissioner is giving us the best care and giving us our chance now.[200] We shall have many things we have not got," he said. "Our agent has been transferred and is going away." He said this before the agent was gone. Think of it! And the agent sure left too! This man said many things about old people. "There is one old woman who has done much good for her own people. She will go away from us." This oldest woman on the reservation did die Friday of last week.

[200] By this time the "New Deal for the Indians" had begun, John Collier had been appointed Commissioner of Indian Affairs, and there were high hopes that his policies would greatly improve the conditions and prospects of the Indians.

The Power That Would Not Be Bossed

There is a woman who picked up her ceremony around Elk Springs. This is the woman I told you about who tried to cure the Pablo family of the "flu." She said she was out gathering piñon nuts one day and she came to a cave that was just like pollen inside. I've been there, and it is all yellow. She told us where this cave was, and many of us saw it. All that she said about it is really true. It looks as if it is a flat place with shrubs and Apache plume plants around it. From the entrance to the bottom it is about twenty feet, a sharp drop. There is just one entrance. It is right on the ridge. You can't see it till you're at the very mouth of the cave. There are deer tracks all around; all kinds of things live there. On the inside one tunnel goes straight to the east. No one else has been in it. I never have. I was afraid of it. It would be too hard to get out of it.

One fellow was riding along one time at this ridge. A black dog with a white ring around its neck came up to him. He saw it with his own eyes. The dog wagged its tail. Then it ran up to the cave and disappeared.[201]

[201] It is claimed that dogs are often seen in the vicinity of the caves or holy homes of supernatural power. These canines are thought to be the pets of the supernaturals.

When this was told I was farming just above the gate that was witched. I thought about it and then saddled the best horse I had. I went along the ridge and missed the cave the first time. I found it the second time. I found it by this black dog. I heard it yelp. I thought it was a dog belonging to one of the Indians. He came up towards me and then went back. I followed him and found the cave. The dog disappeared. I did not see it go into the cave.

I thought, "Suppose I go and stay in the cave four days; I might learn something."[202] I looked and looked, but it was too far to the bottom. Once I nearly made up my mind to jump to the bottom. But it was too far, and I was all alone, so I gave up.

[202] Once more the narrator toys with the idea of attempting to acquire supernatural power.

The piñon nuts the woman was gathering were along the side. This very same dog came to her. Her husband was cutting oats that day. She did not think of going back to him. The dog stayed with her. She camped all alone that night. She had courage. It shows she was pretty strong in power. That's the only thing you can think of a woman like that. She went to bed. The dog stayed right with her. She had fed it and given it water. It lay at her feet. The dog would bark when something would come around. She did not ask the dog for a ceremony.

She heard a growl behind her. Then the dog disappeared. She was about to go to sleep. Something touched her then and told her to get up. She sat up, and before her the coals, when the wind blew, threw light on this animal. She thought it was a mountain lion at first and was deathly afraid. Then in the light she saw it was a wildcat. The eyes showed yellow in the dark, then green, and then red, and then as a shining spot like a star.

The wildcat told her not to be afraid. "I come for a good purpose. I will give you what you seek." She wanted a ceremony and that's why this wildcat came to her.

Now she was not afraid at all. She thought, "Now is the time to get what I have wanted."

The wildcat said, "I came to that cave where you were today. Do you want to be a shaman? Now is the time that everything is changed. We are getting under the white man, even supernatural power, but the white man will not get all the power."[203]

[203] Note that supernatural power is described as identifying itself with the Indian, pledging itself to make a stand against white encroachments.

"All right, then show me the way of the white man."[204]

[204] The woman is here asking for a ceremony which will help her influence and cope with the white man.

"Is that all?"

"No, many times my husband is sick. Often his lungs are in bad shape. Show me the way to cure that man."

"Is that all?" She was given her choice.

"No, there's another thing. What is the best way to be a healer?"

"The best way is to know different herbs, but not only herbs. You must know a ceremony to help you with the herbs."

"I'm glad," she said.

"I cannot give it to you here. Let us go back to the cave."

"All right." And when she said this she found herself inside the cave. And the wildcat transformed itself into a man, and she was led by this man.

Then they went on, and a great door opened, and they got into a place where the sun was shining. The country was beautiful, rough, with springs and different kinds of plants. It was shown to her in a plain way because she was a very strong woman, one of the bravest women who ever came into a ceremonial cave.

Even the power spoke of this and asked, "Why did you come to this cave without the help of a man?"[205]

[205] Note the slight sex inferiority felt by the woman in this ritual context and her need for declaring herself to be as strong and resolute as a man.

She said, "I'm going to be a strong shaman."

She was shown everything about this place very plainly. When she holds her ceremony she never leaves a thing hidden; she tells every bit to the sick person. She always tells first where she got the power, how she got it, and who gave it to her. That's what her power told her to do. "Hide nothing, then perform your ceremony. Tell the parents about it if it is a child you are curing." The power told her, "You will not be the only one to come to this cave then. And your people will always know that this is a ceremonial cave." She called the place "Pollen Home." That's the name of that cave; that's what her power called it.

You remember that Navaho who was singing for Nancy's child? Well, this old woman said he was strong but not as strong as she was. So Nancy hired her. The boy had diarrhea. First they took him to the doctor. He got worse. So they took him away from the doctor. I don't think much of the doctor. It's easy to check diarrhea in a baby. Then they hired the Navaho and after that they got this woman. I wanted to be present and asked, but they said I couldn't be present. They knew what I wanted. That day I carried the child around all over, and in the evening I saw them drive off to get the old lady. I made all kinds of excuses to be present. I had my bed there and said I was going to sleep there that night.[206]

> [206] The narrator is frank about his curiosity concerning the woman's ceremony and his determination to see it.

This woman spoke to Nancy when she came. She said, "That man in there is pretty strong. You know he handles coyotes and bears and owls, and you know what that means. He's likely to carry the whole thing away."[207] She saw that my bed was inside. She's afraid of me.

> [207] The woman is obviously afraid that the narrator has unsavory power and intentions that may nullify her rite.

I said, "I don't see why I can't stay here."
One of the girls said, "I don't think he'll do anything. Let him stay."
But the old woman didn't like it. So I took my bed out and said, "I can sleep out here in the open."
Then she was more afraid and said, "It's all right; you can stay inside, but, my nephew, be good. I do only good things."
"I'm only here for your own good," she told Nancy.
So here was my chance. I said, "I'm always good. If you do good things I'll help you. I'm an old man, and I should know a lot."
That's how I came to see her ceremony and to know all this. I found her out then.
We got in. I felt very good. I did not know how long it would last, but I was going to stay for the end. Nancy asked me if I had any money. I gave her the three dollars I got from you that day. Donald Nalade, his wife, Walt Nalade, his wife, Nancy, the sick boy, his two sisters, the old woman, and I were present.
The old woman said, "I've got to tell you about my power and where I got it first. 'Pollen Home' is a great place," she began, and she told what I have already told you. She looked at me all the time she was talking. I was smiling. She looked at me every time she told how strong her power was and how she had it only for good.
She said a few prayers. In her right hand she had the paw of a wildcat. She worked with it over the child in different ways. She put it to the top of his head and over him. It was a good ceremony. Everybody kept quiet. Everybody was marked. She went about it very quietly.
She said, "Why do you hire me? You've got a man here as strong as anyone. You think he is young, but he knows many things." Then she marked me.

I said, "My aunt, you shouldn't say those things about me. I know nothing."

She said, "You can't fool me. You monkey with snakes and bears and other things. You couldn't do this if you didn't know something. They are dangerous."[208]

[208] The worrisome habits of the narrator are in the forefront of the shaman's mind, and she pauses to voice some of the concern she has about them.

I said, "Go on with your ceremony. You're the one hired." And she stopped talking about me.

She had abalone shell on buckskin. She put it in pollen and put it on her finger. She started her prayer. It had four verses. It was short. Then she put pollen on the child. It was sleeping. She made a noise in imitation of something; she went, "Du, du, du, du." I couldn't make out what it was. It sounded like several things. It could be the chipmunk, the pygmy owl, the kite, or Cooper's hawk. I think it was the hawk. Then she sucked something out, and we each spit into our own can, for we were in a tent with a floor to it.[209]

[209] Whenever a sucking shaman draws some object of witchcraft or some noxious substance from the body of a patient, he spits it into the fire. At the same time all present spit directly ahead four times.

We sat up for quite a while. She started to sing. Then she said, "The child will be all right. But you have one here who is pretty strong through herbs." Then she sang again. She sang very beautifully. I surely liked that song. I started to sing it too. She said, "Hey! It's not for you," and I had to stop.

She asked her power about an herb. Then she said, "My power tells me that lupine is good.[210] There is one here who knows it. You've got to get some and give it to the child. You've got to do it by tomorrow or the child is in danger. It's getting bad inside."

[210] "Lupinus aduncus."

The next day the old lady said to me, "You've got to give it to the child."
I said, "You're not bossing me."
The girl, my sister-in-law, said, "You've got to do it."
I said, "I'll do it after she goes; I won't do it while the old lady is here."
So the old lady went out and then came in. "Did you do it?" she asked.
"Yes," I told her. But I had done nothing. I had just sat there.
I went home. I called my oldest girl. "Go to Nancy," I said, "and tell her that she should know better. No power is going to be bossed. Even though she is my relative, power has to be asked in the right way, and she's old enough to know this."[211]

[211] Though the narrator claims to be no more than an herbalist, medicine, to be most effective, has to be offered with some ceremonial flourish. Moreover, a particular medicine can itself be considered a power source or supernatural

helper. The narrator is making it plain that he will not play a subordinate role to the woman shaman and that he cannot be treated in a casual or undignified manner just because he is a relative of the sick child and her mother. Note that he treats a slight to himself as an affront to supernatural power.

The girl went over and in just a few minutes Nancy came. She asked in a respectful way.

"That's good," I told her. "Remember that. Now I will cure that child. Diarrhea is an easy thing for me to cure. If that white doctor gave it up, he's no good. I'll give the child medicine, and if there is blood in its feces tomorrow you can call me no good and go to someone else."

Then I gave the child the medicine. The next day the child was all right. Nancy came up to my camp early in the morning, before I was up, to tell me that there was no blood in the feces.

The ceremony lasted for four nights. The old lady used the power of the wildcat only. They gave her the three dollars Nancy got from me. They gave her some buckskins too, for there were two there, and I don't see them any more. They took her down to Tularosa and bought her calico and many things. She's still staying with them.

They are all working on that child. The old lady, my mother-in-law, claimed the turtle shell I was saving for you and gave medicine to the little boy in it. They use it because lightning can't strike a turtle. I sent my boy over and tried to get my mother-in-law to tell about her medicine. I know she has cured lots of people. But she wouldn't tell. She said, "It's my work."[212]

[212] In the myths there are episodes in which protagonists are protected from Lightning by Turtle. Consequently a turtle shell is often used as a container for medicine, particularly medicine to counteract Lightning sickness. Since he has to avoid his mother-in-law, the narrator could not himself ask her about her medicine.

The Turn of the Wheel

When you have no children and you are old, you are all alone. It's no good. Look at what my children do for me. My girls were up early this morning to get water. My boy was chopping wood. My oldest girl cooks for me. Children lead you around when you are old.

My smallest girl is just at the age when she is very interesting to watch. I was telling stories. She listened for a while and then she said, "I'm tired," and went out. Pretty soon I heard her talking. I listened. She was telling stories. She had got the children together and was telling them the same stories. One night I sat up telling stories in my camp with some of the men. She was there listening. In the morning I heard her telling her grandmother how Coyote married his own daughter. Then she told the old lady the story of the rock rabbit and made a noise like Coyote did when he hurt his mouth on the rock.[213]

²¹³ In this story a rabbit skin was put over a rock to deceive greedy and foolish Coyote. Coyote leaps and bites at the rock with the results described. Coyote stories are told with all necessary gestures and sound effects. Note that there is no hesitation about allowing children to hear the "funny" stories about the trickster, such as the tale of incest to which reference is made.

One other night a bunch of people were in my camp telling stories. My little girl was there. We all took turns. All of a sudden she walked right out in the middle of all those people. She wasn't a bit bashful. She didn't have a smile on her face at all. "It's my turn to tell a story," she said. "There was a very old man and he went to get a bucket of water to wash his clothes." She just got that far and everyone began to laugh at her. Just as soon as they laughed, she stopped and jumped back like a little chipmunk.

The older children are good-natured with her and show her many things. Her older sister showed her how to make a man by stringing berries. She did it and then asked her sister to make a hat for him.

Though the older people do not like to see it very much, the children play at having a girl's puberty rite and imitate the masked dancers. I saw my little girl and some others playing that way the other day.

In spite of how little she is, she speaks right up. She got angry at my mother-in-law the other day. I heard her say, "If you don't let me do it, I'm going over to my 'grandmother' at Three Rivers."²¹⁴ When I brought her some candy I had promised her she said to me, "Father, you promised me candy and you sure enough brought it for me. Now you must keep all your promises to me. If you don't I'll run away out into the hills and you'll never see me again." She was told that she should say "yes" politely when people spoke to her. Pretty soon I missed out on it myself, and she told me, "Papa, don't say 'eh,' say 'yes.'"

²¹⁴ This woman is actually a paternal great-aunt; the kinship term is used in an extended sense.

I was tired and told her to go away for five minutes and let me sleep. She went away but came right back and began to shake me, saying, "A lazy man doesn't count!"

Later, while she was playing, she got very tired. She said, "Papa, I'm tired and want to sleep for a little while. Will you hold my chewing gum for me?"

My boy Anthony is getting to be a big fellow now. He is strong and a good runner. The other boys say to him, "You know Bear power; that's why. You eat bear." They think he gets it from me.²¹⁵

²¹⁵ The narrator's son is a good hunter and shows much the same interest as his father in outdoor life. His companions are already saying that he must have obtained his father's Bear power just as it has constantly been said of the narrator that he must have acquired his father's Bear ritual.

I had two smokes of Edgeworth left. I was saving it for the night. When I came back it was missing. Anthony had taken it. I caught him by the ear. "Look here,"

I said, "you haven't caught a coyote yet." He is smoking right along now. I caught him chewing tobacco too. One time a while back I missed my cigarettes and found that he had taken them. I made him give them back, and I gave them to Don Nitsigane who was with him. Don is older.

I told Anthony that I was going to put coyote fur on my coat. He said, "No, I wear that coat sometimes. Can't you put something else on it?" He wouldn't let me do it.[216]

[216] In all probability the narrator was teasing his son in this instance.

Anthony is a pretty good shot and will make a good hunter. I made a bow and arrows for him last year. He killed lots of rabbits. Then he got to killing birds. I said, "Now you are getting too bad. You leave those poor birds alone."[217]

[217] The narrator has the older Indian's dislike of wanton killing of animals. He hunts for some specific purpose only.

Another time I let him carry the gun as we were going along. A road-runner went across the road, and he got ready to fire. I told him not to, but he did and brought it down. Then he was ashamed. I thought of how to punish him. I said, "You're not going to waste that, are you? Pick it up and take it back to camp to eat."
"I didn't know that it is good to eat."
"Sure it is."
So he took it back to camp. The old lady, my mother-in-law, got after him right away. These old people don't want the road-runner around camp because they say it kills and eats snakes.[218] She made him take it far away.

[218] The Mescalero consider the food habits of an animal or bird in deciding whether that animal or bird is clean or polluting, edible or forbidden food.

"My father said it was good to eat," he told her.
"They are no good! Take that nasty thing out of here and hurry up!" the old woman told him.
He asked me for fifty cents. He said he wanted to buy something to eat with it. I gave it to him, and he went off to the store and bought a watermelon and a deck of cards. When he came back with these, I took the cards and began chewing them. "Is this good to eat?" I asked him. He laughed at me.
Once lately he came in at 3:00 A.M. His shirt was torn too. I scolded him and asked him how he tore his shirt. His sister said, "He probably tore it on the floor of someone's house."[219]

[219] The implication is that the boy was having an affair with some girl.

He got after her right away. "Here," he said, "don't you talk to me like that! I'm a good man and don't do such things."

I've been telling him, "You can't sit around."

He said, "All right, I'll look for something to do."

He went down to that white man, the agency farmer, and asked for work. The farmer said he had all the help he needed right now. He tried all the others, and they all said the same. He came back and told me.

I pointed to the trees. "You see that wood?" I told him. "There's money in that." He said he'd try again and if he can't get a job he'll saw wood. But I guess he'll be going away to school pretty soon. Yesterday some of the boys who are going to the Santa Fe school were up here teasing me to let him go with them.[220]

[220] This is an indication of the change of attitude toward off-reservation schooling. It is not so long ago that the possibility of being sent to an off-reservation boarding school was dreaded and resisted by both the prospective pupils and parents.

He's at Three Rivers now. He said, "I'm going to see my grandmother[221] before I go off to school. It might be the last time I'll see her."

[221] This woman is the boy's maternal grandfather's sister.

Bibliography

Annual Reports of the Commissioner of Indian Affairs, 1851–1935.

AUBRY, FELIX X., 1942,"Apache Golden Bullets," *Masterkey*, Vol. XVI, No. 5, p. 174.

BANCROFT, HUBERT HOWE, 1884–1889, *History of the North Mexican States and Texas* (2 vols.). (Vols. XV and XVI of *The Works of Hubert Howe Bancroft*). San Francisco: A. L. Bancroft & Company (Vol. XV); San Francisco: The History Company (Vol. XVI).

————, 1889, *History of Arizona and New Mexico* (Vol. XVII of *The Works of Hubert Howe Bancroft*). San Francisco: The History Company.

BETZINEZ, JASON AND WILBUR STURTEVANT NYE, 1959, *I Fought with Geronimo*. Harrisburg, Pa.: The Stackpole Company.

BOLTON, HERBERT E., 1915, *Texas in the Middle Eighteenth Century: Studies in Spanish Colonial History and Administration*. Berkeley: University of California Press.

CASTETTER, EDWARD F. AND MORRIS E. OPLER, 1936, *The Ethnobiology of the Chiricahua and Mescalero Apache* (University of New Mexico Bulletin, Ethnobiological Studies in the American Southwest, No. III; Biological Series, Vol. IV, No. 5). Albuquerque: University of New Mexico Press.

COLYER, VINCENT, 1872, *Peace with the Apaches of New Mexico and Arizona: Report of Vincent Colyer, Member of the Board of Indian Commissioners, 1871*. Washington, D.C.: U.S. Government Printing Office.

DUNN, WILLIAM EDWARD, 1911, "Apache Relations in Texas, 1718–1750," *The Quarterly of the Texas State Historical Association*, Vol. XIV, No. 3, pp. 198–274.

FLANNERY, REGINA, 1932, "The Position of Woman among the Mescalero Apache," *Primitive Man*, Vol. V, Nos. 2–3, pp. 26–32.

FORBES, JACK D., 1960, *Apache, Navaho, and Spaniard*. Norman: University of Oklahoma Press.

GARRETT, PAT F., 1954, *The Authentic Life of Billy, the Kid*. Norman: University of Oklahoma Press.

GODDARD, PLINY EARLE, 1909, "Gotal—a Mescalero Apache Ceremony," in Franz Boas (ed.), *Putnam Anniversary Volume*. New York: G. E. Stechert & Co., Publishers, pp. 385–394.

————, 1916, "The Masked Dancers of the Apache," in F. W. Hodge (ed.), *Holmes Anniversary Volume*. Washington, D.C.: J. W. Bryan Press, pp. 132–136.

GREGG, JOSIAH, 1954, *Commerce of the Prairies* (edited by Max L. Moorhead). Norman: University of Oklahoma Press.

HODGE, FREDERICK WEBB, 1907, "Mescaleros," in Frederick Webb Hodge (ed.), *Handbook of American Indians North of Mexico, Part 1* (Bureau of American Ethnology Bulletin 30), p. 846. Washington, D.C.: U.S. Government Printing Office.

HOIJER, HARRY, 1938, *Chiricahua and Mescalero Apache Texts* (with Ethnological Notes by Morris Edward Opler). Chicago: University of Chicago Press.

McNEIL, IRVING, 1944, "Indian Justice," *New Mexico Historical Review*, Vol. XIX, No. 4, pp. 261–270.

MECHEM, G. B., 1890, "Mescalero Agency," in *Report on Indians Taxed and Indians Not Taxed, United States Department of the Interior, Census Office, Eleventh Census*. Washington, D.C.: U.S. Government Printing Office, pp. 398–404.

MOORHEAD, MAX L., 1968, *The Apache Frontier: Jacobo Ugarte and Spanish-Indian Relations in Northern New Spain, 1769–1791*. Norman: University of Oklahoma Press.

NEWCOMB, W. W., 1961, *The Indians of Texas: From Prehistoric to Modern Times*. Austin: University of Texas Press.

OPLER, MORRIS E., 1933, "An Analysis of Mescalero and Chiricahua Apache Social Organization in the Light of Their Systems of Relationship." Unpublished Ph.D. thesis, University of Chicago, Chicago, Illinois.

———, 1935a, "The Concept of Supernatural Power among the Chiricahua and Mescalero Apaches," *American Anthropologist*, Vol. 37, No. 1, pp. 65–70.

———, 1935b, "The Mescalero Apache Bow-Drill," *American Anthropologist*, Vol. 37, No. 2, p. 370.

———, 1935c, "A Note on the Cultural Affiliations of Northern Mexican Nomads," *American Anthropologist*, Vol. 37, No. 4, pp. 702–706.

———, 1936a, "The Influence of Aboriginal Pattern and White Contact on a Recently Introduced Ceremony, the Mescalero Peyote Rite," *Journal of American Folk-Lore*, Vol. 49, Nos. 191–192, pp. 143–166.

———, 1936b, "An Interpretation of Ambivalence of Two American Indian Tribes," *Journal of Social Psychology*, Vol. 7, pp. 82–116.

———, 1936c, "The Kinship Systems of the Southern Athabaskan-Speaking Tribes," *American Anthropologist*, Vol. 38, No. 4, pp. 620–633.

———, 1936d, "Some Points of Comparison and Contrast between the Treatment of Functional Disorders by Apache Shamans and Modern Psychiatric Practice," *American Journal of Psychiatry*, Vol. 92, No. 6, pp. 1371–1387.

———, 1938a, "Further Comparative Anthropological Data Bearing on the Solution of a Psychological Problem," *Journal of Social Psychology*, Vol. 9 (November), pp. 477–483.

———, 1938b, "Humor and Wisdom of Some American Indian Tribes," *New Mexico Anthropologist*, Vol. III, No. 1, pp. 3–10.

———, 1938c, *Myths and Tales of the Jicarilla Apache Indians* (Memoirs of the American Folk-Lore Society, Vol. XXXI). New York: G. E. Stechert Co.

———, 1938d, "Personality and Culture: A Methodological Suggestion for the Study of their Interrelations," *Psychiatry*, Vol. I, No. 2, pp. 217–220.

———, 1938e, "The Sacred Clowns of the Chiricahua and Mescalero Indians," *El Palacio*, Vol. XLIV, Nos. 10–12, pp. 75–79.

———, 1938f, "The Use of Peyote by the Carrizo and Lipan Apache Tribes," *American Anthropologist*, Vol. 40, No. 2, pp. 271–285.

———, 1940, *Myths and Legends of the Lipan Apache Indians* (Memoirs of the American Folk-Lore Society, Vol. XXXVI). New York: J. J. Augustin.

———, 1941a, *An Apache Life-Way: The Economic, Social, and Religious Institutions of the Chiricahua Indians*. Chicago: University of Chicago Press. (Reissued in 1965 by Cooper Square Publishers, Inc., New York.)

———, 1941b, "Three Types of Variation and Their Relation to Culture Change," in Leslie Spier, A. Irving Hallowell, and Stanley S. Newman (eds.), *Language, Culture, and Personality: Essays in Memory of Edward Sapir*. Menasha, Wis.: George Banta Publishing Co., pp. 146–157.

———, 1942a, "Examples of Ceremonial Interchanges among Southwestern Tribes," *The Masterkey*, Vol. XVI, No. 3, pp. 77–80.

———, 1942b, *Myths and Tales of the Chiricahua Apache Indians* (Memoirs of the American Folk-Lore Society, Vol. XXXVII). Menasha, Wis.: George Banta Publishing Co.

———, 1945, "A Mescalero Apache Account of the Origin of the Peyote Ceremony," *El Palacio*, Vol. LII, No. 10, pp. 210–212.

———, 1946a, "The Creative Role of Shamanism in Mescalero Apache Mythology," *Journal of American Folklore*, Vol. 59, No. 233, pp. 268–281.

——, 1946b, "Reaction to Death among the Mescalero Apache," *Southwestern Journal of Anthropology*, Vol. 2, No. 4, pp. 454–467.

——, 1946c, "The Slaying of the Monsters, A Mescalero Apache Myth," *El Palacio*, LIII, No. 8, pp. 215–225, and No. 9, pp. 242–258.

——, 1947, "Mythology and Folk Belief in the Maintenance of Jicarilla Apache Tribal Endogamy," *Journal of American Folklore*, Vol. 60, No. 236, pp. 126–129.

OPLER, MORRIS E., AND HARRY HOIJER, 1940, "The Raid and War-Path Language of the Chiricahua Apache," *American Anthropologist*, Vol. 42, No. 4, pp. 617–634.

OPLER, MORRIS E., AND CATHERINE H. OPLER, 1950, "Mescalero Apache History in the Southwest," *New Mexico Historical Review*, Vol. XXV, No. 1, pp. 1–36.

SABIN, EDWIN L., 1935, *Kit Carson Days* (2 vols.). New York: Press of the Pioneers.

SCHOOLCRAFT, HENRY ROWE, 1855, "Apaches," in H. R. Schoolcraft (ed.), *Historical and Statistical Information Respecting the History, Condition, and Prospects of the Indian Tribes of the United States*, Vol. V. Philadelphia: Lippincott, Grambo, pp. 202–214.

SONNICHSEN, C. L., 1958, *The Mescalero Apaches*. Norman: University of Oklahoma Press.

STOTTLER, V. E., 1897, "Pressure as a Civilizer of Wild Indians," *The Outlook*, Vol. LVI (January 12), pp. 397–400.

THRAPP, DAN L., 1967, *The Conquest of Apacheria*. Norman: University of Oklahoma Press.

TWITCHELL, RALPH EMERSON, 1911–1917, *The Leading Facts of New Mexican History* (5 vols.). Cedar Rapids, Iowa: The Torch Press.

Index